Spiritual Tattoo Symbols

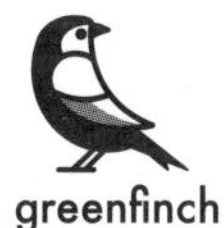

greenfinch

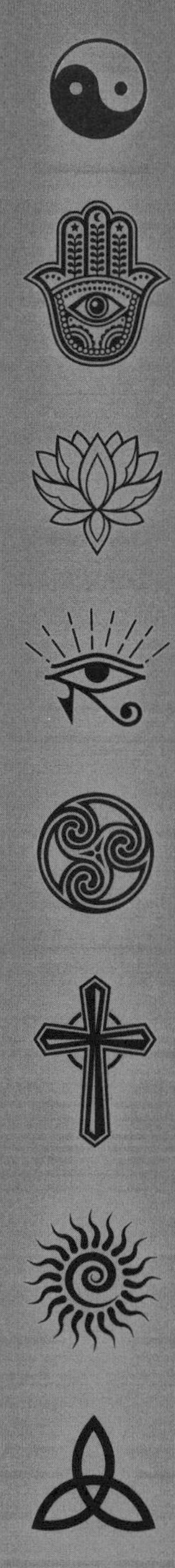

Spiritual Tattoo Symbols

A directory of over 500 sacred symbols and their meanings

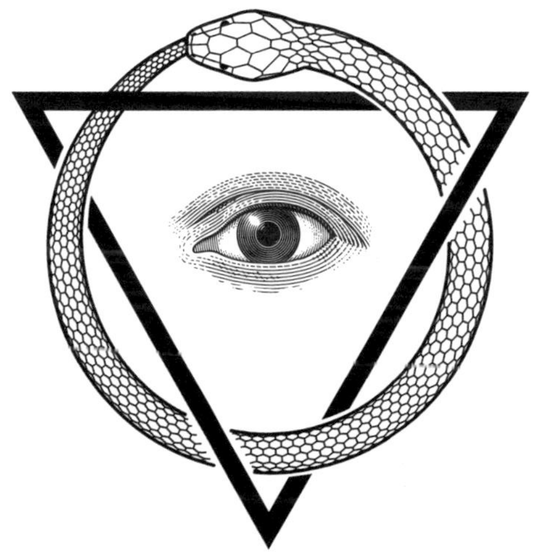

Alison Davies
and Oliver Munden

First published in Great Britain in 2025 by

Greenfinch
An imprint of Quercus Editions Limited
Carmelite House
50 Victoria Embankment
London EC4Y 0DZ

An Hachette UK company
The authorised representative in the EEA is Hachette Ireland, 8 Castlecourt Centre,
Dublin 15, D15 XTP3, Ireland (email: info@hbgi.ie)

A CIP catalogue record for this book is available from the British Library

HB ISBN 978-1-52944-256-4

Quercus Editions Limited hereby exclude all liability to the extent permitted by law for
any errors or omissions in this book and for any loss, damage or expense (whether direct
or indirect) suffered by a third party relying on any information contained in this book.

10 9 8 7 6 5 4 3 2 1

Printed and bound in China by 1010 Printing International Limited

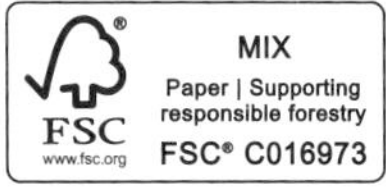

Papers used by Greenfinch are from well-managed forests and other responsible sources.

Conceived, designed and produced by
The Bright Press, an imprint of the Quarto Group

1 Triptych Place
London SE1 9SH
United Kingdom
www.quarto.com

Publisher: James Evans
Editorial Director: Isheeta Mustafi
Commissioning Editor: Sorrel Wood
Managing Editor: Lucy Tipton
Art Director: Emily Nazer
Senior Editor: Joanna Bentley
Project Editor: Lindsay Kaubi
Design and Picture Research: Paul Sloman | Subtract

Contents

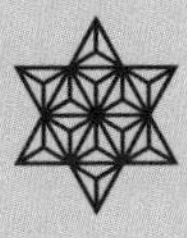

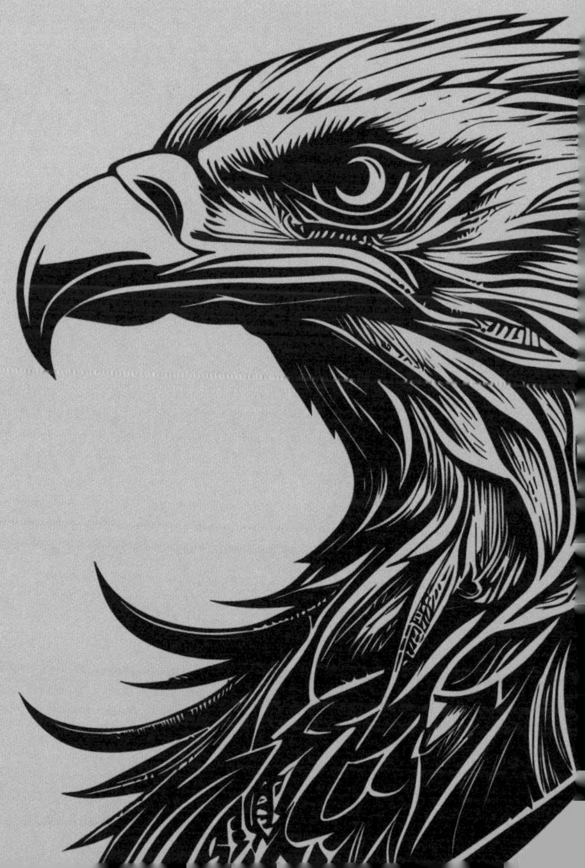

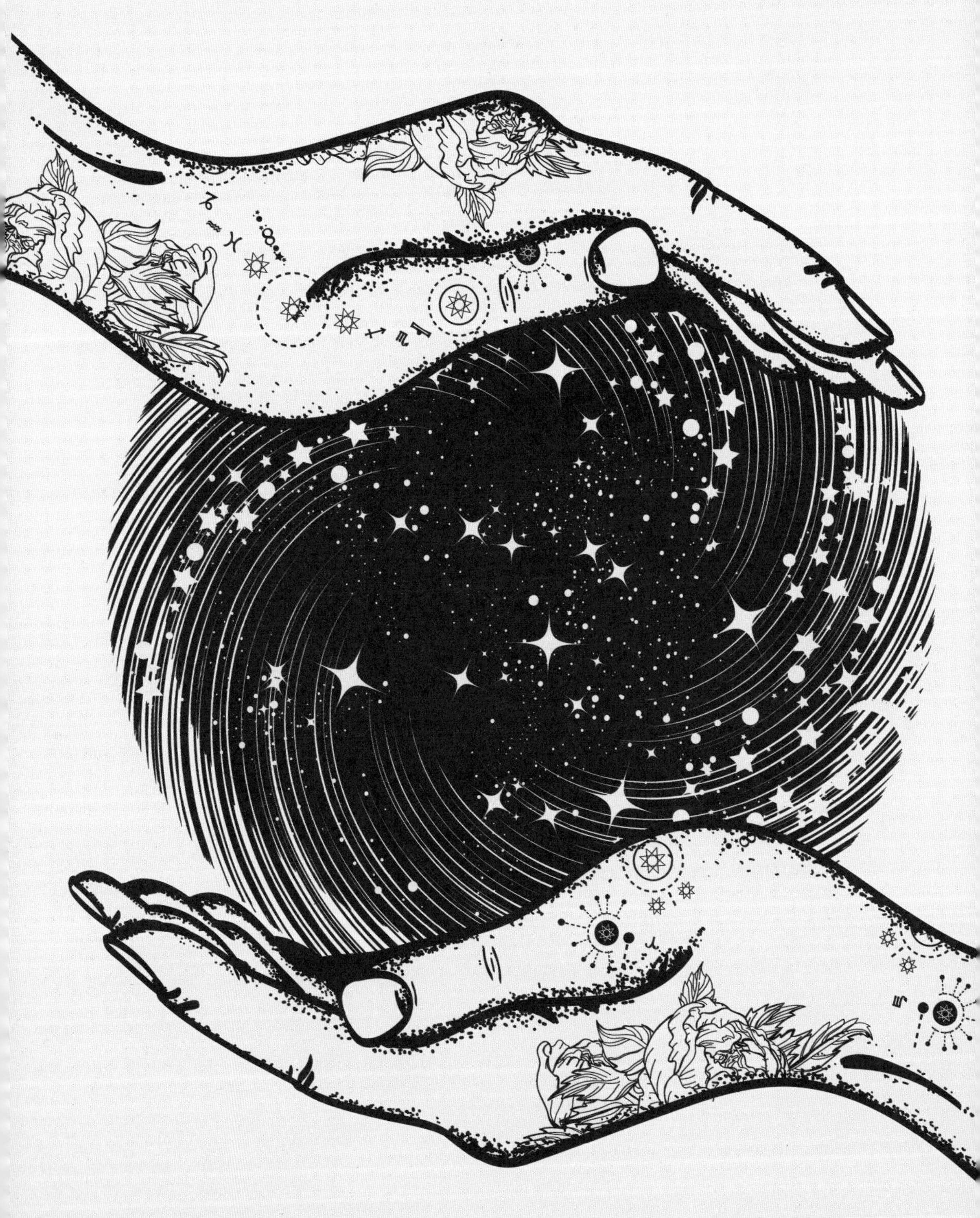

Introduction

Tattooing is an art that has endured the test of time, for it is both primal and universal. From the shores of the Nile to the Pacific islands of Polynesia, and further still to China's Taklamakan desert, the act of marking flesh in a significant way was inherent. Early humans were intuitive, making sense of the world in their own way and finding meaning where they could. Every part of nature was a canvas on which to ruminate and draw, so it was only natural to represent their beliefs upon the skin.

The discovery of Ötzi the Iceman, on the Italian–Austrian border, provides more proof of the eternal nature of the tattoo. This glacier mummy from the Copper Age was adorned with line markings in the most unique places. These tiny dots and crosses were positioned at ankle and knee joints and at the base of the spine, to cure the wear and tear of old age in what is likely the earliest form of acupuncture. Indeed, many early tattoos were created with a medicinal purpose in mind, symbols imbued with healing energy.

The inking of skin using implements crafted from bronze and flattened to a point might seem crude to the modern eye, but it was every bit as effective as today's techniques and served a purpose. By marking themselves with symbols of power, our ancestors enhanced their experience of the world and formed a deeper connection with nature. They harnessed the energy of each carefully crafted motif, turning the tattoo into a talisman to attract their greatest desires and repel evil, creating a link between the sacred and mortal with a symbol.

In the pages of this book, you will find a selection of tattoo symbols from around the world, carefully chosen for their potency and spiritual meaning – motifs that have existed for thousands of years and continue to capture the imagination. Grouped by shape and style to make it easy for you to find what you are looking for, these iconic images cover an array of themes. You'll learn their history and origins, along with any myths or folklore associated with them, and discover what makes them so special. Each symbol comes with key words which highlight its true meaning, along with a selection of designs for inspiration, and some ideas on how to wear it. It's important to carefully research a tattoo design before you commit to it. Some of the symbols contained in these pages are considered sacred by their culture of origin, and it's vital to respect the spiritual importance they hold, and understand any messages your tattoo design might communicate.

Whether you're a symbol seeker, looking for your next tattoo and wanting to learn more about the tattoos you have, or hoping to broaden your portfolio of designs, you'll find something of interest here. The spiritual nature of symbols lives on in the hearts and minds of those who choose to embellish their body with these emblems.

Visual key to tattoo styles

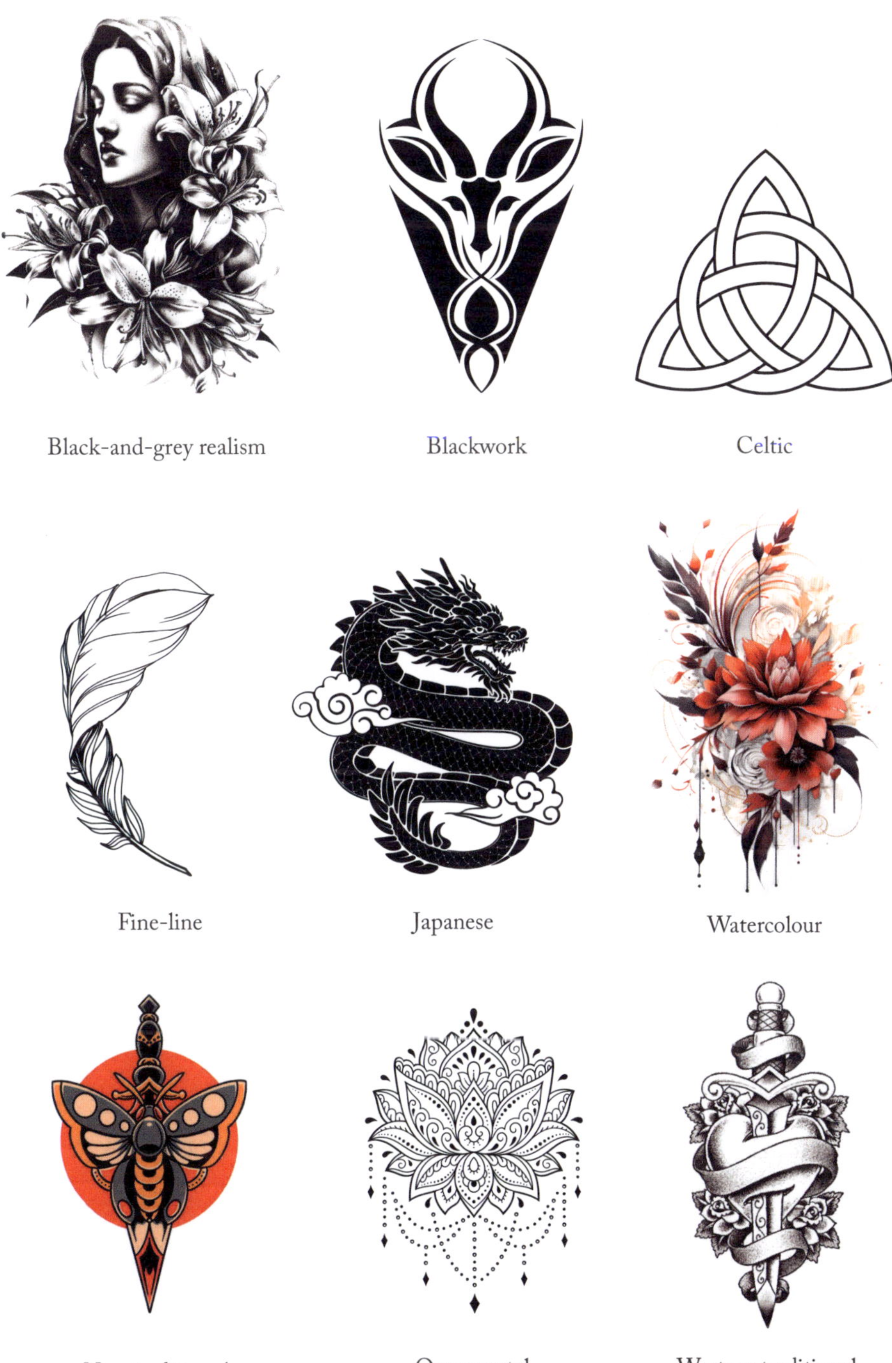

Black-and-grey realism

Blackwork

Celtic

Fine-line

Japanese

Watercolour

Neo-traditional

Ornamental

Western traditional

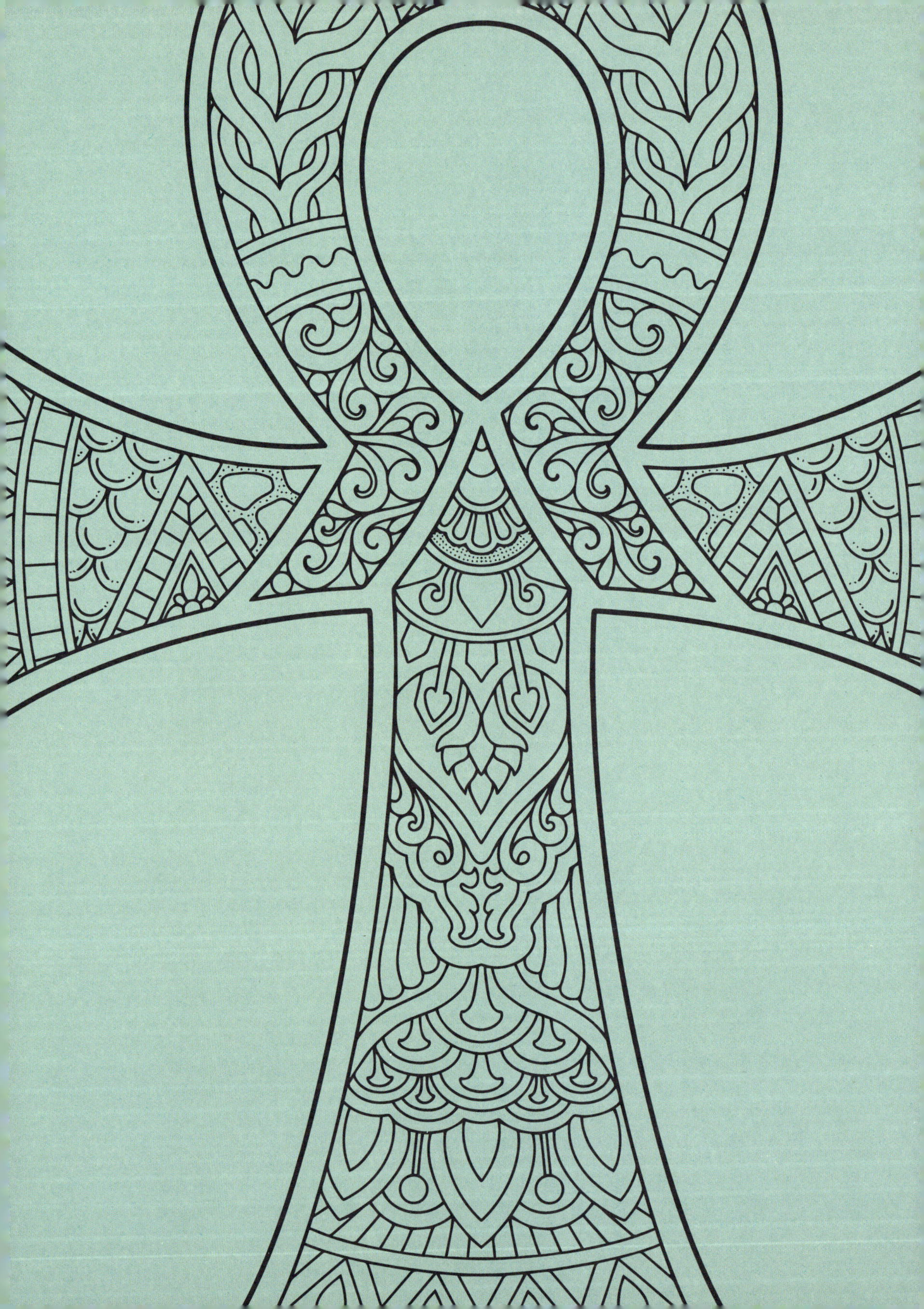

1

Crosses and Lines

Since the beginning of time, humans have used tools to make their mark. From stone and flint to bone, wood and horn, they have shaped and crafted implements with which they could create lines in stone and sand. Those early civilizations would have taken note of the linear forms in nature: the skyline or the towering tree pointing upwards; the lithe and lengthy snake as it moves through the undergrowth. They would have seen these shapes and copied them, and once they mastered this, they progressed to crosses and more angular constructions with pointed ends.

These markings were eventually coupled with meaning, and given more significance, with the introduction of belief systems. Over time, narratives evolved, and shapes which may at first have been simple instructions, like an arrow to 'move forwards' or a method of bringing order to the world using lines to count the days, became powerful talismans and a way of evoking the gods. And so it was that lines and the symbols created from them were transformed into sacred emblems. This chapter introduces some of the most prominent. Featured in a variety of spiritual beliefs from around the world, these designs will catch your eye and help you see that simple can be significant and stylish too.

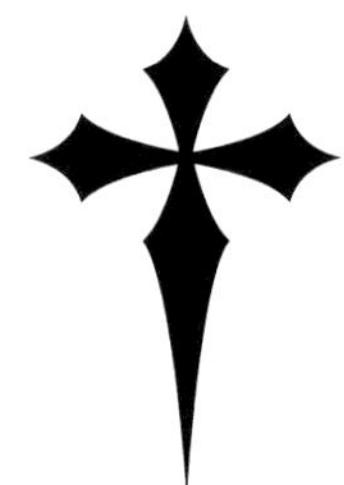

Cross

Faith | Hope | Strength | Guidance | Resurrection

Sacred Origins
Greek, Roman,
Egyptian, Christian

Used Since
Stone Age

Tattoo Styles
Black-and-grey realism
Fine-line
Blackwork
Western traditional

Opposite: This selection of simple and more ornate crosses (top) demonstrates the many different styles associated with this symbol. Crosses are commonly associated with hope, faith, honour and unity. The ornate floral decoration on this Christian-style cross (bottom) signifies faith and beauty.

A symbol of faith, hope and belief for many people around the world, the cross can be seen in myriad forms in architecture, artwork and mathematics.

A symbol of faith

While it is commonly associated with the Christian faith, in truth the cross predates this and has existed since the Stone Age. The first crude inscriptions of cross-like symbols can be seen in petroglyph drawings found in caves in Europe. Indeed, before the Christians adopted the symbol, it had a variety of forms and meanings.

From lightning bolts to bulls

The swastika, which first appeared in Eurasia, was an early interpretation of the cross. With crossed sticks which have ends that are at right angles, this motif was synonymous with peace and often associated with the Greek god Zeus. It was thought that the shape emulated his lightning bolts as they lit up the night sky. In its early incarnation this symbol was also a prominent feature in the Hindu faith. The tau was another version of an early cross. This simple marking which looks like the Greek letter 'T' has also been called the Cross of St Francis. Linked to the Roman god Mithras, whose cult worshipped in underground temples, the main practice of followers was the ritual slaughter of the bull to emulate an early myth associated with the god. Unsurprisingly, the tau has astrological ties to the zodiac sign Taurus (see page 192).

Compass and cross combined

It was the ancient Egyptians who played a key role in the belief that the cross was a symbol of rebirth. Their version, the ankh (see page 28), is based upon the

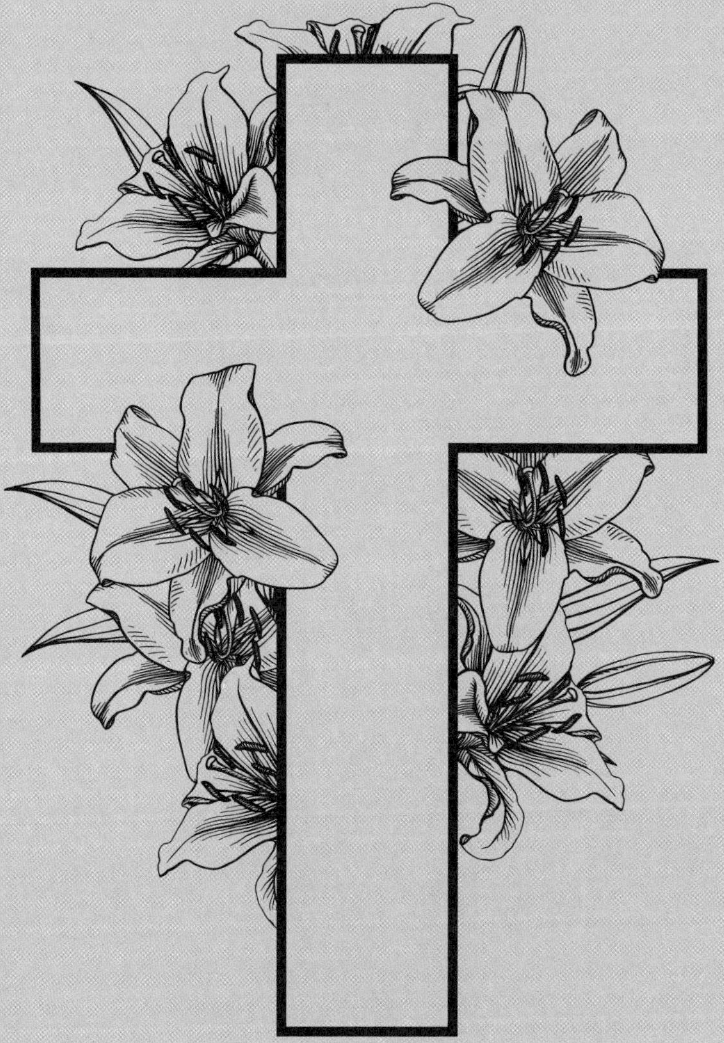

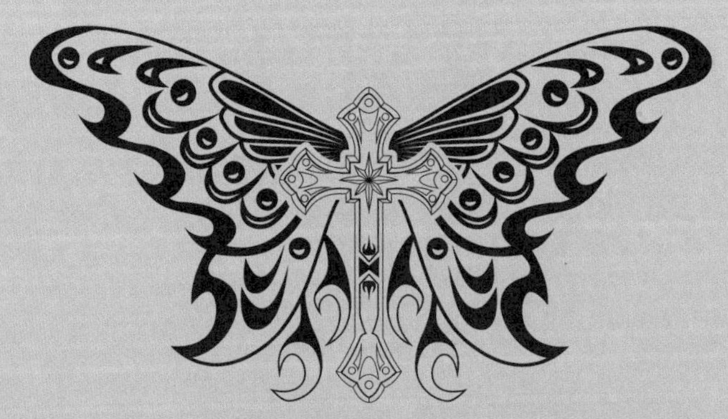

cross shape in its simplest form and was synonymous with life, death and the afterlife. One of the most popular symbols at the time, it was adopted by the Coptic Christians of Egypt, who embraced the idea of life after death and took it as a symbol of faith and the resurrection of the son of God. When Emperor Constantine became the new ruler of the Roman Empire, Christianity was no longer outlawed and the cross of Christ, also known as the 'wood of life', became a common sight. The Celtic cross is another version of the early cross, similar to the ankh; it bears a circular nimbus which encircles the upper part of the cross and symbolizes a compass, to guide and promote movement and strength.

How to wear it

The beauty of the cross is that it can be tattooed in a number of ways, from ornate and elaborate interpretations – frequently seen in black and grey – to simple linear executions, often tattooed on fingers or even tucked discreetly on the ribs. The Celtic cross, with its knotwork patterning, is a popular choice for those seeking guidance and strength, while simpler versions imbue the wearer with peace and compassion.

Opposite: **Lilies surrounding a cross (top) add purity to this symbol of faith, while combining the cross with a butterfly (bottom) can signify a journey to spiritual awakening.**

Right: **A cross decorated with Celtic-style patterns can signify Irish connections.**

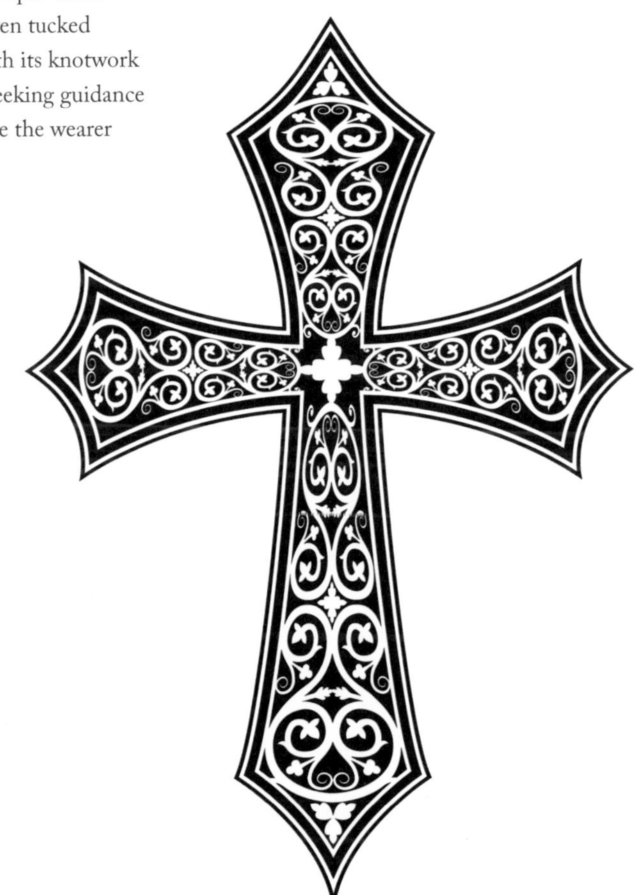

Anchor

Stability | Strength | Balance | Hope | Faith

Sacred Origins
Christian, Greek

Used Since
End of the
1st century

Tattoo Styles
Western traditional
Fine-line
Blackwork

Opposite: Traditional anchor tattoos (left column) denote strength and stability. The addition of a squid (top right) or a serpent (bottom right) provides a link to the power of the natural world.

Synonymous with stability, strength and hope, the anchor is a popular choice of tattoo, often worn to show that a person has reached a state of balance.

A nautical link

Originally sported by sailors, who first started tattooing it in the late 18th century as a way of showing their love for the sea, the anchor was a symbol of achievement and associated with those who had sailed across the Atlantic Ocean.

Hidden meanings

First invented by the ancient Greeks, who used a bucket filled with stones to hold their vessels in place upon the seabed, the anchor evolved over time and now comes in a range of designs and shapes but all with the same purpose – to provide support, safety and stability. To early Christians, the anchor was used as a hidden symbol to represent the cross and a way of showing their faith. Indeed, anchors were discovered carved into ancient catacombs near Rome, and have since been used on gravestones as a way of declaring that someone is steadfast in their beliefs.

How to wear it

Traditional iterations of the anchor include a bold outline and classic colour palette; in contrast, fine-line interpretations transform this recognizable symbol into a more elegant form. Either style is often seen accompanied by flowers and/or a banner displaying a loved one's name. This symbol works well on prominent areas of the arms and legs, the forearm being a popular choice.

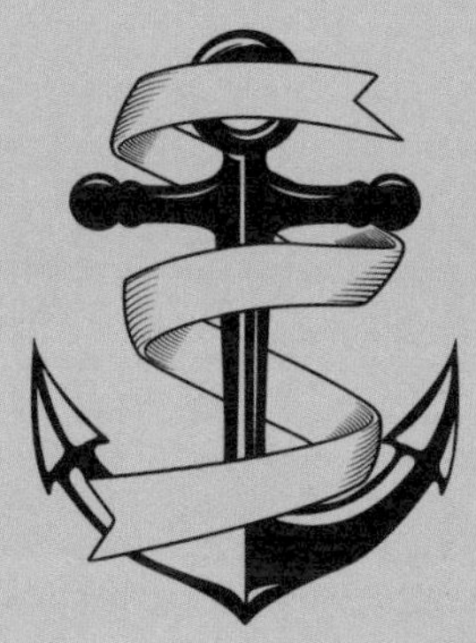

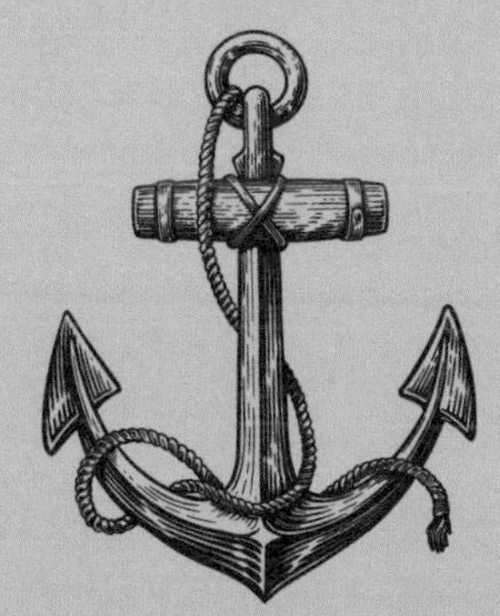

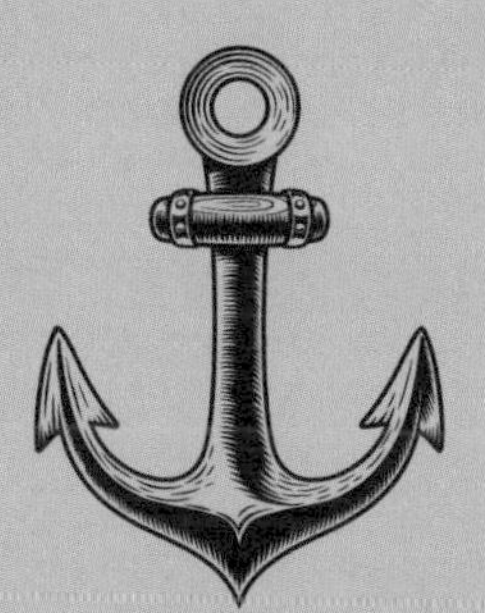

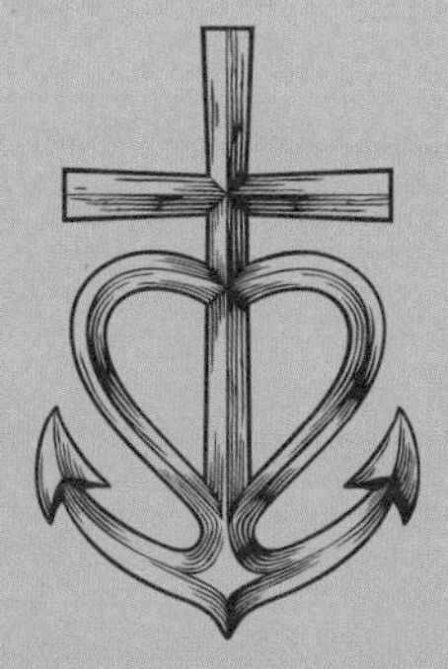

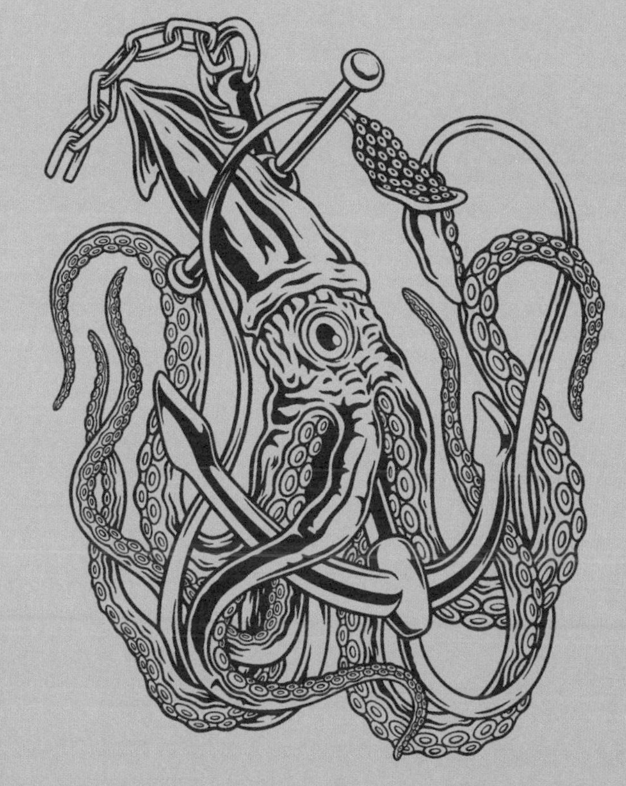

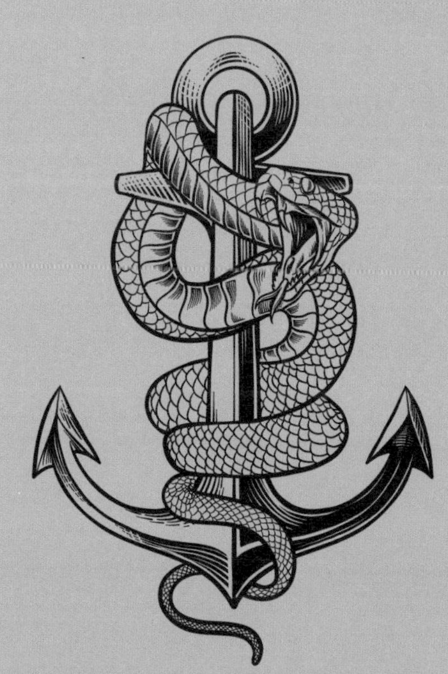

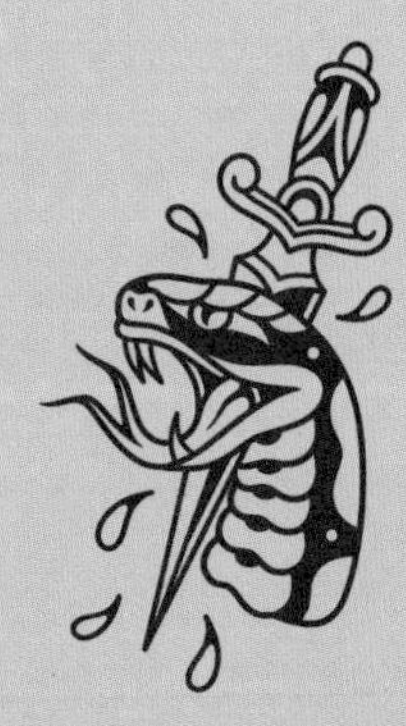

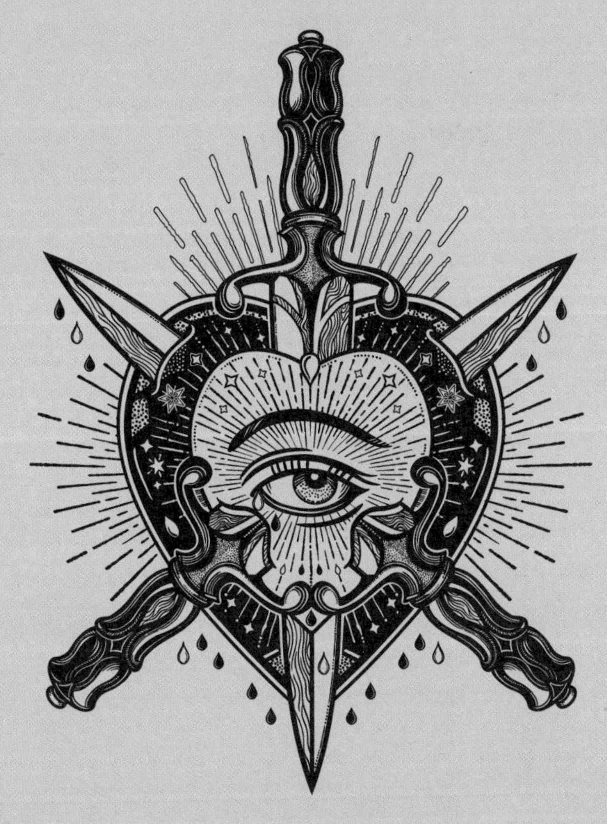

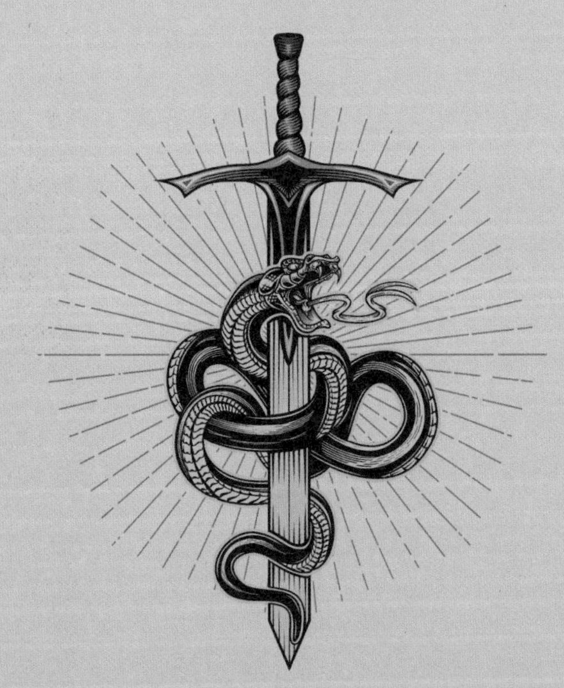

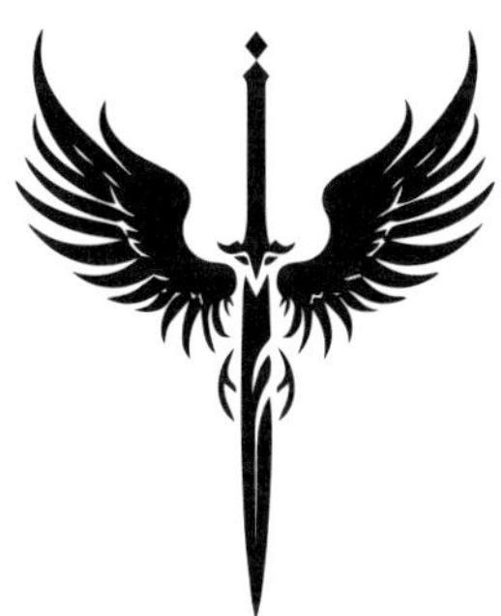

Dagger

Honour | Courage | Loyalty | Freedom | Power

Sacred Origins
Egyptian, Roman,
Norse, Celtic, Sikh

Used Since
Stone Age

Tattoo Styles
Western traditional
Neo-traditional
Fine-line
Blackwork

Opposite: Three small daggers (left column), each piercing an object or creature, denote power and courage. A dagger penetrating a heart (top right) implies heartache, while the evil eye repels harm, suggesting that this symbol is a talisman to keep bad luck at bay. The dragon/serpent entwined around a blade (bottom right) enhances this symbol's power.

A complex and intriguing symbol, the dagger has a long history of use dating back to the Stone Age.

Cloak and dagger

The first daggers were crudely fashioned from flint, horn and bone, and served a purpose – enabling early humans to hunt. During the Bronze Age, daggers were fashioned from copper and had evolved in shape and function; being symmetrical and double edged, they were used in close proximity but could also be tied to spears to make a savage throwing weapon. By the dawn of the Iron Age, daggers transformed again and became sturdier, cast from iron and steel. This made them more practical and easily concealed, the perfect illustration of the 18th-century phrase 'cloak and dagger', meaning to deceive or behave surreptitiously.

From practical to ornate

Every civilization had its version of these miniature swords. Nordic warriors carried seax, which were hardy and functional, while the soldiers of Rome kept a pugio about their person. These shorter blades were an emergency backup to the less manageable sword. The ancient Egyptians were the first to consider the look of the dagger, crafting them from gold for use in their temples in ritual sacrifices, and over time this concept grew. Daggers became less about weaponry and more symbolic in appearance. Elaborately decorated with jewels and ornate carvings, they were emblems of wealth and status. The South Asian katar is a good example of this, often used in worship and given as a sacred gift. With its 'H'-shaped grip and shorter, punchier blade, this ceremonial tool is carefully engraved and often fashioned from gold or silver, while the Sikh kirpan, a small, curved dagger worn in a sheath and strap, is a reminder to the bearer of their duty to protect and serve humanity. It symbolizes power and the need to fight injustice and oppression while showing compassion for others.

Synonymous with loyalty and strength of spirit, the dagger may have been used in numerous crimes throughout history, but its main purpose has always been to defend those in need and stand up for what is right and honourable.

How to wear it

Dagger tattoos are often slender, meaning they work well when tattooed on the forearm or lower leg. While some people wear them as they are, many choose designs that combine daggers with other elements to highlight the positive connotations of this symbol. For example, a heart accentuates courage or the trials of love, while the addition of a rose may illustrate honour, pride or courage. Daggers work well in black and grey, a traditional palette, or psychedelic colours. The dagger can be rendered to suit almost any request the wearer might have.

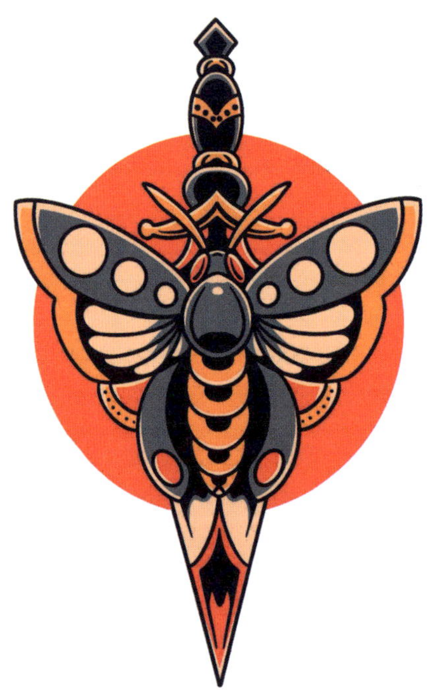

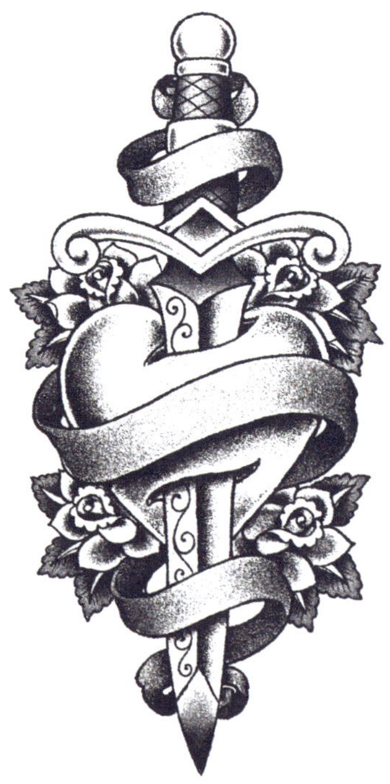

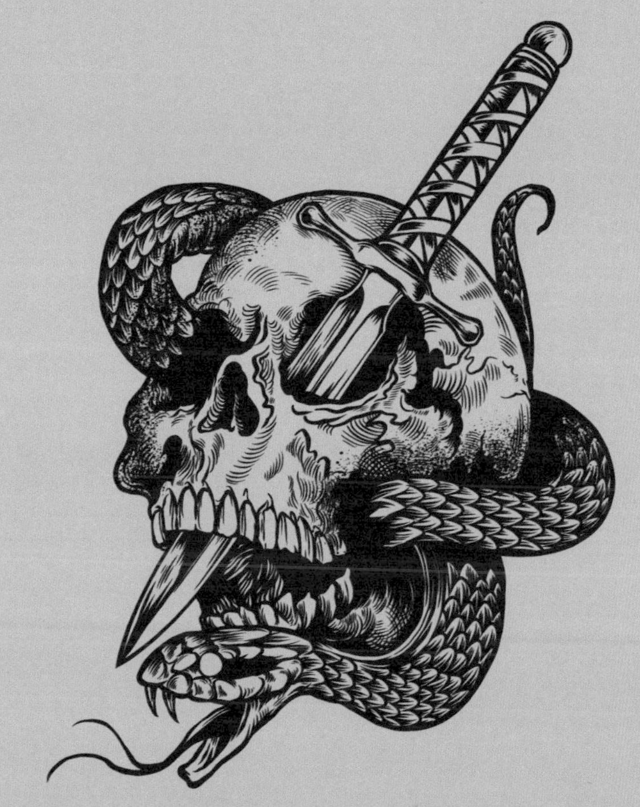

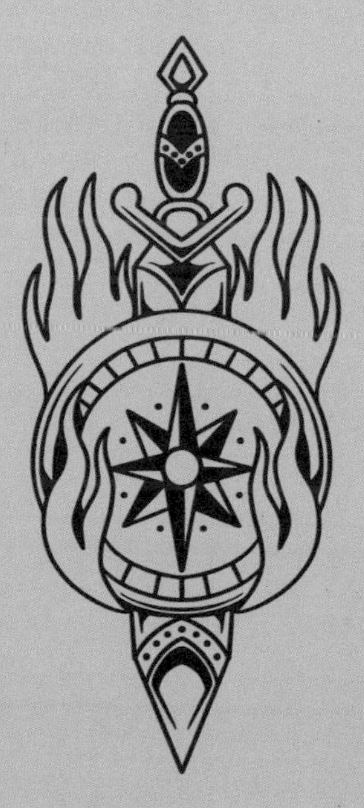

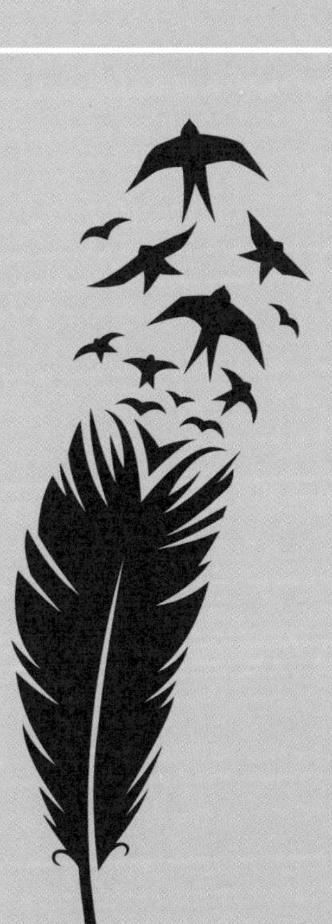

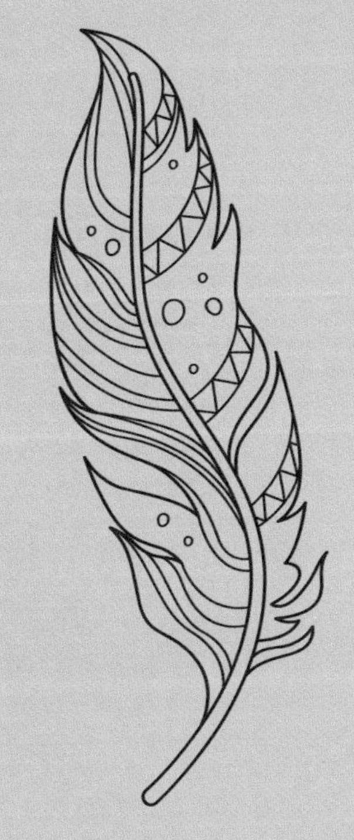

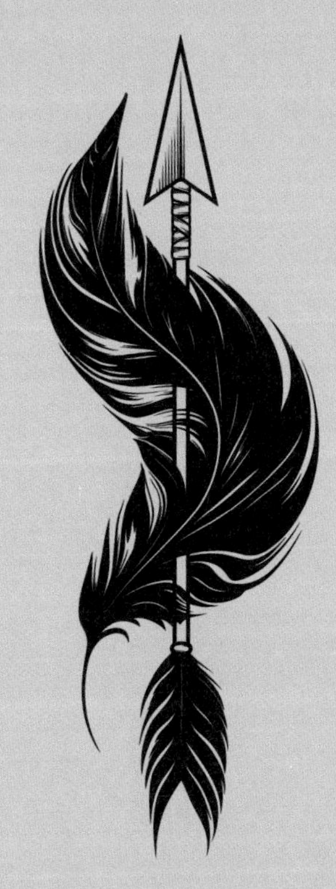

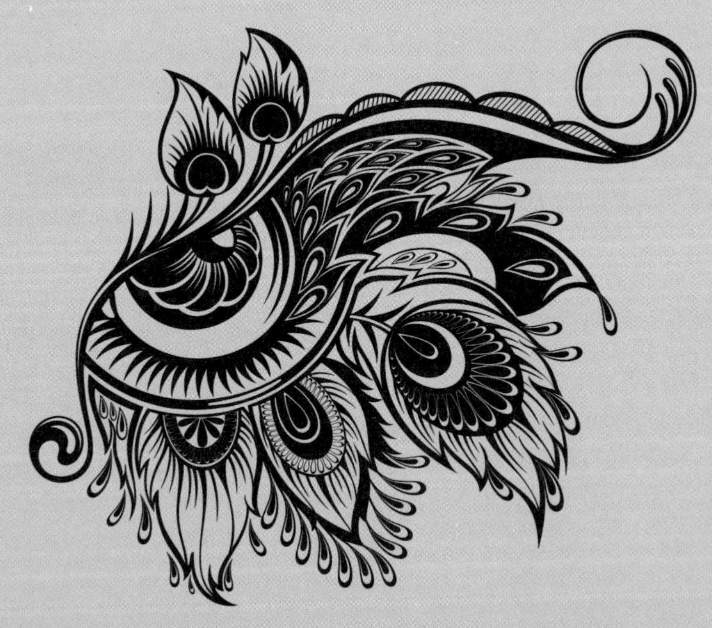

Feather

Peace | Faith | Freedom | Spirituality | Guidance

Sacred Origins
Egyptian, Native
American, Christian

Used Since
Dawn of time

Tattoo Styles
Fine-line
Black-and-grey realism
Ornamental

Opposite: The arrow
piercing a feather (top
right) suggests direction
and enhances the theme
of guidance, while the
birds (bottom left) denote
freedom and faith in
their flight. A feather
image in the shape of an
eye (bottom right) watches
over the wearer. This
is a symbol of spiritual
protection and guidance.

Rooted in spiritual significance, the feather is widely acknowledged as a symbol of peace, purity and hope.

The element of air

The feather represents a lightness of being which comes with faith and spiritual development. This is not surprising when you consider its structure. Delicate fibres combine to form this airy tool that provides insulation and can assist a bird's flight. No wonder it's synonymous with the element of air.

A spiritual totem

In many Indigenous cultures, feathers are held in high regard, providing a spiritual link to each specific bird and connecting the wearer to the creator. In Christianity, they are a symbol of faith and often seen as a sign that angels are present. It's a common belief throughout the world that feathers are a gift from lost loved ones in spirit. Ancient Egyptians believed feathers were significant in matters of justice and honour. Their goddess of truth, Maat, was thought to wield an ostrich feather, which she used to weigh the souls of the dead.

Shamanic tools

The Celts also held feathers in high regard. They associated them with the Irish goddess of summer and wealth, Áine. This beautiful deity was depicted wearing a cloak of pure white swan feathers and was thought to be able to shape-shift into a bird. Druidic priests borrowed this look for their shamanic journeys, often donning a cloak adorned with bird feathers for the practice. As such, feathers in any shape and form were seen as tools to transcend other realms.

How to wear it

Often intricate in style, but working equally well in a bold, traditional style, the meaning of this tattoo can change depending on where on the body it is tattooed. A single feather on the arm or wrist usually indicates a sense of freedom and peace. Larger feathers on the back can be used to form a design representative of angel wings, which are synonymous with protection and guidance. The feather is also a way for the wearer to pay homage to their favourite bird without having the full animal tattooed on them.

Opposite: **A decorative tattoo design featuring feathers and other elements speaks of those classic feather associations: freedom, peace, spirituality and faith.**

Bottom: **Feathers depicted as a part of full wings, in particular angel wings, emphasize protection and guidance.**

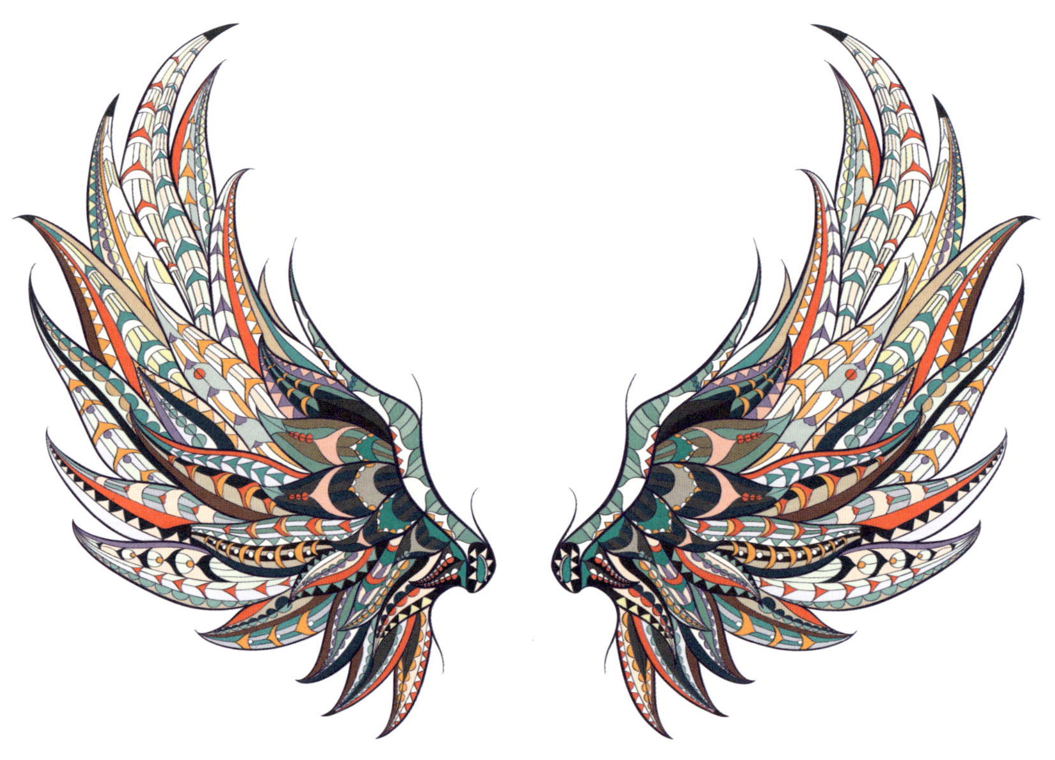

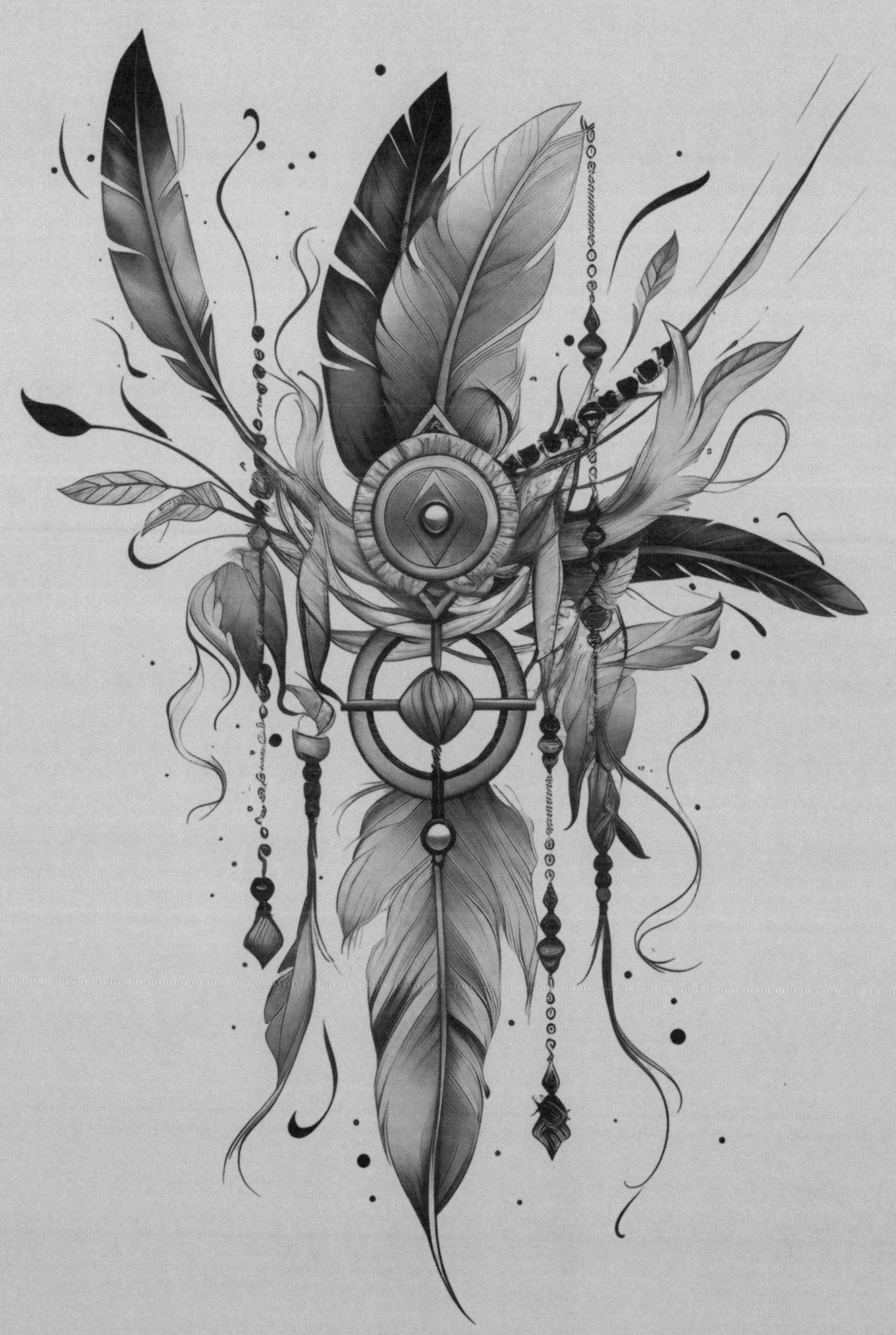

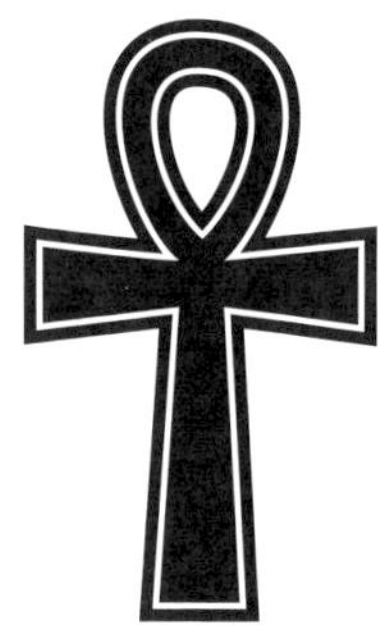

Ankh

Afterlife | Resurrection | Rebirth | Strength | Protection

Sacred Origins
Egyptian, Coptic
Christian

Used Since
c. 3150 BCE

Tattoo Styles
Fine-line
Blackwork
Ornamental

Opposite: The Egyptian ankh (left column) symbolizes life or eternal life. A mandala-style ankh (top right) with ornate decoration denotes spiritual rebirth and the cycles of life. An ankh within a circular pattern that resembles the sun (bottom right) is associated with strength of spirit and new life.

The ancient Egyptians believed that the hieroglyphic symbol of the ankh could imbue a person with a long life, also offering protection and guidance.

The key to eternal life

Dating back to the Early Dynastic period of ancient Egypt, the ankh, otherwise known as the 'key of life' or the 'cross of life', is a symbol with a contradictory history. This simple motif featuring a traditional cross with a loop at the top was associated with a number of key deities and was often carried or worn as an amulet. A symbol of eternal life and the journey of the soul as it moves on to the afterlife, it was also revered by the Coptic Church of Egypt when it emerged in around the 4th century BCE. This ancient school of Christianity embraced the link between the ankh and the resurrection of Christ, which is thought to have influenced the creation of the Christian cross.

Footwear to belt buckles

There are a number of theories as to where the ankh originated from. The famous Egyptologist Sir Alan H Gardiner believed the symbol evolved from the strap of a type of sandal which would have been worn at that time. The loop at the top of the cross was a representation of the strap as it curved around the ankle, while the Egyptian word for sandal, *nkh*, forms part of its name. Other scholars disagree with this theory, believing that the sigil is based upon 'the knot of Isis', also known as the tyet, a prominent belt buckle for a girdle belonging to the goddess of magic and healing. The girdle was associated with female genitalia and fertility, linking it to the source of all life, which is at the core of the ankh's power.

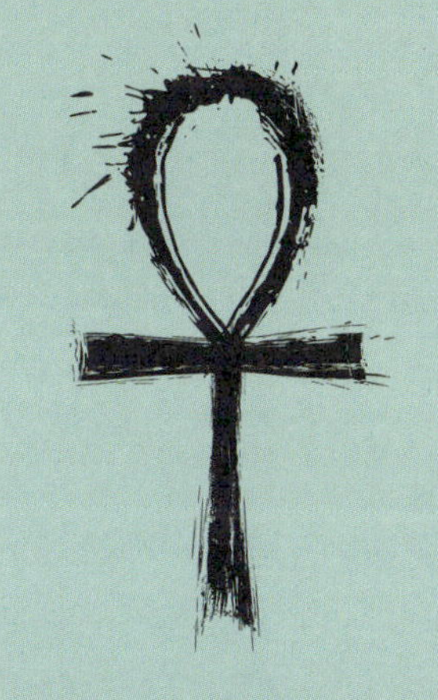

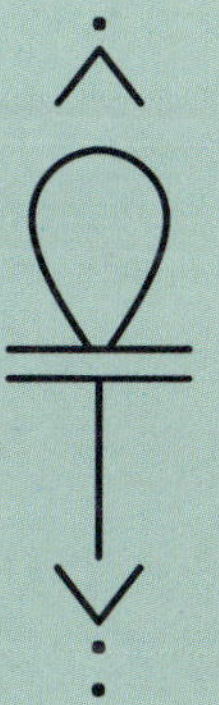

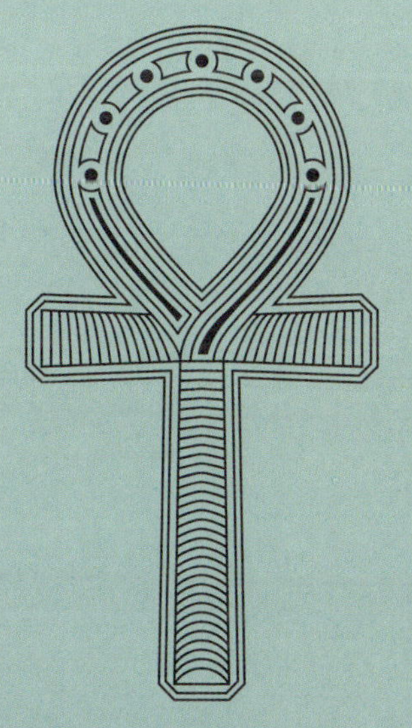

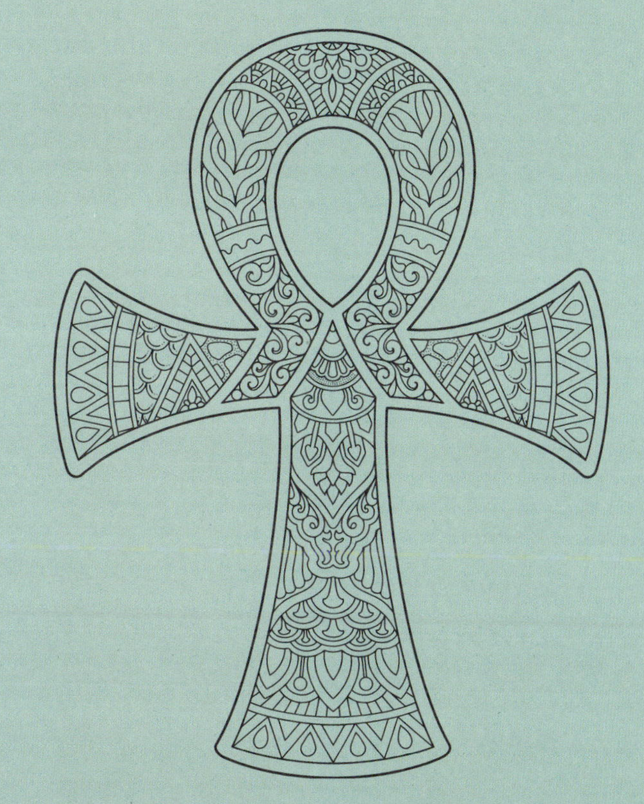

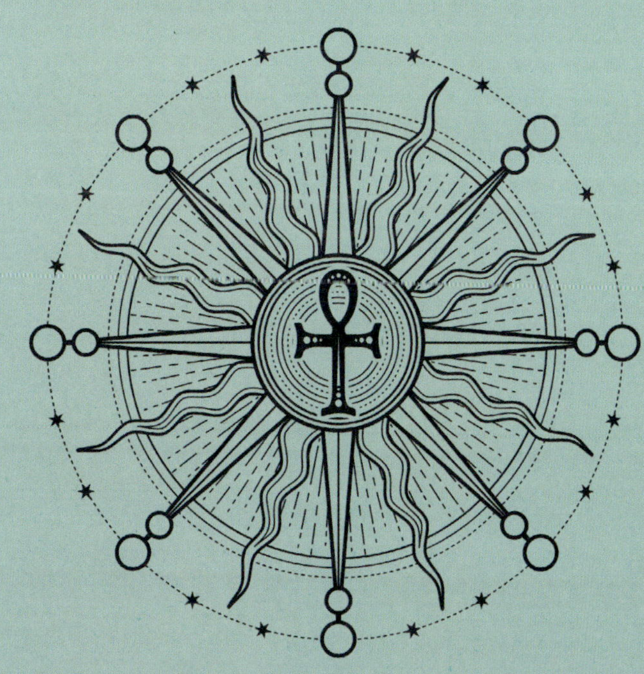

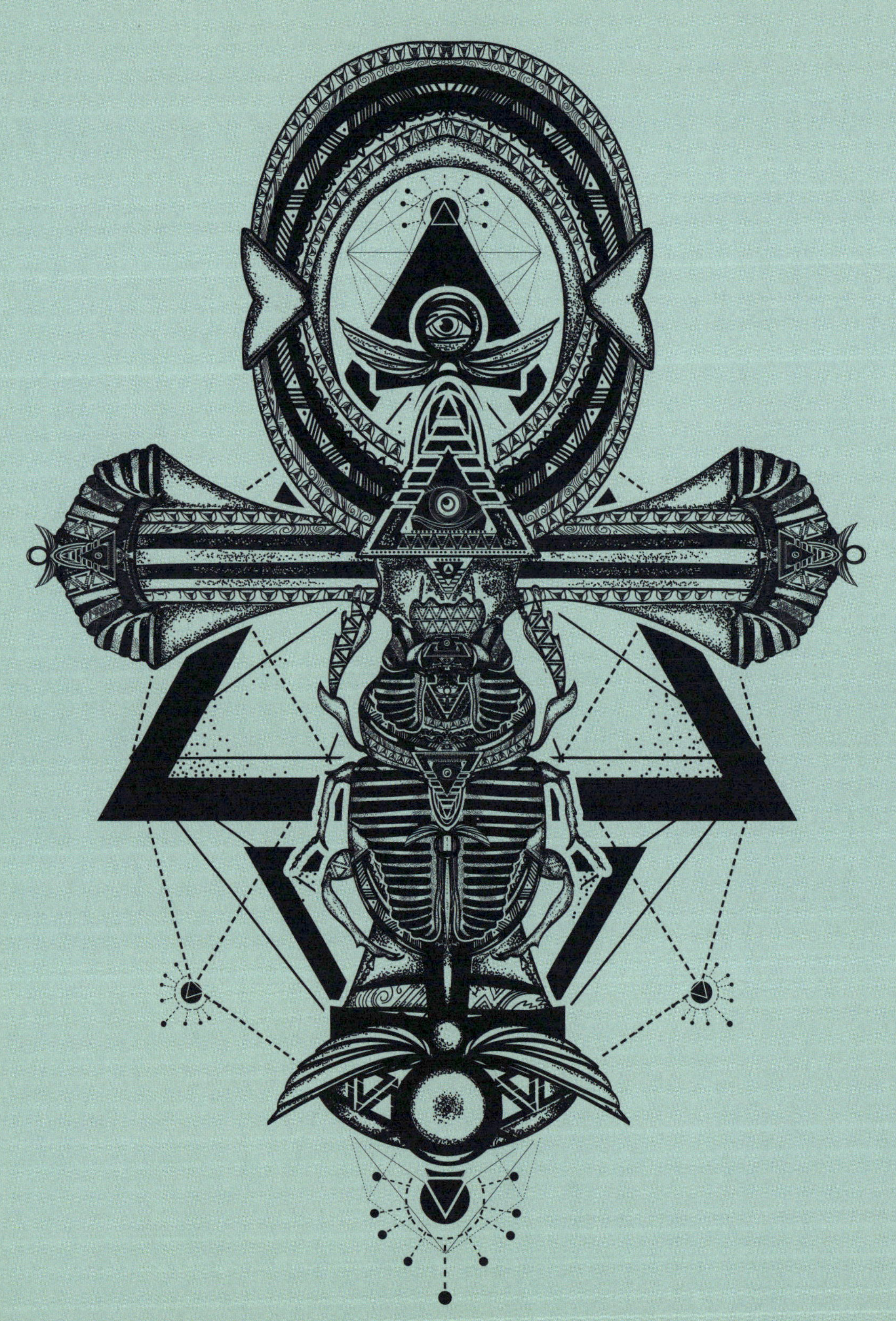

Tomb paintings show a number of deities wielding the symbol, including the goddess of justice and balance, Maat; the god of the dead, Anubis; and the great god Osiris. As the narratives in these depictions unfold, it's clear the ankh was used to revive the souls of the dead, being placed upon the lips of the deceased in a bid to raise them from eternal sleep.

How to wear it

This is a popular tattoo choice because it is malleable and works well on many parts of the body. The ankh is most commonly tattooed in solid black, or black and grey if more embellishment is added, and is often seen as a small to medium-sized tattoo. The ankh can be combined with script and other symbols like the Eye of Horus (at the centre of the ankh design, left) – this combination amplifies the strength and power of the original symbol.

Opposite: **A symbol of protection and strength, the eye and scarab beetle combined make this ankh a powerful talisman to repel evil.**

Right: **An ankh incorporating a scarab signifies protection and safe passage for the dead.**

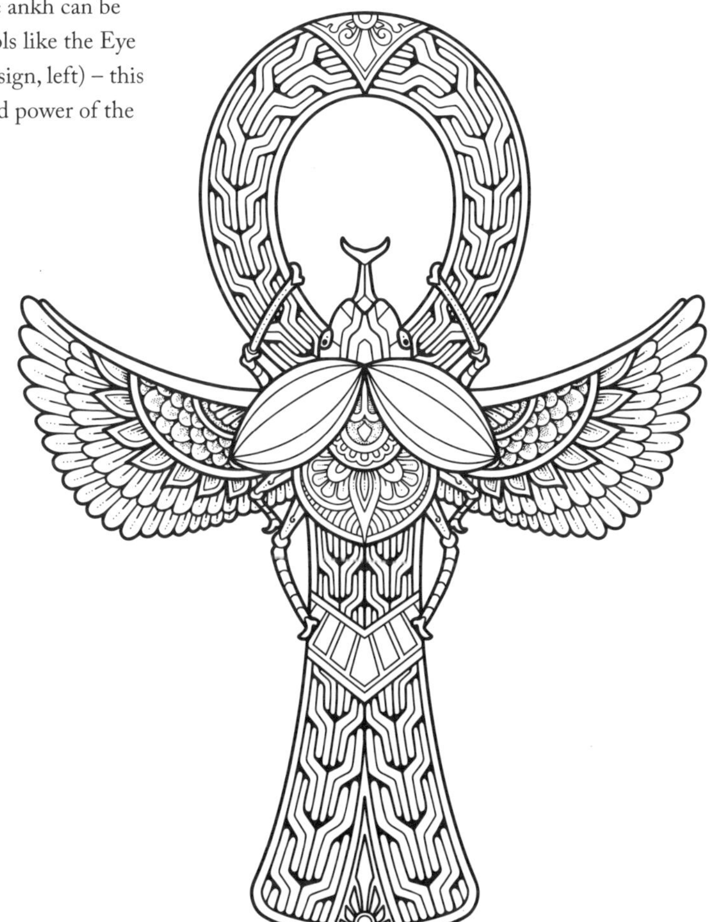

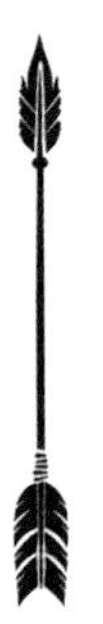

Arrow

Movement | Focus | Courage | Resilience | Achievement

Sacred Origins
African

Used Since
18th century

Tattoo Styles
Fine-line
Blackwork
Western traditional

A symbol of movement, action and direction, the image of an arrow can carry many meanings.

A tool for survival

To truly understand the weight of this symbol's meaning, we must step back in time to when arrows were first used as a tool for hunter-gatherers. Crudely shaped from flint and stone, those early arrowheads made the difference between life and death, allowing humans to hunt for sustenance and protect themselves from some of the larger carnivorous beasts. This alone imbues the motif with courage and resilience.

The oldest known examples are remnants of arrows found at Sibudu Cave in South Africa. These prehistoric tools were crafted from bone around 61,000 years ago. While there's a long history of arrow use, the symbol itself has been in existence for around 400 years. It was in the 18th century that it made its first appearance in a set of engineering papers, where it indicated the flow and direction of a waterwheel.

How to wear it

Depending on how the arrow is tattooed, different meanings are implied. Crossed arrows indicate an alliance between tribes or, in a modern context, between friends. A broken arrow is considered a symbol of peace, while an arrow pulled back in its bow can indicate the wearer is facing a struggle.

The arrow is a hugely versatile tattoo design: it can be used as the perfect 'gap filler', or it can be tattooed to appear as if it is piercing the skin, through one side of the neck and out of the other, for example.

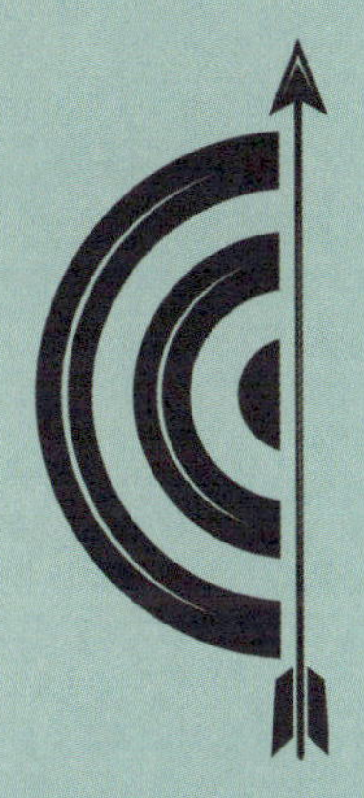
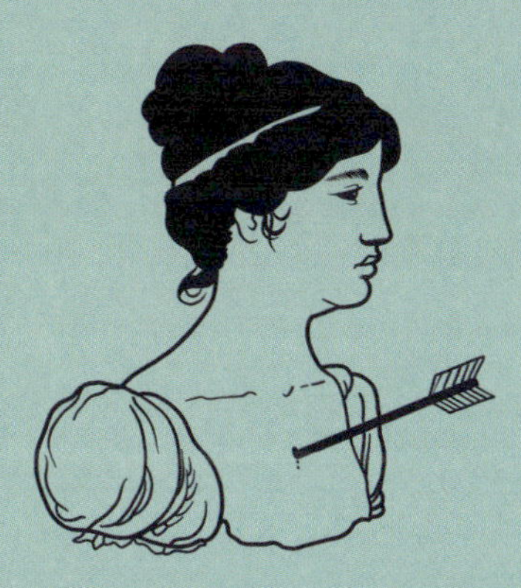
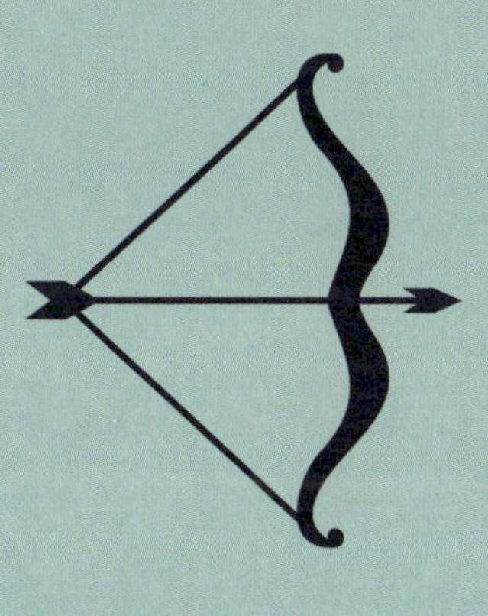
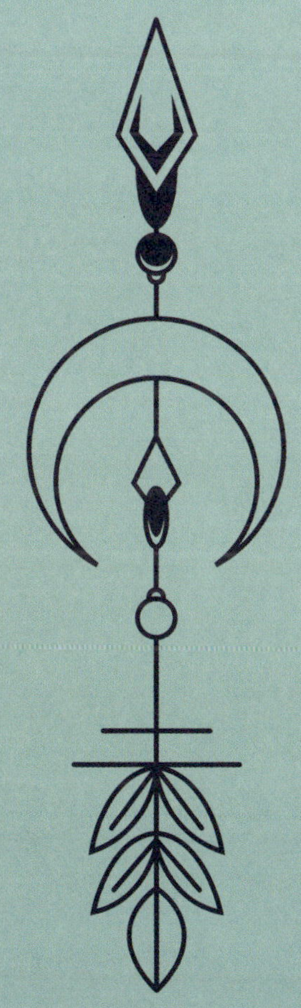
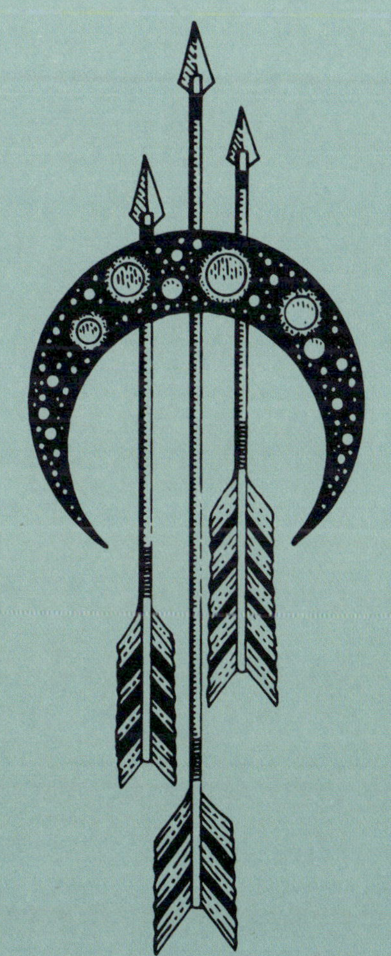

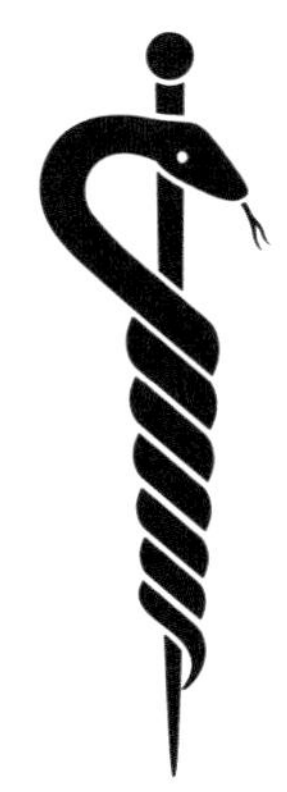

Staff of Asclepius

Medicine | Healing | Purification | Peace | Victory

Sacred Origins
Roman, Greek

Used Since
8th century BCE

Tattoo Styles
Fine-line
Blackwork
Black-and-grey realism

Opposite: The rod of Asclepius (top left and right) is associated with medicine and healing. Wings combined with the rod (bottom left) add spiritual significance and seek to enhance its healing power.

The staff or rod of Asclepius, also known as the asklepian, features a heavy wooden staff entwined by a snake, used to represent medicine and healing since 800 BCE.

Two snakes or one?

The staff of Asclepius is often confused with the caduceus (from the Greek word meaning 'herald's wand'). The caduceus had two serpents intertwined along the length of the staff and belonged to the Greek messenger god Hermes, while the staff of Asclepius belonged to the Roman god of healing, who then transmuted into a Greek deity.

God of medicine and healing

According to legend, Asclepius was originally a mortal man and a keen physician with an aptitude for medicine. He later became a deity and son of the sun god Apollo. With the ability to heal and even raise the dead, Asclepius was much loved by the ancient Romans and Greeks, and a cult soon evolved around his worship which spread throughout Europe during the 5th century BCE. Followers would gather at sacred temples to perform various rites and conduct healing and purification rituals. These places became a font of medical knowledge, and over time patients gathered and participated in curative practices, many of which involved the use of snakes, a nod to Asclepius's rod.

Interestingly, snakes were believed to have healing properties, mainly because of their ability to shed their skin and be 'reborn'.

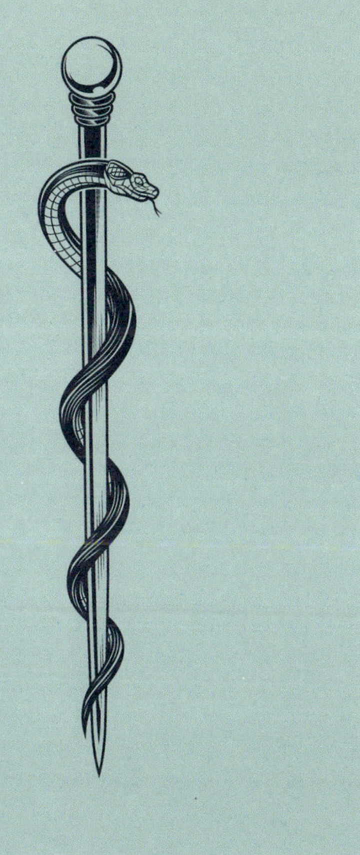

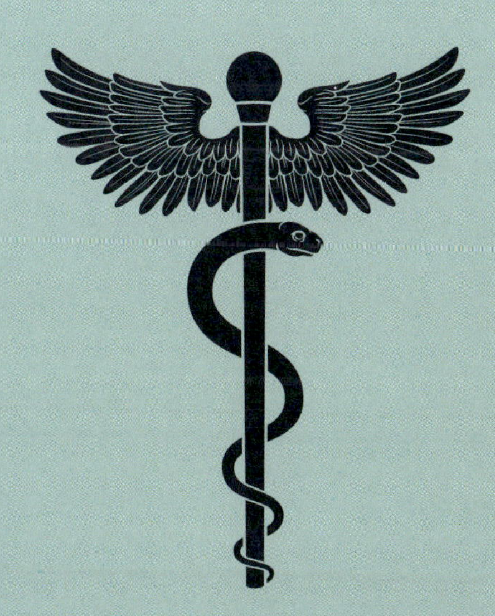

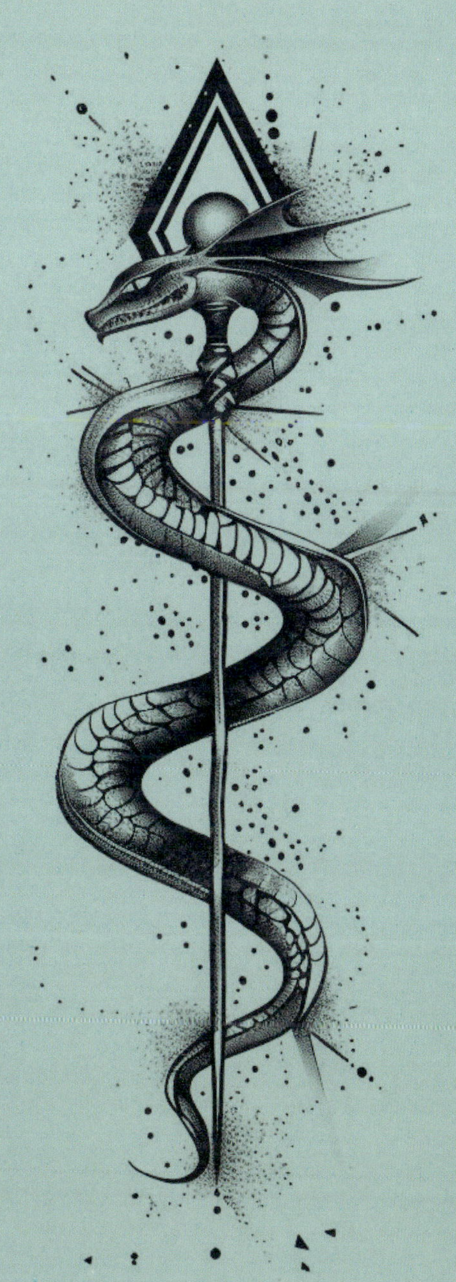

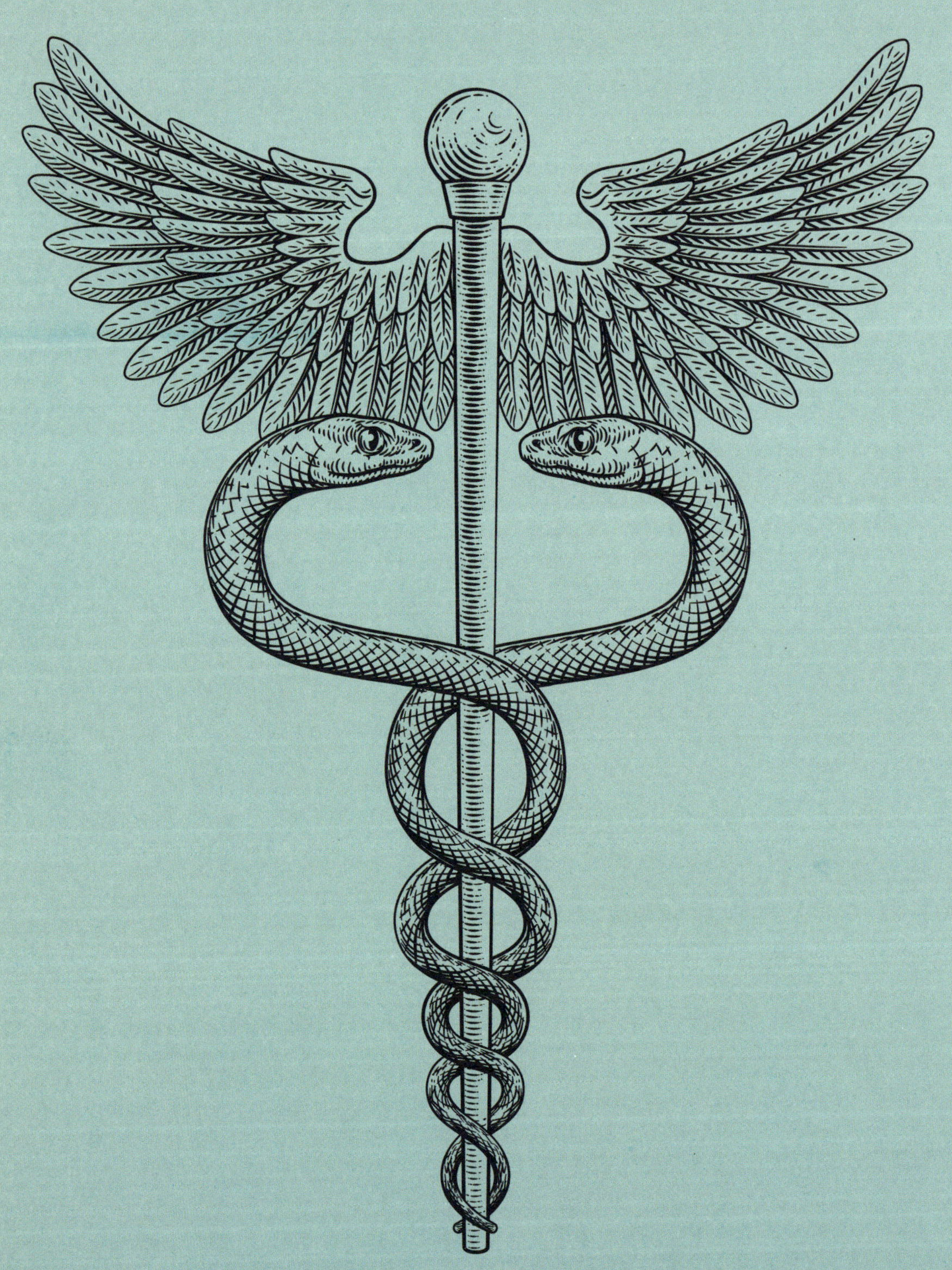

Modern medical emblem

Asclepius, who was depicted as a bearded old man to reinforce his image as
a learned scholar, was often pictured with his daughter Hygieia. She was the
goddess of health, cleanliness and sanitation, and it is from her name that we
get the word 'hygiene'. She too favoured snakes in her healing practices and was
associated with the bowl of Hygieia, a symbol for cleanliness and purification,
which was adorned with a snake.

The rod of Asclepius is used as an emblem by many medical
institutions, including The New England Journal of Medicine,
The American College of Physicians and the World Health
Organization. While the caduceus is sometimes used to represent
medical institutions, it is primarily an emblem associated with
peace and commerce, while the rod remains the true motif for
all kinds of healing and medicine.

How to wear it

There is a clear link between the rod of Asclepius
and careers in medicine and healing, and many
doctors and nurses choose this tattoo as a way
of honouring the work they do. The design can
also symbolize that a person has been through a
healing situation and emerged triumphant. The
length of this tattoo makes it the ideal choice for
calves, forearms and the outer bicep. While it can
be successful when tattooed in a simple fashion,
the inclusion of a snake in the symbol means
this design lends itself to an ornate approach.

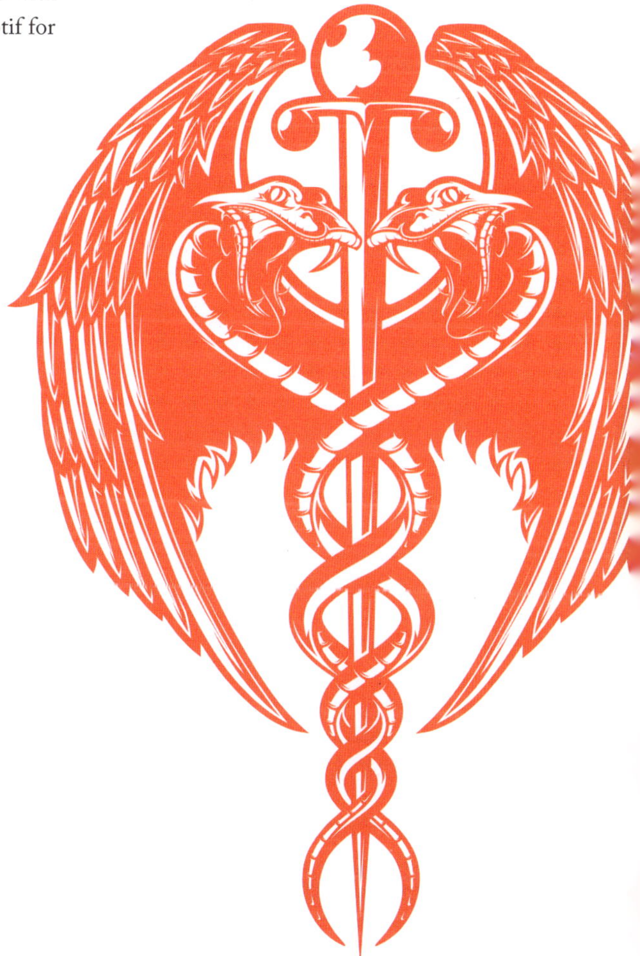

**Opposite and right: The staff
of Caduceus – often confused
with the rod of Asclepius
– was carried by the Greek
god Hermes. It is considered
a symbol of peace and is
synonymous with heralds
and messengers.**

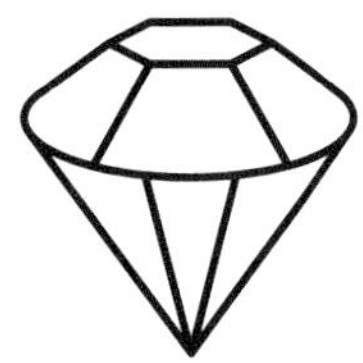

Diamond

Beauty | Magic | Invincibility | Divine power | Wealth

Sacred Origins
Greek, Roman,
Chinese, Egyptian

Used Since
8th century BCE

Tattoo Styles
Western traditional
Fine-line
Blackwork

Opposite: Diamond tattoos (top left) can be used to communicate glamour, strength and power, among other qualities. Swallows pictured with a diamond (middle) make this symbol synonymous with faith, beauty and hope, while wings combined with a diamond (bottom and top right) give the symbol spiritual significance.

The diamond's role in history and the beliefs attributed to the jewel that inspired the symbol go some way to explain its significance and why it is a popular tattoo choice.

More than a gem
Early civilizations noted the beauty of the diamond and its reflective properties, which must have given it an otherworldly charm. To them, the diamond was so much more than a magnificent jewel.

Teardrops of the gods
The ancient Greeks believed these faceted stones were the teardrops of the gods that had fallen to earth and were imbued with magical powers. Indeed, Plato went a step further when he suggested that they were alive and had the ability to reproduce. He believed that each stone contained a heavenly spirit which could be petitioned for assistance. The Romans prized the diamond for its strength, and often included these gems in the breastplates of armour, to protect and endow the wearer with invincibility. In the Far East, the diamond's mirror-like sheen made it a common charm to ward off evil and repel bad luck.

How to wear it
The diamond's compact proportions make it suitable for tattooing at a small scale. It is often accompanied by additional decoration, such as flowers or a wreath; however, this symbol holds equal, if not more, power when tattooed on its own with some simple lines to hint at its sparkle and indestructible properties. Diamond tattoos work well as gap fillers anywhere an awkward space has been created, but equally well in a prominent location such as the top of the hand or the inner wrist.

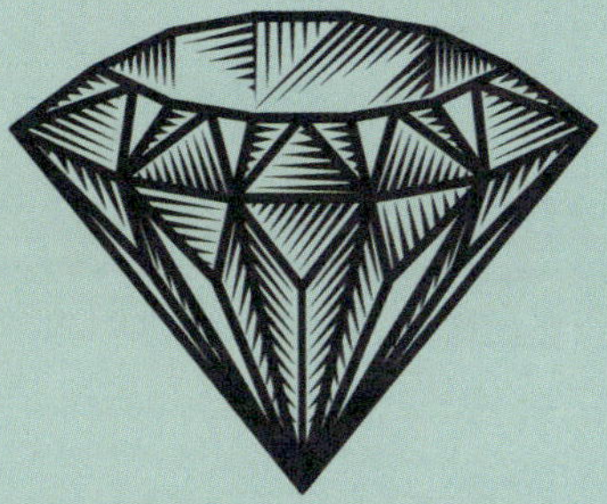

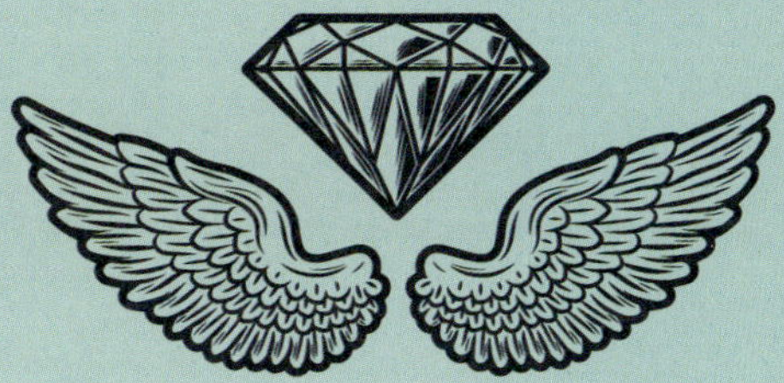

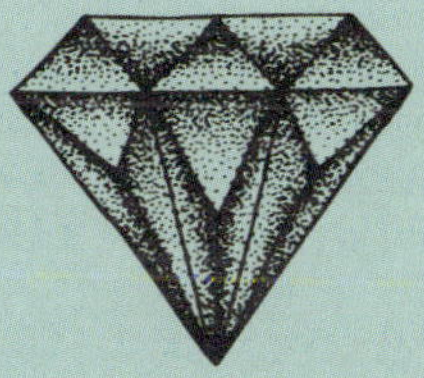

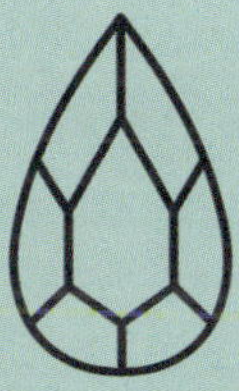

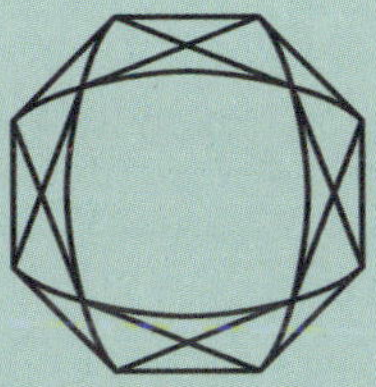

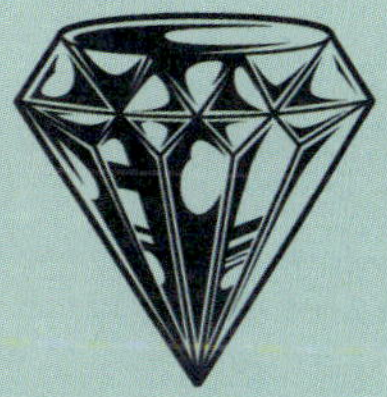

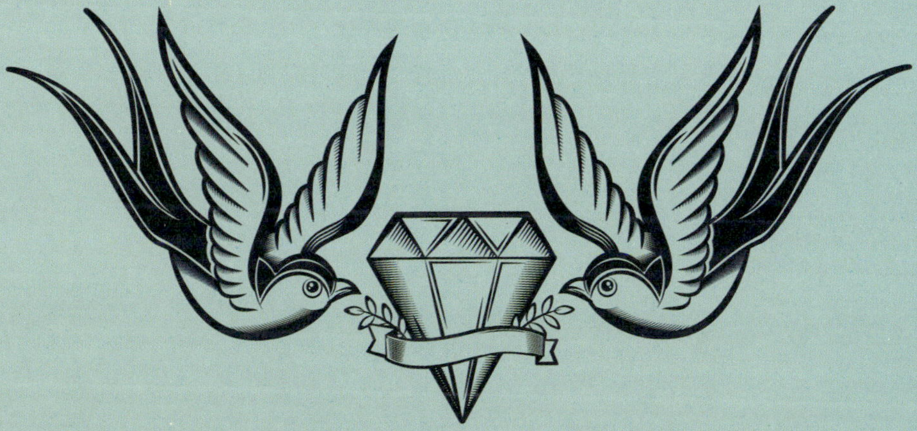

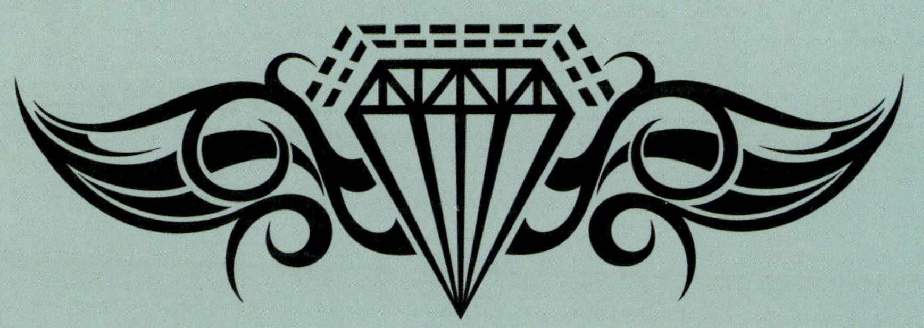

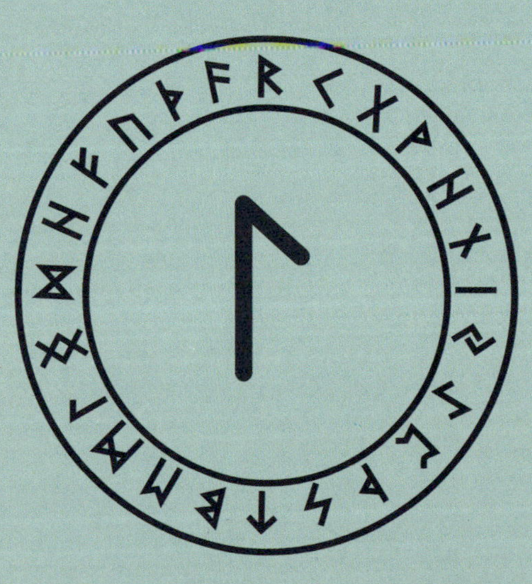

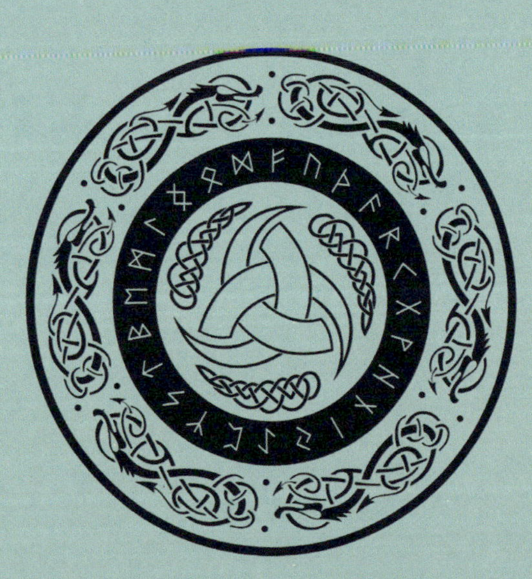

Laguz

Flexibility | Sustenance | Power | Intuition | Grace

Sacred Origins
Germany, Scandinavia

Used Since
2nd century

Tattoo Styles
Fine-line
Blackwork

This symbol is associated with intuition and the subconscious mind, urging the wearer to go within when seeking answers, and to trust their innate wisdom.

An early form of communication

Laguz, meaning 'water' or 'lake', is the 21st rune of the ancient Germanic alphabet known as the Elder Futhark, which was used between the 2nd and 8th centuries. This tool for communication, more commonly known as the runes, was a Nordic creation used to mark burial mounds and record great moments in history. The laguz symbol itself, which looks like half an arrow pointing upwards, captures the essence of fluidity and the importance of going with the flow. The word *lagu* in Old English means ocean or sea, while the Norse interpretation *lögr* translates as waterfall.

Nature's lessons

Essential to survival of early tribes, water was key to sustaining life as well as providing a bridge to new worlds and transporting essential items. Ancient civilizations would have watched the way water moves around objects to overcome any obstacle and how it can be absorbed. The rune laguz was a reminder to embrace change, to create and nurture, but also to adapt and accept the twists and turns of fate with grace.

How to wear it

This simple form is best tattooed in a minimalist way and is often worn on the finger, hand or perhaps the wrist or ankle. It can be combined with other runes and/or feature as a design detail within a larger tattoo.

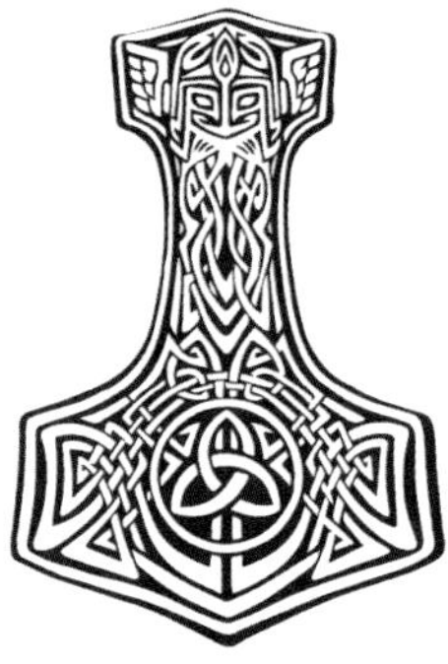

Thor's Hammer

Courage | Strength | Fortitude | Blessings | Good fortune

Sacred Origins
Norse/Viking

Used Since
11th century

Tattoo Styles
Western traditional
Neo-traditional
Black-and-grey realism
Blackwork

Opposite: Thor's hammer displayed in a circular symbol (top middle) encompassing the runic alphabet amplifies sacred power and strength. The hammer combined with two birds (bottom) – most likely ravens – strengthens the association of the symbol with the Norse peoples, who revered the birds, and linked them to the god Odin. The use of Celtic knotwork in the design can be used to indicate a personal link to that culture.

Known in Old Norse as Mjöllnir, the hammer of the god of thunder and lightning, Thor, was one of the most prolific and popular symbols of the Viking era.

A weapon with magical power

To truly understand the sacred meaning of this symbol, it's important to delve deeper into the pantheon of gods and their significance to those early Nordic tribes.

Thor was a mighty warrior god, the son of the father of all, Odin. His main responsibility was to guard the Aesir, a tribe of deities within the pantheon who lived in the celestial realm of Asgard. According to Viking myth, the hammer was crafted by the dwarves and made from an unusually strong iron. Gifted with magical powers, it could only be wielded by Thor himself, and only when he was pure of heart and honest in his intentions. The hammer rarely missed its target and would always return like a boomerang to its master. It's thought that it was a representation of the bolts of lightning that the god had at his disposal.

Blessings and consecration

Thor was considered the strongest of all the Norse gods, and the people regularly petitioned him for assistance and protection. It was thought that the hammer was a key part of this worship, for although it was a weapon it was also used in rites to provide consecration and blessing. Indeed, Thor used it on many occasions to bring souls back to life. In one tale he kills and eats his goats, then in a moment of penance hallows the bones with Mjöllnir and brings them back to life. Medieval historians documented evidence of giant hammers kept as instruments of ritual in Thor's temples. These were used to bang enormous drums, to create a thunderous sound to ward off evil spirits.

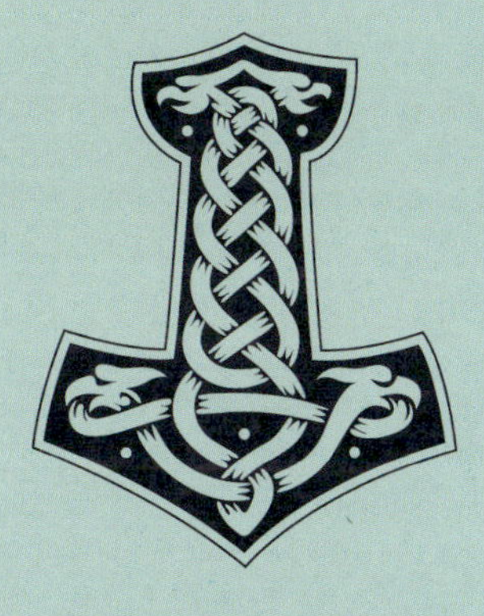 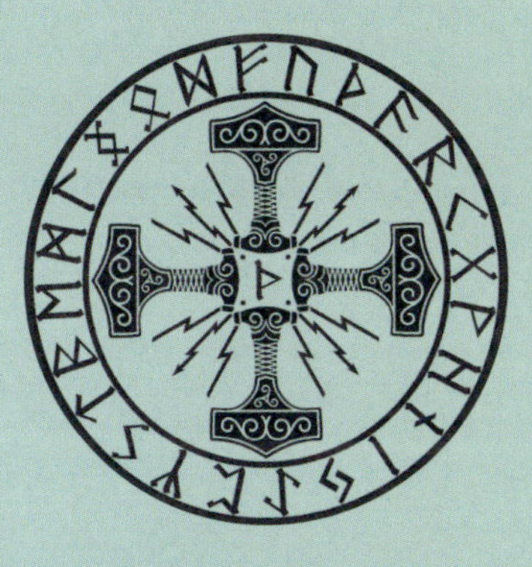 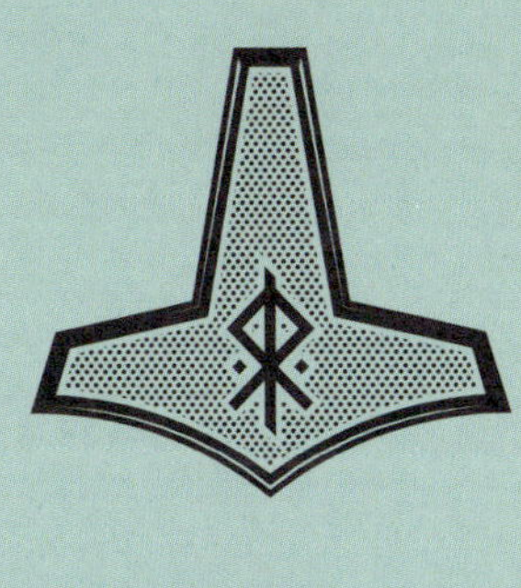

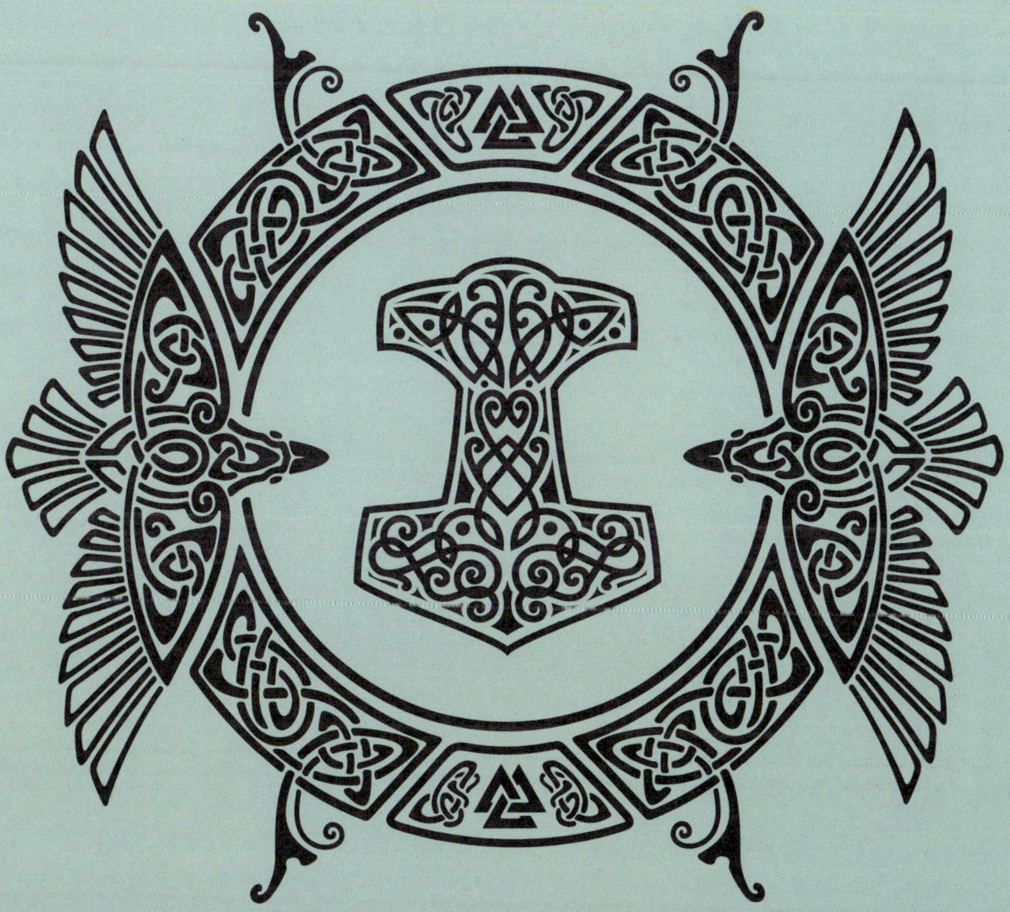

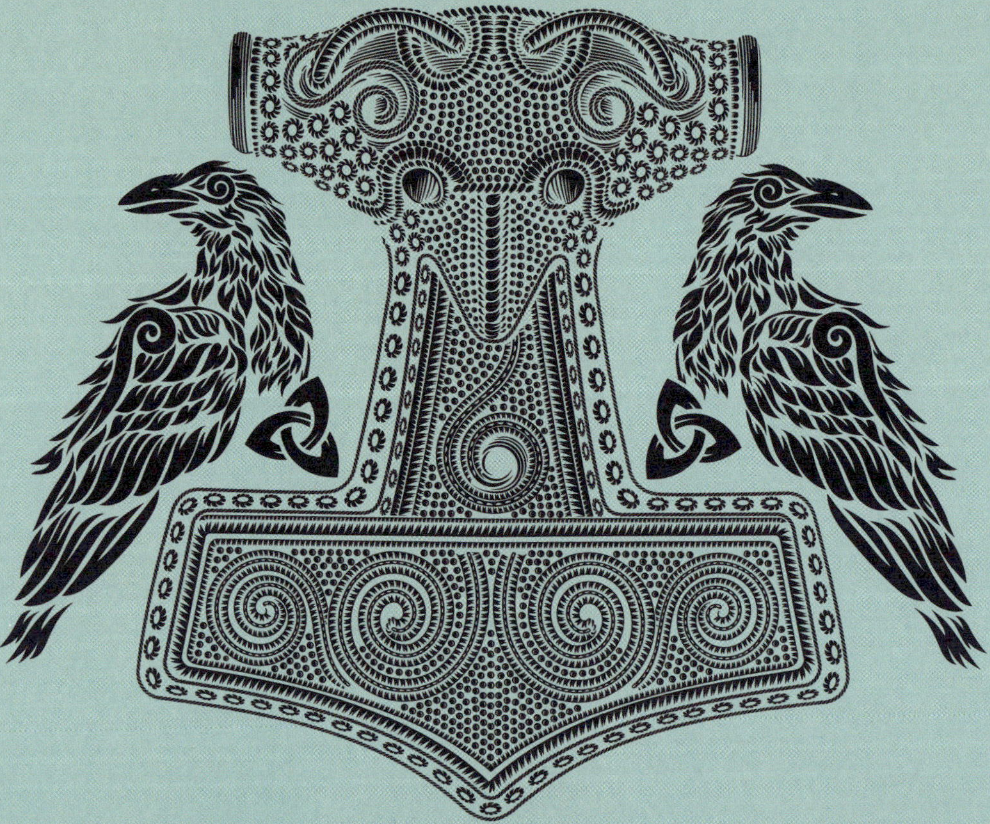

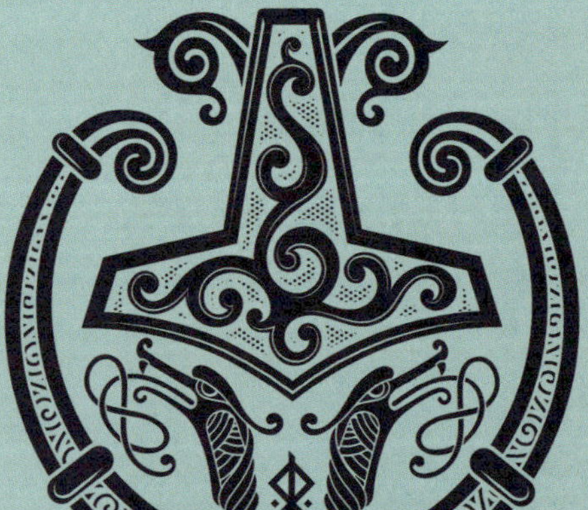

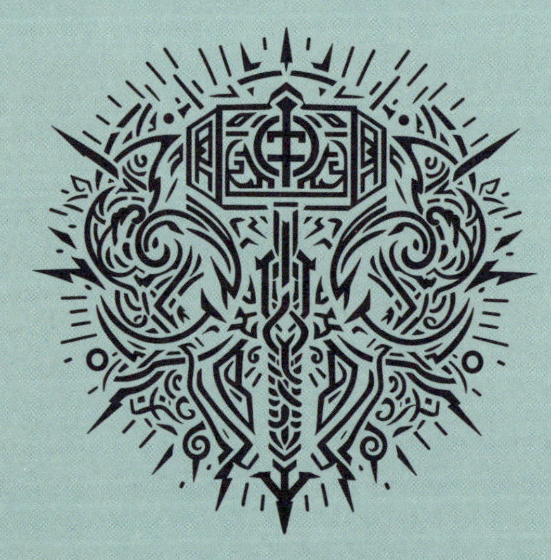

Versatile votive

The symbol was also used to bless sacred unions, with an early stone carving discovered in Scandinavia which clearly depicts a betrothed couple being blessed by a giant hammer. Thor's hammer was used in a variety of ways around the home, with miniature votives displayed to keep evil at bay, or worn as talismans for strength, protection and courage.

How to wear it

The power this symbol possesses means it earns a prominent spot on the body – whether it be the outer bicep, back or chest, this design works best at a considerable scale. Heavy line weights in the Western traditional style are suitable, or the use of black-and-grey realism can produce successful tattoos, as many nuanced narratives from Norse mythology can be weaved in effortlessly. The addition of Thor's hand and/or lightning is a popular choice, as is Norse patterning within the hammer itself.

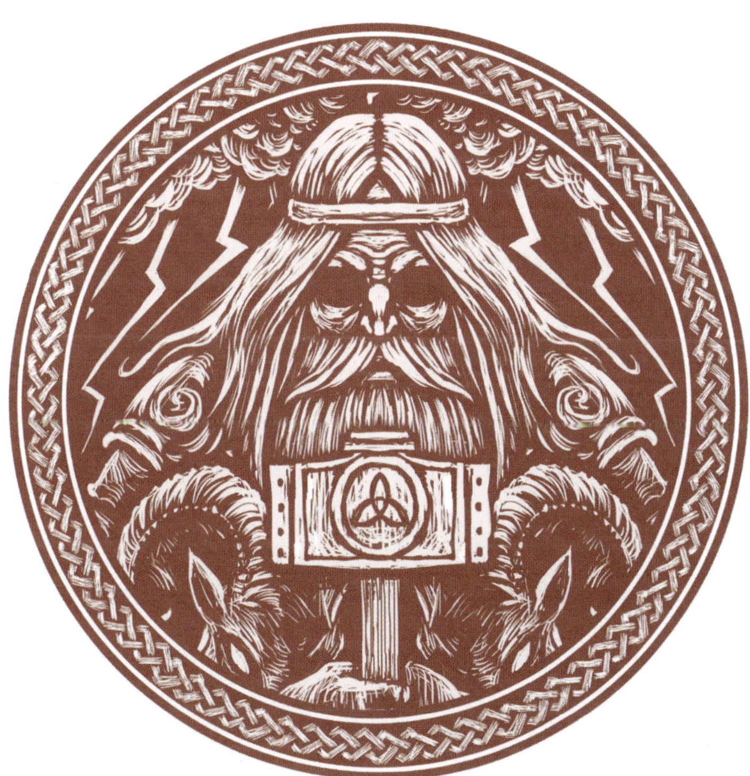

Left: Thor wielding his hammer is a symbol of purity of heart and good intentions.

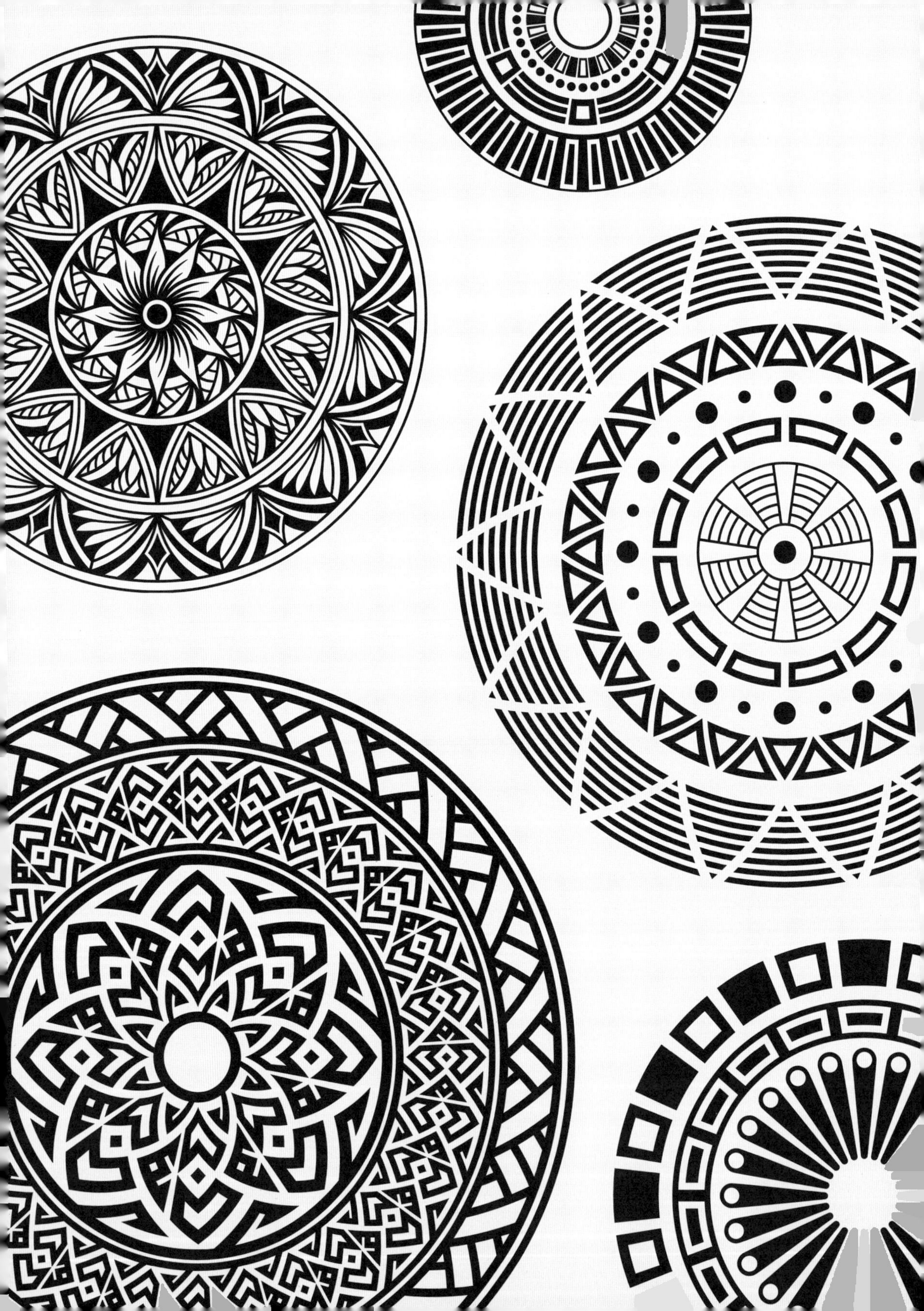

2

Circular Designs

The natural world is full of circles – from seeds to mushrooms and the patterns on a butterfly's wing, this shape takes precedence above all others. It greets us every morning from the sky as the radiant glowing fireball of the sun, and watches over us at night, when the moon is full and an almost perfect circle of illumination. No wonder early civilizations recognized the beauty and significance of the sphere and believed it to be a symbol of wholeness and unity.

The word 'circle' comes from the Latin *circus*, meaning ring or circular line, a concept that was borrowed by the Romans, who used it to describe their arenas. Like the Greeks, they were fascinated by this shape, and they weren't the first. The Babylonians studied round structures and were one of the first civilizations to develop a method for calculating the area of a circle, while the ancient Egyptians and Mesopotamians were equally captivated with its geometry.

Today, circular shapes are at the heart of some of the most elaborate tattoo symbols. Within these pages you will find a selection of emblems that embrace this outline, from willow-woven rings that catch bad dreams to the earth itself, a planet spinning around the sun, another spherical wonder. Circular designs have much to offer and, like the symbols they are based on, can make a powerful impression.

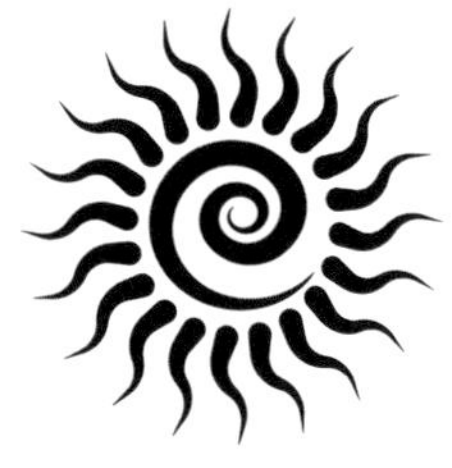

Sun

Vitality | Joy | Light | Power | Creativity

Sacred Origins
Every civilization

Used Since
Dawn of time

Tattoo Styles
Japanese
Fine-line
Western traditional

Opposite: The moon peeping from within the sun (top left) is synonymous with balance, inferring that light and dark are interconnected. A sun emerging from clouds (bottom left) suggests that even on the darkest day there is light and joy to be found. The cosmic landscape of sun, moon and stars (bottom right) denotes the power of the universe.

A symbol of light, energy and joy, this fiery orb has captivated humans since the dawn of time.

The sun's journey

From sunrise to sunset, ancient civilizations were fascinated by the movements of the sun. They recognized its power and presence, aware that it was key to their survival, providing warmth and light and nurturing the land. Its journey through the sky each day was the subject of much interest and each mythology had a story to explain this.

Chariots and chases

To the ancient Egyptians, the sun was the god Ra, or Re, who rode his chariot accompanied by his daughter Bastet. Each day, they were pursued by the demon serpent Apep, who eventually stole the light of the sun, causing darkness to sweep through the land. The following morning Ra would rise again, resplendent and ready to outwit his attacker. In Norse mythology, the sun was represented by the goddess Sunna, or Sol. A beautiful being with a golden halo of hair, she would race through the sky upon her chariot pulled by two giant steeds. The hungry wolf Skoll would chase her and sometimes get so close that he was able to take a bite from the sun, causing an eclipse.

How to wear it

A sun tattoo can be big, bold and filled with colour – this approach is seen in Japanese tattooing, often as a background element on the shoulder in a sleeve design or as a framing device in a full-back piece. This symbol can also be tattooed small and discreetly. Like some moon-themed tattoos, the sun is often personified. Another notable sun-themed tattoo is 'The Sun' Tarot card.

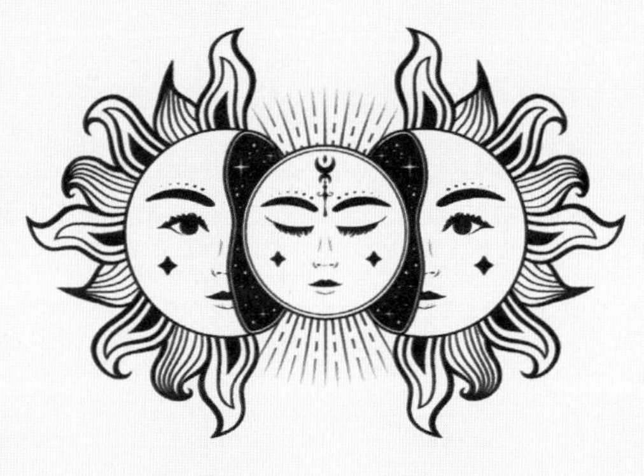

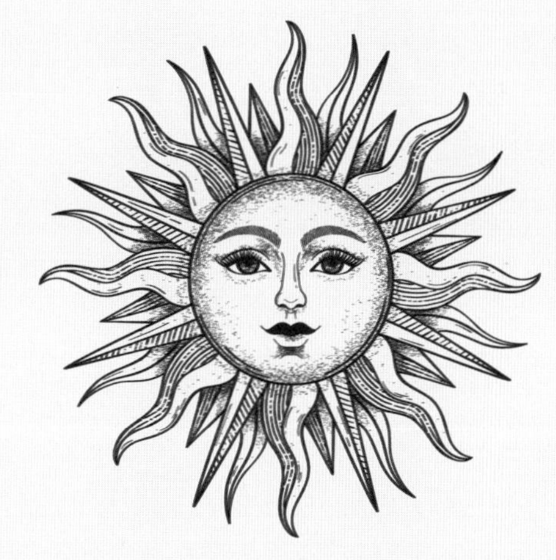

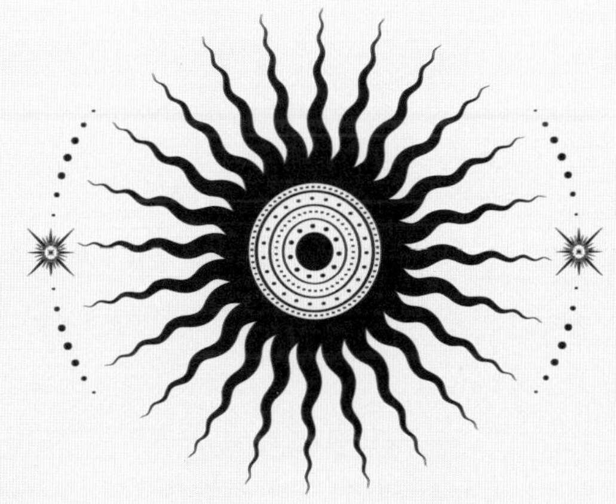

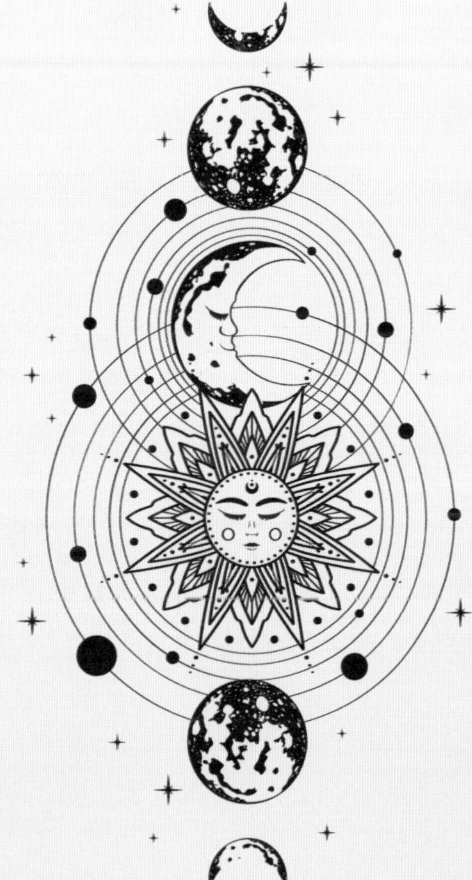

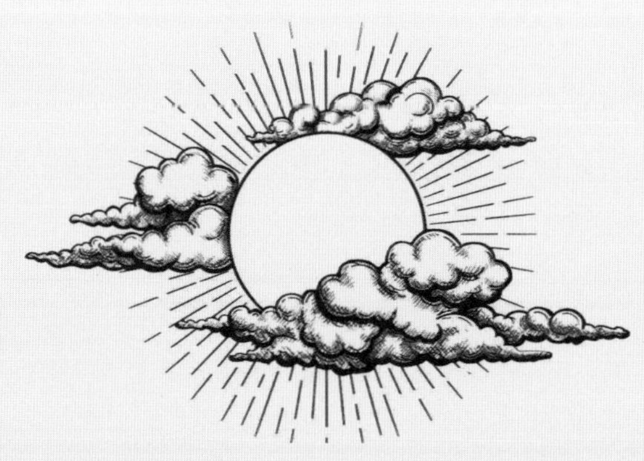

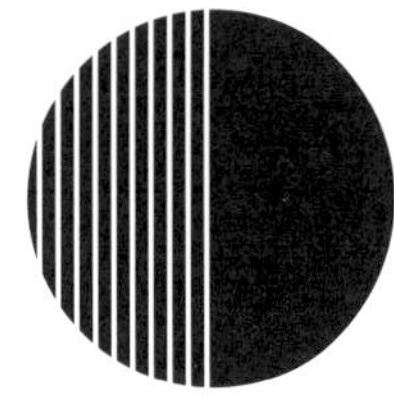

Moon

Imagination | Intuition | Creativity | Mystery | Magic

Sacred Origins
Every civilization

Used Since
Dawn of time

Tattoo Styles
Fine-line
Western traditional
Neo-traditional

Mysterious and somewhat elusive, the moon is a symbol of illumination, the glowing orb that lights up the night sky.

Illuminating orb

The moon offers us a glimpse of the unseen while maintaining an air of mystery. No wonder ancient civilizations associated it with intuition, power and feminine energy. They watched in awe as it shifted shape each month, seemingly growing to the full height of its powers, then fading away to darkness. To explain this, they came up with a number of theories and created magical myths to celebrate its magnificence.

Moon myths and deities

To the Romans, the moon was the goddess Luna, often depicted with a crescent moon upon her head. While this deity was renowned for her serenity, the word 'lunacy' sprang from her name, giving rise to the belief that the moon could affect the mood and cause erratic behaviour thanks to its shifting patterns. The Greek version of this deity was the beautiful goddess Selene, a passionate deity who embraced the power of love and fell head over heels with a mortal man named Endymion. Every night she would visit him as he slept, invading his dreams and satiating her love, a union that would result in the birth of 50 daughters known as the Menai. It was commonplace for the moon to be associated with passion, from romantic leanings to the wilder passions that might cause a person to lose their mind. Artemis was another Greek goddess of the moon; associated with nature and the hunt, she represented the nurturing side of the planet, linked to fertility and motherhood. Indeed, the moon in her fullness was said to represent a woman about to give birth.

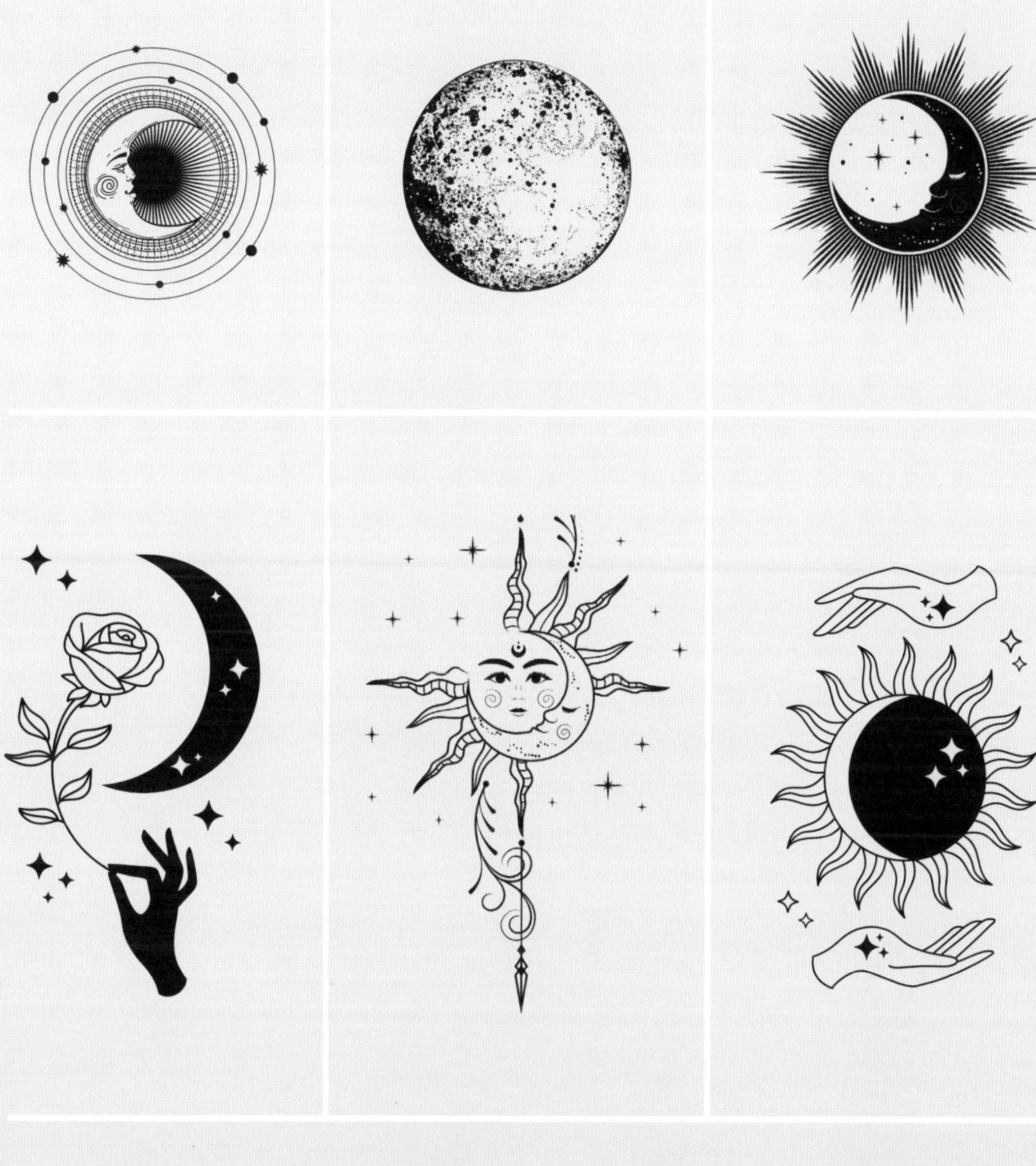

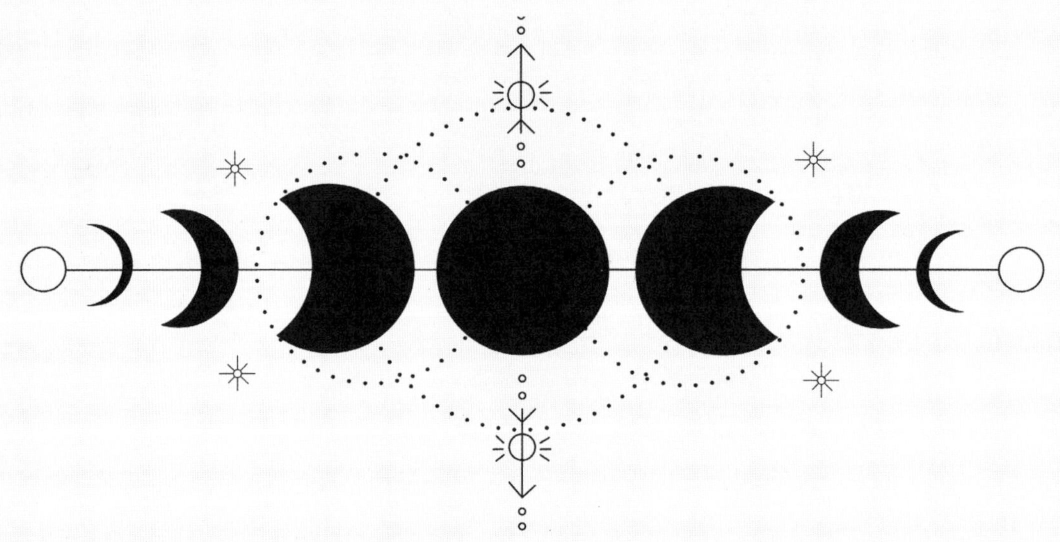

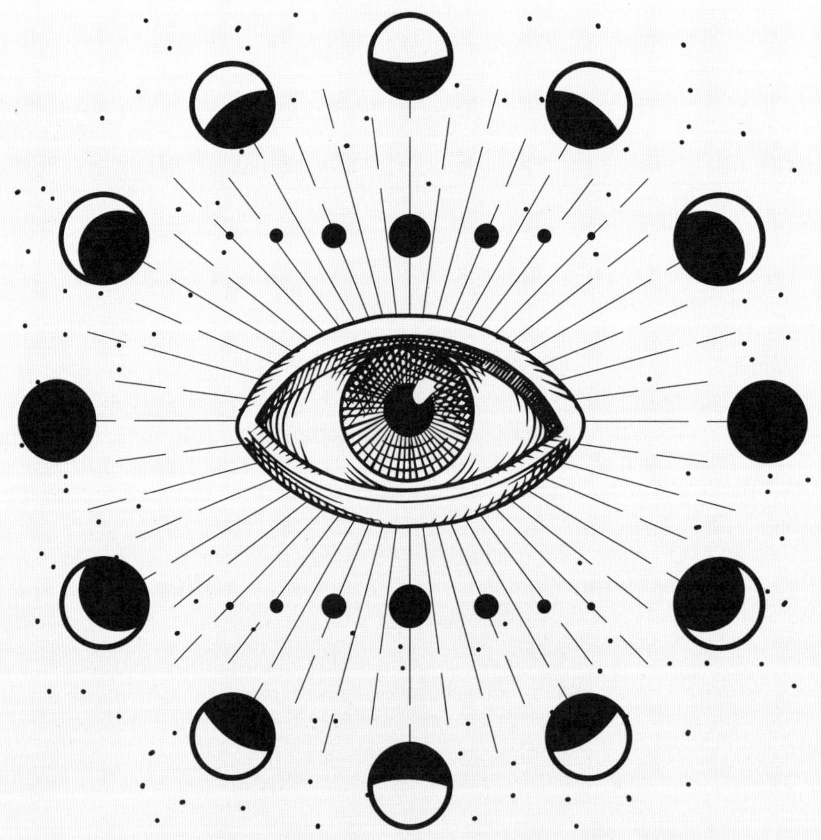

Psychic power and mystery

A symbol of mystery and magic, the moon is often
linked to mystical rites. Early civilizations performed
rituals to the deities under the light of the moon,
believing it would enhance their success. Today, the
moon has many meanings. As a tattoo it is often
chosen to represent feminine power and strength.
It is a symbol of creativity, synonymous with
transformation and illumination. It is also thought to
be associated with psychic potential.

How to wear it

The moon can be tattooed in various ways to represent
its many phases, from crescent to full. It can also be
worn as the symbol of the Triple Goddess: in this
form it has the waxing moon on the left, the full moon
in the middle and the waning moon on the right. The
addition of a face can often be seen in neo-traditional,
fine-line and traditional half-moon tattoos, adding
another layer of character to this recognizable symbol.

Opposite: The lunar phases
(top) are a nod to the cycles
we all go through from day
to day. An eye at the centre
of a lunar phase (bottom)
denotes esoteric wisdom.

Right: A feminine
silhouette with moons
and lotus flower
symbolizes the connection
between the monthly cyles
of the moon and fertility.

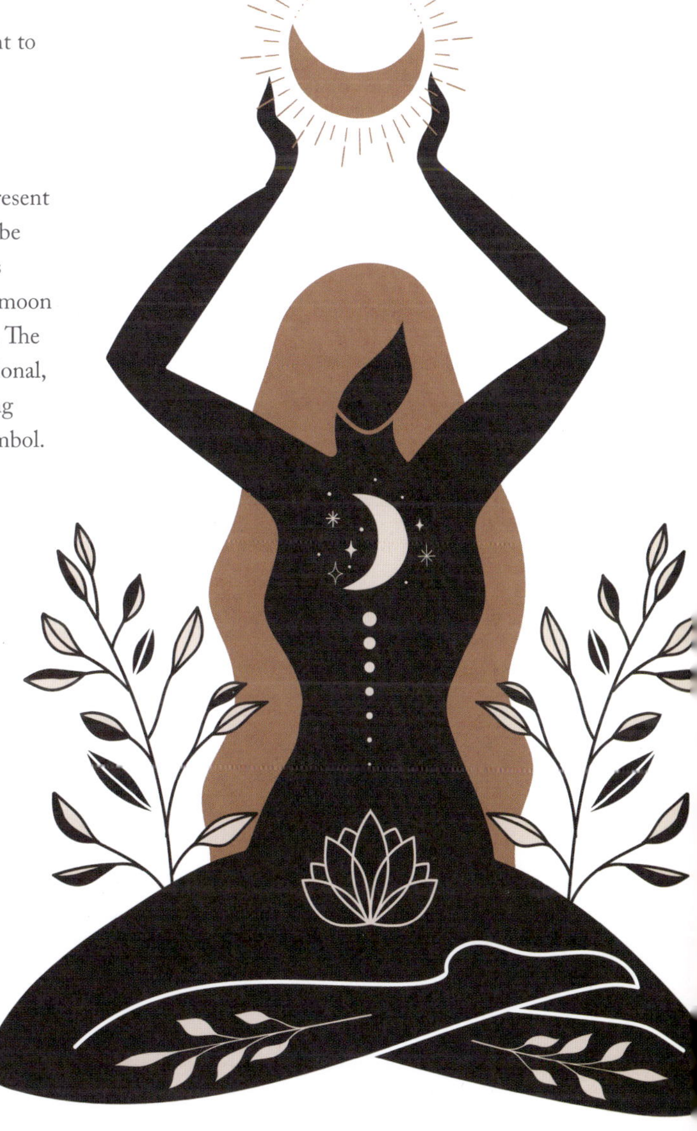

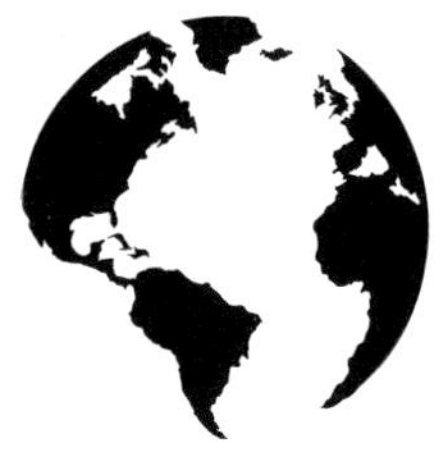

Earth

Adventure | Freedom | Creativity | Fertility | Balance

Sacred Origins
A key concept to many cultures around the world

Used Since
Dawn of time

Tattoo Styles
Fine-line
Blackwork

The earth is a symbol with many connotations, from freedom and adventure to being stable and grounded.

Adventure and travel

At first glance this symbol exudes adventure and indicates a free spirit who enjoys travel and exploration, but there are many layers to this motif. Being 'of the earth' means to be grounded, and this symbol is synonymous with balance, structure and stability, as it is one of the four elements. The alchemical symbol for the earth is a downward-pointing triangle with a horizontal line across the tip – this is often used to show a link to this element and to the environment.

A feminine force

The earth as a planet is considered feminine by many cultures. It is a nurturing force embodied by the divine feminine, the ultimate Mother Goddess and a symbol of creativity. To the ancient Greeks, the earth was associated with the goddess Gaia. This primordial deity stepped out of the chaos of nothingness and gave birth to the world. She created the sky, known as Uranus, and gave rise to the race of gods known as the Titans. In Hindu mythology, the earth itself is viewed as a mother goddess called Bhumi, who is seen as a personification of the earth.

How to wear it

Tattoos of the earth work best at a small scale. When tattooed in a monochrome, fine-line style, they are often given a diagrammatic look, illustrating earth's rotation or how the moon orbits. If tattooed in a bolder traditional style, it's often the case that the earth is shown as a tabletop globe on a stand, frequently accompanied by flowers or a banner with an evocative slogan – 'Wanderlust', for example – to convey the wearer's passion for travel.

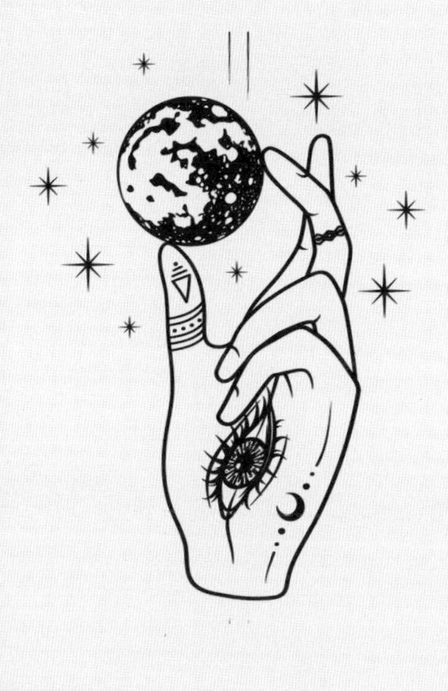

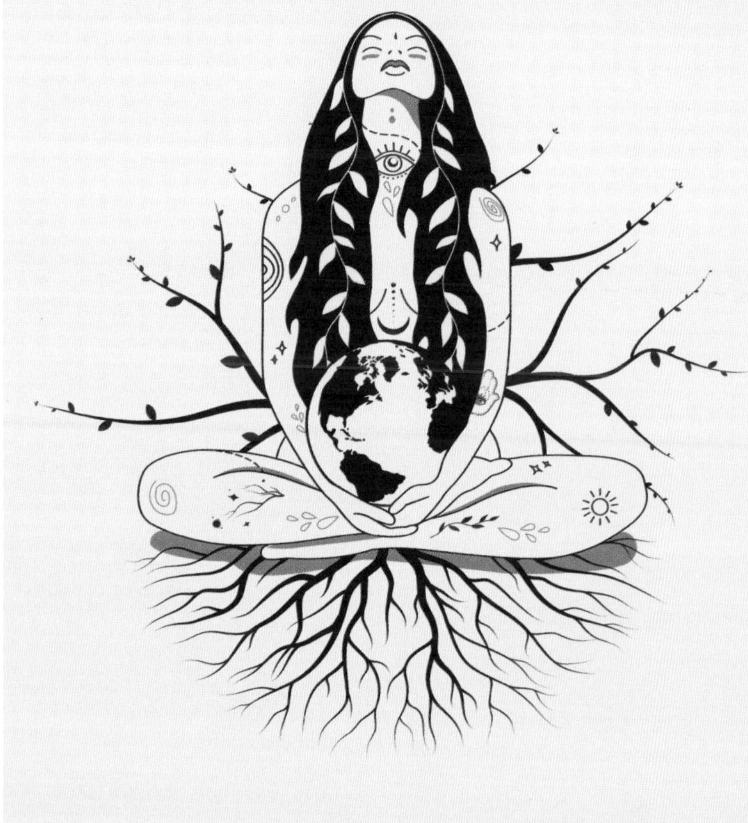

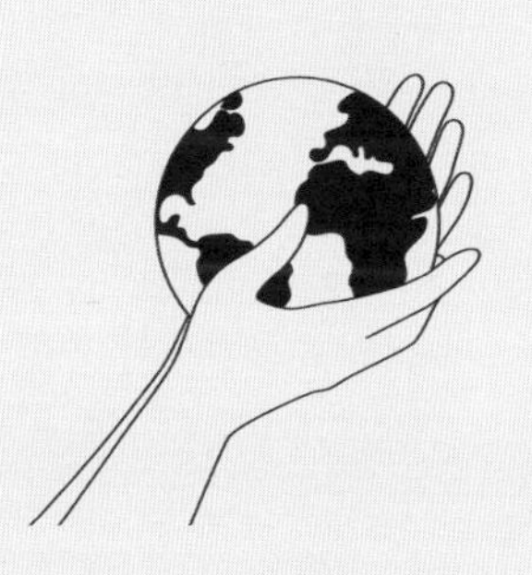

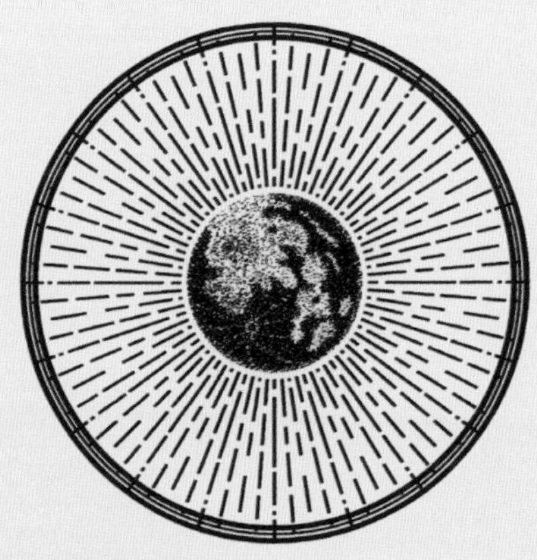

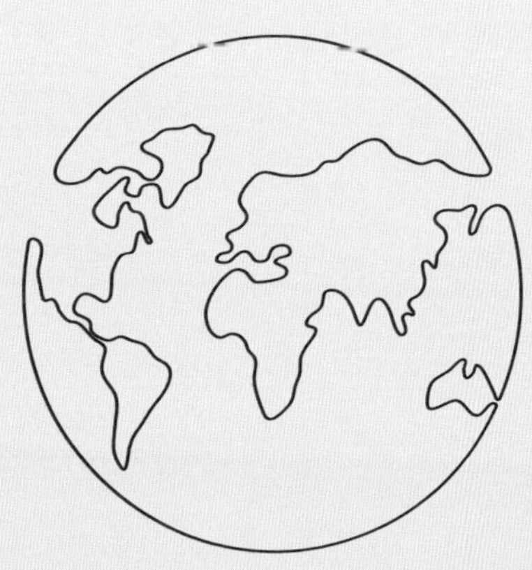

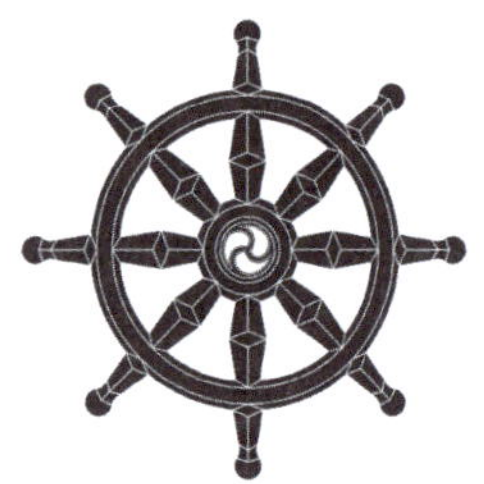

Wheel of Life

Life | Death | Rebirth | Enlightenment | Liberation

Sacred Origins
Buddhist

Used Since
9th century BCE

Tattoo Styles
Ornamental
Fine-line
Blackwork

Opposite: A wheel of life tattoo (top right and left) is a symbol of the cycle of existence. An ornate wheel in the style of a ship's helm (bottom) signifies direction and freedom of movement.

The wheel of life was thought to have been created by Lord Buddha as a tool to help people navigate the many cycles they would experience on the path to enlightenment.

A navigation tool

Also known as the bhavacakra and the Buddhist wheel of life, this symbol is a visual representation of the cyclical pattern of life and gives an overview of the Buddhist philosophy, looking at the effects of karma and the eventual path to enlightenment. The symbol itself is divided into three sections.

The cycle of suffering

The outer circle is where the 12 links to dependent origination reside. These are split into the categories of past, present and future. The core concept here is one of causation: each link is dependent on the previous one, creating a new cycle of cause and effect. As such, all actions are dependent on previous actions. This key insight provides the tools needed to attain an enlightened state of being.

Poisons and passions

The inner circle of the wheel represents the six realms of existence, each of which has its own section within the circle. These realms represent different states of being which are dependent on karma. The hub of the wheel is where the three poisons of ignorance, attachment and aversion can be found; together, they power the wheel onwards. Thought to be the primary obstacles to enlightenment, each poison is represented by an animal which is portrayed in a loop, biting the tail of the previous creature to show the perpetual chase that they create in the human psyche. The pig relates to ignorance, the rooster is linked to attachment and the snake is associated with aversion.

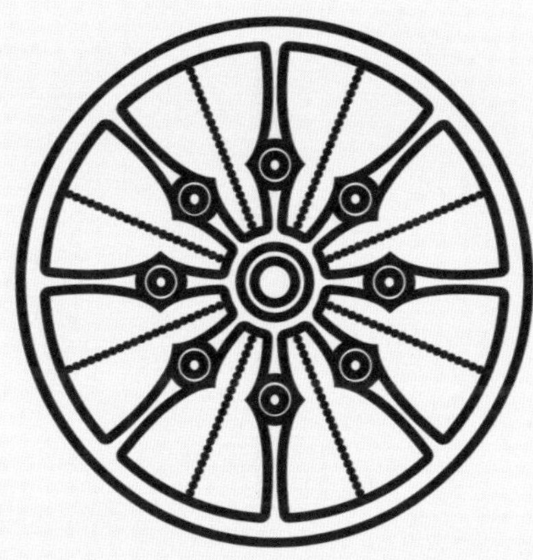
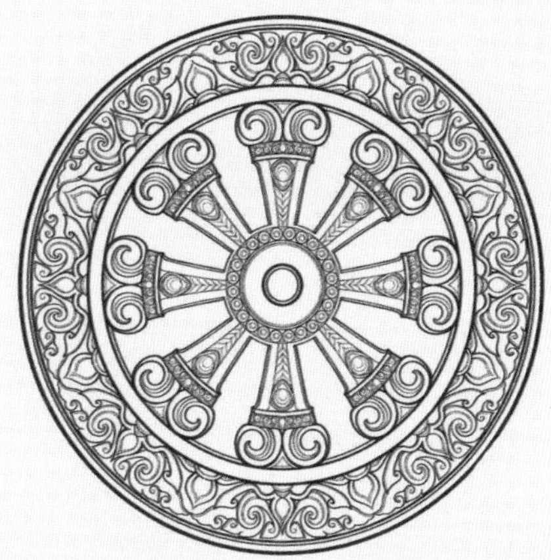

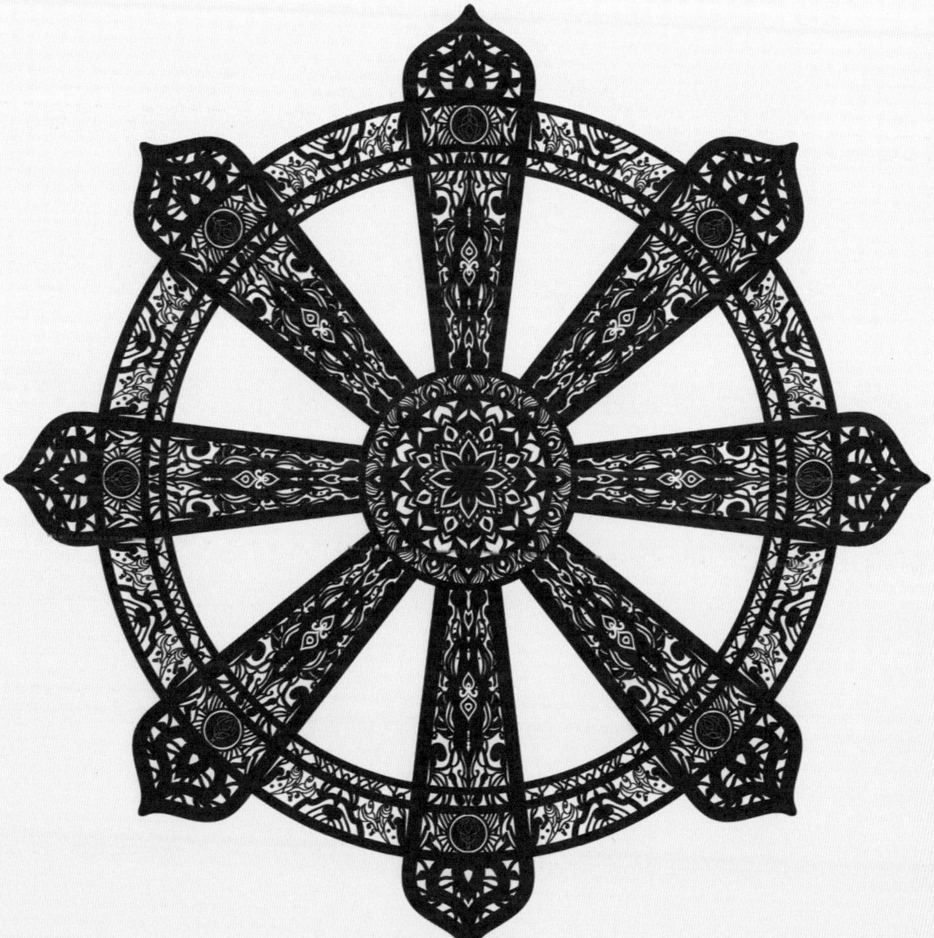

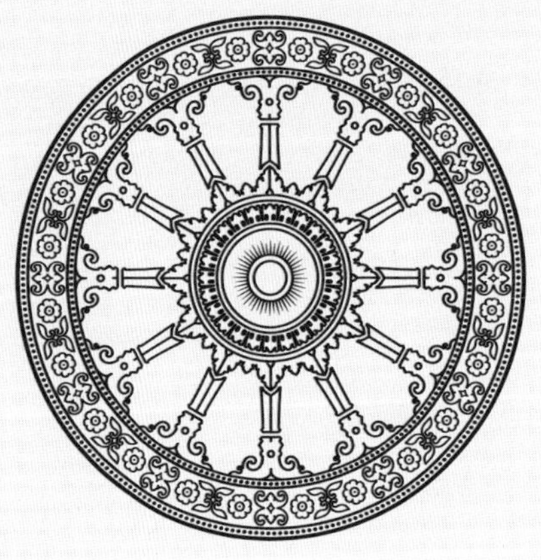
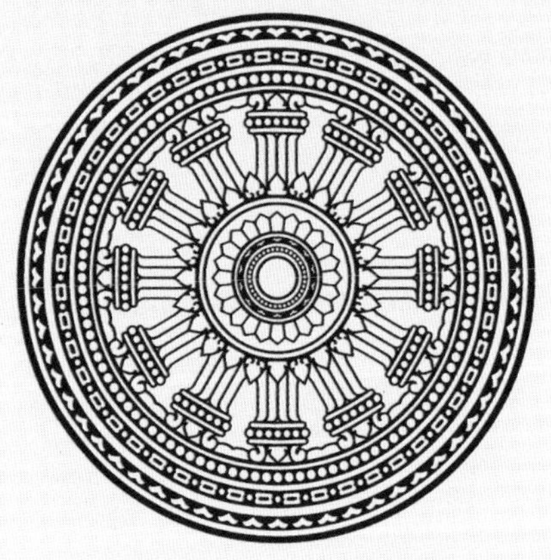

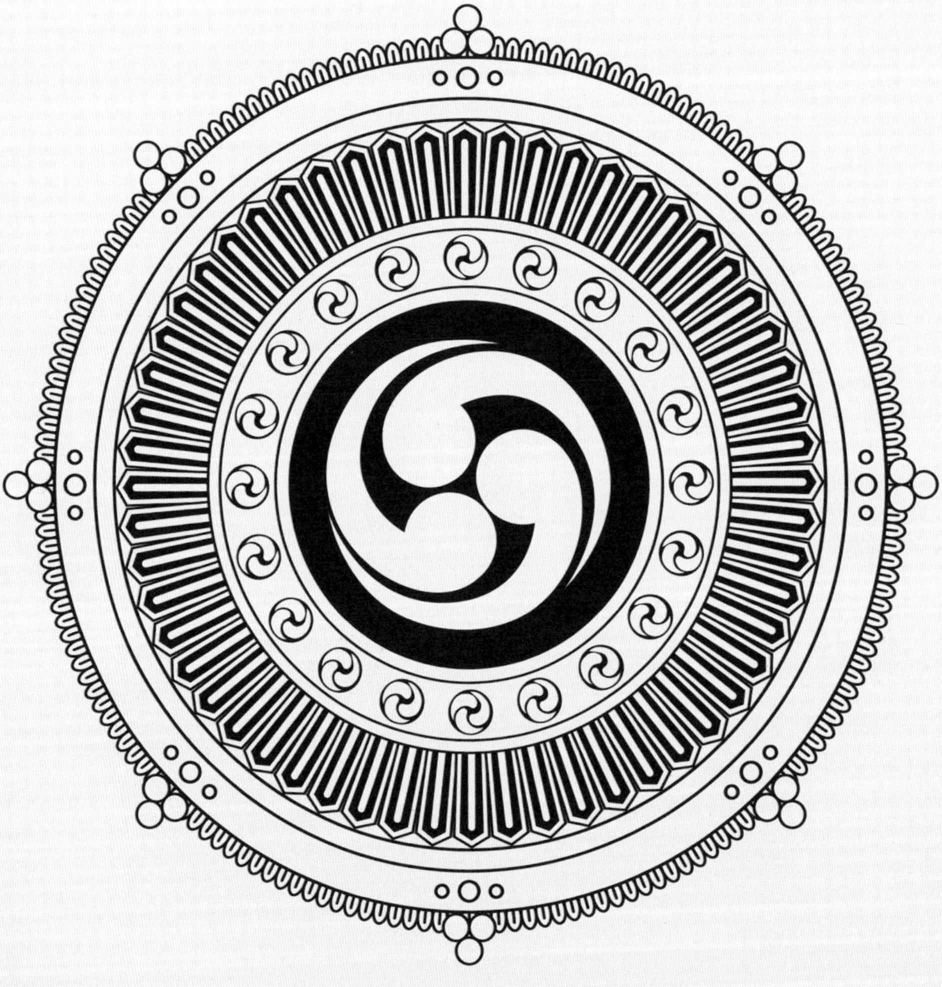

The wheel portrays the inevitable cycles of life that all creatures must go through, from birth to death and rebirth, and shows that enlightenment is the key to escaping this never-ending loop. The wheel itself is held by the lord of death, Yama, while the snake that entwines the circumference represents life and death. The sun and the moon in the distance are symbols of the dual nature of life. Visual representations of the wheel of life appeared in the 9th century BCE, and have provided a focus for the mind during meditation for thousands of years.

How to wear it

Although simplified versions are possible, the wheel of life's complexity means it is most suited to being tattooed at a large scale – a full-back or front piece being most popular. While it can be tattooed monotone, it is at its most beautiful when in full colour. The symbol is often pictured with flames behind Yama, and the creatures within the central hub can vary.

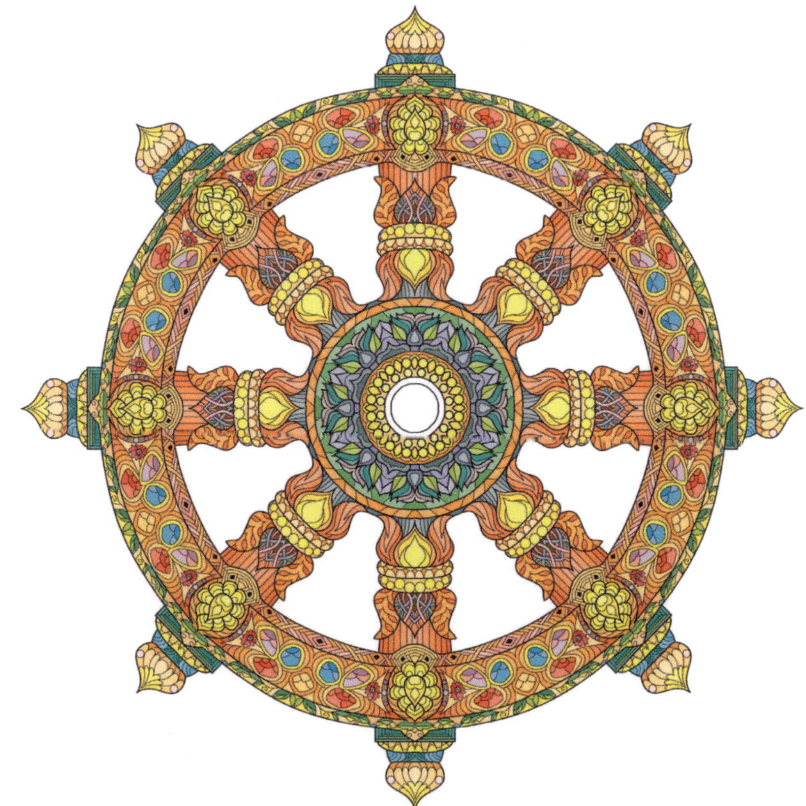

Opposite: The mitsudomoe at the centre of this wheel (bottom) links the symbol to Shintoism and the threefold division at the heart of the religion: human, earth and sky.

Right: The intricate beauty of this colourful wheel invokes the joy that comes with enlightenment.

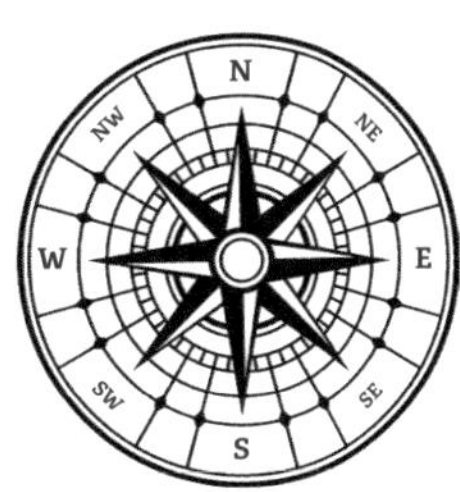

Compass

Safety | Good fortune | Protection | Guidance | Inner wisdom

Sacred Origins
Chinese, Greek, Roman

Used Since
12th century

Tattoo Styles
Western traditional
Neo-traditional
Fine-line
Black-and-grey realism

Opposite: Compass symbols have a strong association with exploration and adventure. An anchor attached to a compass (middle left) shows that the wearer is grounded, while the bird indicates that there is still freedom to roam. A compass with wings (bottom) suggests liberation and freedom to seek new adventures.

A symbol of protection, the compass is also associated with spiritual guidance, referring to the inner journey of the soul and discovering life's true purpose.

Sailing emblem
A cherished motif of sailors, the compass is associated with safety and good fortune while travelling at sea. As a practical tool it offers guidance and direction to those who are lost, and the ability to find a way home, wherever you might find yourself in the world.

A needle and a piece of wood
The Chinese were the first to create a navigational tool, in around the 12th century, using an iron needle and a piece of lodestone, which has magnetic properties. Those early compasses may have been a simple affair, but they were just as effective as their modern counterparts. Ancient civilizations used a dish of water with a piece of wood or cork floating inside which had a magnetized needle attached to it. Once the needle had settled, it would point northwards. This would have been of great significance to those first explorers who were charting a path around the world.

How to wear it
The compass is a staple of the tattoo vocabulary. It is most often seen in a bold traditional style, in a muted palette accompanied by flowers, an anchor, a banner, or perhaps all of the above. The symbol also works well when a fine-line approach is employed, which often simplifies the design, highlighting only the N, E, S and W initials, along with arrows to indicate direction. It's an incredibly versatile motif that can be tattooed on the arm, leg, chest and elsewhere, but is not often seen larger than palm size.

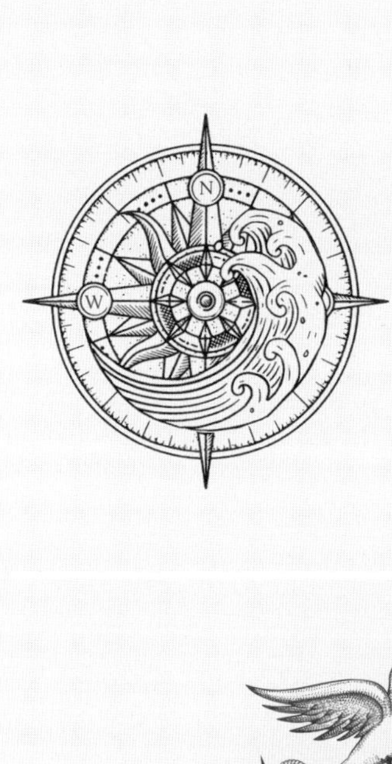

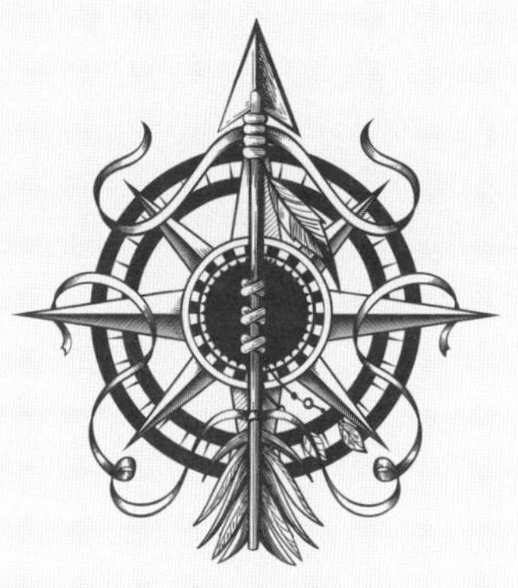

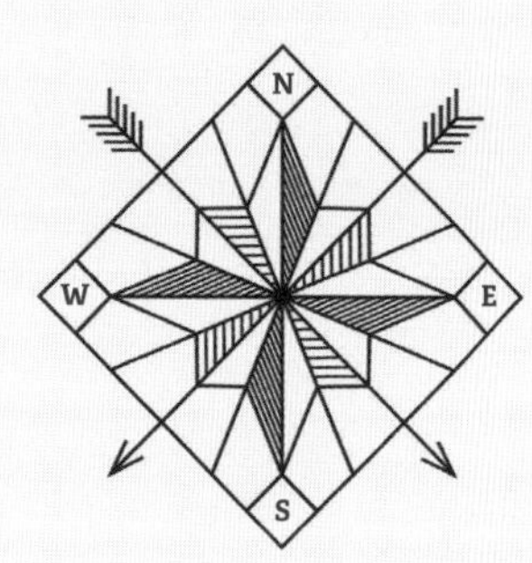

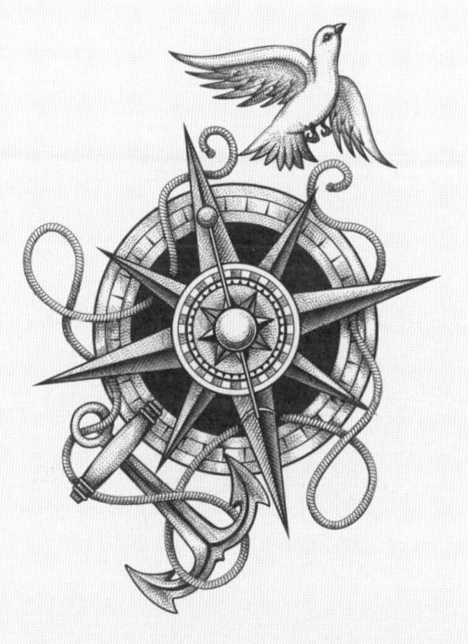

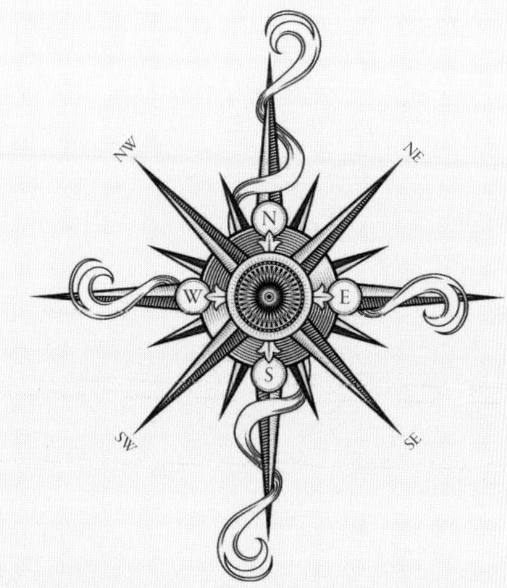

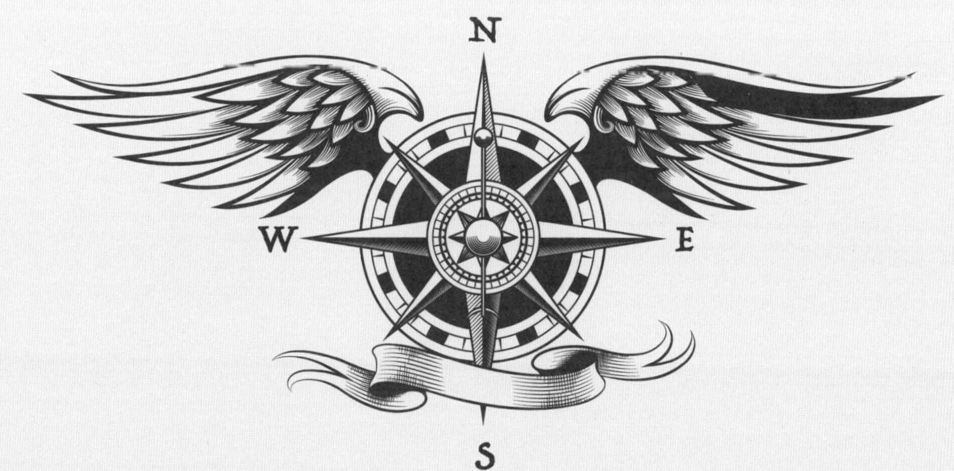

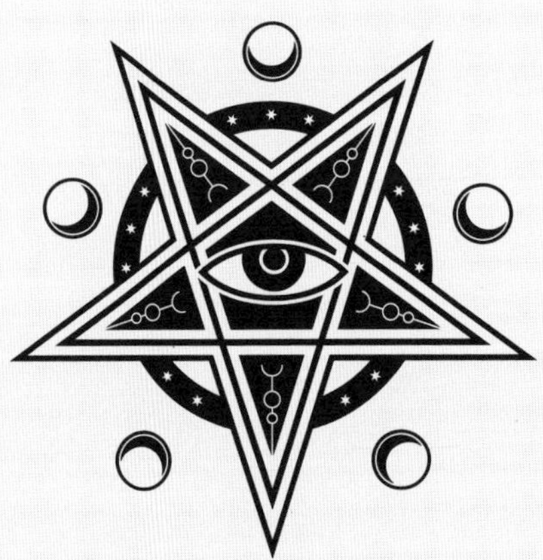

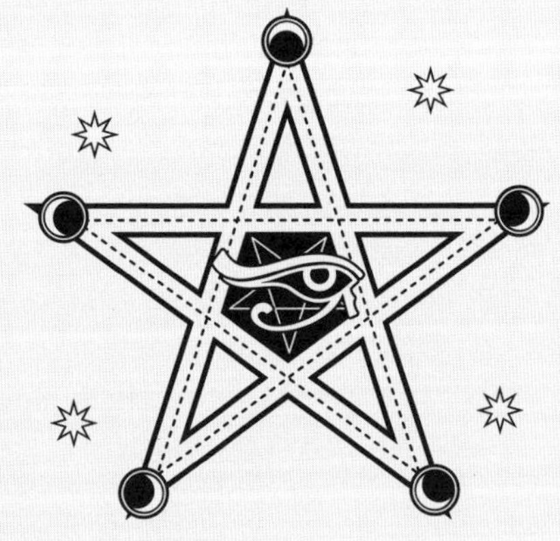

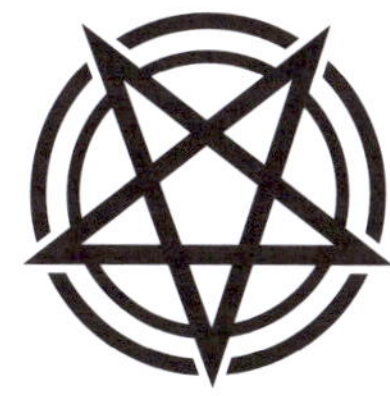

Pentagram

Protection | Balance | Knowledge | Power | Magic

Sacred Origins
Egyptian,
Mesopotamian,
Chinese, Greek

Used Since
7th century BCE

Tattoo Styles
Fine-line
Blackwork
Ornamental

The pentagram is an ancient symbol that has been used worldwide with many different interpretations.

An early motif
Early manifestations of this motif have been found engraved into tombs and seals in Egypt and Mesopotamia, where the markings were believed to ward off evil. Representations can also be seen on shards of pottery from the ancient kingdom of Judaea. In this form, it was thought to be the mark of tax collectors.

Elemental energy
The pentagram was a popular symbol in Chinese philosophy, each point representing one of the 'five agents' – fire, water, wood, metal and earth. The intersections where these elements crossed illustrate a harmonious interaction between each of the agents. Pentagrams are often pictured within a circle in oriental artwork to show that everything is in balance. The Japanese held a similar view; the pentagram, or gobousei, was used to mark the entrances to temples. It was associated with a particular school of esoteric thought known as Onmyōdō, which relates to the Yin and Yang concept, originally borrowed from China. The pentagram symbol was also adopted and became a mystical emblem for protection and balance.

The cult of Pythagoras
While the symbol has ancient roots, it wasn't until the Greek philosopher and mathematician Pythagoras became intrigued by its aesthetically pleasing appearance that it really came to the fore. It was thought that he associated it with health and knowledge, and even placed the letters of the Greek word for

'health' at each of the five points. Soon the entire cult
of Pythagoras was on board, using the symbol as their
insignia and a way of recognizing fellow members.

In the Middle Ages, the pentagram was thought to be
a depiction of the five knightly virtues and was used
to signify loyalty and honour. While nobles revered
the symbol, everyday folk in Europe used it as a way
to keep evil forces at bay, believing it had the power
to repel witches and dark spirits. Those in the Muslim
faith associated it with the Seal of Solomon, while
the Christians believed that each point was one of the
wounds of Christ.

Today the pentagram is often associated with the
Wiccan faith and considered pagan. In this form the
symbol represents the elements, including the spirit,
and balances masculine and feminine energies, while
being synonymous with power and protection.

How to wear it

The pentagram can be rendered in many different
forms when it comes to tattooing. A design may
feature decorative patterning, dots and fine-line work.
It could be tattooed to appear as if carved in stone,
or a torn, skin effect can be used to make it appear as
if the pentagram is ingrained under the skin of the
wearer, hinting at their fascination with witchcraft or
the desire for the symbol to protect.

Opposite: The cross at the
heart of this pentagram (top)
suggests a link to religion and
enhances its sacred nature.
The moon and sun combined
indicate unity, and connect
the wearer to the power of
the universe.

Below: Pentagrams incorporating
arcane symbols and runes amplify the
magical energy of the symbol.

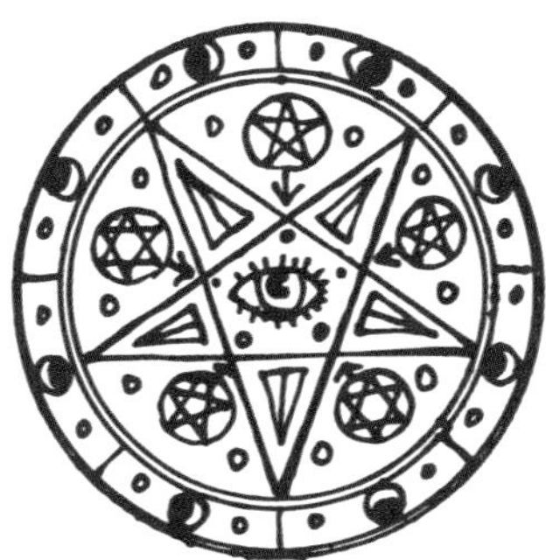

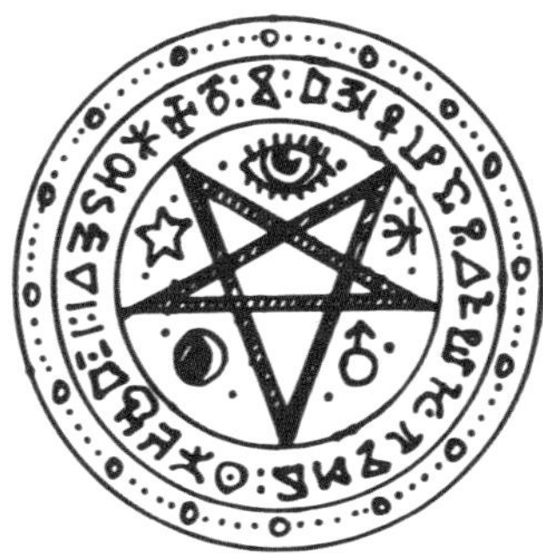

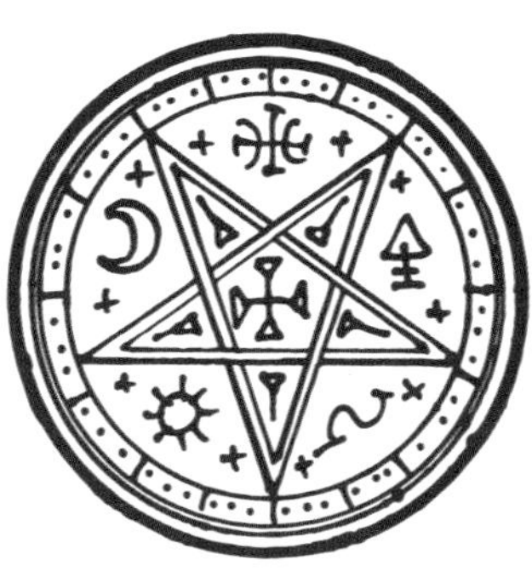

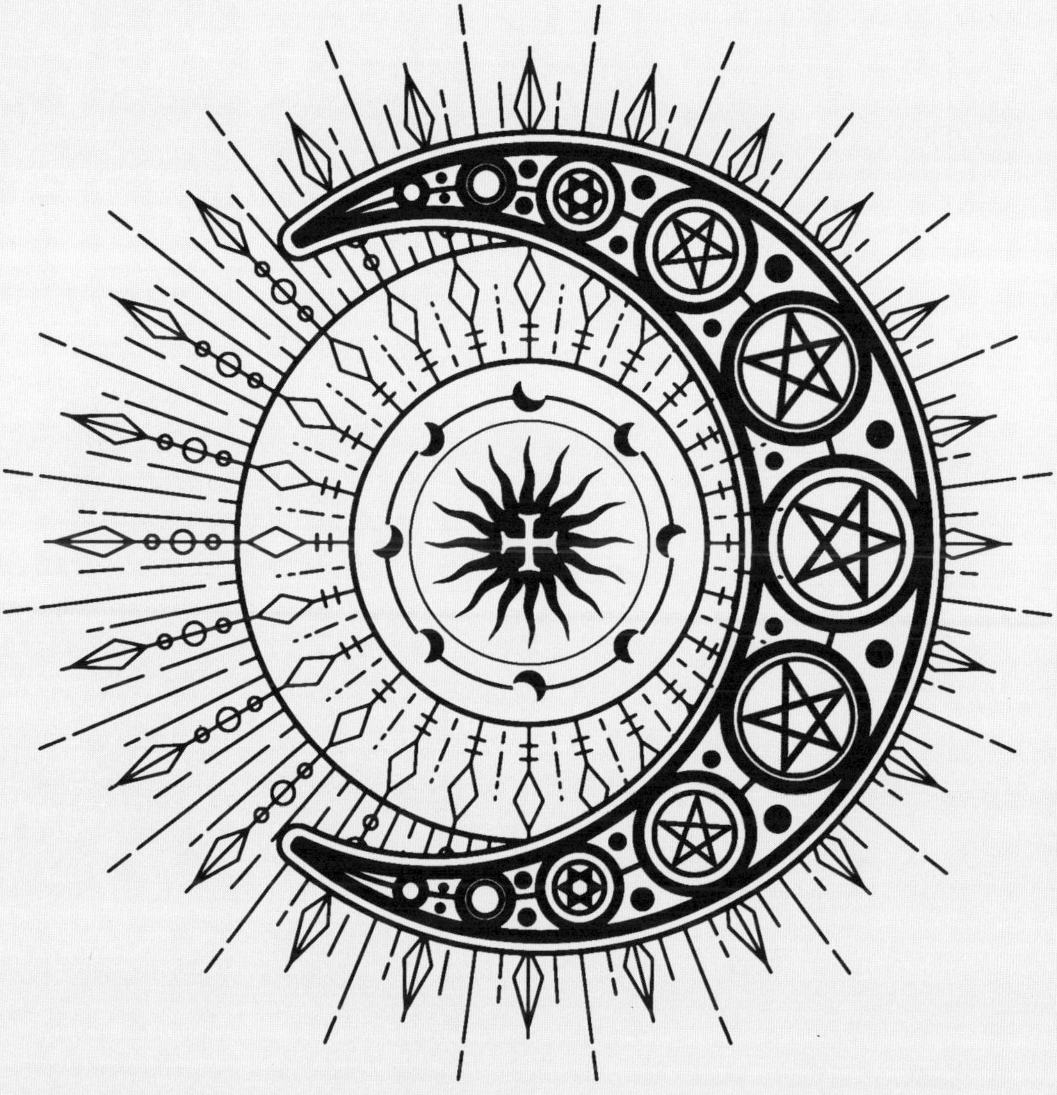

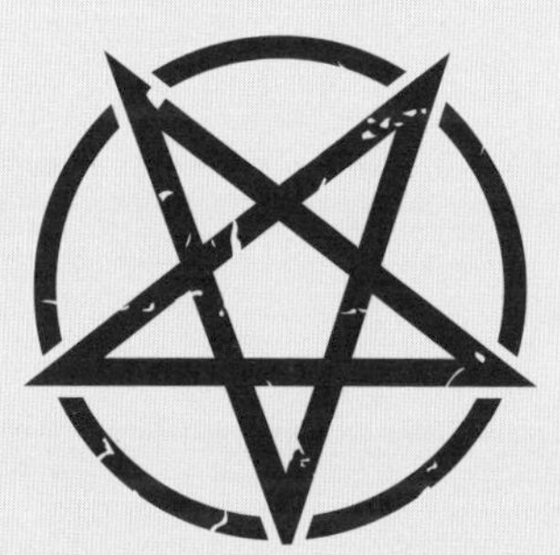  

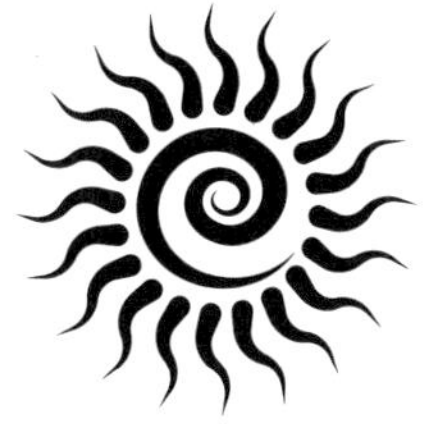

Sacred Spiral

Life | Death | Rebirth | Cosmic power | Fate | Magic

Sacred Origins
Celtic, Greek,
Mycenaean

Used Since
Stone Age

Tattoo Styles
Ornamental
Fine-line

As a key part of nature, many ancient civilizations believed that the spiral was a manifestation of the force at the heart of every living being.

A natural image

One of the oldest geometric shapes in the world, the sacred spiral is a common pattern featured in nature. Appearing in the whorl of shells, fingerprints, pinecones and horns, it's also present in hurricanes and whirlpools, and the double helix of our DNA. To ancient civilizations it was everywhere, and that meant it was of great significance. Petroglyphs of the spiral have been found dating back to the Stone Age, and one of the earliest versions of this symbol was found etched into the entrance stone at Newgrange, a prehistoric collection of monuments at County Meath, Ireland. This example dates back to around 3200 BCE. Other representations of the sacred spiral were discovered on the Greek island of Naxos, dating back to the early Bronze Age.

The point of all creation

It's no surprise the spiral was so popular. An ever-continuing loop, unbroken and seemingly unending, it's hard to trace the exact pattern of the spiral without returning to the starting point. The sacred spiral rotates around a singular fixed point, each rotation moving further away from the centre to show the interconnection between all things. It illustrates that everything comes from this initial point of creation and represents the inner journey that we take to discover our true potential. The whirling pattern, so intrinsic to the natural world, represents the cycles of birth, life and rebirth in a continuous loop. To the Celts, the spiral was an important symbol and central to their spiritual path. They called it the spiral of life, because it showed in the simplest form that life is a

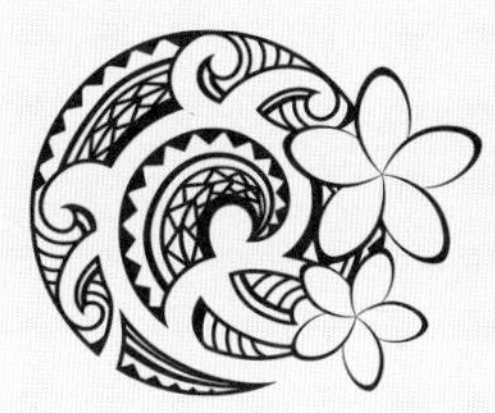
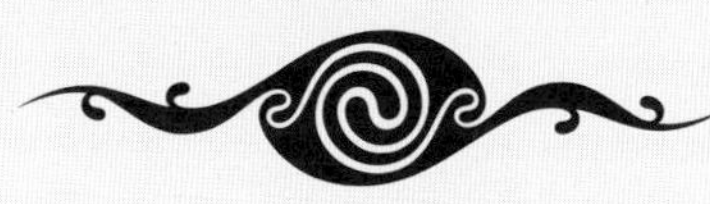
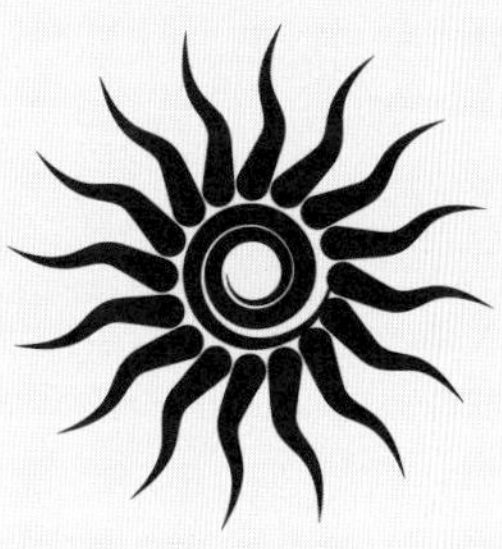

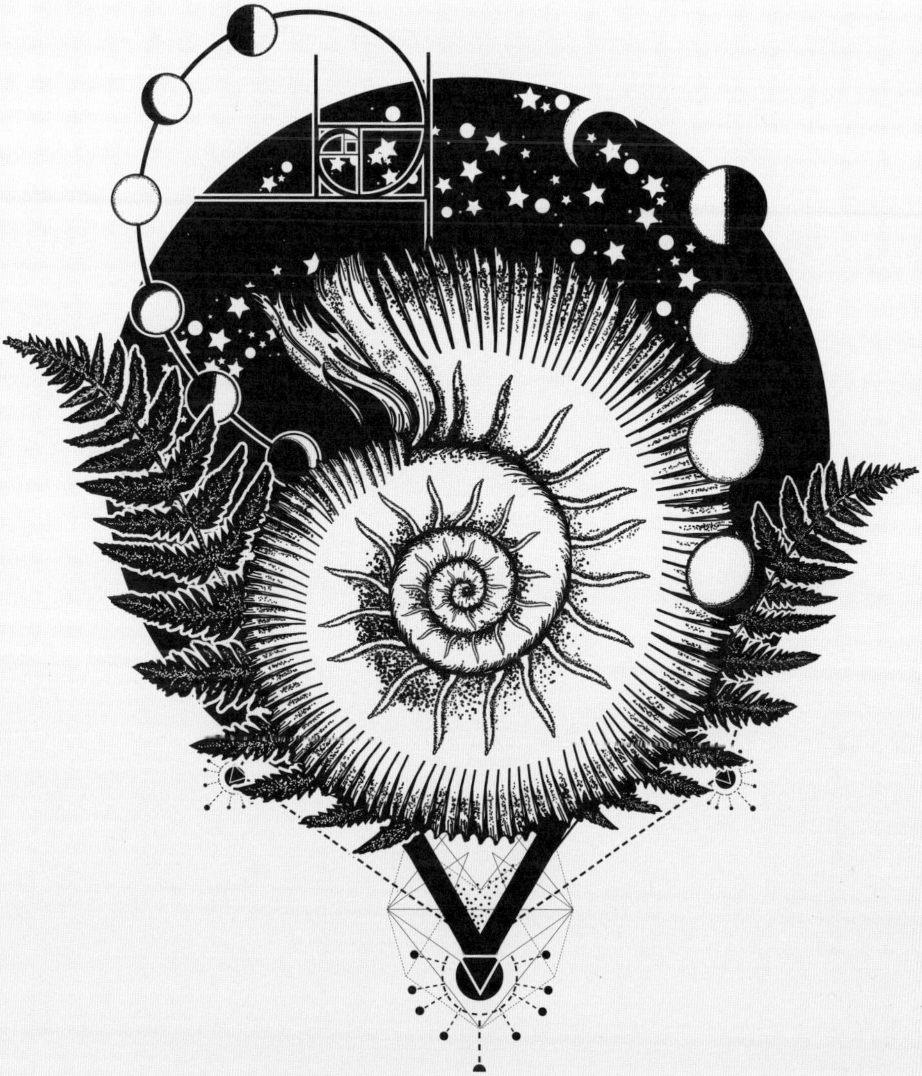

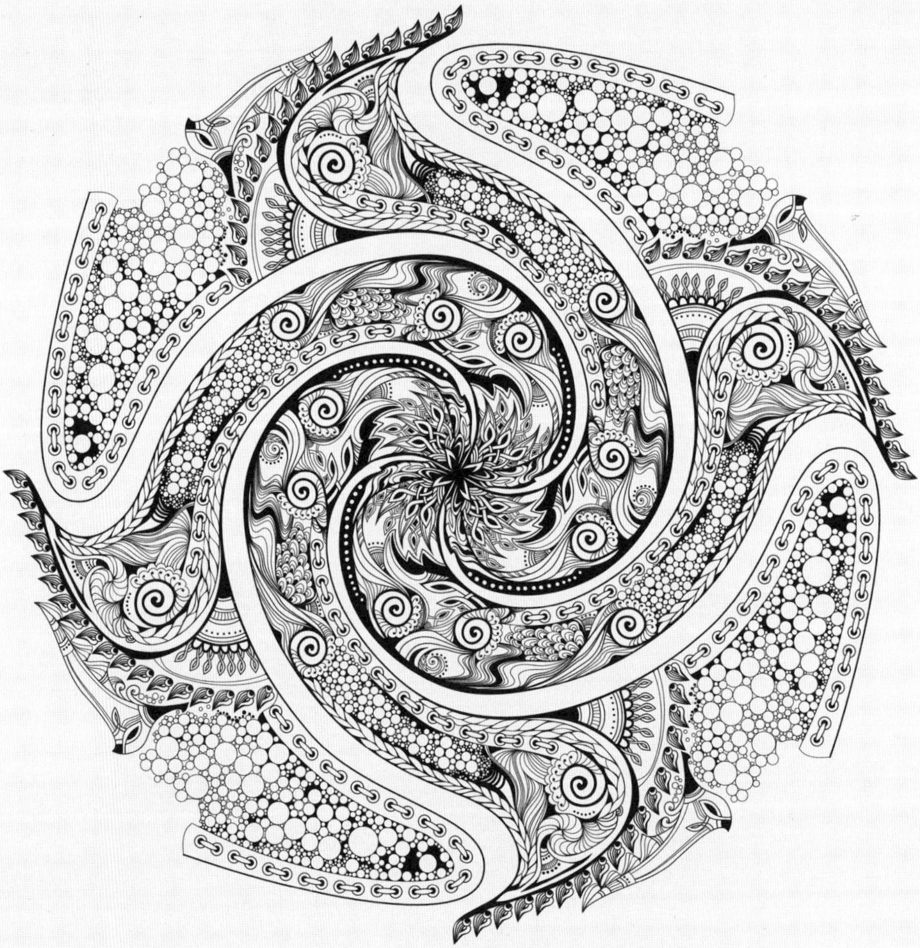

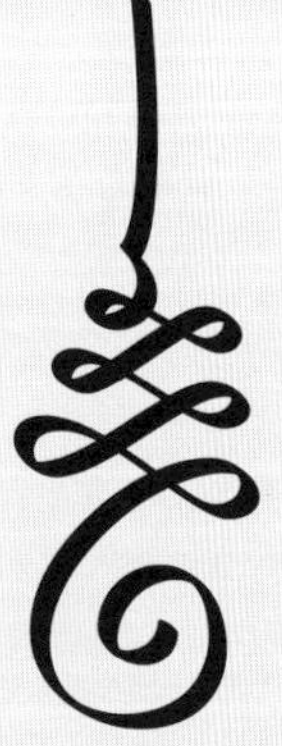
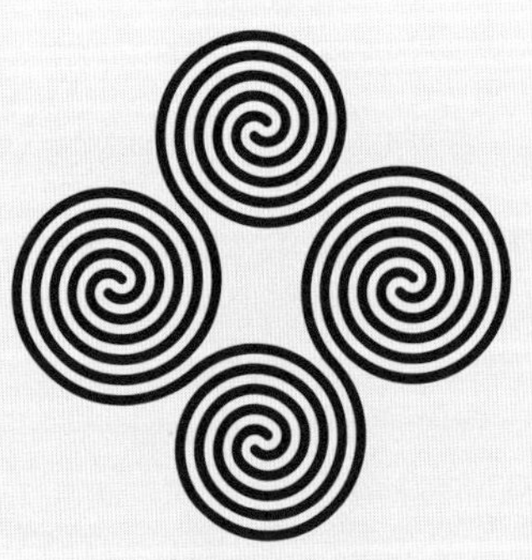
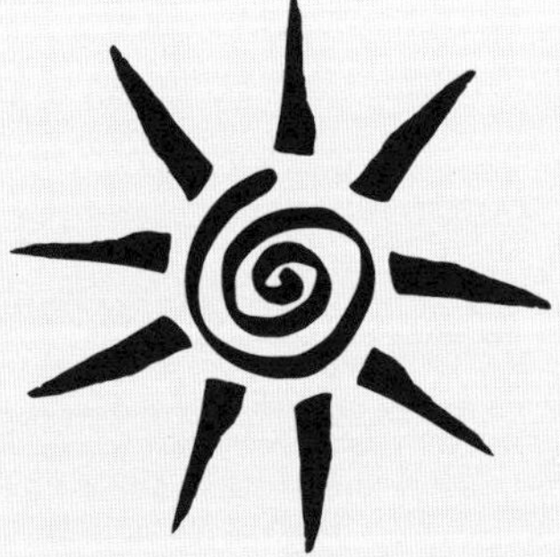

never-ending journey and as we evolve we continually repeat ourselves, facing the same challenges until we finally reach resolution.

Many Native American tribes also revered the spiral shape – it featured in their paintings and pottery. The Puebloan people associated it with the power of the sun, while elsewhere it was used as a representation of a tornado.

How to wear it

The sacred spiral is incredibly flexible as a tattoo design: it can be rendered as a circular, mazelike design that fits well on the shoulder, shoulder blade, inner forearm or most areas of the leg. The symbol can also be elongated into an oval shape to fit a specific body part. Some people choose to accentuate the geometric patterns, while others incorporate flora and fauna to highlight the link to the natural world. Celtic style renditions are popular, as they enhance the link to the spiritual nature of the symbol.

Opposite: **A mandala-style spiral (top) signifies the wearer is on a journey of finding inner wisdom and peace.**

Right: **A spiral within the fertility goddess implies a connection with creativity and the earth.**

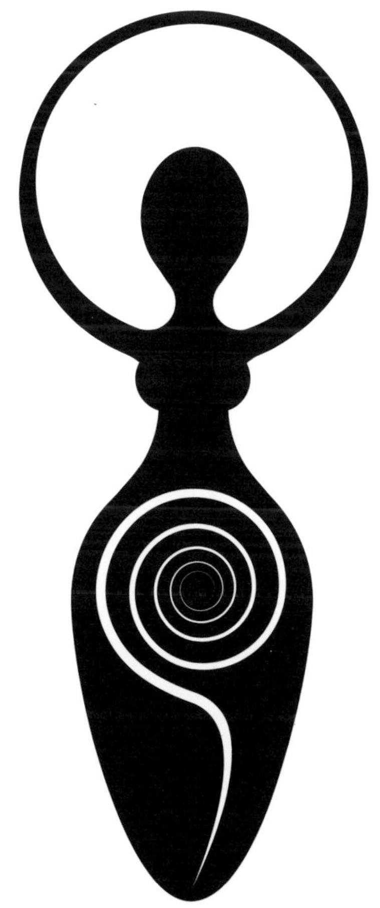

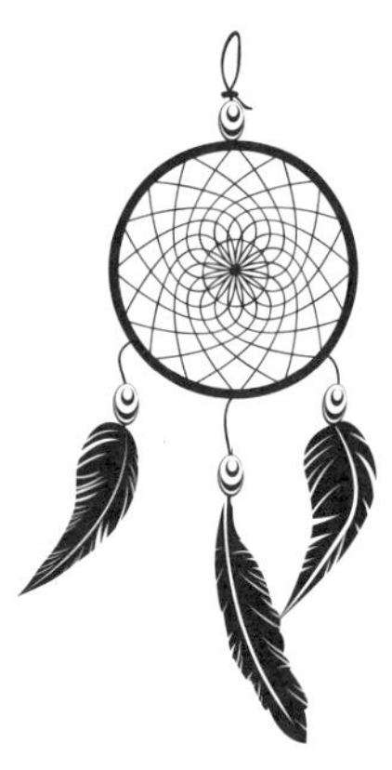

Dreamcatcher

Hope | Healing | Positivity | Light | Dreams

Sacred Origins
Native American

Used Since
The 1920s

Tattoo Styles
Black-and-grey realism
Fine-line
Western traditional

Opposite: A dreamcatcher is a symbol of both protection and positivity. A dreamcatcher which incorporates a triangle shape and the crescent moon (top left) suggests a mystical influence, linking it to esoteric wisdom. A lotus flower within the heart of a dreamcatcher (bottom left) connects it to inner peace and wisdom.

Over time the dreamcatcher has become a popular symbol synonymous with the light of the sun and healing, and an emblem of hope and positive energy.

Caring origins

Dreamcatchers are deeply rooted in Native American cultures, and while each tribe has its own origin story, it's thought the Ojibwe people were responsible for their creation. According to legend, at the beginning of time Spider Woman was responsible for taking care of the Ojibwe, and while this was within her capabilities, as the tribe grew and spread it became harder for her to look after everyone. In her quest to be there for her beloved children, she made the dreamcatcher, a tool which hung over the bed and caught any bad dreams, keeping little ones safe as they slept.

A web and a ladder

The willow hoop of the catcher is circular to represent the earth and woven with a net like a spider's web, to ensnare any nightmares floating in the air. The feathers that hang from the central hoop are a ladder, allowing good dreams to descend upon the sleeping infant.

How to wear it

There is so much scope for customization with this design: further iconography can be incorporated into the pattern within the willow hoop, or additional items can be added to the feathers hanging below. This versatility makes the the dreamcatcher a popular choice, often seen tattooed on the upper outer arm, forearm or shoulder blade. While the dreamcatcher has become widely used as a spiritual symbol, it must be remembered that it is a sacred item to many Native American cultures, and designs featuring it need to respect this.

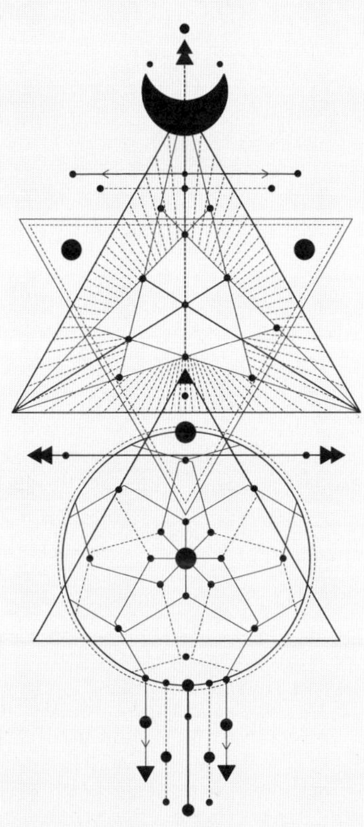
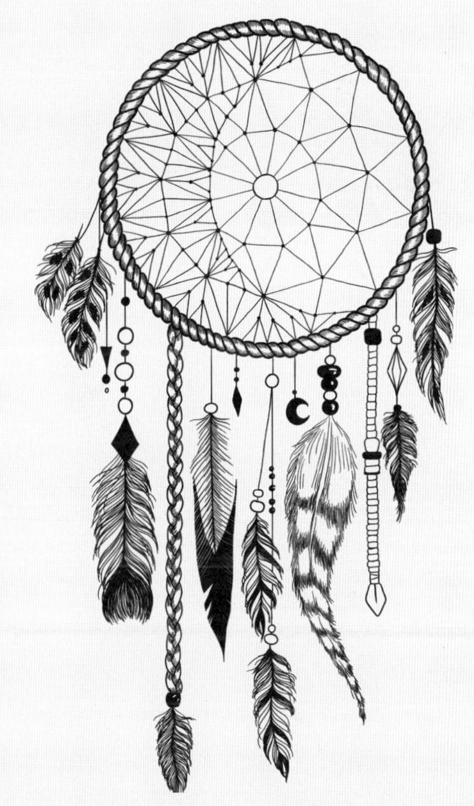
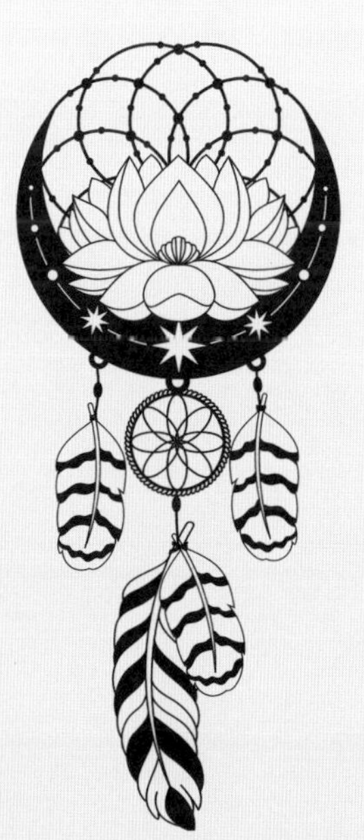
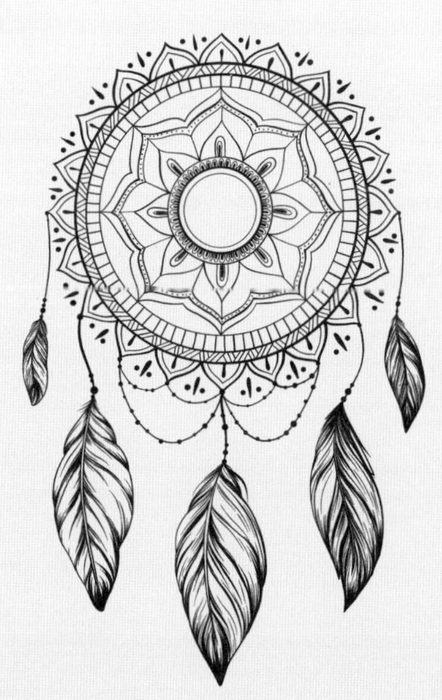
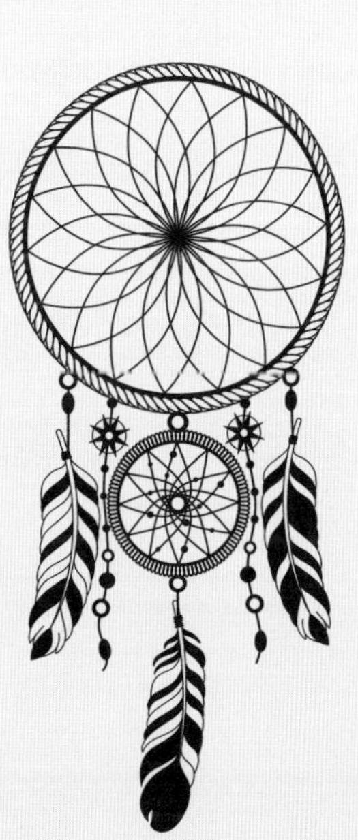

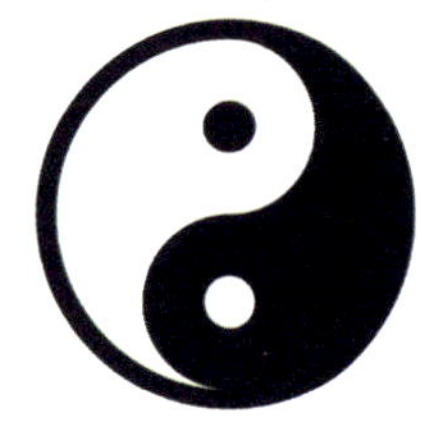

Yin and Yang

Balance | Wholeness | Harmony | Nature | Union

Sacred Origins
Chinese, Taoist

Used Since
14th century BCE

Tattoo Styles
Blackwork
Fine-line

Opposite: Yin and Yang is a symbol of the balance between two opposing but complementary forces. The sun and moon within a Yin and Yang (top), helps to emphasize the influence of light and dark and how the two are interconnected.

In Chinese philosophy the Yin and Yang symbol refers to the dual nature of life, the concept that two opposites come together and become whole to create a sense of balance.

Opposites attract

The Yin and Yang symbol, which is circular to represent the eternal flow of the universe, has two teardrop-shaped halves, one which is black and the other which is white. Both halves feature a small dot which bears the colour of the opposite half and are curved to represent the fluid, ever-changing motion that is required to create balance. The black half is Yin and thought to be feminine. It is associated with darkness, passivity and rest, while the white half is Yang and has a masculine energy. It is associated with light, activity and movement.

Light and dark

The concept of Yin and Yang is an old one. Archaeologists have discovered oracle bones inscribed with Yin and Yang in parts of China that date back to the 14th century BCE, used as a form of divination and to represent the constant flux of the weather and the shifting pattern of night and day. To those early farmers, the transition of light to dark was key. Yang represented the daytime and the arrival of the sun. It was a time of great activity when people could tend to the land and harvest their crops. Yin symbolized the coming of night, when darkness prevailed. This was the time to withdraw, to go home and rest in readiness for the next day.

The book of changes

While the origins of the Yin and Yang symbol are shrouded in mystery, it's generally thought that the key to its invention lies with the infamous *I-Ching*,

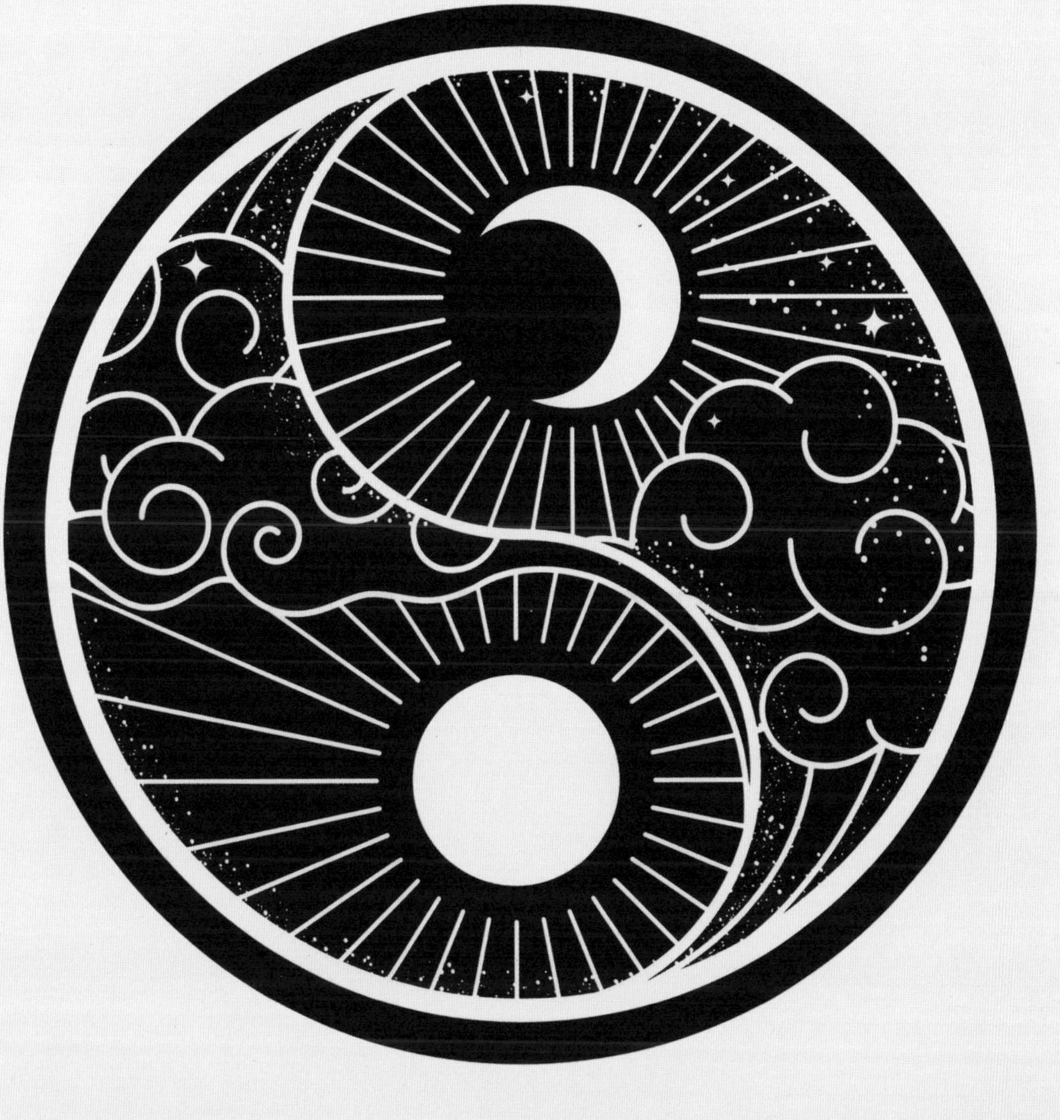

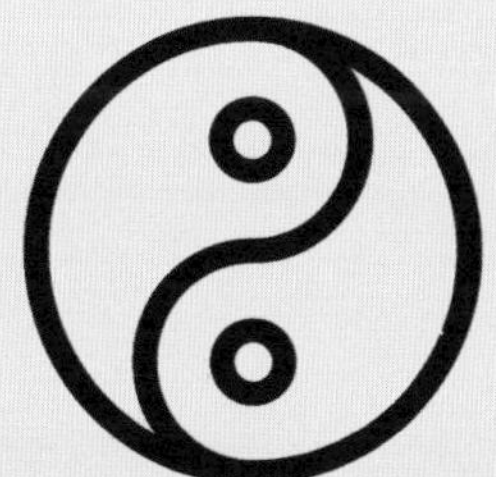 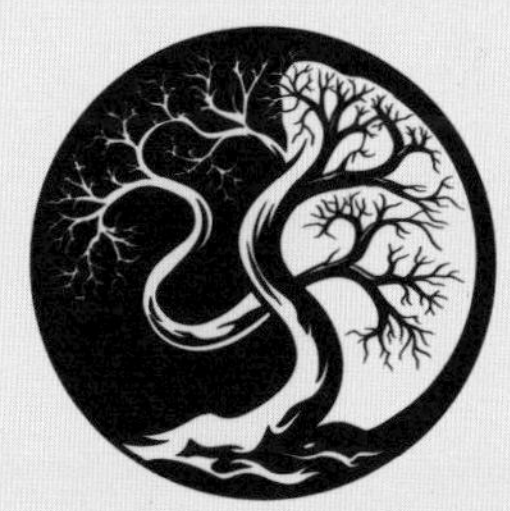 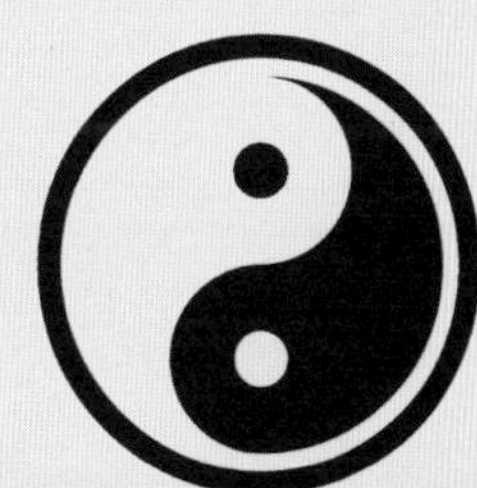

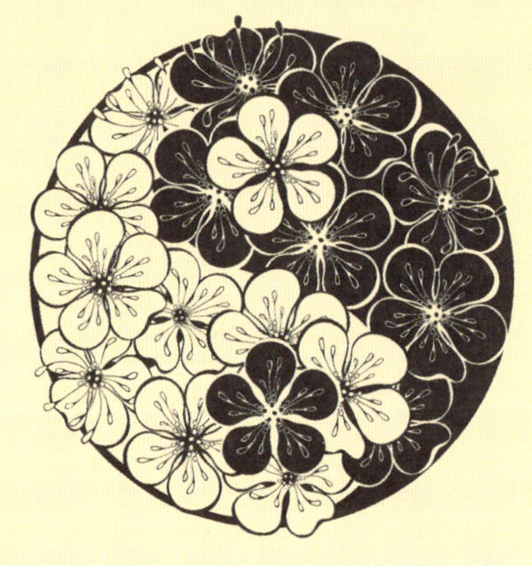

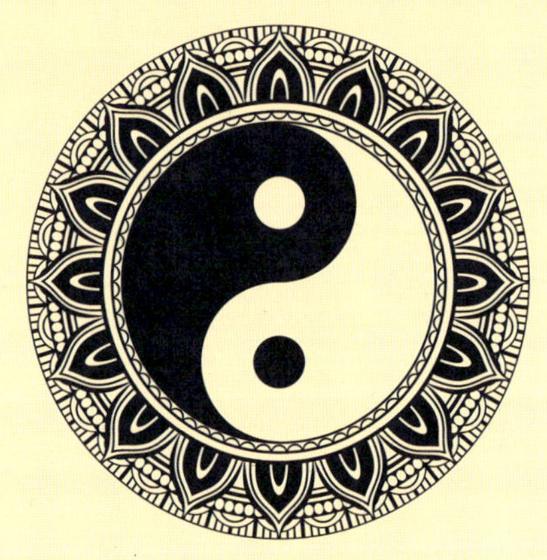

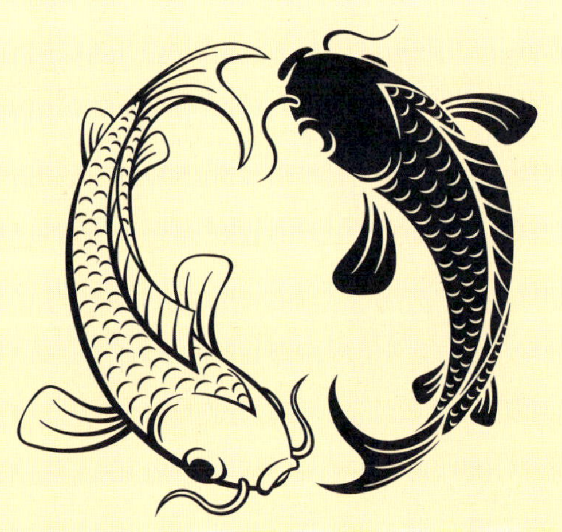

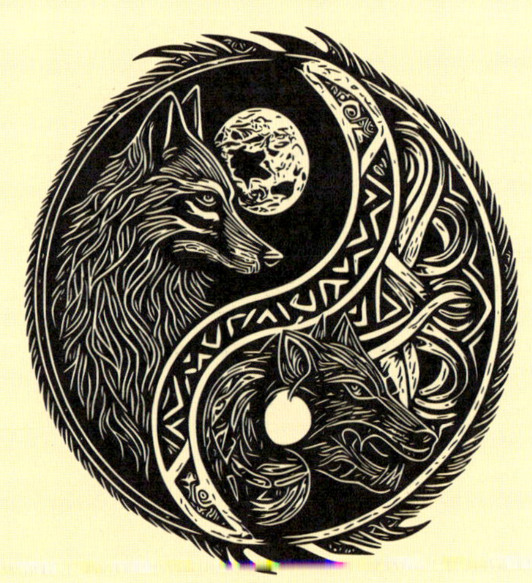

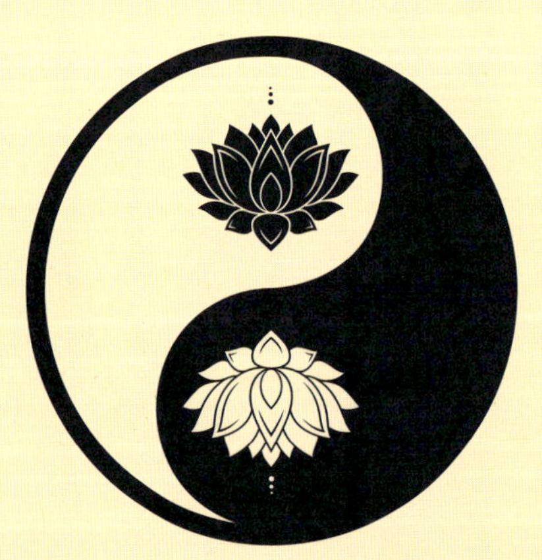

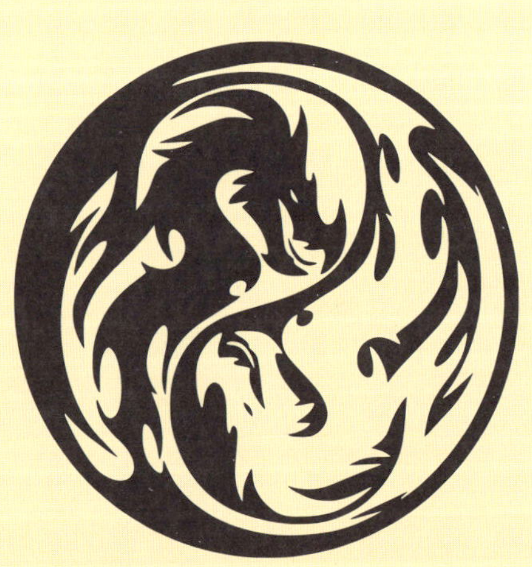

which translates as the 'Book of Changes'. This ancient manuscript looks at the transformational power of nature. In particular, it looks to the cosmos for inspiration in charting the path of earth around the sun. It is this journey, and the resulting seasons, that form the basis of the symbol we recognize today.

How to wear it

Synonymous with balance and harmony, the Yin and Yang symbol is a popular tattoo choice. In its simplest form it works well at a small size; however, many elaborate versions are seen in the tattoo world, often including heavily and lightly shaded animals associated with Eastern tattooing. Tigers, dragons or koi feature widely in these versions, and for more complex designs a larger scale is required. White ink, or a clever use of the wearer's skin tone, can be used to create the high contrast required to communicate the Yin and Yang concept.

Opposite: Yin and Yang can be combined with elements from different cultures and mythologies. The floral style (top left) depicts natural beauty, while the carp (middle left) suggests a link to the zodiac sign Pisces. A Viking-style wolf (middle right) links to Norse mythology.

Right: The woman and the dog at the heart of this Yin and Yang suggest a bond between human and animal.

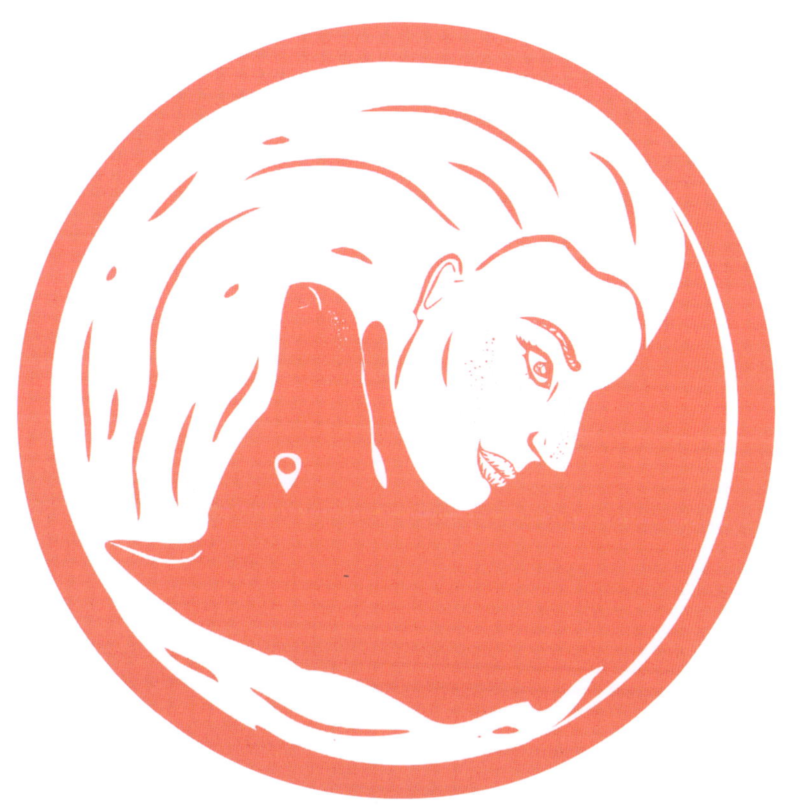

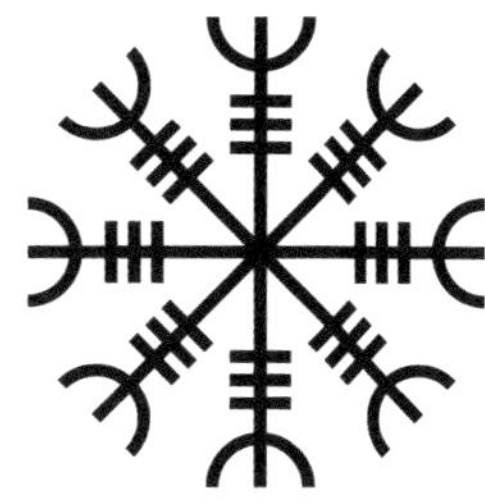

Helm of Awe

Defence | Protection | Strength | Resilience | Invincibility

Sacred Origins
Icelandic, Norse

Used Since
Late 10th century

Tattoo Styles
Blackwork
Fine-line

Opposite: The Helm of Awe symbol is synonymous with protection, courage and overcoming enemies. It can be depicted in a variety of styles which link the wearer to different movements and cultures. Celtic knots (middle left) imply a Celtic link.

Also known as the Ægishjálmr, the Helm of Awe was thought to strike fear into the heart of anyone who laid eyes upon it.

The power of serpents

To understand the true nature of this mighty motif carried by Viking warriors, we must look to early folk tales. According to the *Poetic Edda*, a collection of epic poems narrated by Norse bards, the Helm of Awe was worn by the worm-like dragon Fàfnir to protect his treasure from hoarders. The symbol made him invincible against the weapons of men. It's thought that the Helm of Awe holds the power of many serpents at its heart and renders those who gaze upon it paralysed by otherworldly poison.

A shield of protection

The power of the symbol is evident when looking at its structure. Eight spiked arms protrude from a central point, to create a circular pattern which resembles a shield. The tridents point like weapons outwards, warding off attack. Some interpretations have only four or six spiked arms with less adornments. Either way, the true meaning of the Helm of Awe is one of defence. Historians have concluded that the pattern itself is made up of a number of different runes, the most prominent being the arms of the Helm which resemble the rune Algiz. While the meaning of this rune is sketchy, it's thought to be synonymous with protection and the ability to withstand attack.

Spells and sigils

The Helm of Awe, which was thought to have been crafted by the god of all, Odin, was considered a spell in its own right, used by Norse magicians who

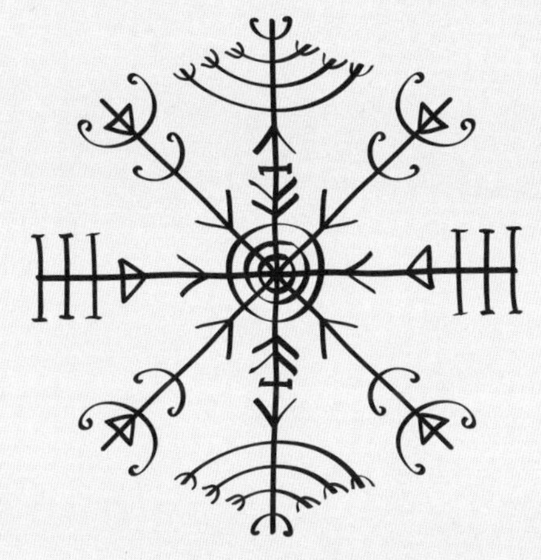

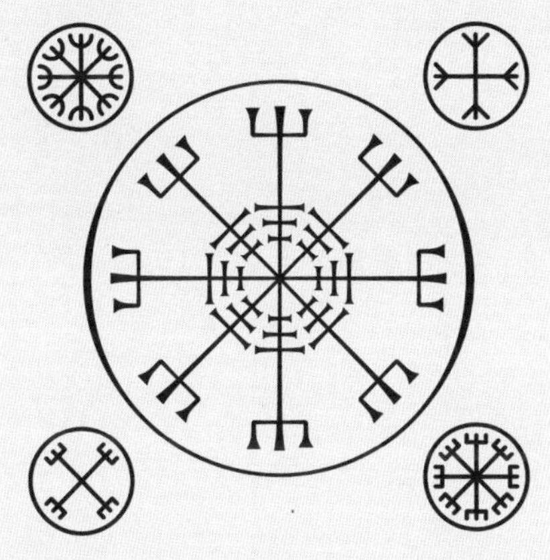

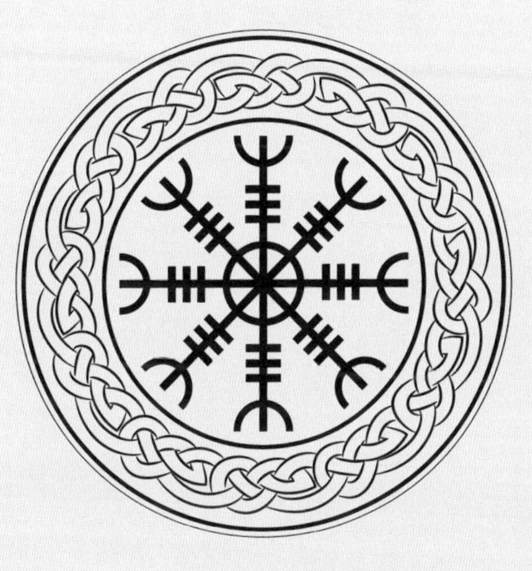

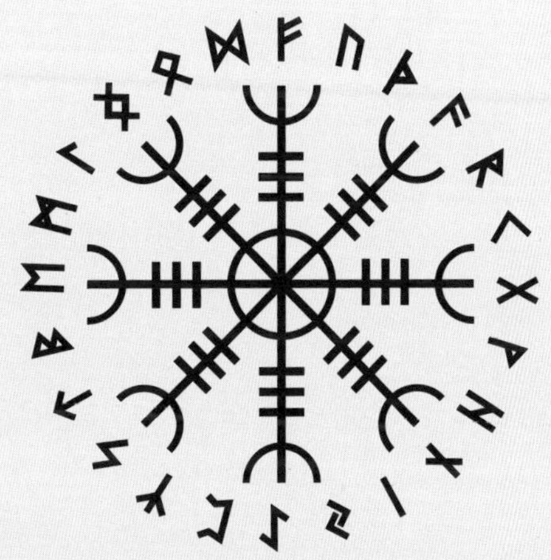

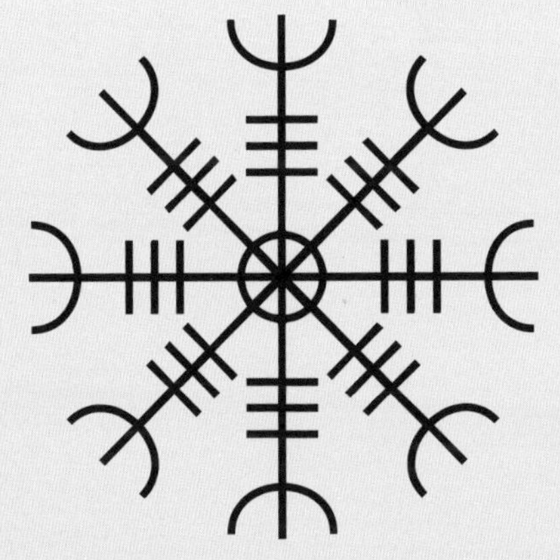

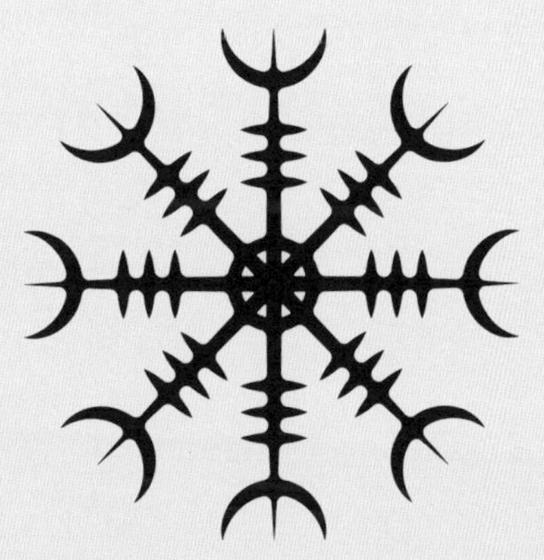

were usually female, known as *völva*. It was etched into stone and bark, carved
into bone, and even painted on the body as a form of protection. The image varied
depending on the power that the seer wished to summon. It's thought that the
elaborate eight-armed Helm referred to the eight divisions of the sky and earth.
Symbols with only six arms represented the four cardinal points and a vertical
axis, while the four-armed motif is a simplistic version of the cardinal points. The
labyrinth-like appearance of the symbol relates to the journey of self-discovery that
every person takes, which ultimately leads to renewed strength and self-belief.

How to wear it

It is thought that this symbol would have been worn by warriors upon the forearm.
The main pattern would wrap around the limb to imbue the sword arm with
strength. Today, the symbol can be seen tattooed in other locations as well as on
the forearm, giving the wearer an inner sense of strength or protection from life's
challenges. The Helm of Awe can also be found in among elaborate, large-scale
Nordic designs for the arm, leg and torso.

Opposite: **The Helm of Awe**
sits at the heart of a giant
triquetra (see page 92),
suggesting a link to the power
of three and unity.

Right: **The dragon, which**
is present in numerous,
mythologies, adds power,
good fortune and strength to
this Helm.

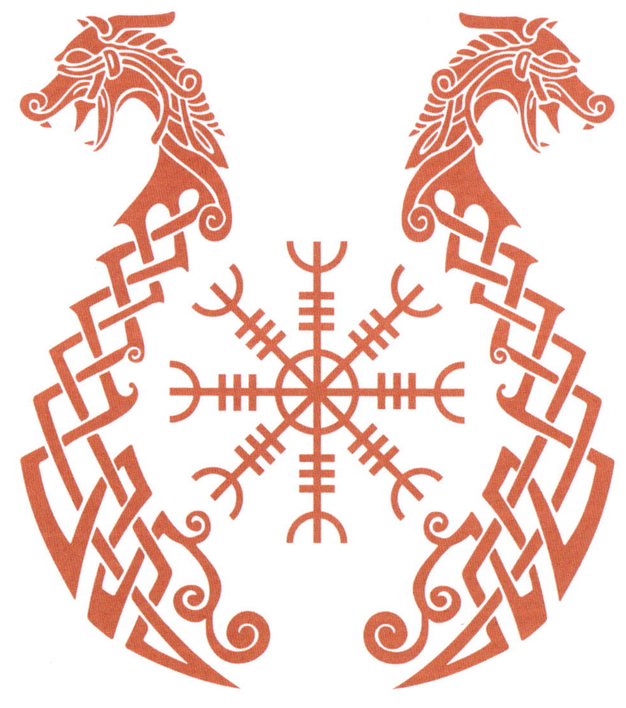

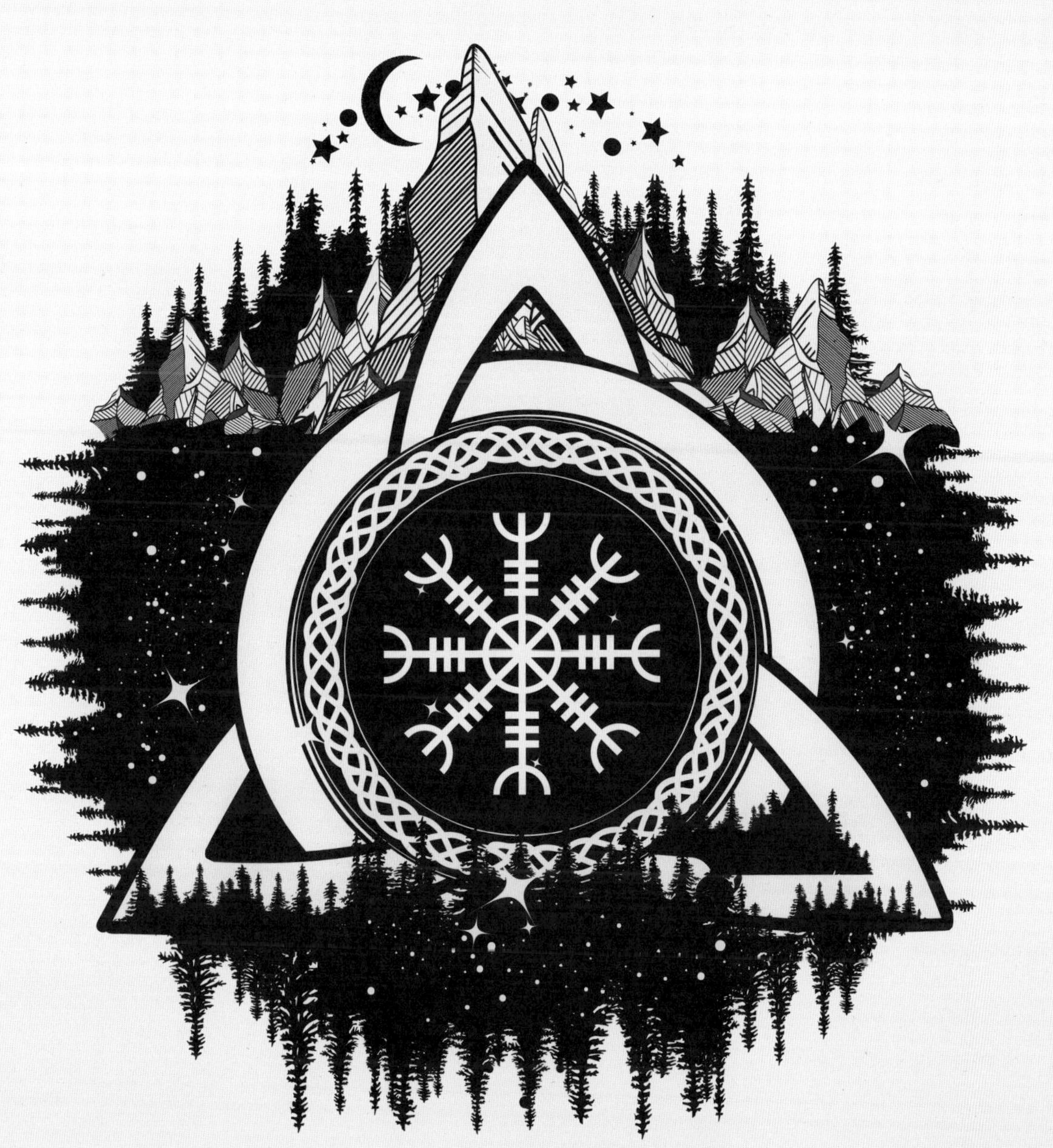

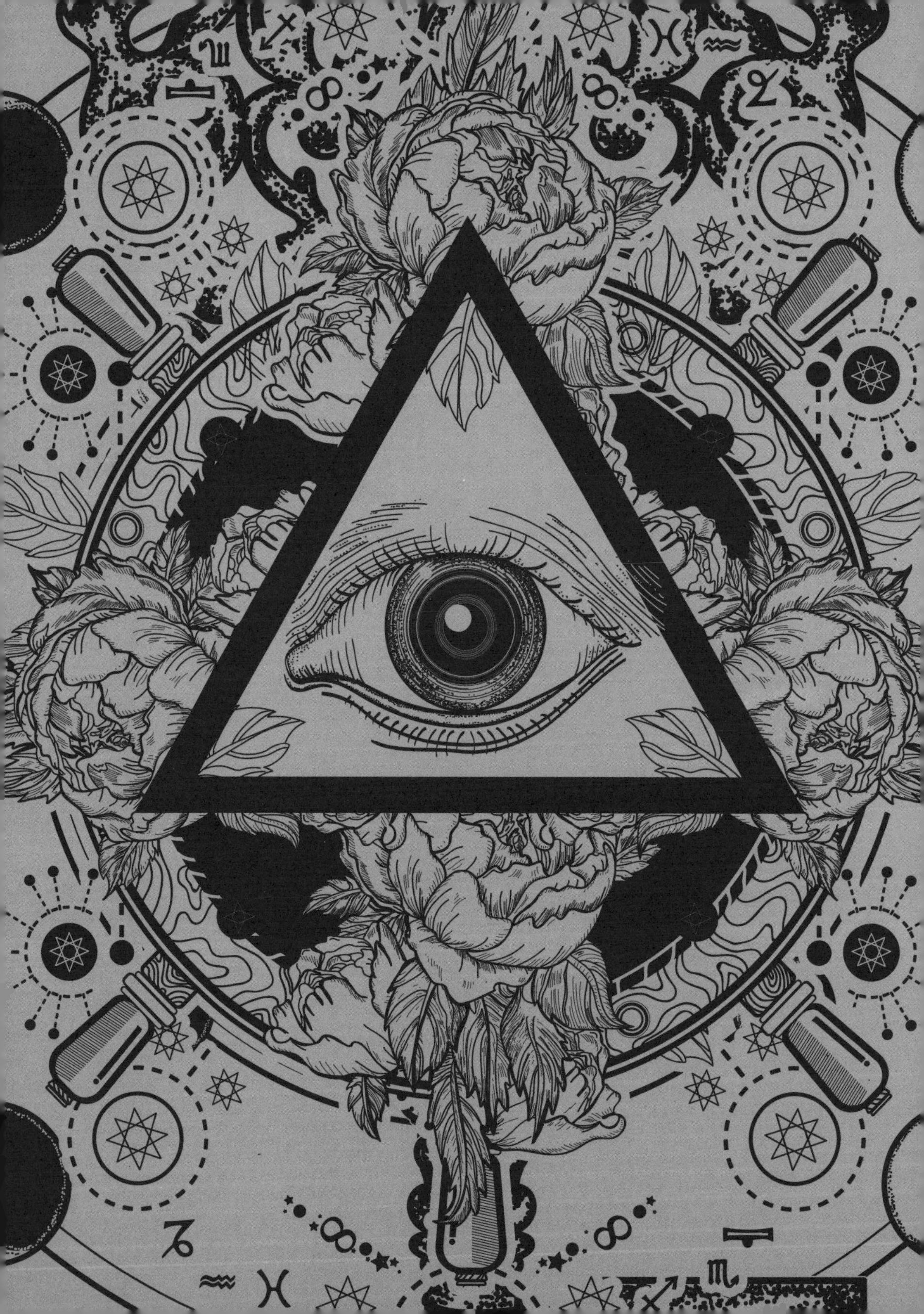

3

Triangles

Ancient civilizations often observed triangular shapes in nature, from lobed leaves and fronds to succulents that grew into a pyramid-like structure, or towering fir trees, with their abundance of spiny branches at the base which eventually narrowed with height. They recognized the power of this form – how the sturdy base could support more weight, how the pointed tip had the capacity to reach to the heavens, and used this in some of their earliest constructions.

They realized that the triangle could be helpful in other ways too. From its use to create perfect corners using knots in a rope to mark out a right angle, a trick both the Egyptians and Babylonians favoured, to measuring the distance a ship was moored from the shore. They revered the power of three, because they could see its effectiveness and harness it for themselves. Over time the triangle became potent and sacred, and at the core of many powerful symbols, some of which feature in the following pages. Here you will find a plethora of delights from the many faceted and deeply spiritual Sri Yantra, to the simple, solid structure of a mountain, sacred to so many cultures, a beacon of hope and potential.

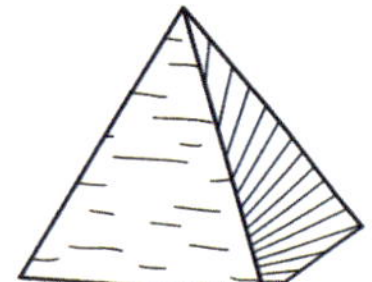

Pyramid

Wisdom | Enlightenment | Transition | Higher power | Mysticism

Sacred Origins
Egyptian

Used Since
Early 3rd millennium BCE

Tattoo Styles
Western traditional
Neo-traditional
Fine-line
Blackwork

Opposite: Pyramids symbolize the connection between heaven and earth. The eyes at the heart of these pyramid images (top left and right) are a link to the esoteric power of the Eye of Providence, the All-Seeing Eye.

The intricate knowledge, planning and spiritual beliefs used by early civilizations in the construction of pyramids goes some way to explaining their prominence as symbols of transition, wisdom and mysticism.

A bridge between heaven and earth

The shape of the pyramid reveals much of its sacred significance. The flat, sturdy base is said to represent the earth, while the pointed tip reaches towards the heavens for spiritual enlightenment. As such, the pyramid connects the earth, the primordial source of all creation, with the higher cosmic realms.

Tombs and burial chambers

The ancient Egyptians were the first to create these impressive structures using the triangular shape to distribute the enormous weight evenly. It was Pharaoh Djoser who commissioned his architect to design a tomb-like structure using bench-shaped stones called mastabas, placing one on top of the other to create a step pyramid. This prototype was built around 2780 BCE, but it wasn't until the reign of the founder of the 4th dynasty, Pharaoh Snefru, that the pyramid evolved to have smoother sides.

How to wear it

Pyramids often feature in the background of large-scale work. If, for example, the theme is Egyptian, a pyramid would be a popular element to help set the scene. However, there are many examples where the pyramid takes centre stage and the symbol's triangular space can be used to incorporate other Egyptian motifs, like the Eye of Horus – which represents protection, health and restoration – to enhance the meaning.

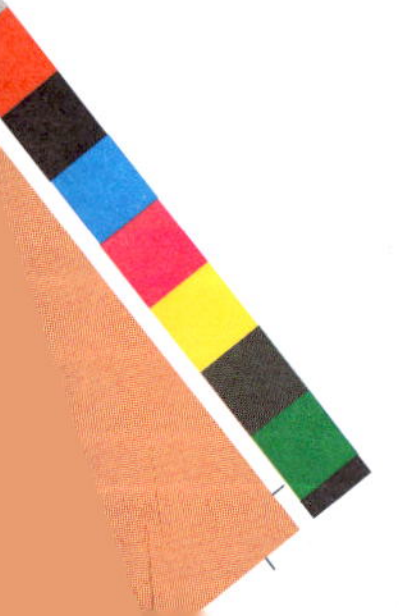

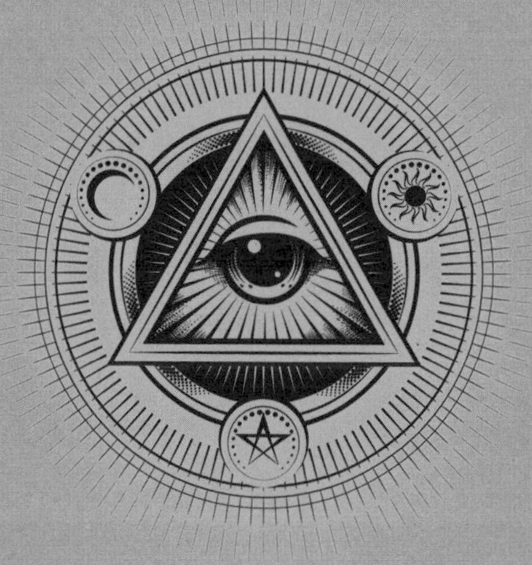

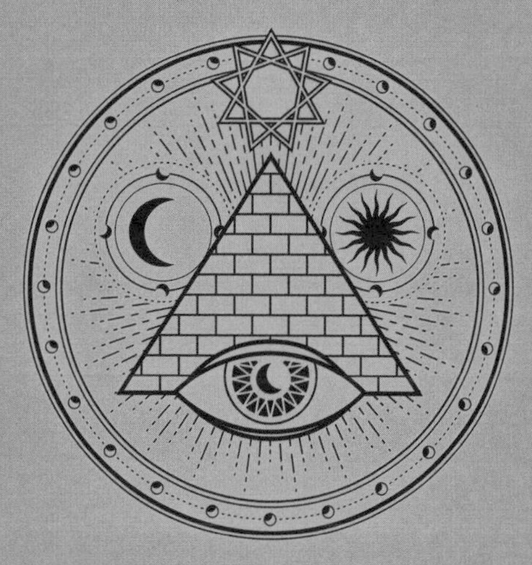

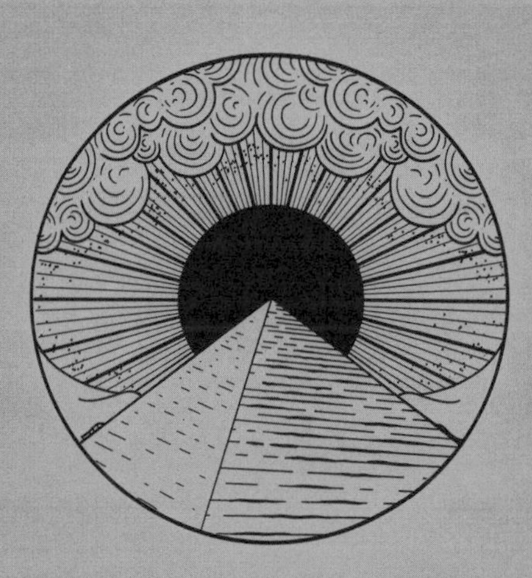

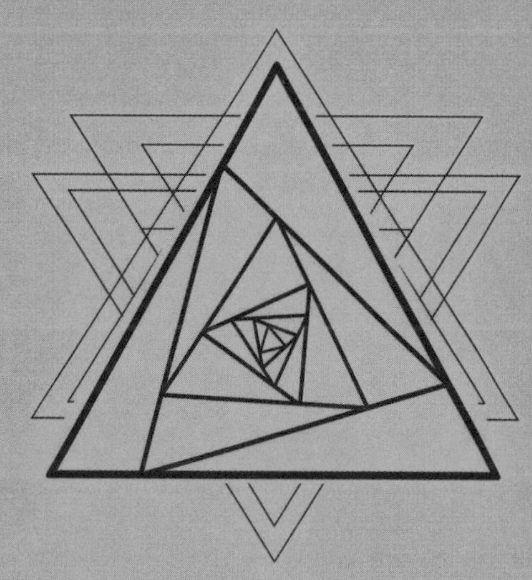

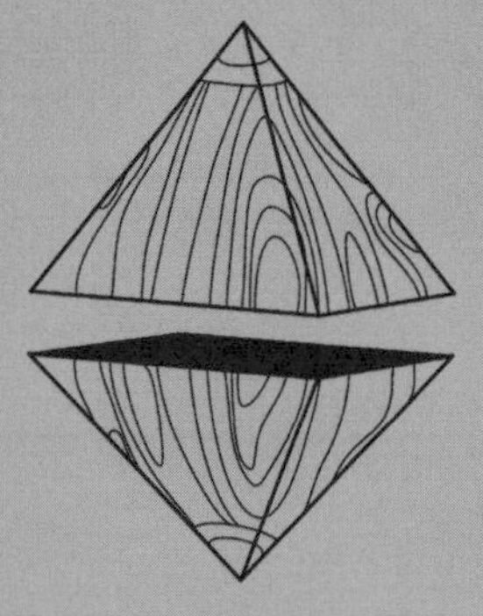

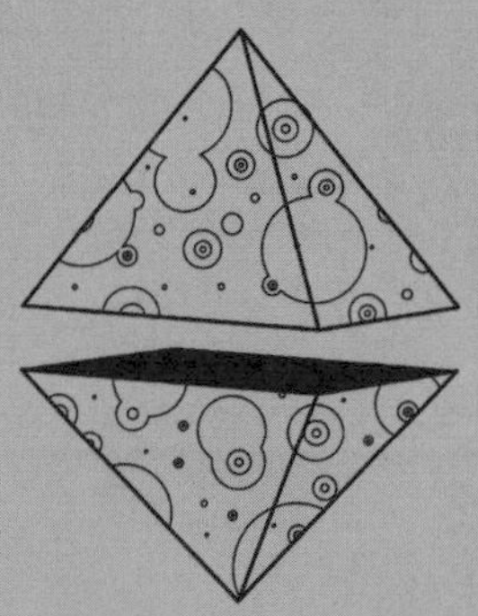

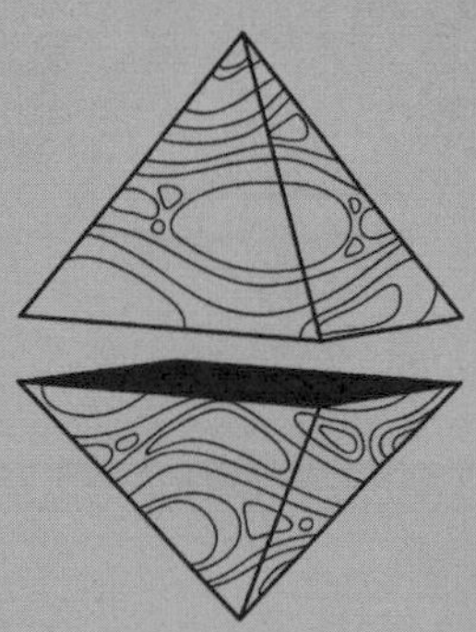

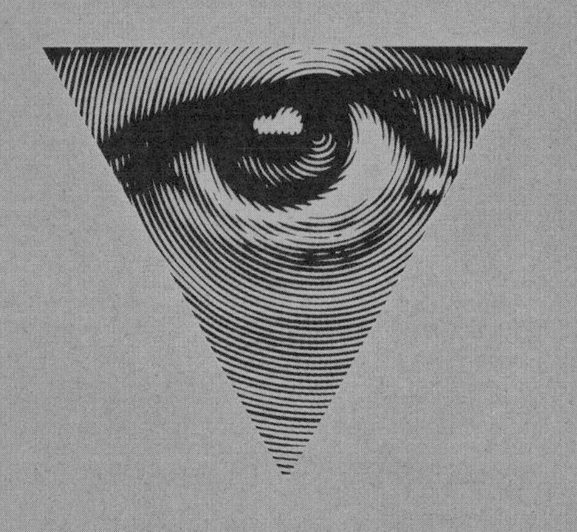

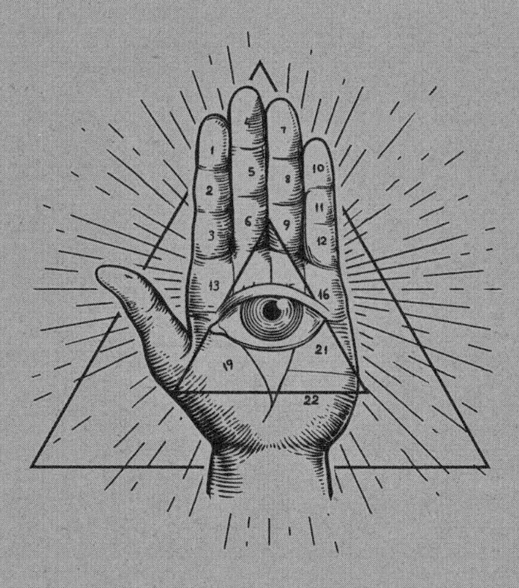

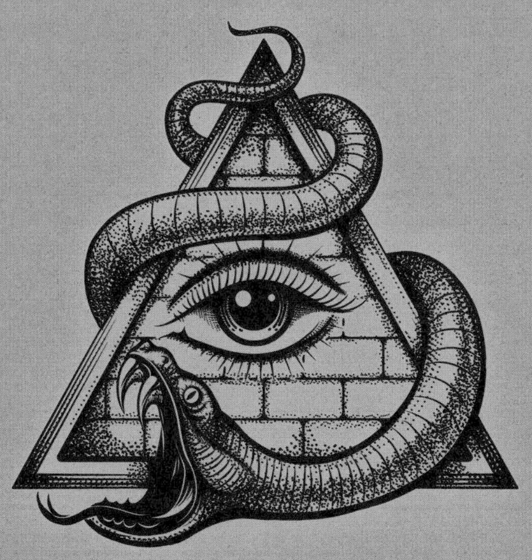

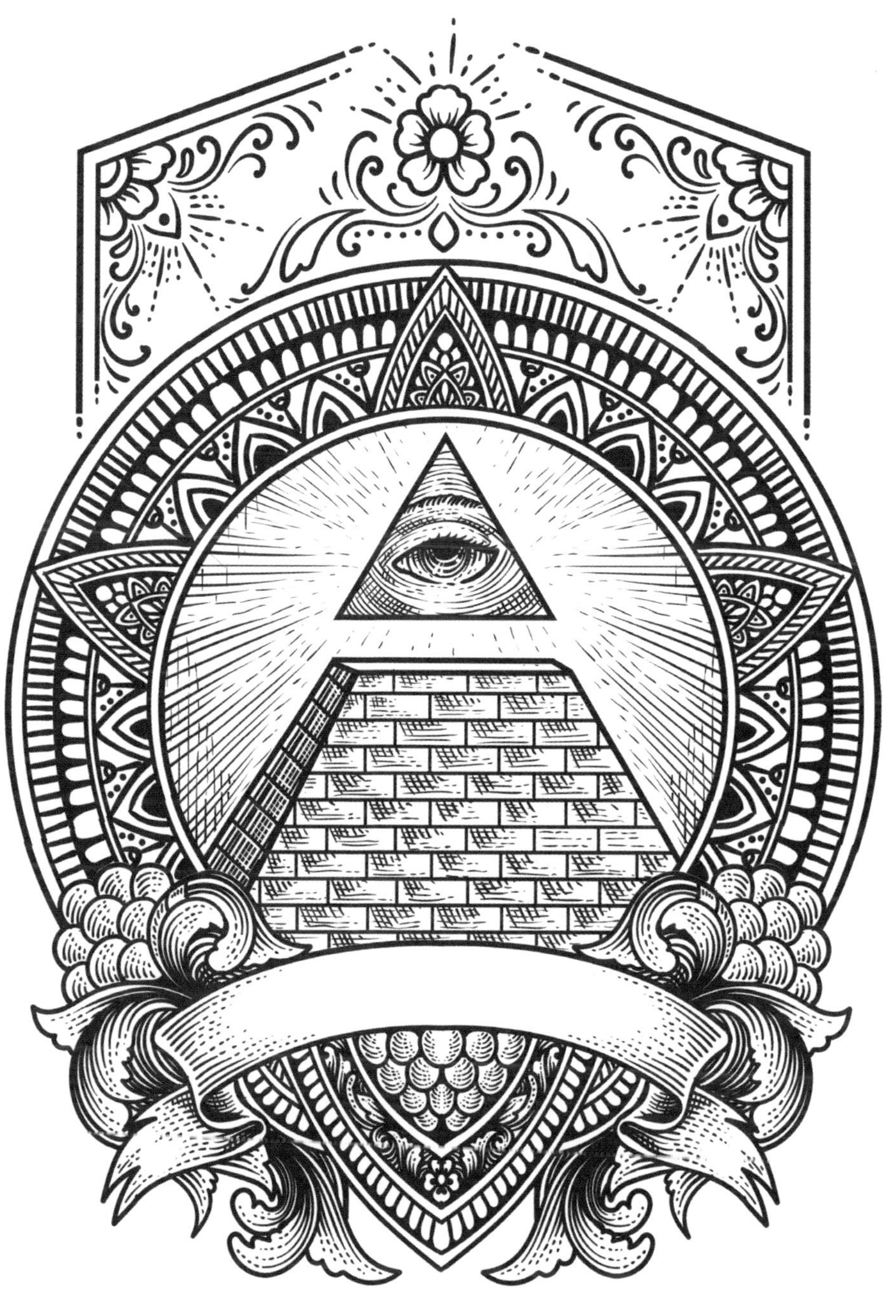

Above: This split pyramid with the All-Seeing Eye in the top half suggests an eternal mystical presence overlooking everything.

Opposite: The snake that encircles the pyramid (middle) denotes power and strength, while the Egyptian-influenced pyramid (bottom) has wings, which suggest otherworldly guidance and protection.

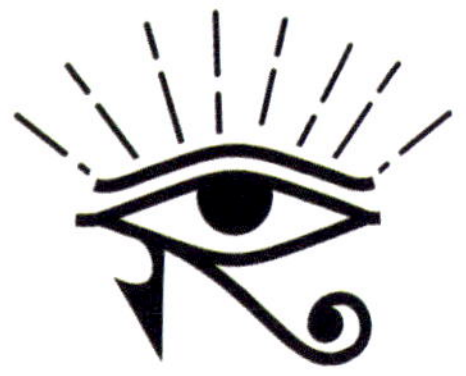

Eye of Providence

Divinity | Protection | Spiritual guidance | Esoteric wisdom

Sacred Origins
Sumerian, Egyptian, Christian

Used Since
Late 1800s

Tattoo Styles
Fine-line
Blackwork
Western traditional
Neo-traditional

Right: The eye surrounded by three snakes in a triple knot design (top) connects the symbol with the eternal cycles of life. Different eye designs can accentuate mystical energy. The moon and stars (middle left) connect the eye with the universe, while the lotus petals (middle right) infer inner wisdom and peace.

A haunting image, the Eye of Providence is a composition using multiple sacred symbols from different origins.

A composition of cosmic power

The symbol of the Eye of Providence, or All-Seeing Eye, shows a disembodied eye aloft within a triangle, sometimes portrayed as a pyramid, and often features clouds or a burst of light to add to the impression of cosmic power. A common motif, which is used on the Great Seal of the United States and appears in artwork and stained-glass windows, it has curious roots that incorporate a number of different beliefs. While the author of the original remains a mystery, the combination of symbols used gives some insight into the deeper meaning.

The Eye of Horus

The motif is often likened to the Eye of Horus, an important symbol to the ancient Egyptians, used in amulets and talismans for protection. Horus, a god and king, lost both of his eyes in battle but was later healed by the god of wisdom and writing, Thoth. As such, the eye was considered important, associated with rebirth and renewal.

Divinity and the power of three

Being a central feature of the face and usually the first thing that connects us with another person, eyes were deemed highly significant. Depictions of enlarged eyes were used by the Sumerians as early as 4500–1900 BCE, to show a watchful nature and a heightened state of being. Eyes were linked to the ability to see beyond the surface. Couple this with the three-pronged approach of the triangle, linked to divinity and recognized as a Christian emblem, and an

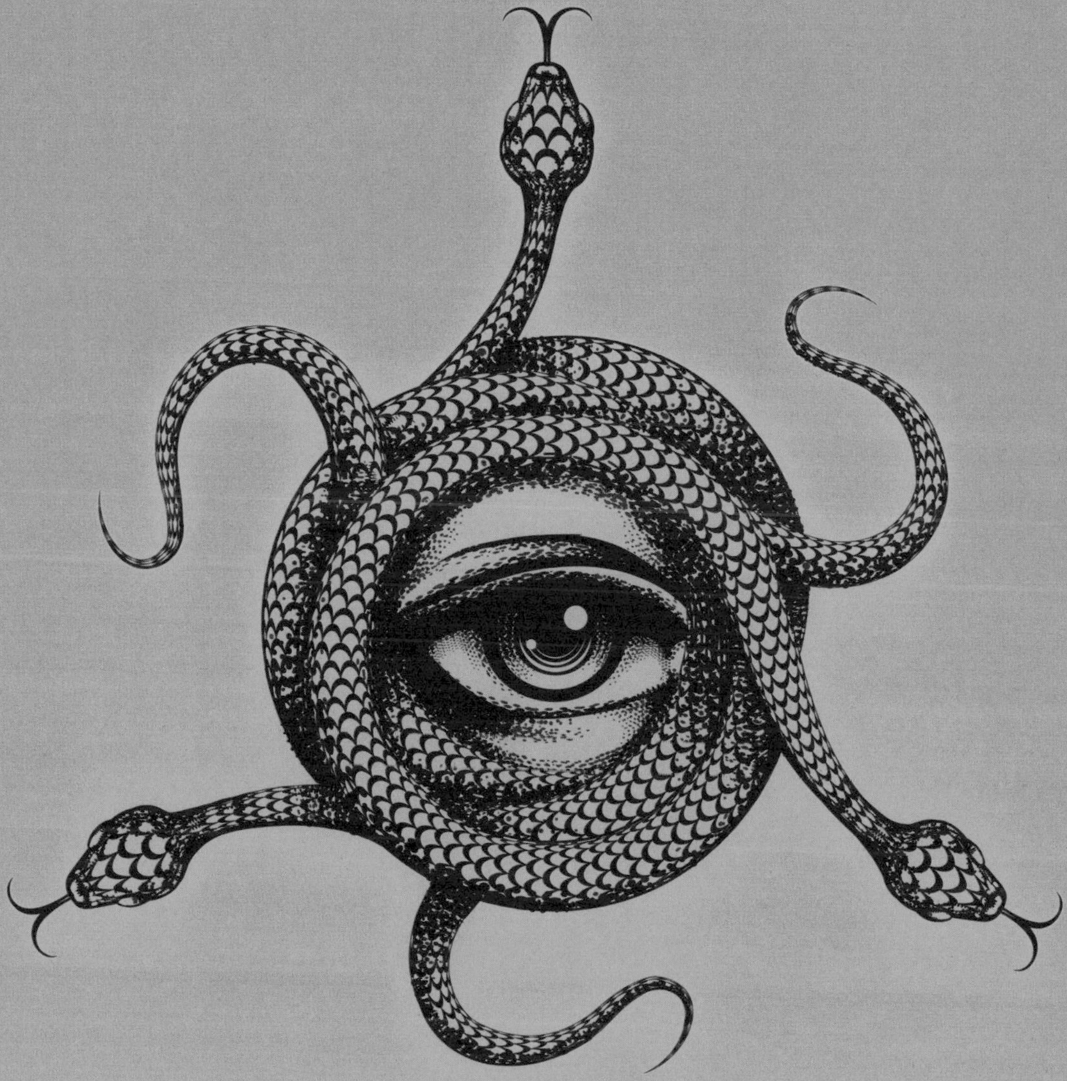

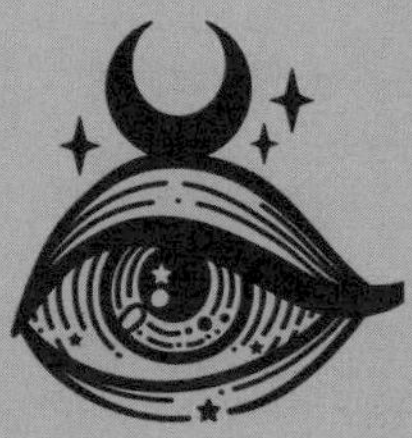

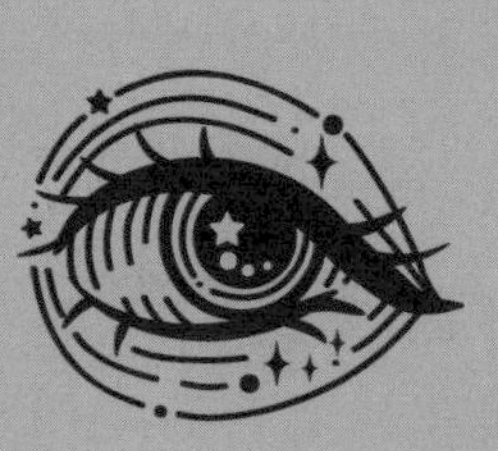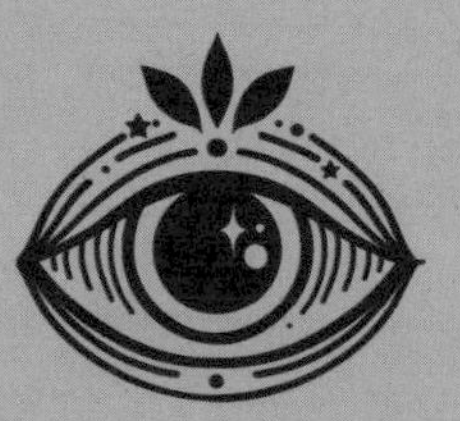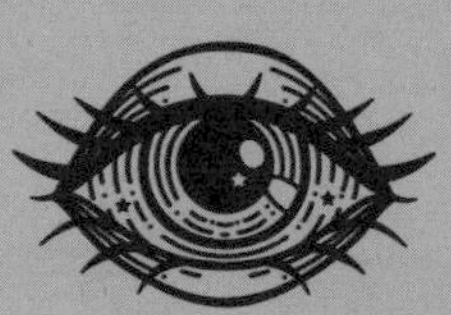

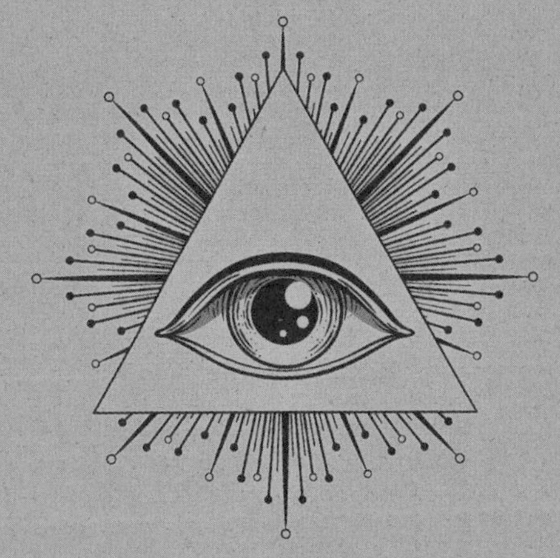

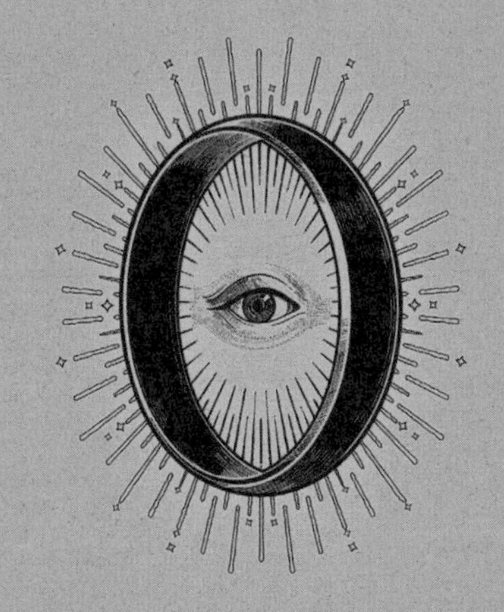

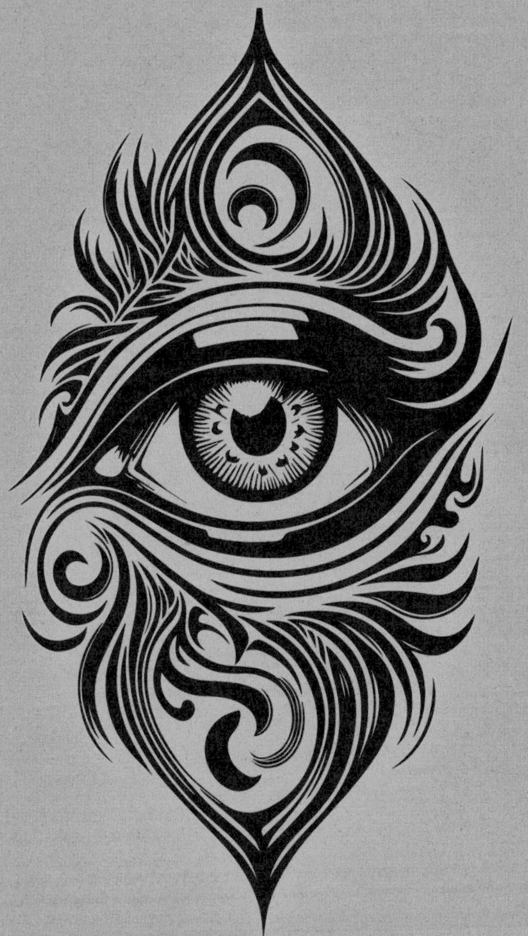

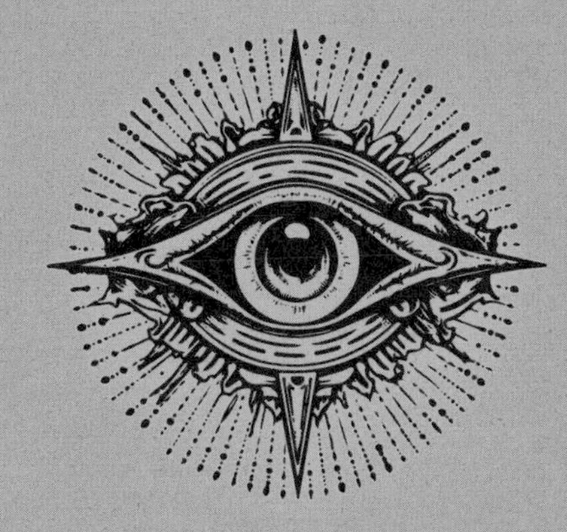

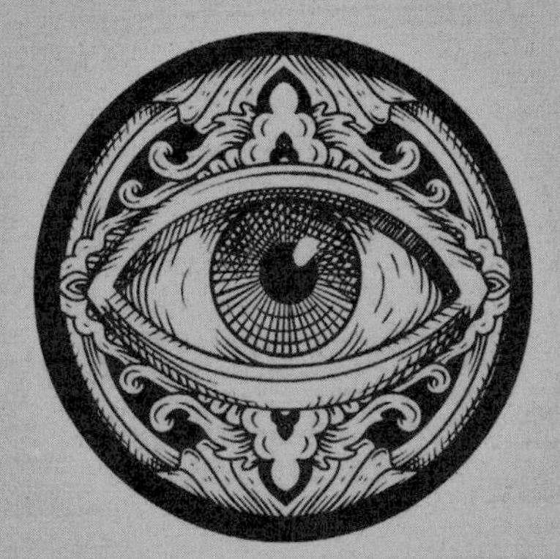

illustration of the Holy Trinity – the Father, the Son and the Holy Spirit – and it becomes evident that this symbol was meant to personify the ever-present and all-powerful eye of God.

The triangle has other connotations too: while it encompasses three ways or aspects of being, it also represents unity. To the Freemasons, the Eye of Providence was the perfect embodiment of divine power – it portrayed the watchful care of the Supreme Architect, God. They began using the symbol in the late 18th century, taking their lead from churches and Renaissance artwork to come up with their own version.

How to wear it

With so many variations, this symbol can be tattooed in many ways. Some artists use a pyramid with the eye floating above it, while others choose to place the eye in the centre of the triangle. Other elements are often added, including bursts of radiating light, clouds or wings, to help elevate the symbolism. This design is most often seen in black and grey fine-line. However, if it's tattooed in a bold traditional style, the addition of colour works well.

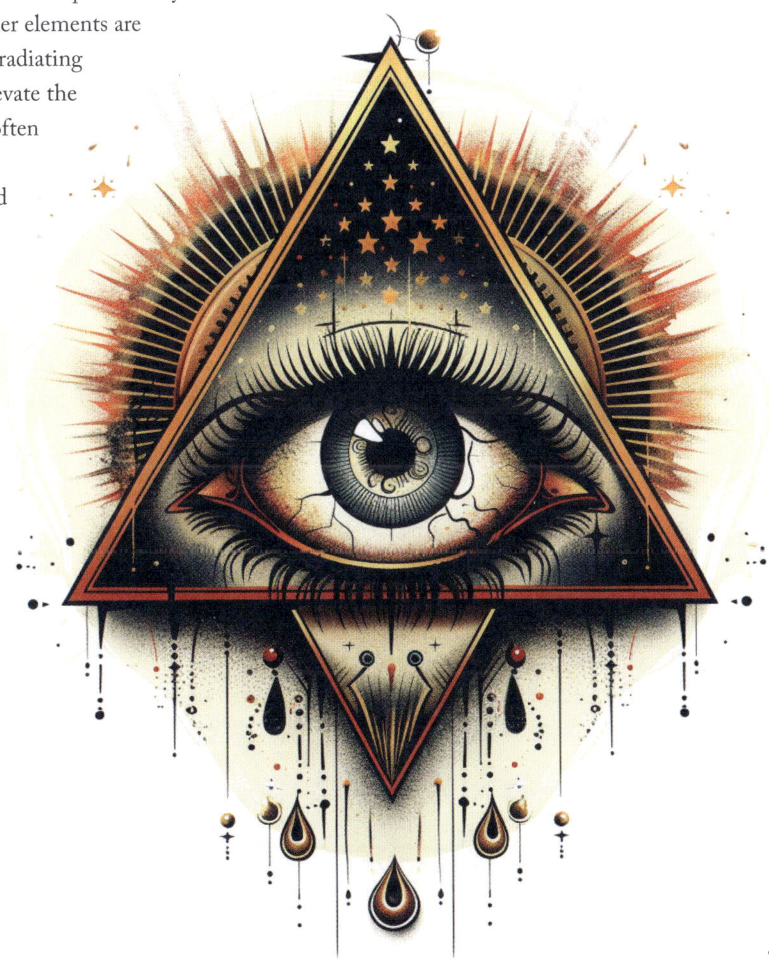

Opposite: The eye displayed within a circular frame (right column) is associated with strength and rebirth.

Right: This Eye of Providence is incredibly detailed, which makes it a powerful symbol of protection.

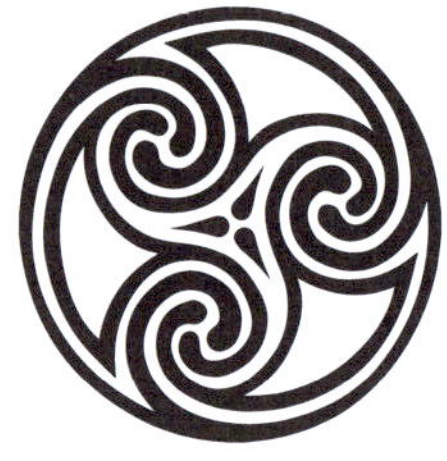

Triskelion

Rebirth | Renewal | Energy | Movement | Fate

Sacred Origins
Celtic, Greek

Used Since
c. 3200 BCE

Tattoo Styles
Ornamental
Blackwork

Opposite: The Triskelion lends itself to a variety of decorative styles. When encircled (top middle), it becomes even more powerful and links to the eternal cycles of life.

Also known as the triskele or the spiral triskele, this eye-catching motif is a popular Celtic emblem, appearing in jewellery, artwork and home décor.

Ancient roots

While it's a favourite with many modern designers, the triskelion is steeped in history. The name itself comes from the Greek word *triskeles* meaning 'many legs', but the symbol dates back to the Stone Age, first appearing around 5,000 years ago etched into the stone at Newgrange, an ancient site of monuments in the Boyne Valley, County Meath, Ireland. Here, it represents the ongoing cycles of life.

The power of three

To the Greeks, the symbol meant movement and action, and this can be seen in the rotating legs which were often used to form the spirals. The Celts placed their focus on the triplicate nature of the symbol, believing the number three was sacred because it was used to describe key concepts, from birth, life and death, to mind, body and spirit, and past, present and future. Today the triskelion features on the flag of Sicily and is also used as a powerful meditation symbol in Buddhism.

How to wear it

This symbol can be styled according to whichever mythology the wearer wishes to highlight. It can be formed from Celtic-inspired knots, surrounded by a Greek-influenced pattern or rendered in solid black in its simplest form. The triskelion is often seen on the centre of the back between the shoulder blades but works equally well on the forearm, wrist or shoulder.

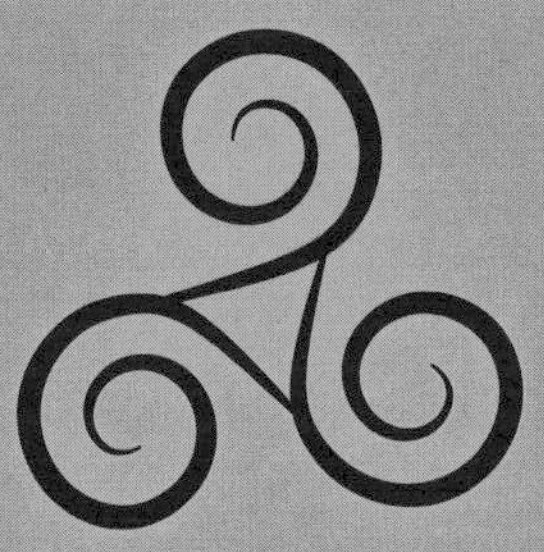

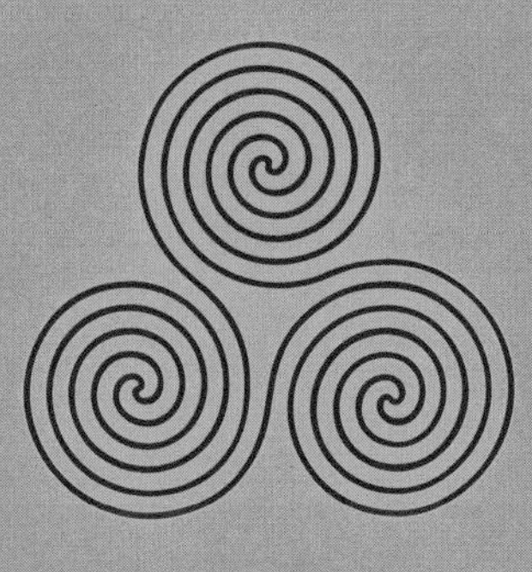

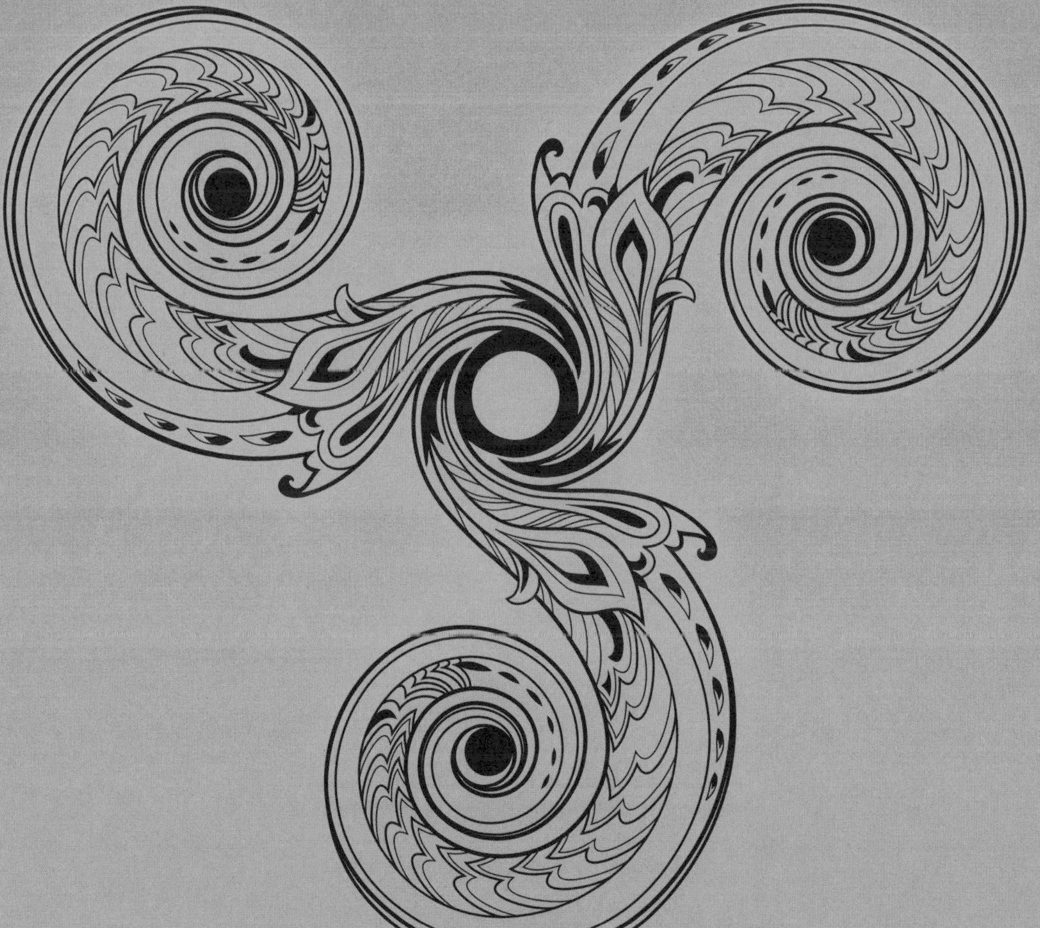

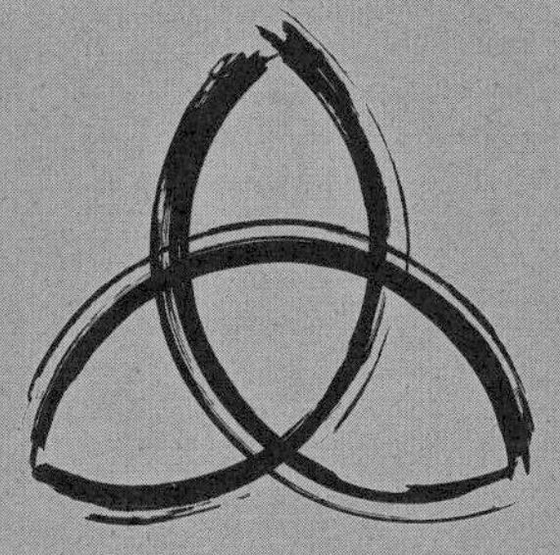 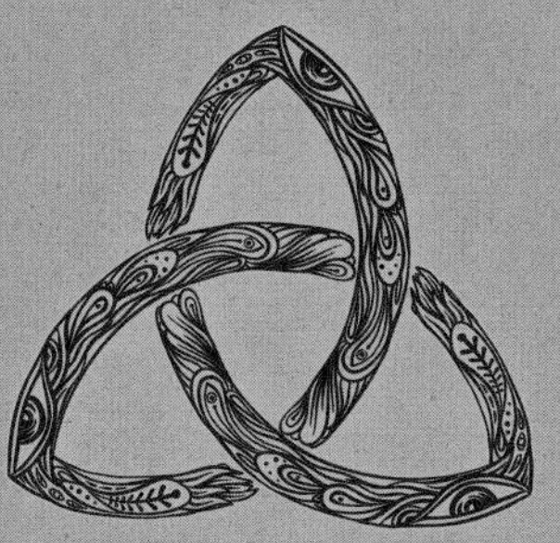 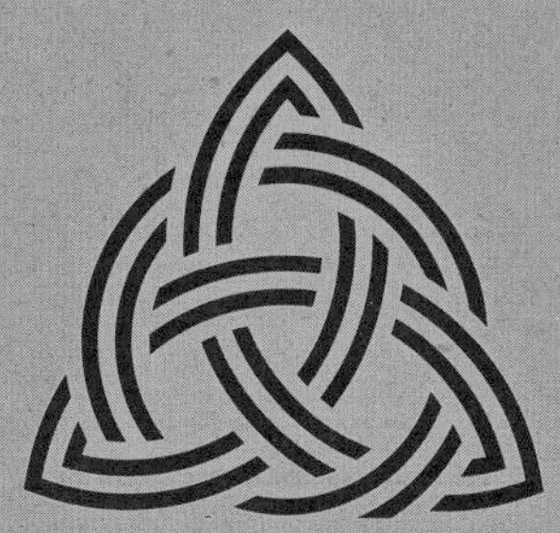

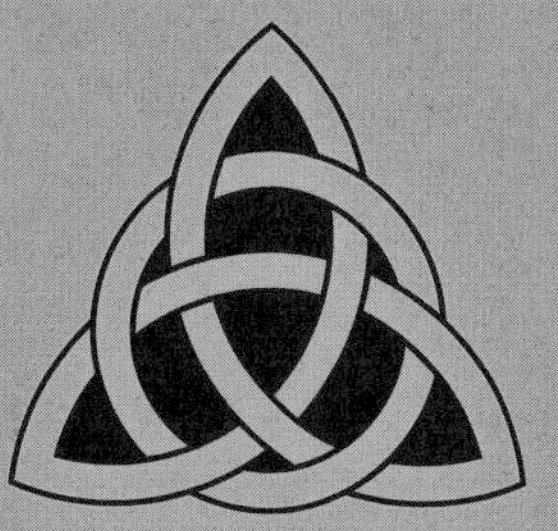 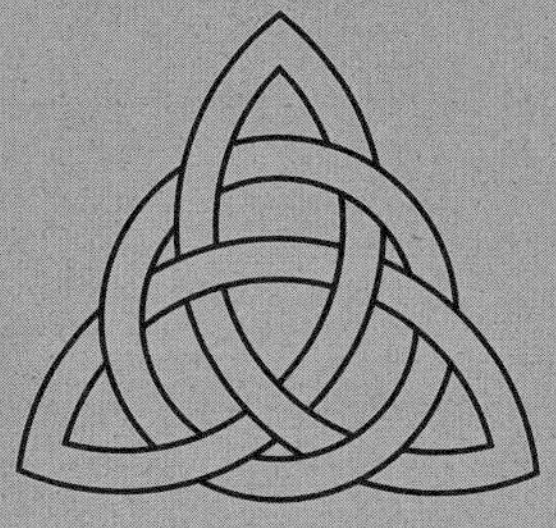 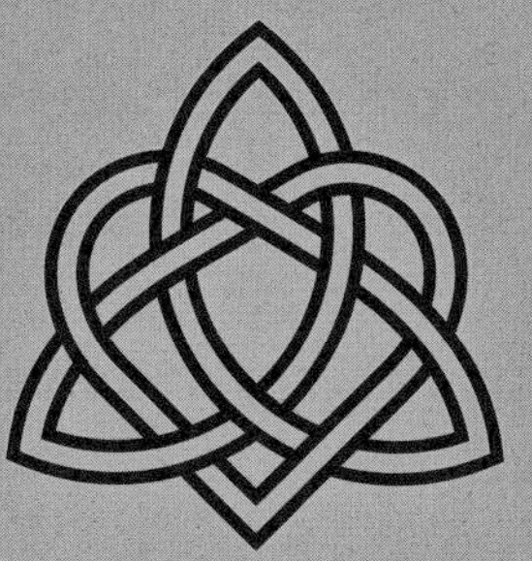

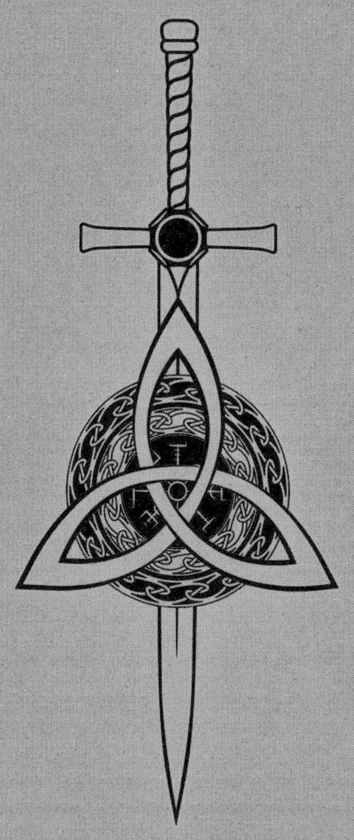 

Triquetra

The power of three | Unity | Wholeness | Protection

Sacred Origins
Celtic, Norse,
Pre-Christian

Used Since
4th century BCE

Tattoo Styles
Fine-line
Blackwork

Opposite: Traditional triquetra designs (top), highlight the symbol's core message of the power of three. A sword plunging into the heart of the triquetra (bottom left) adds power and enhances the symbol's protective energy. The triquetra floating above a mountain backdrop (bottom right) links the wearer to the heavenly otherworld.

The name comes from the Latin adjective *triquetrus*, meaning 'three cornered' — each arc slides neatly into the next, giving the appearance of a never-ending knot.

A unifying power

A mysterious symbol, it is often assumed that the triquetra is of Celtic origin, and while it does date back to the Pre-Christian era, being at least 5,000 years old, it was used by a wide range of cultures. Versions of this symbol appear on a range of artefacts originating from the Gauls, Scythians and Vikings. Indeed, it was popular with the Norse peoples and often used alongside runes on everyday objects.

The symbol, which is comprised of three overlapping and interconnected arcs, is also known as the vesica pisces. While each loop is separate it is also intrinsically connected to the other two, making the triquetra a symbol which brings together three elements and unifies their power.

The maiden, the mother and the crone

To the Celts, the triquetra was a representation of the triple goddess and used to illustrate the three aspects of her form: the maiden, the mother and the crone. Each element was important and tied to the cycles of a woman's life. It embodied the qualities and strengths of each unique phase, which when combined in a trinity created a deity of immense power.

In addition, the symbol came to represent any significant grouping of three that worked together to create a concept, for example the past, present and future, or the cycles of life from birth to death and then rebirth. This was incredibly important to those early tribes who embraced the idea that life was an eternal loop and used the triquetra to mark graves, burial mounds and sites of worship. The knot was also thought to signify the union of land, sea and sky. A deeply protective symbol, it is used today by pagan and Wiccan groups in rituals, seals and talismans to represent the body, mind and spirit working in harmony.

How to wear it

The simplicity of the triquetra means that it is usually tattooed at a small scale, suitable for areas such as wrists, ankles and centrally on the sternum. If the motif is woven into a large-scale design, it's often featured in sleeves or back pieces.

The triquetra is frequently adorned with ornate Celtic knotwork or decorated with plants and flowers. It's most often seen tattooed in black unless embellishment has been added, which opens up the design to a larger palette.

Opposite: This symbol features a reflection of the original triquetra and sends a powerful message of 'as above, so below', meaning what we do in the physical realm will reflect in the spiritual.

Right: The Helm of Awe in this triquetra amplifies the protective energy of the symbol and brings together two different cultures, the Norse and the Celtic.

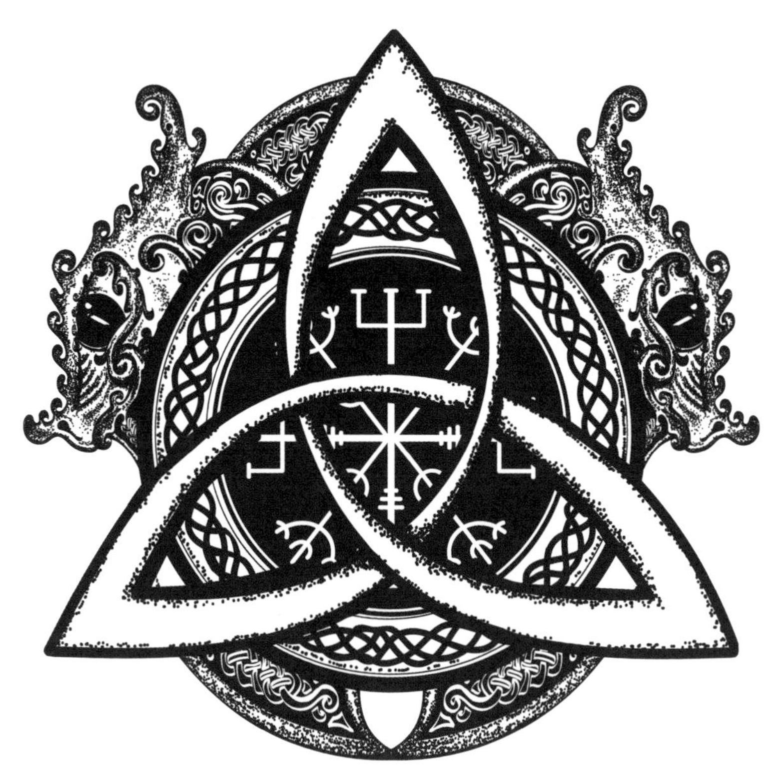

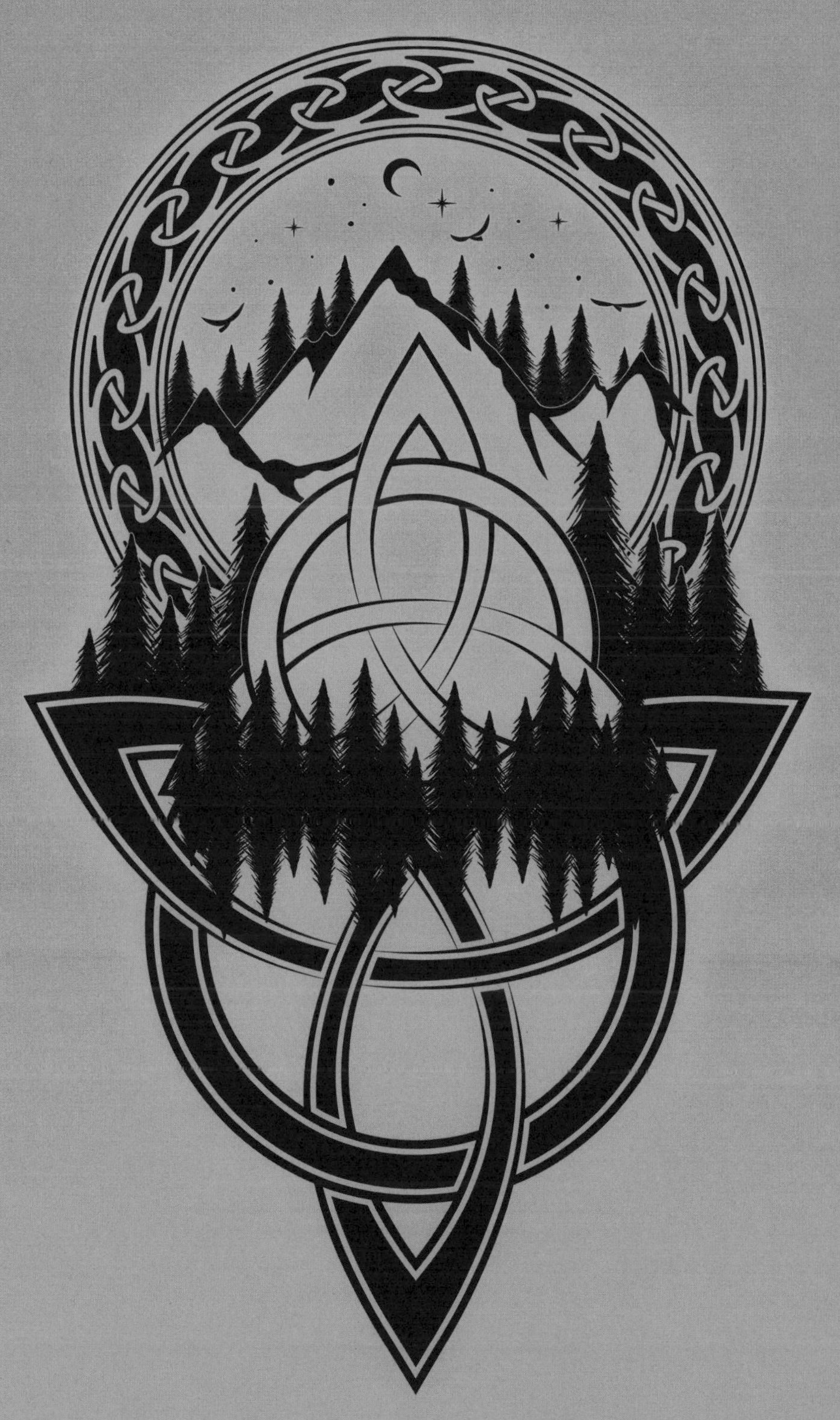

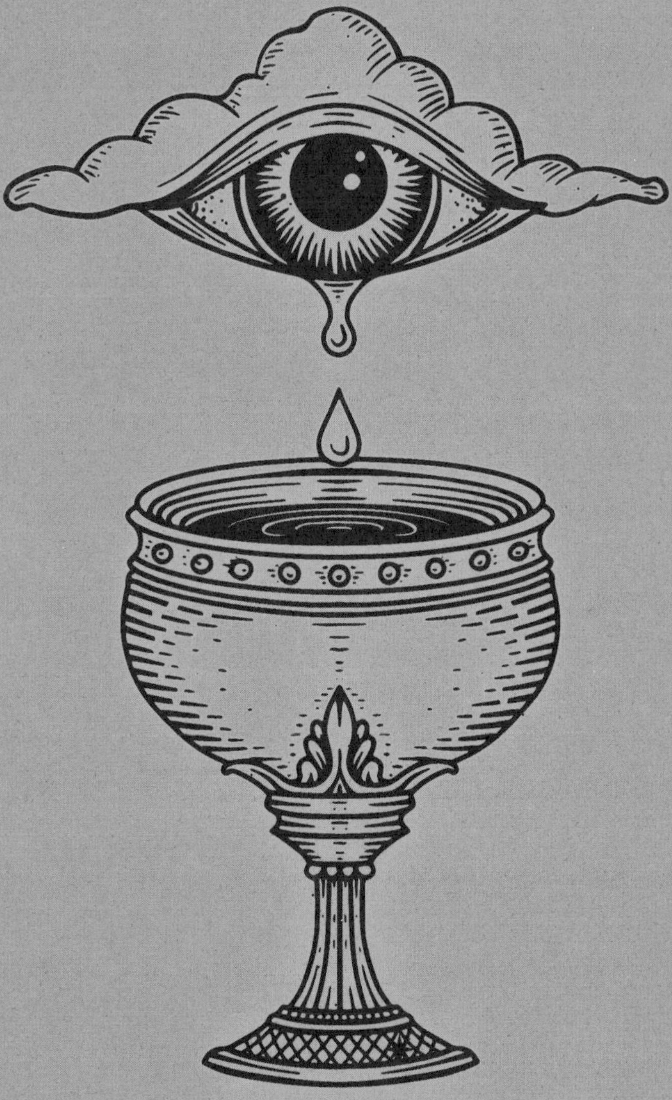

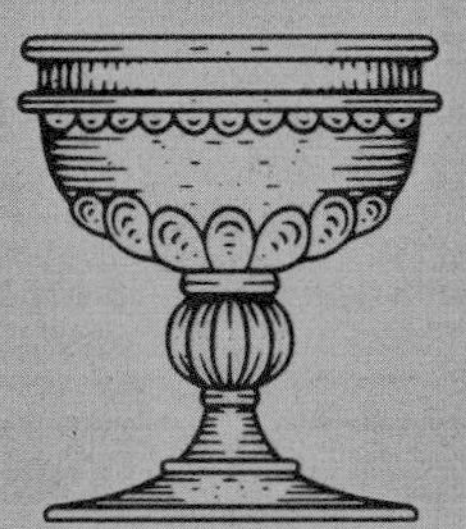

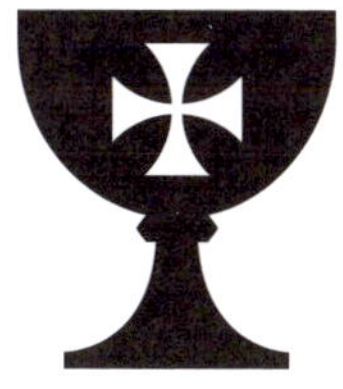

Holy Grail

Healing | Eternal youth | Love | Fulfilment | Truth

Sacred Origins
Celtic, Greek, Roman, Christian

Used Since
12th century

Tattoo Styles
Fine-line
Black-and-grey realism
Blackwork

Opposite: The Eye of Providence cries tears of knowledge into the Holy Grail (top), which suggests the cup holds infinite wisdom of an otherworldly nature. The grail encompassed by wings (bottom left) indicates heavenly guidance and amplifies the sacred energy of the symbol.

This cup-shaped vessel, triangular in form, being wide-mouthed at the brim and dwindling to a point, is thought to have its roots in Greek, Roman and Celtic mythology.

The healing cup
Likely based on earlier symbols like the cornucopia, the grail is the overflowing cup of the gods and a symbol associated with youth and everlasting love. Perhaps this was why early poets and writers were fascinated with the idea of a specific cup or vessel that held the purest essence of life.

An eternal quest
Pre-Christian writers were so inspired by the idea that they wrote epic narratives and poems which highlighted the grail's prominence. The quest to find it was first mentioned in the unfinished romantic tale, *Perceval, ou Le Conte du Graal* (*Perceval, or the Romance of the Grail*) written around 1180 by the French poet Chrétien de Troyes. Here the young knight Perceval is enamoured by the idea of the relic and goes on a quest to retrieve it. It was the 13th-century poet Robert de Boron who first established a link with Christianity. His verse trilogy *Joseph d'Arimathie, Merlin, and Perceval* (often called the *Estoire dou Graal*) cited the grail as the drinking vessel which Christ used at the Last Supper, and the same cup that Joseph d'Arimathie used to catch the blood flowing from Christ's wounds as he hung upon the cross. As such, this made the grail a sacred object and the subject of many conspiracy theories.

The mystery continues...
While King Arthur's knights did their best to acquire it in a number of narratives, the artefact's whereabouts remained a mystery. According to one

myth, Joseph d'Arimathie spirited the grail away to Glastonbury in England, where he hid it beneath the ground. It's thought that the stream runs red at this point, as it's imbued with the blood of Christ, but this is most likely a result of the red iron oxide in the soil. Other stories hint at a secret order of knights, known as the Knights Templar, who seized the vessel to protect it from falling into the wrong hands.

Whatever the truth, the Holy Grail remains an emblem of the quest for enlightenment. Drinking from the cup is thought to heal all wounds and grant a person eternal youth and happiness.

How to wear it

The grail is versatile and can be tattooed in a variety of styles, incorporating anything from Celtic to Nordic decoration. A classic Renaissance style, using intricate line work and stippled shading, also works well for this symbol. The vertical orientation and relatively slender proportions means many choose to tattoo it on their arms or legs. Those looking for strengthened meaning may opt to wear it on the chest so that the grail is next to the heart.

Opposite: The mystical geometry at work within this encircled symbol (bottom) speaks of esoteric power and magic. The grail itself sits within a star, which is associated with hope and faith.

Right: This ornate, floral Holy Grail is associated with beauty and grace. The flame bursting from within represents the Holy Spirit.

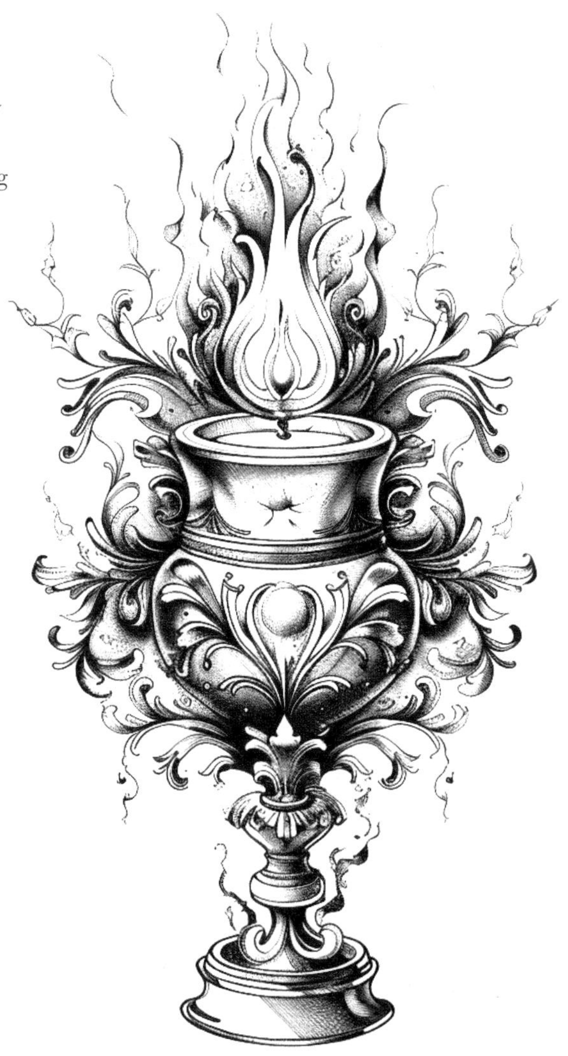

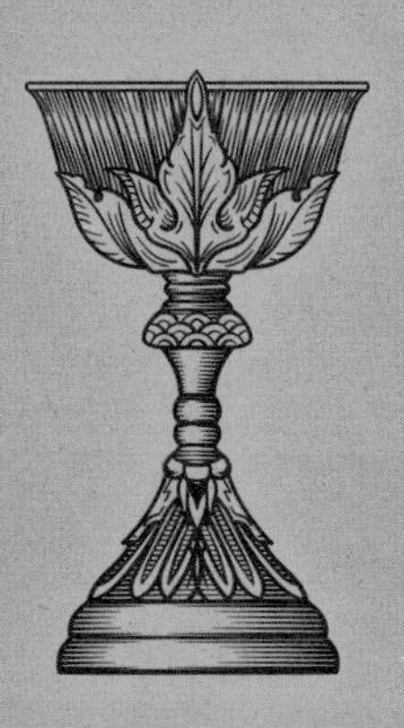 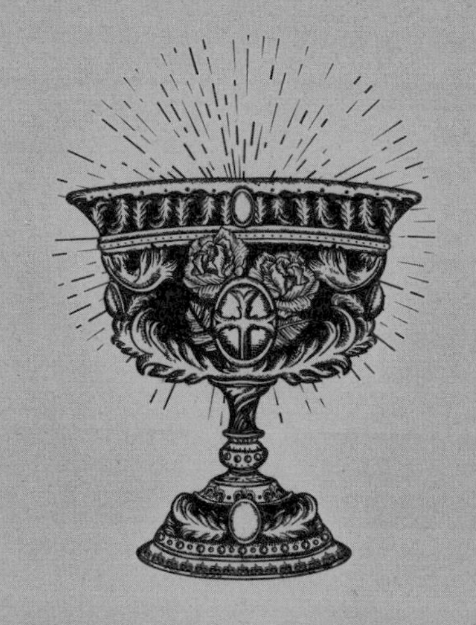 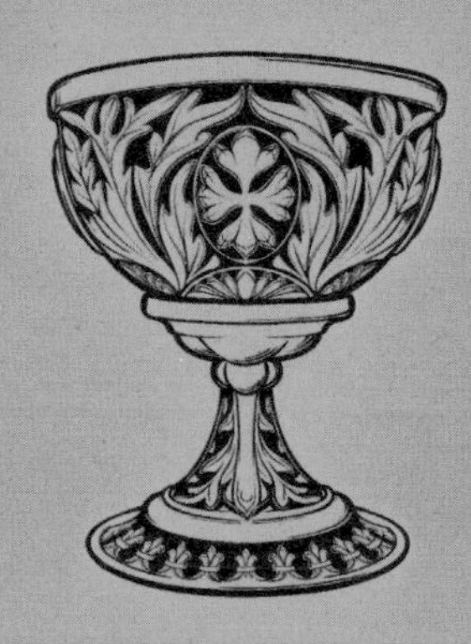

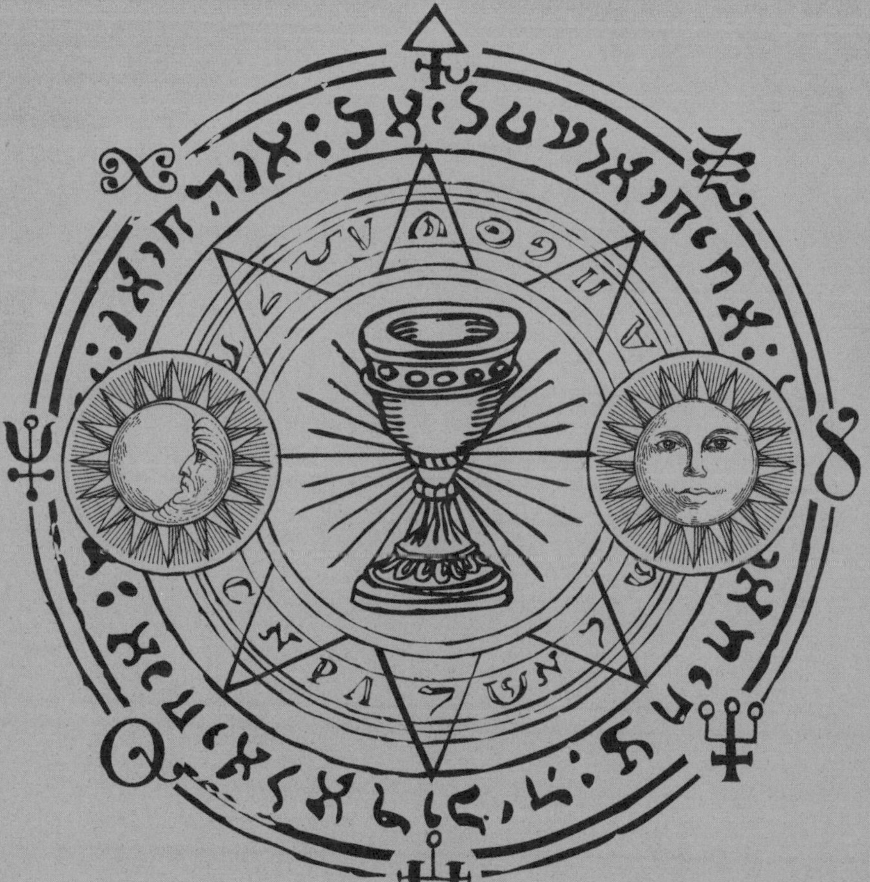

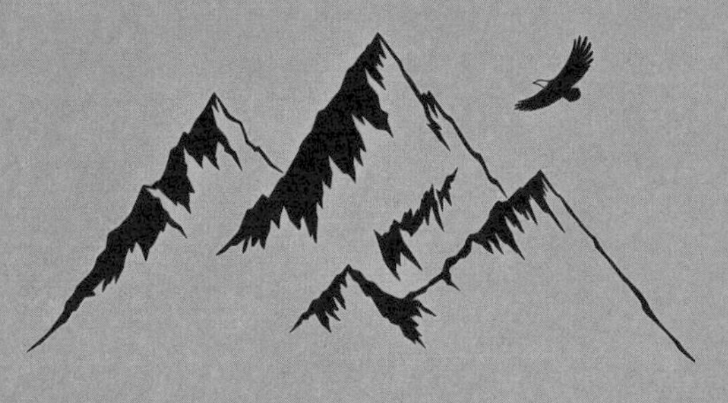

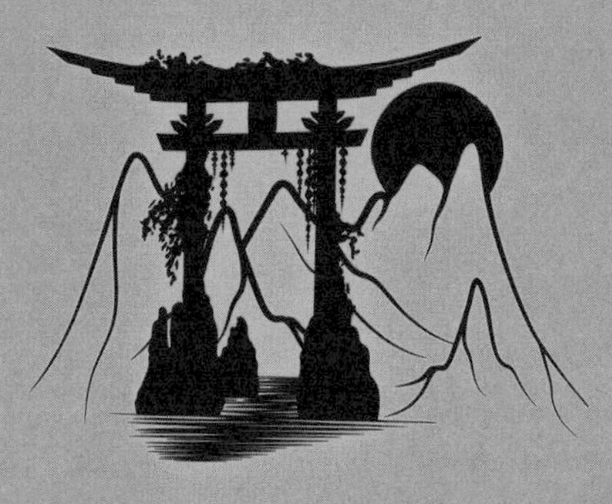

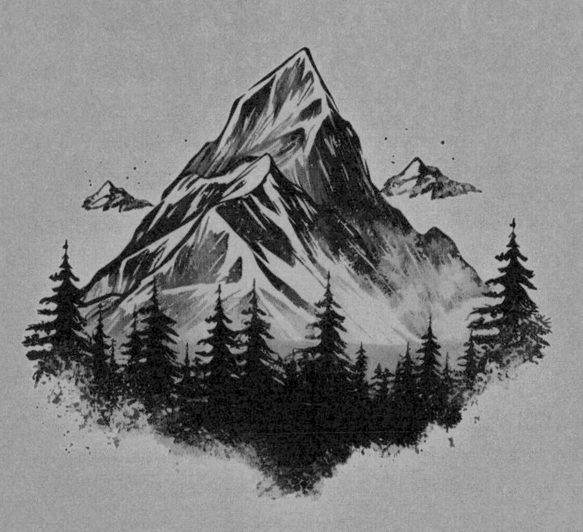

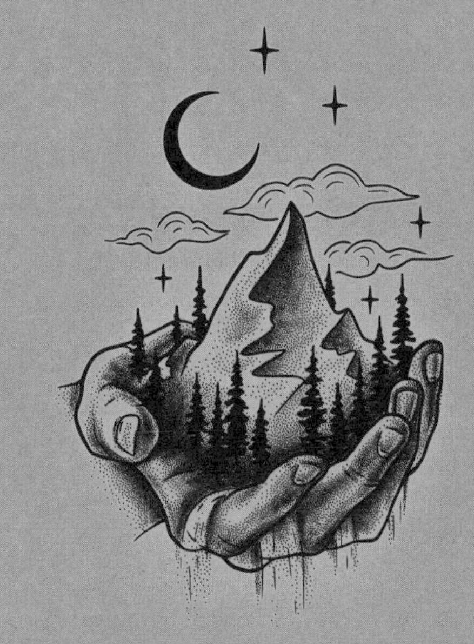

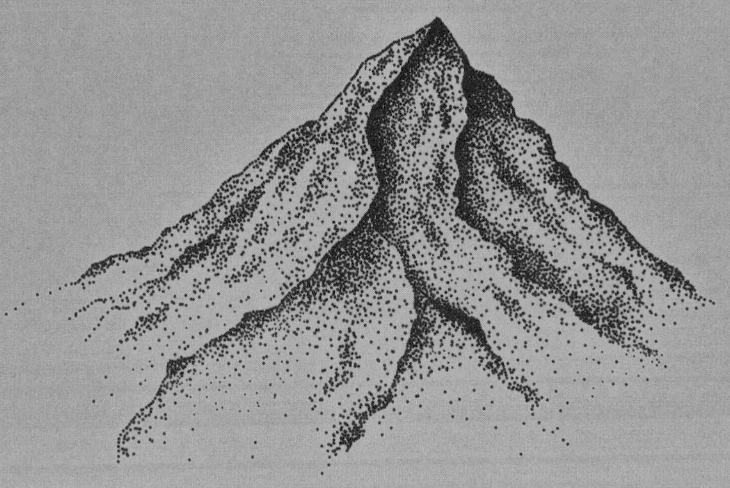

Mountain

Travel, adventure | Resilience | Potential | Power

Sacred Origins
Universal – mountains
appear in most
mythologies

Used Since
Dawn of time

Tattoo Styles
Fine-line
Black-and-grey realism
Blackwork

Opposite: A pagoda within a mountain landscape (top right) adds strength and structure and suggests resilience. A soaring bird above the mountains (top left) signifies the ability to fly free and attain fulfilment. A mountain offered up by a hand (middle right) seems to say, 'this is where you need to be, this is your challenge.'

The mountain is a popular tattoo choice signifying the wearer's ability to overcome obstacles and reach the height of their potential.

The peak of potential

While the image of a mountain is synonymous with travel and new adventures, most people choose it as a focal point to showcase their determination to reach their goals and indicate resilience during tough times.

Myths and mountains

Sacred mountains feature in mythology from around the world, one of the most predominant being Mount Olympus. Although it is a real mountain located between central and northern Greece, according to myth this snowy-peaked ethereal realm was the home of the gods. Littered with ornately adorned palaces, it was the seat of the pantheon's power and a place from which the deities could watch the affairs of humans. In Chinese mythology, Mount Penglai was the spiritual home of eight immortals, a heavenly paradise swathed in white with golden palaces and trees laden with jewel-like fruit. Mount Meru in Tanzania is the sacred five-peaked golden mountain at the heart of all existence, a feature of Hindu mythology and the centre of the Universe.

How to wear it

Mountains can be reduced to a very simple rendering; equally they can be highly illustrated and the focal point of a piece, especially if the mountain depicted is a real location with a strong connection to the wearer. In large-scale work – full sleeves or full front/back pieces – mountain ranges can be used to communicate a sense of depth, drawing the eye to the focal element of the tattoo.

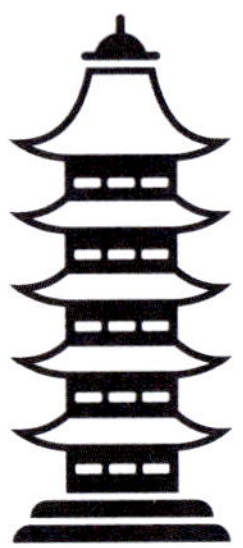

Pagoda

Spirituality | Inner peace | Enlightenment | Protection | Guidance

Sacred Origins
Japanese, Indian,
Chinese

Used Since
17th century

Tattoo Styles
Japanese
Black-and-grey realism
Blackwork

Opposite: The simplicity of traditional pagoda designs (top) accentuates the meaning of practical guidance and inner strength. The detailed realism of this pagoda design (bottom) enhances the spiritual power of the symbol – it would work well on a large scale.

This temple, which has a multi-level structure, is found throughout Asia and has become a popular tattoo choice for those seeking spiritual succour.

The five elements

The earliest Japanese pagodas were built in the middle of the 6th century to coincide with the spread of Buddhism. These lofty structures were made from wood and stone, and usually had five roof levels to represent the five basic elements of the universe, which are earth, air, fire, water and space or sky.

Home of sacred relics

Originally based upon the stupa, a domed monument which houses sacred relics, the pagoda evolved over time with variations in style depending on its region of origin. Japanese versions are tower-like in structure and have little interior room, while those that hail from China often have an underground chamber known as the 'dragon cave'.

How to wear it

The pagoda can be found in many Japanese-style tattoos. The nature of this style lends itself to large-scale work, in some cases covering the entire body. The pagoda is most often found as an accompanying background element to help set the scene and could hint at an element of protection or guidance for the wearer. In rarer cases, this symbol can be seen as the focal point of a piece, covering the entire back or possibly large-scale on a leg or arm sleeve.

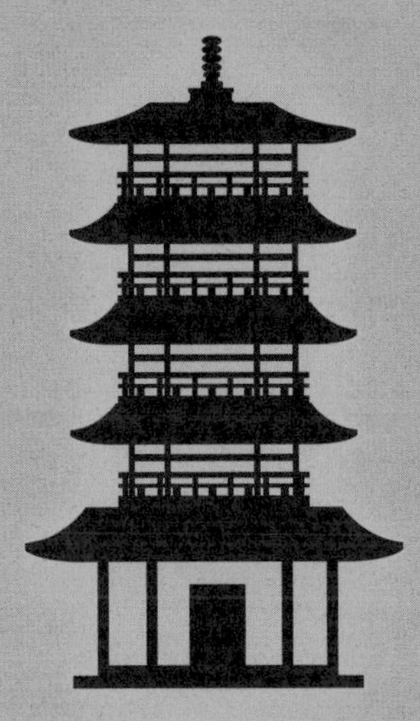 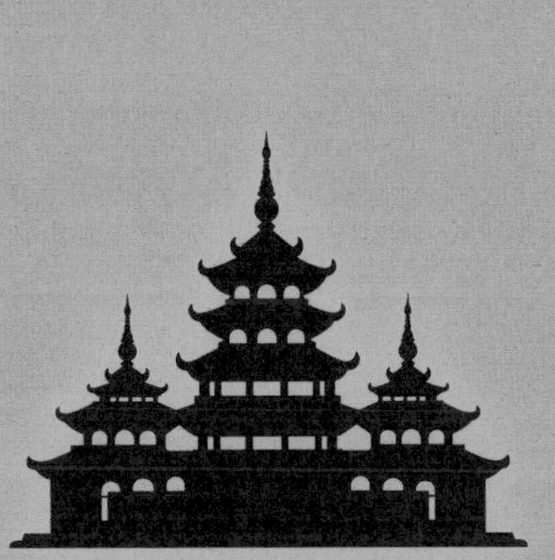 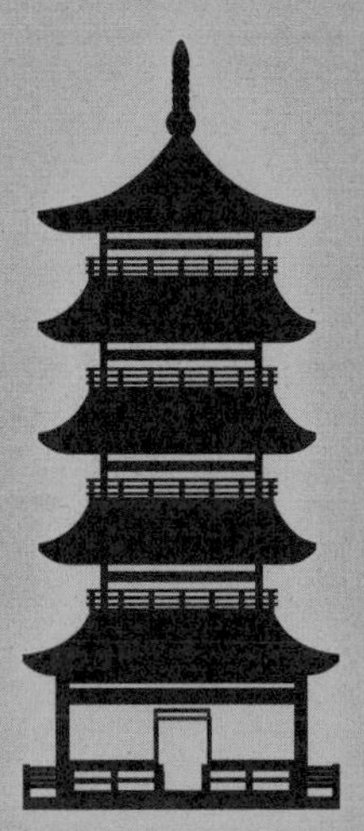

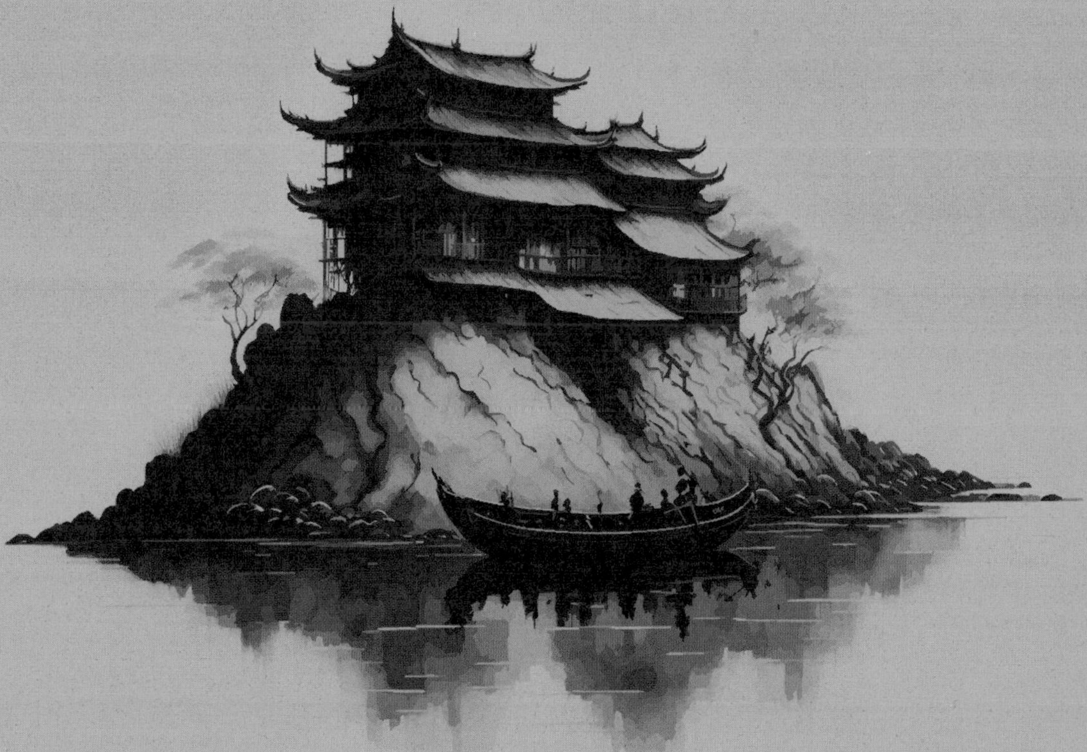

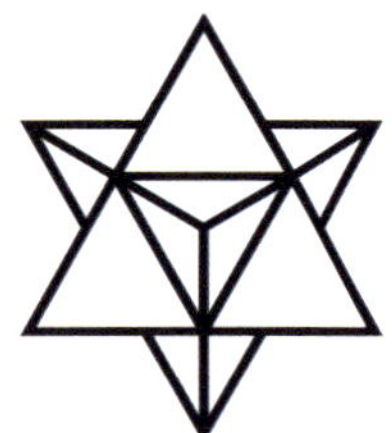

Merkaba Star

Transformation | Ascension | Enlightenment | Protection | Balance

Sacred Origins
Hebrew, Egyptian

Used Since
2nd century

Tattoo Styles
Fine-line
Blackwork
Ornamental

Opposite: The triquetra which sits at the centre of this star (top left) amplifies the protective energy of the symbol and connects it to the power of three. The fine dot work used in this design (bottom), makes each triangle of the star appear three-dimensional, connecting the symbol with the power of transition and enlightenment.

A powerful symbol in sacred geometry, the Merkaba star is widely used as a meditation tool to access cosmic realms and instigate healing.

A chariot of body, mind and spirit

The Merkaba star has many connotations, which is no surprise for a symbol which encompasses all aspects of body, mind and soul. The word 'Merkaba' has two meanings depending on the language used. In ancient Hebrew it means chariot or vehicle, while to the Egyptians it was the embodiment of being human and was broken down into three parts: 'mer', meaning light; 'ka', meaning spirit and 'ba', which translates as body. In essence, Merkaba is the vehicle used to transport the physical consciousness to higher dimensions.

A symbol of unity

The symbol itself is comprised of two intersecting star tetrahedrons which spin in opposite directions. This generates a field of light, which is thought to be protective. The tetrahedron represents the 'light body', which creates the physical body and is also known as the Star of David. According to those who have studied the symbol in detail, the top tetrahedron is synonymous with masculine energy and represents action and logic, while the bottom tetrahedron relates to feminine energy and is linked to intuition and emotion. As the two come together they create balance in all things. There are other interpretations of the intersecting stars: some believe that the top tetrahedron represents spirituality, while the bottom is rooted in the earth. The junction where they cross creates wholeness and the ability to connect with the divine.

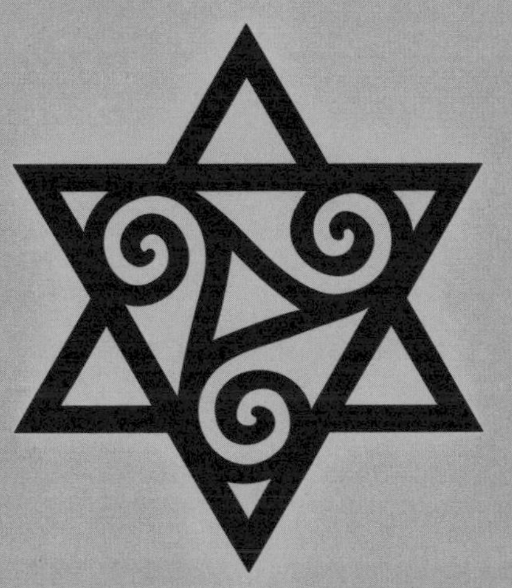

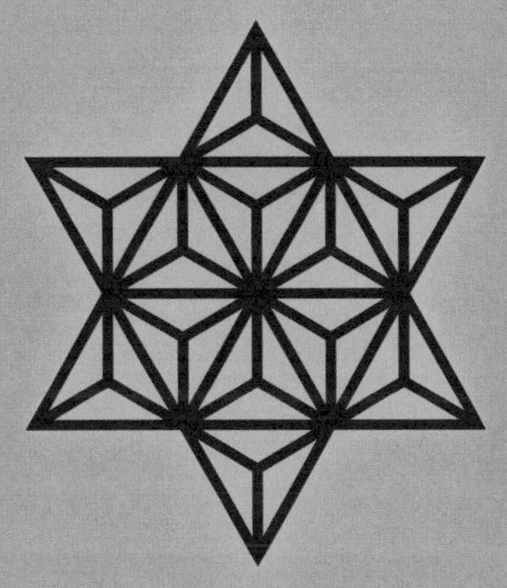

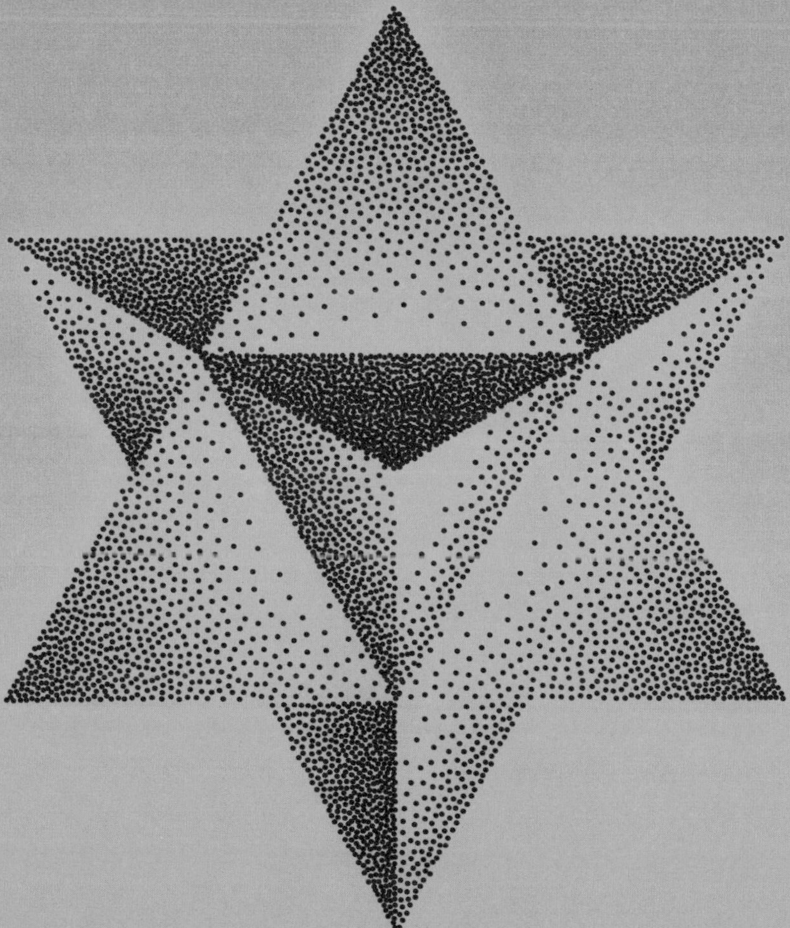

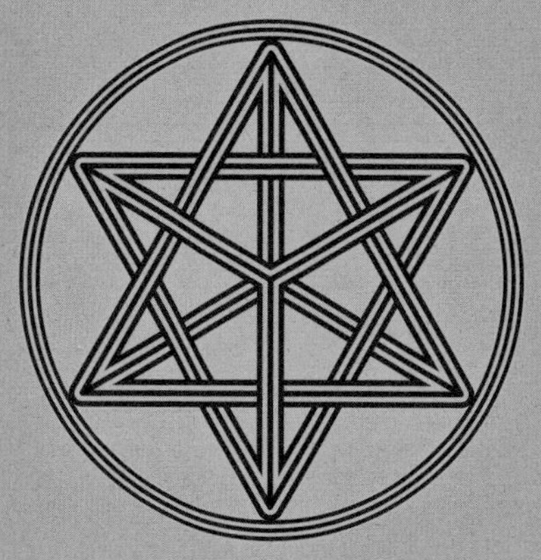

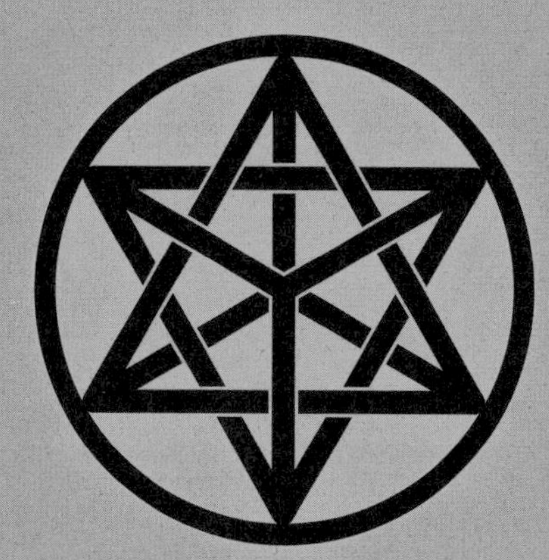

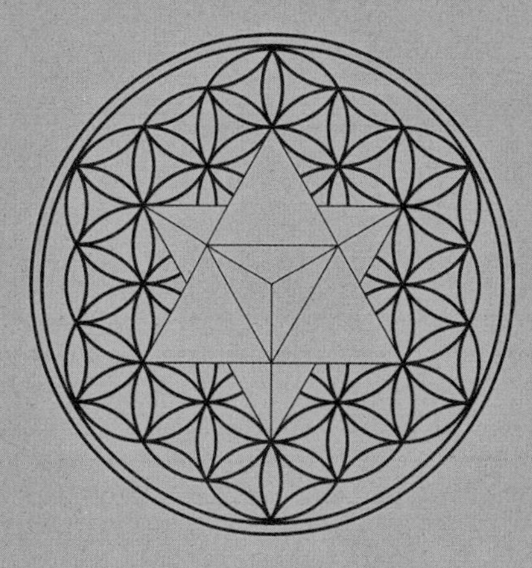

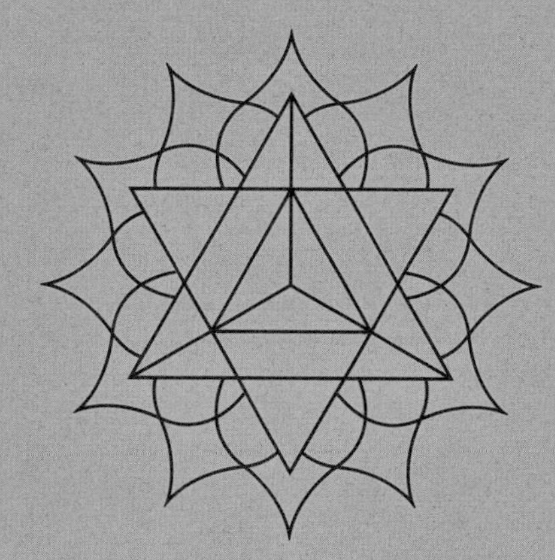

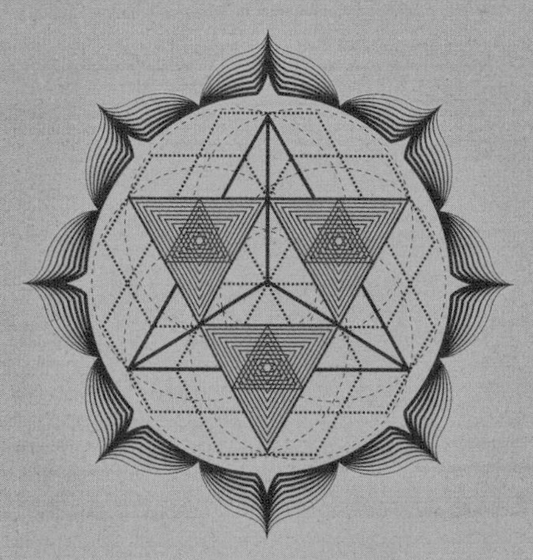

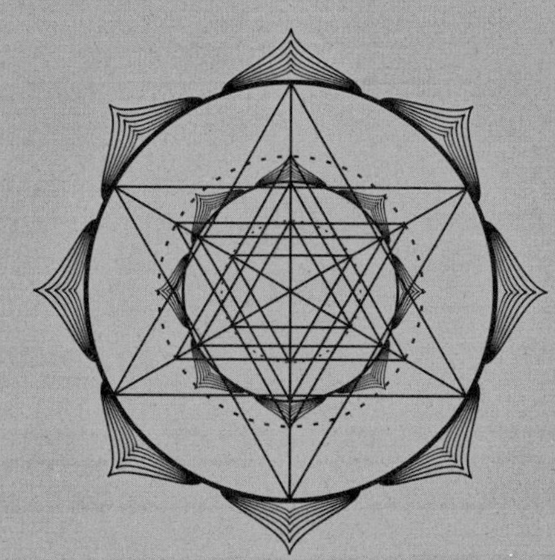

An ancient school of mysticism

The symbol itself is rooted in Merkaba mysticism which was first practised by an ancient Jewish school of thought. Writings on the subject, mainly in Hebrew and Aramaic, have been discovered going back as early as the 2nd century, although it wasn't until centuries later that it was studied more openly and in greater detail. It was the Old Testament prophet Ezekiel who first mentioned Merkaba, citing it as the chariot or throne of God and speaking of his visionary quest, which transported him through the heavens. Since then, many Jewish scholars have attempted to follow in his footsteps using the star symbol as inspiration for their visionary journeys.

How to wear it

The scale chosen for this tattoo should relate to the level of embellishment in the design, and this really rings true for all tattoo designs. The Merkaba star is a moderately complex design but it does work at a small scale if it's kept to simple line work. More elaborate versions work well on the inner or outer forearm as well as the upper outer arm or the shoulder, the outer hip or on the wider section of the calf muscle.

Opposite: The mandala star (middle left) is the ideal tool for those seeking inner wisdom and fulfilment, as it can be used as a meditation tool. The lotus star (middle right) imbues the symbol with peaceful energy.

Right: The star rendered with thick lines resembling the strokes of a paintbrush.

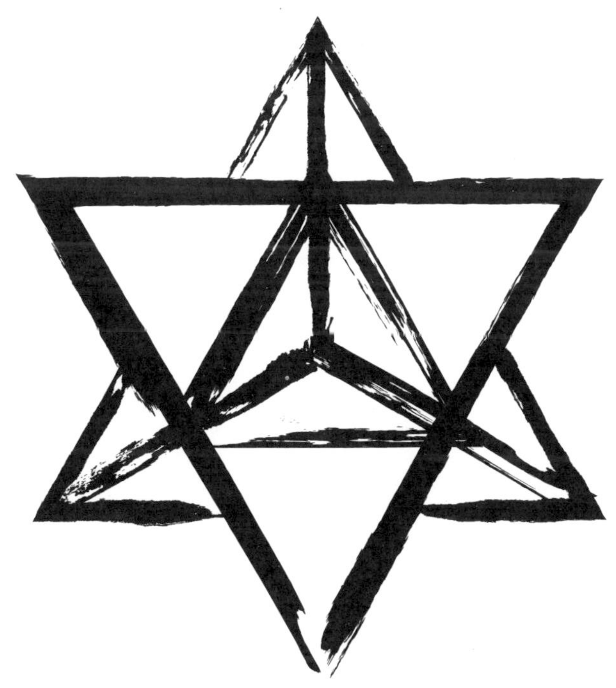

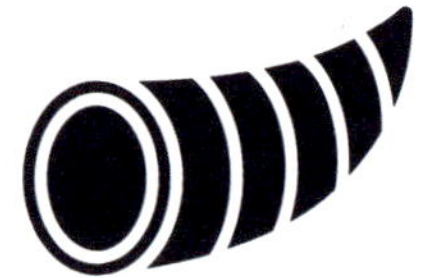

Cornucopia

Abundance | Nourishment | Gratitude | Good fortune | Success

Sacred Origins
Greek, Roman

Used Since
8th century BCE

Tattoo Styles
Fine-line
Western tradtional
Neo-traditional

Opposite: Cornucopias depicted with fruit, vegetables and foliage represent the abundance of nature and promote good fortune and fertility.

Synonymous with abundance and usually depicted as a woven horn-shaped basket overflowing with ripe fruits, grains and vegetables, this symbol has its origins in Greek myth.

The goat and the baby Zeus

According to legend, when the god Zeus was a tiny baby, he was spirited away to a cave on the island of Crete to keep him safe from his paranoid father Cronus. During this time the infant was cared for by Almathea; part she-goat, part nymph, she was a magical being who suckled the babe and protected him. One day, while feeding Zeus, Almathea's horn severed and the broken remnant began to pour forth with nourishment. From that moment on the horn was a symbol of abundance, nurturing energy and prosperity.

A favourite of the gods

Aligned with a variety of deities in the Greek and Roman pantheon, the horn was also associated with Demeter, goddess of the harvest, and Dionysus, the god of revelry and excess. The Roman goddess of chance, Fortuna, was also linked to this symbol, adding a further layer of meaning to the motif and associating it with good fortune and success.

How to wear it

A cornucopia design is deeply meaningful as it highlights a sense of gratitude for life's blessings. The vast array of ingredients within the horn, including fruits, vegetables, seeds and gold coins allows for the use of lots of bright colours; however, it can also work well in a fine-line style using just black and grey. While this design is often fairly elaborate, it is well suited to being tattooed at a medium scale on the arm, leg or torso.

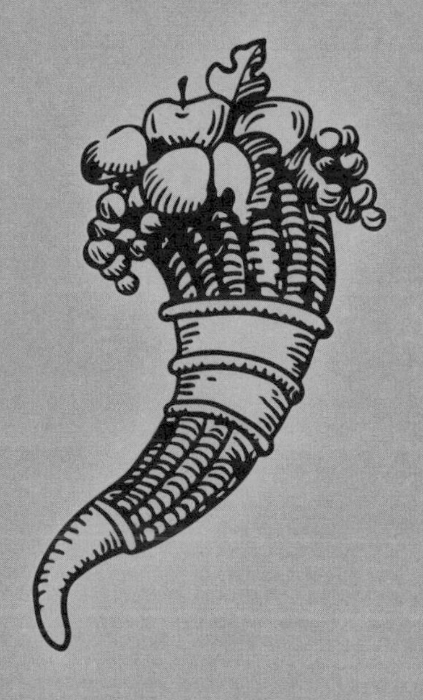

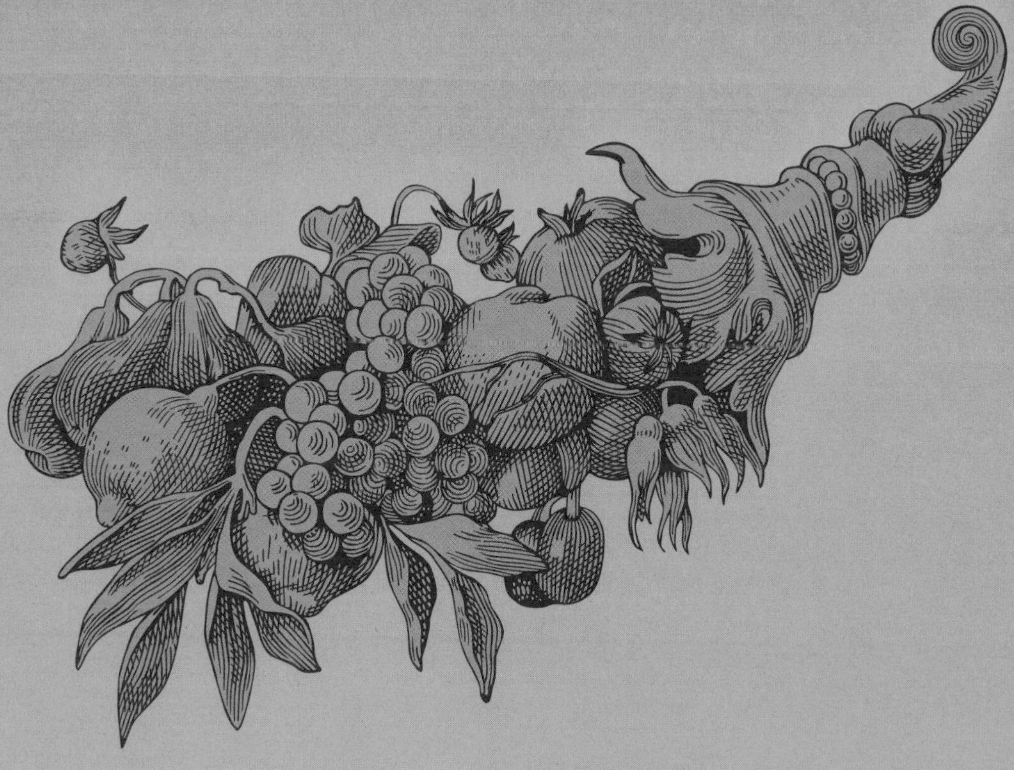

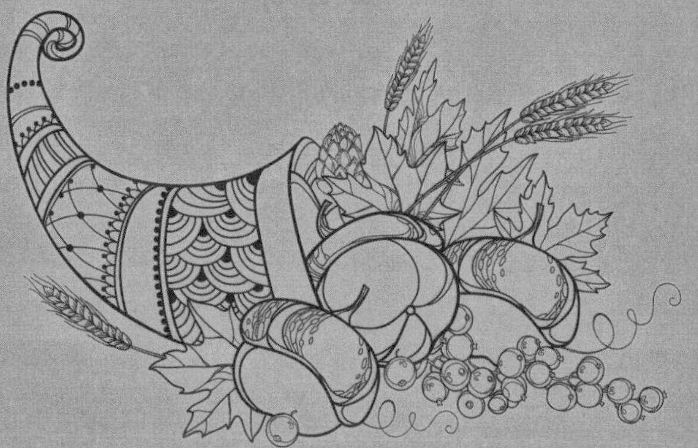

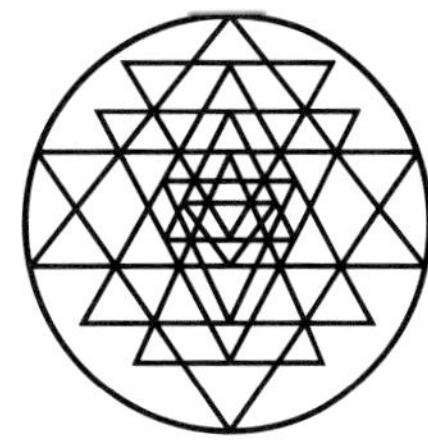

Sri Yantra

Wellbeing | Abundance | Positive energy | Attainment | Wisdom

Sacred Origins
Vedic, Buddhist, Hindu

Used Since
8th century

Tattoo Styles
Fine-line
Blackwork
Ornamental

Opposite: Sri Yantra (top) represents the union of masculine and feminine energies. This Sri Yantra symbol (bottom) has a flower-like appearance, linking it to the beauty of life.

This is a complex geometric symbol comprised of nine interlaced triangles which embody both male and female energy and radiate from a central point.

Queen of yantras

Also known as the Shri Yantra and the Shri Chakra, this sacred symbol has many layers of meaning and features in the Shri Vidya School of Hinduism, but its spiritual significance is such that it is prominent in a number of faiths and belief systems, including Hinduism, Jainism and Buddhism. To add even further weight to its auspicious reputation, it is known as the 'queen of yantras'. This is because all other yantras are said to have evolved from this primordial version.

To fully understand its potency, we must first look to the meaning of its moniker. 'Sri' is associated with wealth and wellbeing, while 'yan' comes from the Sanskrit 'yam', meaning instrument. 'Tra' comes from 'trana', meaning liberation from bondage. Together the Sri Yantra becomes a tool for spiritual liberation and good fortune.

The divine feminine

Those who have studied the symbol in detail believe it expresses the sum totality of the Universe, and the flow of positive energy that comes from this. It is a representation of all the gods and goddesses within the Hindu religion. Others suggest it is actually the divine feminine principle that sits at the heart of the symbol, in the form of the beautiful goddess Tripura Sundari. A deeply revered deity, she is synonymous with power and wisdom, and thought to be the goddess of creation.

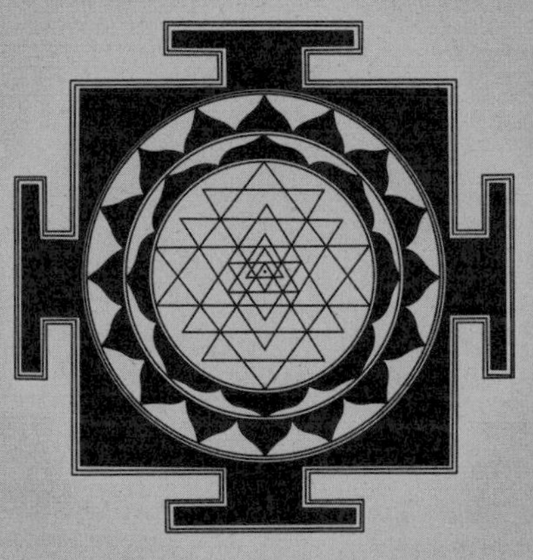 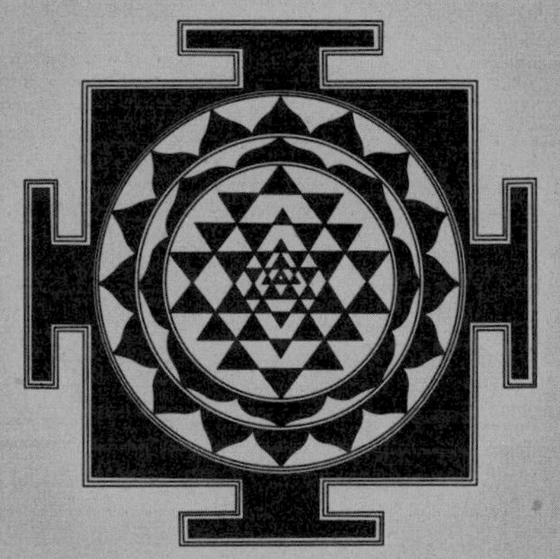

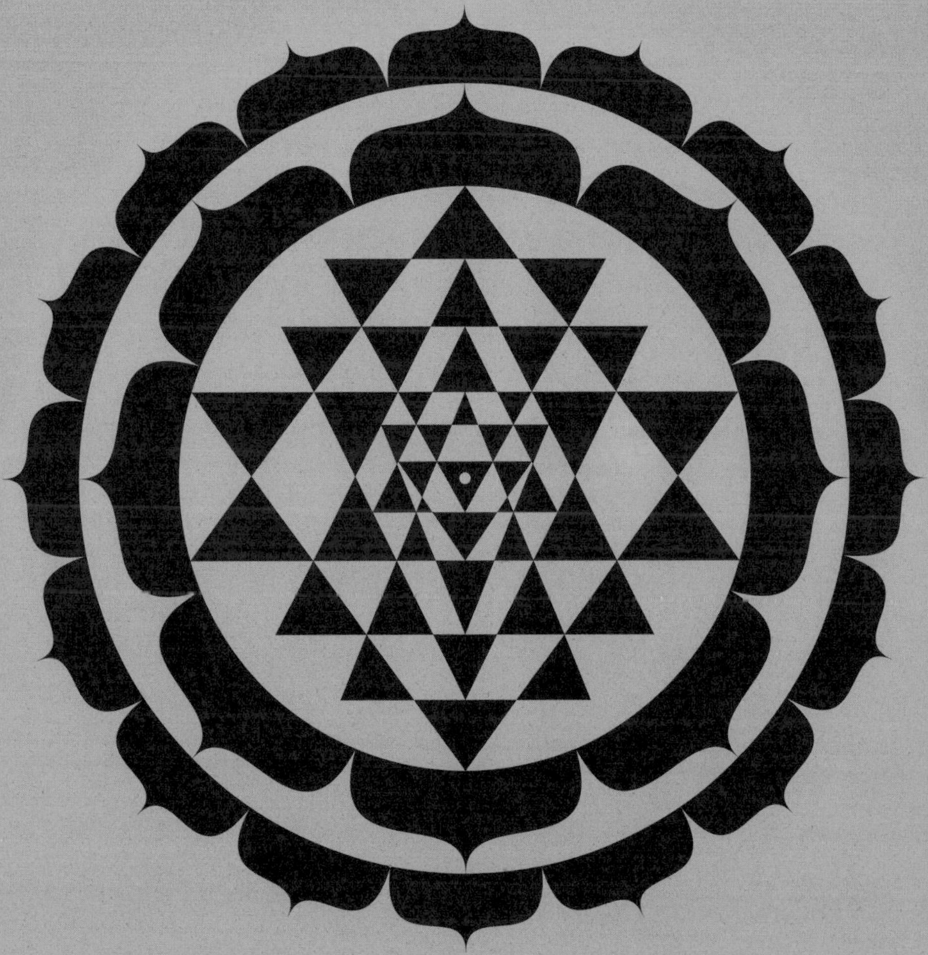

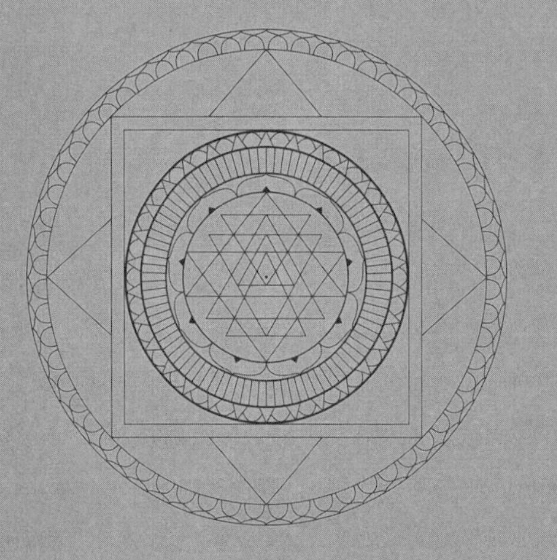

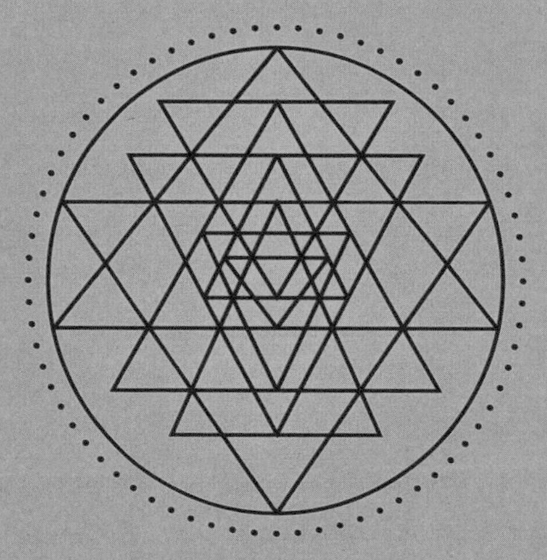

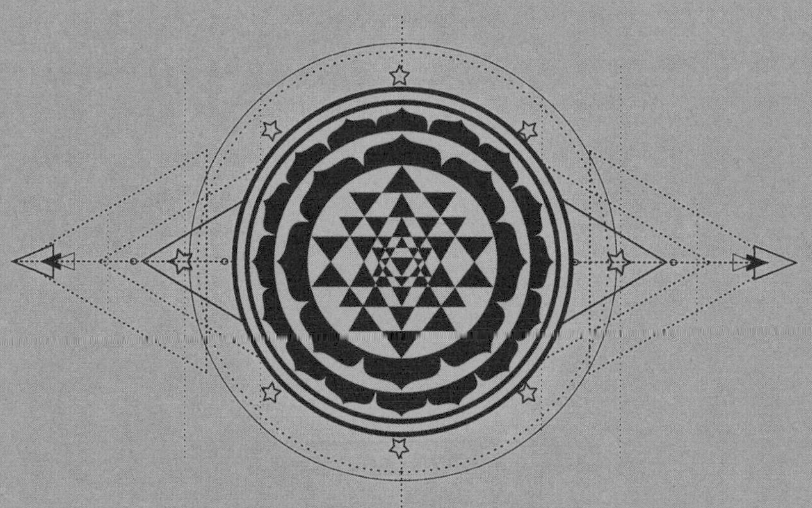

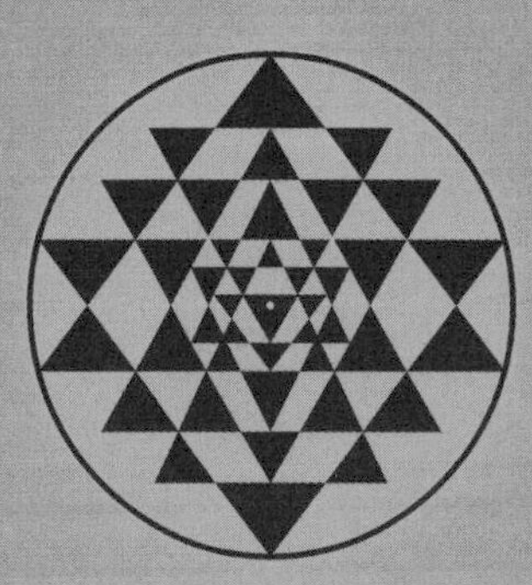

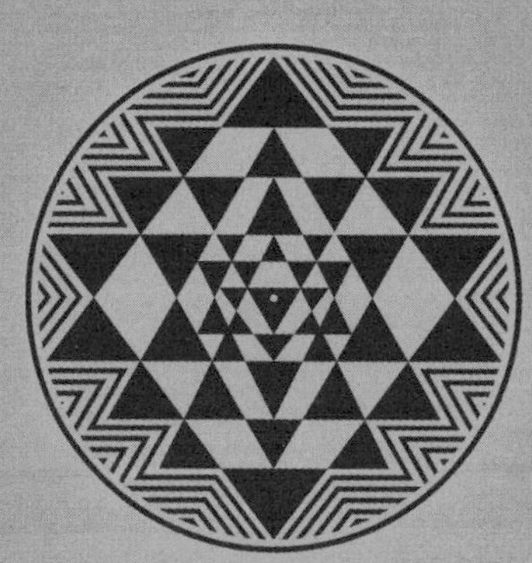

A gift from the gods

According to myth, the symbol was first created by Lord Shiva, a supreme being
in the Hindu faith. He gave 64 chakras and their mantras to the world and the Sri
Yantra was the sum of this knowledge. Based upon sacred geometry, the symbol has
been in use for thousands of years, but its origins are somewhat sketchy. The earliest
depiction was thought to have come from the Spigari Majha, a religious institution
established in the 8th century by the renowned philosopher Sankara. Some scholars
believe the yantra's roots lie in Vedic Sanskrit texts which contain ancient religious
concepts. Either way, it is said to hold the key to a happy, fulfilled and peaceful
existence and plays an important role in many spiritual practices today, including
ceremonies and rituals within the Hindu religion.

How to wear it

Sri Yantra is a highly spiritual symbol and getting one tattooed can involve
a religious ceremony. Due to the complexity of line art involved, it's best not
to embellish the Sri Yantra itself too heavily, as it risks a weaker depiction of
the symbol. Tattooists often choose to embellish the area
around or behind the symbol, or include it as part
of a larger pattern-based design for a sleeve,
back or chest piece. A mandala-inspired
style can be achieved by using the same
embellishment approach and gives a
striking result.

Opposite: The use of lines
and triangles in these
designs creates a link
with sacred geometry,
while the circular frames
are associated with the
ongoing nature of life and
the universe.

Right: The compass-style
setting of this Sri Yantra
suggests direction and
guidance when seeking
inner wisdom.

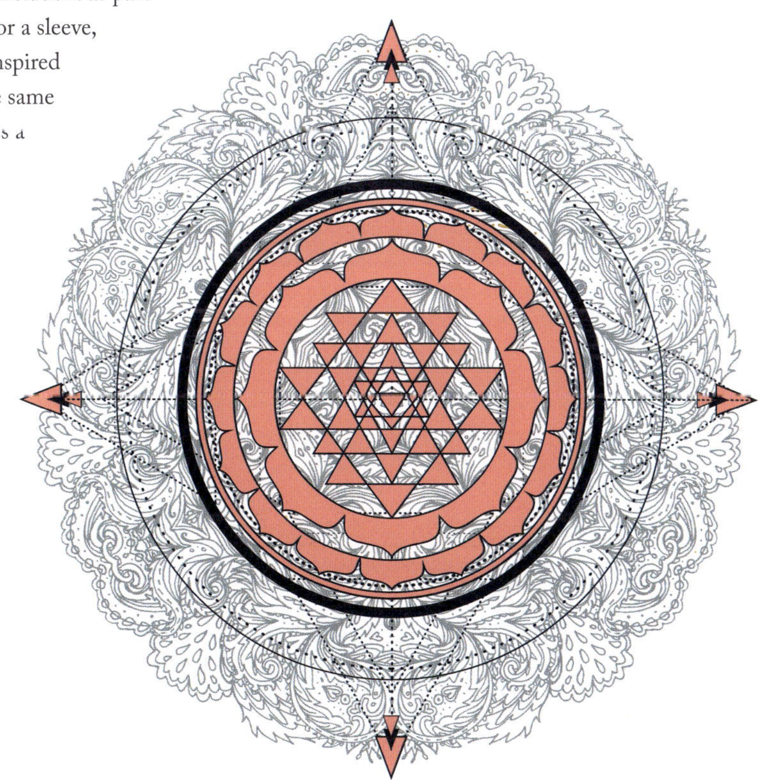

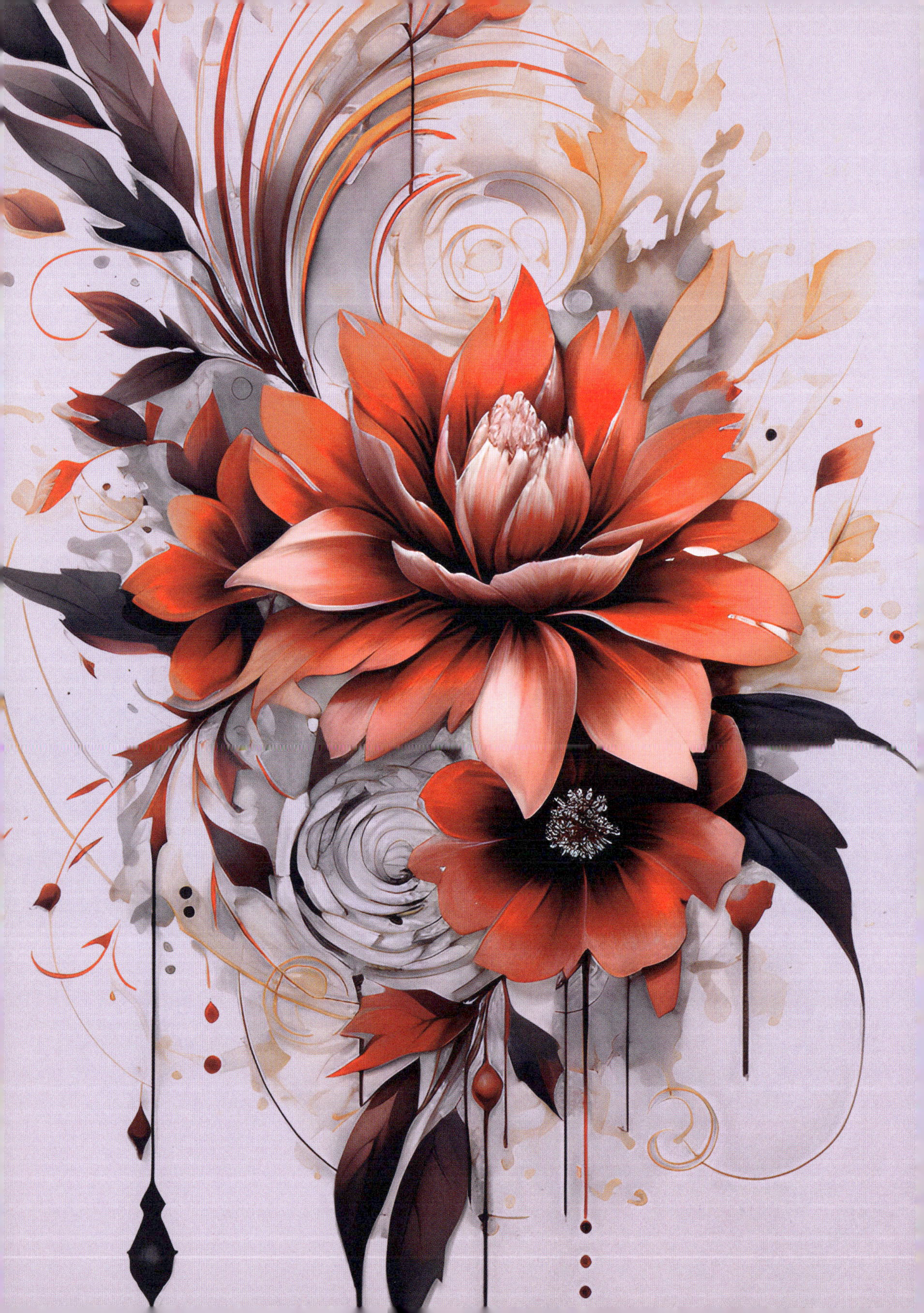

4

Florals and Patterns

Flowers have always been seen as a gift from the gods because of their unique beauty. Their ability to survive and thrive in the strangest of places, against the odds, imbues them with appeal and power. Each bloom has a distinctive pattern, shape and colour, and the way they grow – whether trailing snugly against the belly of the earth, scaling walls and trees, or reaching dizzying heights for a glimpse of afternoon sun – adds to their otherworldly reputation.

Early humans studied the floral form and the many associated patterns that they could see in nature, like the swirling loops of a falling snowflake or the indentations upon a leaf. They believed they were synonymous with new life and growth, and so they took the shapes that they saw and created new narratives, giving them sacred significance. It was the ancient Greeks who really took flowers to heart, creating colourful myths and linking specific plants to deities. They were enamoured and examined the patterns intensely, believing the many-faceted layers of petals to be like the layers between spiritual realms.

From the resilient and always beautiful lotus, a divine flower that rises above the mud and mire to bloom, to the elegant lily, born from the milk of one goddess and cursed by another, the symbols within these pages are based upon floral designs and shapes that have captured the imagination for thousands of years.

Lotus

Enlightenment | Purity | Resilience | Peace | Prosperity

Sacred Origins
Egyptian, Hindu,
Buddhist

Used Since
Dawn of time

Tattoo Styles
Japanese
Fine-line
Ornamental

Opposite: No matter what size the lotus symbol is, it can be embellished with additional details to hint at its link to purity, prosperity and peace. Combining the lotus with mandala-style patterns (bottom) links the symbol to spiritual rebirth and the cycles of life.

While the symmetrical beauty of the lotus cannot be denied, it is its desire to live that elevates its spiritual status.

Emerging from the mud

The indomitable power of this symbol can be found in the way the flower blooms on a daily basis. Submerged in murky water, the lotus dips below the surface overnight and is consumed by the grimy depths only to re-emerge in the morning in all its glory. The waxy layer on each of the petals protects the flower from getting mud-soaked, ensuring it retains its vivid hue. No wonder ancient civilizations associated this bloom with resurrection and rebirth. The Egyptians in particular were mesmerized with its ability to re-invent itself each day and used it in a number of transformation spells which appeared in the *Book of the Dead*. They believed that the flower held the power of the Universe within.

Blooming in the most unlikely places, the lotus can go for years without water, only to germinate centuries later. This remarkable fact explains why it is associated with resilience and strength.

A symbol of creation

Other Eastern cultures revere the bloom and use it as a prominent symbol of faith. To Hindus, the lotus represents enlightenment and prosperity. It is the seat of the gods, associated with the deities Lakshmi and Vishnu. According to one creation story, at the dawn of time, when there was only a vast sea of nothingness, Lord Vishnu awoke to find a lotus flower growing from his naval. Sitting within the giant petals was the first god Brahma, the creator of the universe. With his powers he split the flower into three parts, the first being the heavens, the second the earth and the third the sky.

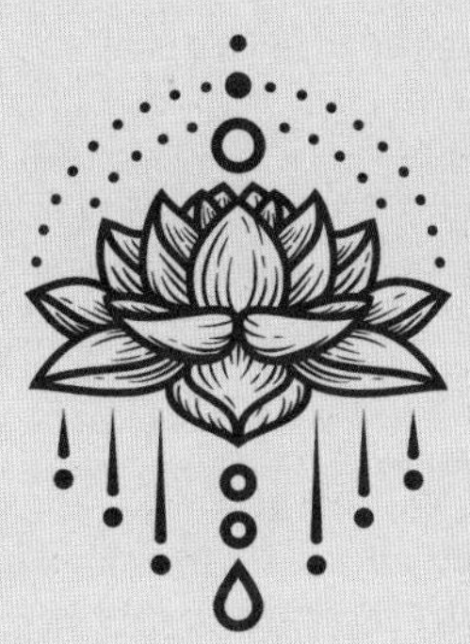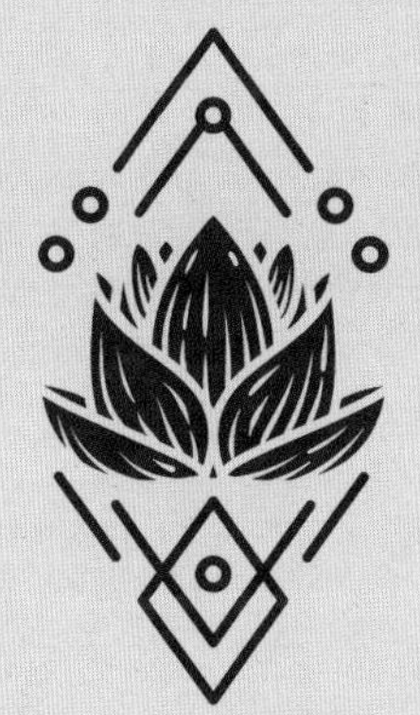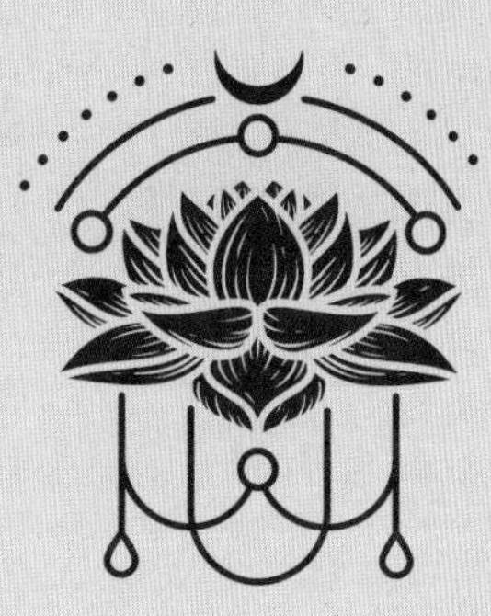

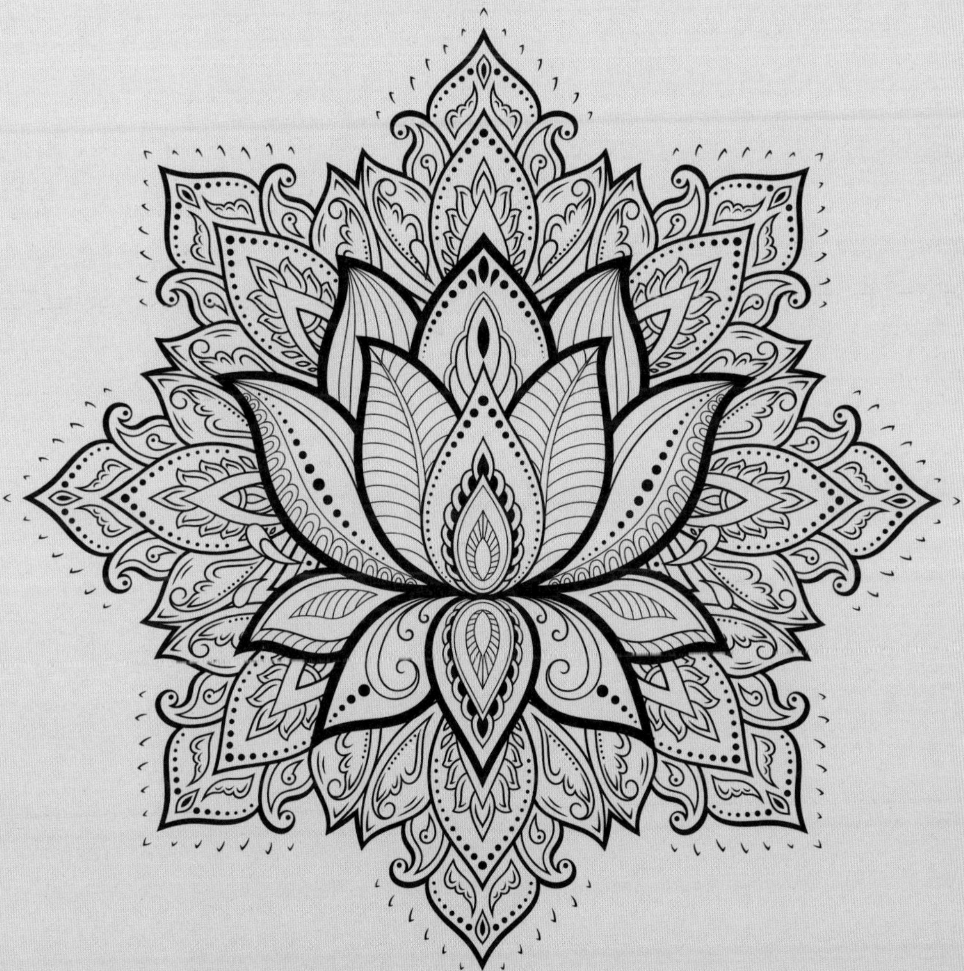

The Buddha's footsteps

Buddhists also have a sacred relationship with the
lotus. They believe it is synonymous with purity and
enlightenment, thanks to its ability to thrive in the
mire. It was thought that Buddha first appeared aloft
a giant lotus flower, and his footsteps upon the earth
left behind a stream of its petals. It is one of the eight
auspicious symbols of Buddhism and an important
part of its teachings.

How to wear it

The lotus can be tattooed in a variety of colours, each
with a different association. White is synonymous
with purity and spiritual enlightenment, blue is
associated with wisdom, purple exudes mystical energy
and pink is linked to love and beauty. Although this
flower is often incorporated into mandala designs, it is
most prolific in Japanese-style tattooing. The lotus is
often paired with Buddhist deities, as well as koi fish
on sleeves or back tattoos.

Opposite: **The lotus is often
found as a structural element
within ornamental tattoo
designs (bottom row),
where qualities like purity
and enlightenment can
be emphasized.**

Right: **A lotus combined
with a diamond signifies
resilience. The pink petals
on the flower hint at love
and beauty.**

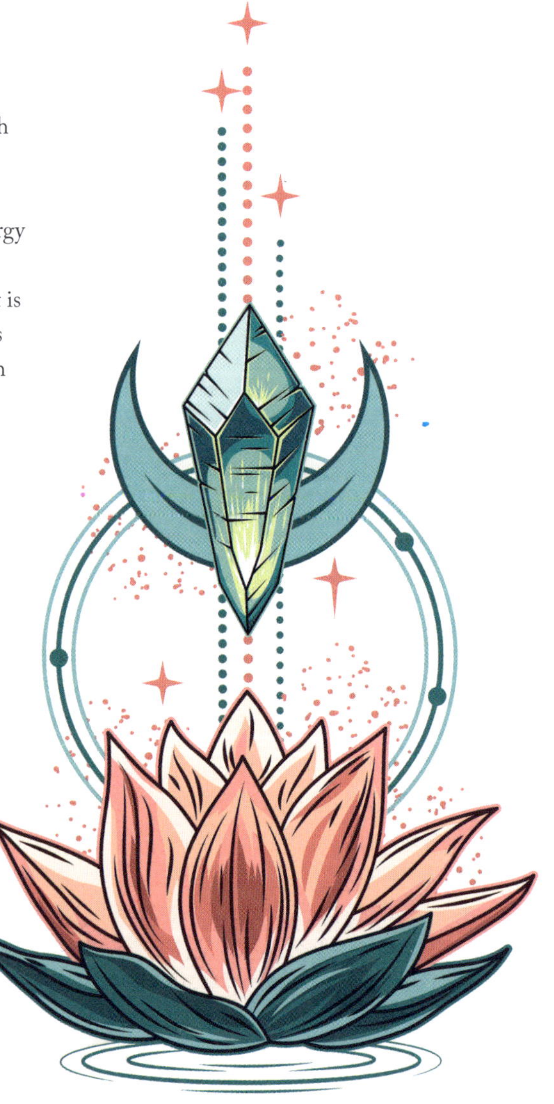

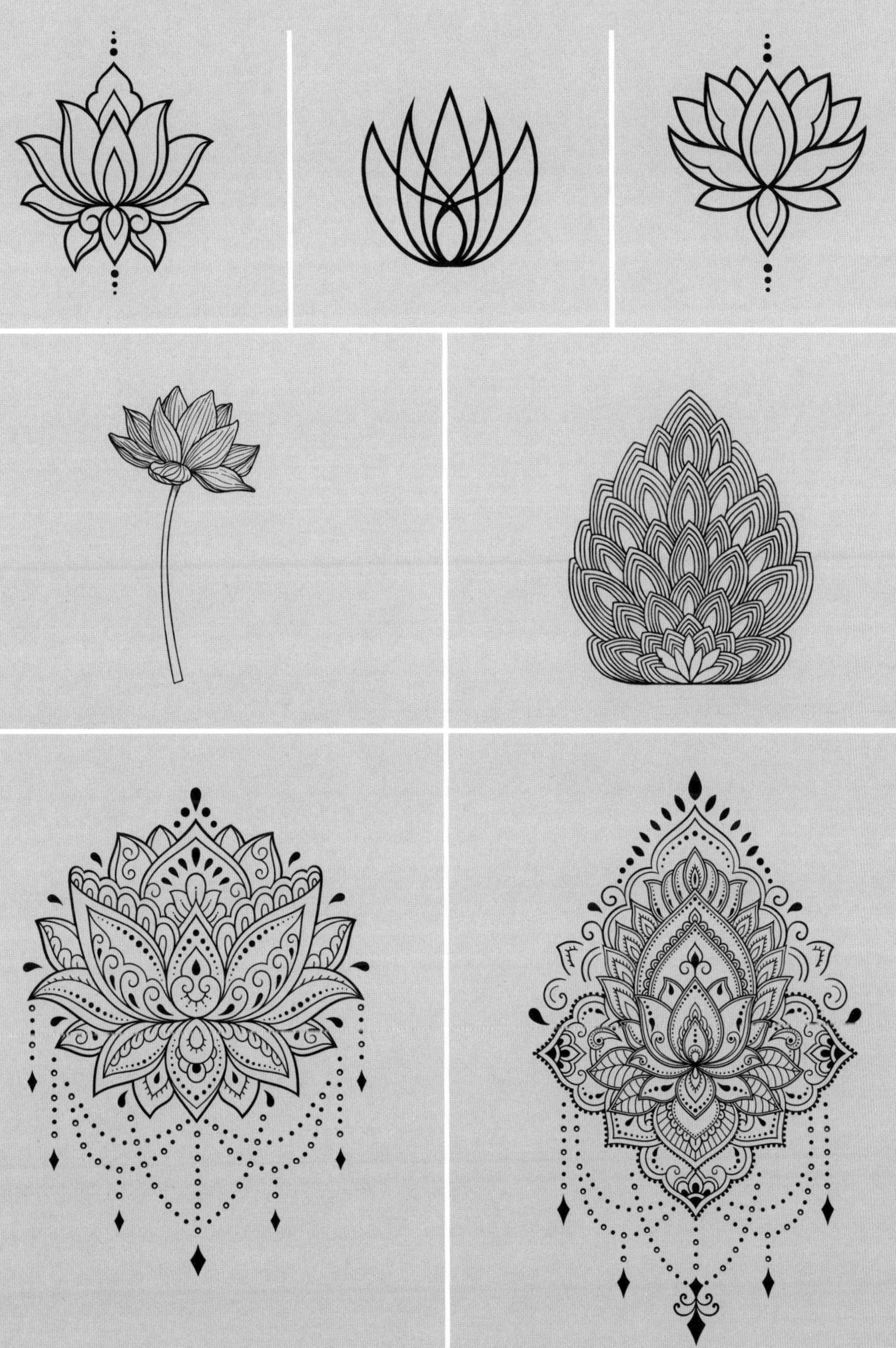

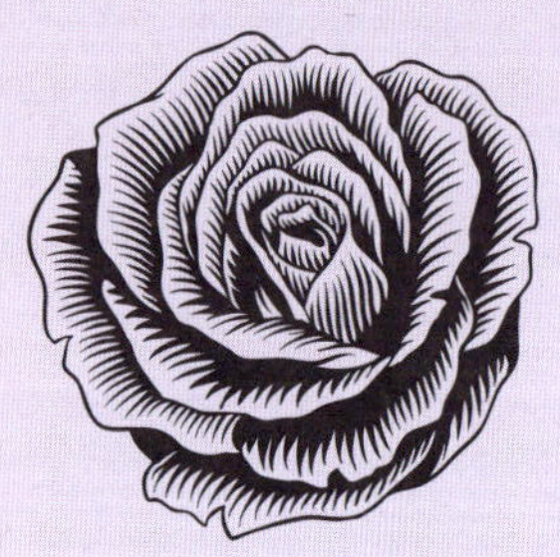
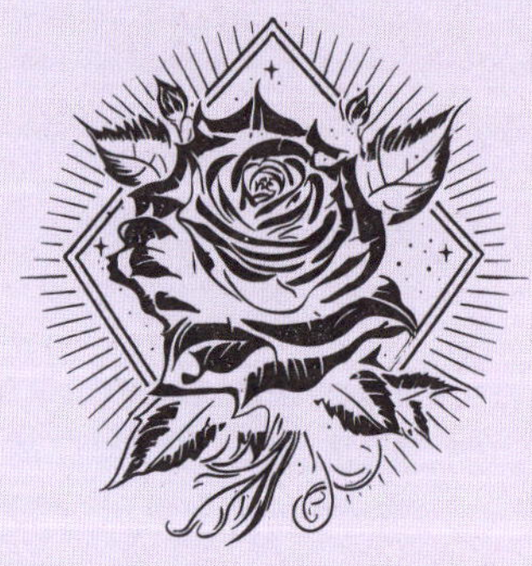
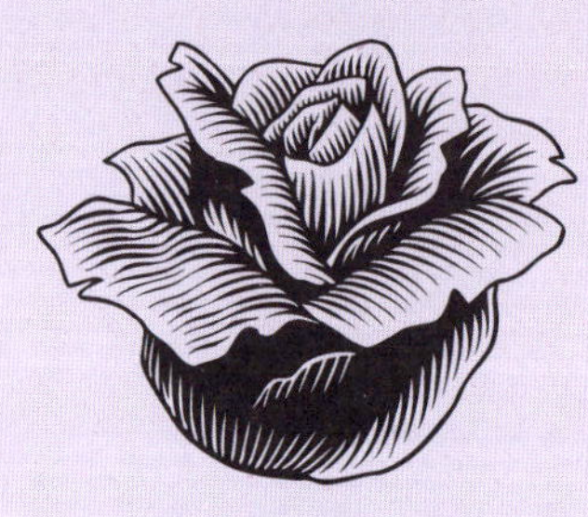
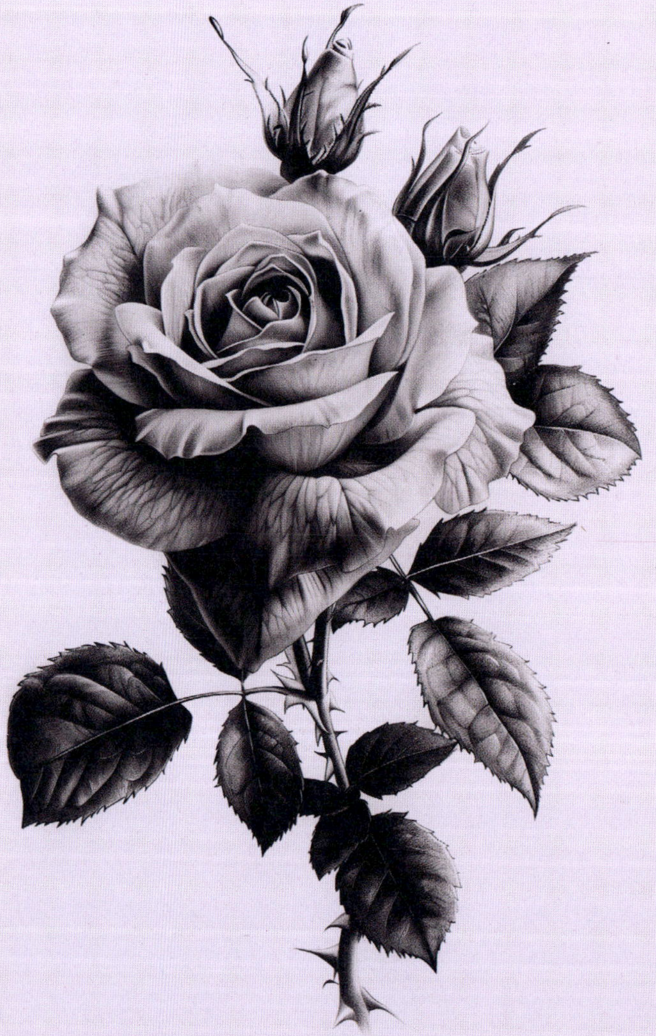
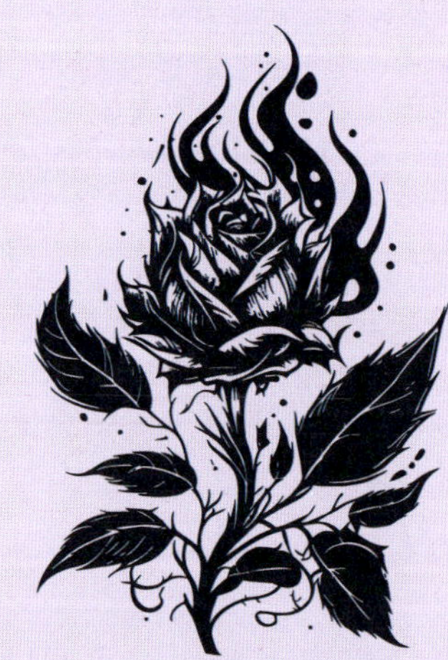

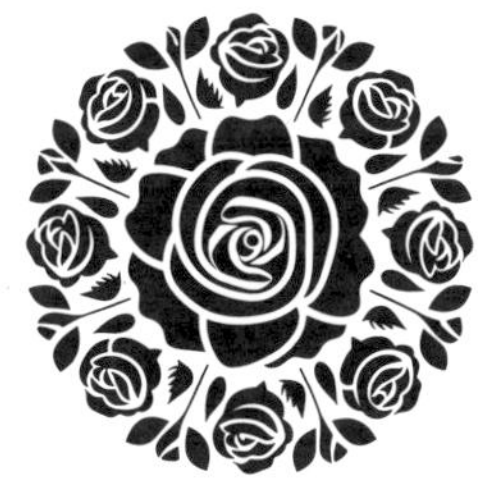

Rose

Love | Passion | Divinity | Beauty | Romance | Prosperity

Sacred Origins
Christian, Persian,
Greek, Roman,
Egyptian

Used Since
3rd millennium BCE

Tattoo Styles
Western traditional
Black-and-grey realism
Blackwork

Opposite: Roses have long been associated with romance and love; a rose with thorns (bottom left) can be used to symbolize the pain of lost love. The addition of flames to a rose (right middle) strengthens the idea of passion, which is already associated with this symbol.

The epitome of love and romance, the rose is a symbol of beauty with a long history.

Years of blooming

Palaeontologists have discovered rose petal fossils which are around 35 million years old. Cultivated for the last 5,000 years, this bloom features in artwork from around the world. Indeed, many ancient civilizations revered the power of this flower, believing it to be sacred. To the Greeks, it was associated with their goddess of love and beauty, Aphrodite, who stepped forth from a scallop shell the colour of rose petals. The ancient Egyptians attributed the rose to their goddess of love and magic, Isis. An escort of the souls of the dead, she would ensure that those recently passed reached the afterlife. The rose became her symbol because of the way it died and then bloomed again, making it the perfect emblem for the never-ending cycles of life.

A nightingale's love

In the Middle East it was a popular flower not only because of the way it looked but also for its sweet, distinctive scent. One Persian folk tale tells how the red rose gained its colour when a nightingale fell in love with a white bud. After many days of wooing the flower with its pretty song, the bird finally embraced it in full bloom. As it did, a sharp thorn pierced its tiny heart and the blood that flowed turned the petals ruby red.

The flower of the soul

In Sufism the rose is likened to the human soul. One famous philosopher claimed that the rose, which goes from tiny bud to a beautiful fully fledged flower, is like the soul opening up to the power of God. In the Christian faith the red rose is believed to be stained by the blood of Christ, and white roses are often associated with the Virgin Mary, while to Muslims this flower is sacred, believed to have sprouted from drops of sweat which fell from the Prophet Muhammad's brow. Many mosques and temple gardens are filled with roses, in honour of this. More recently, it has become a national symbol and the flower of England, while the US adopted the rose as its national emblem in 1986.

How to wear it

The rose is a very popular tattoo choice, often used to represent everlasting love. The addition of a banner and name can be used to either show devotion to a loved one or to pay homage to those who have passed. The colour of a rose can hold special significance, with red symbolizing passion, pink associated with romance, white linked to purity or peace and yellow synonymous with friendship and joy. A rose can be tattooed in many styles, but prominent styles are the Western traditional style or the highly rendered black-and-grey versions.

Opposite: The rose can be tattooed in so many ways, from the very simplistic (bottom right) to the ultra detailed (middle right). Pierced by a dagger, a rose tattoo (top middle) signifies the sacrifice required for love, or perhaps the pain of love lost.

Right: This realistic, thorny rose twined around a Christian cross describes the love and sacrifice of religious faith.

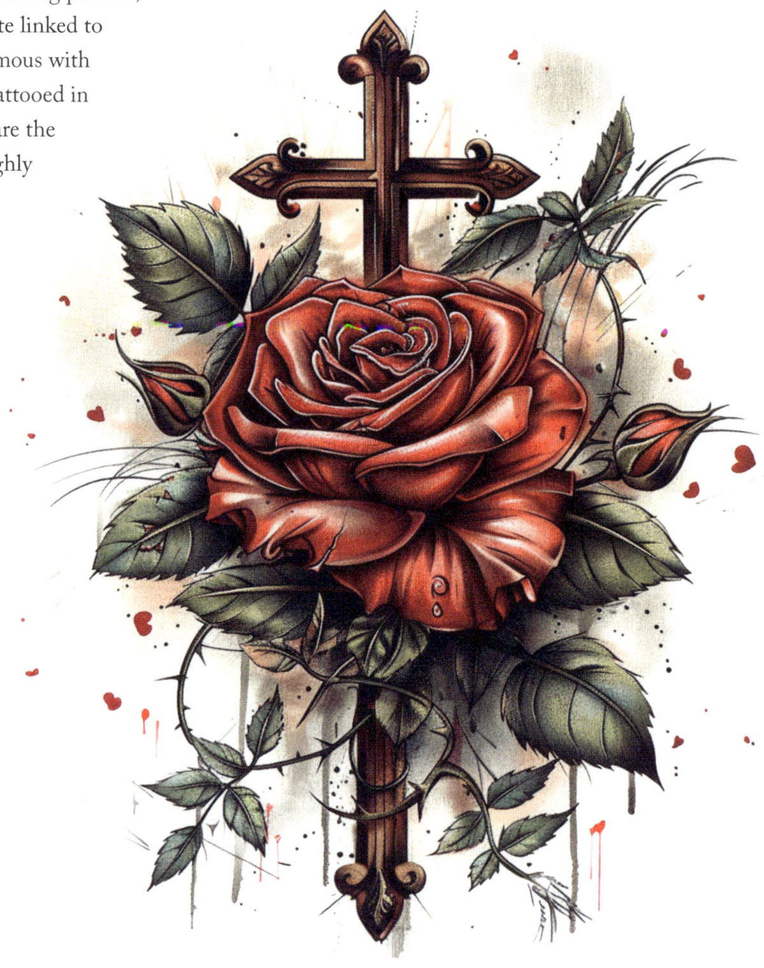

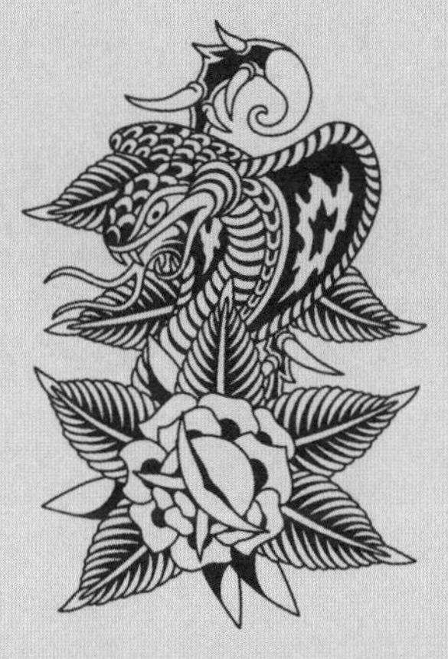

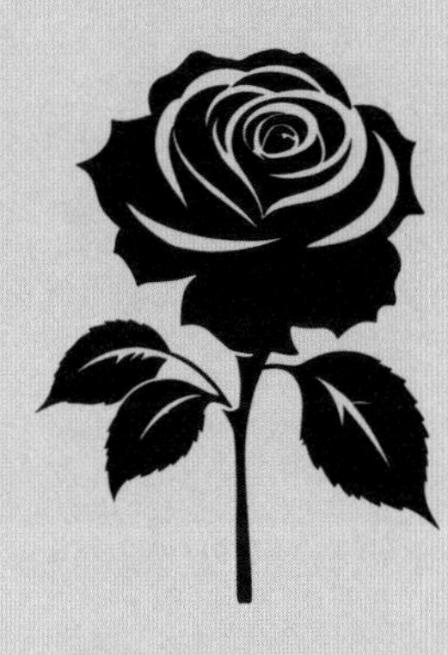

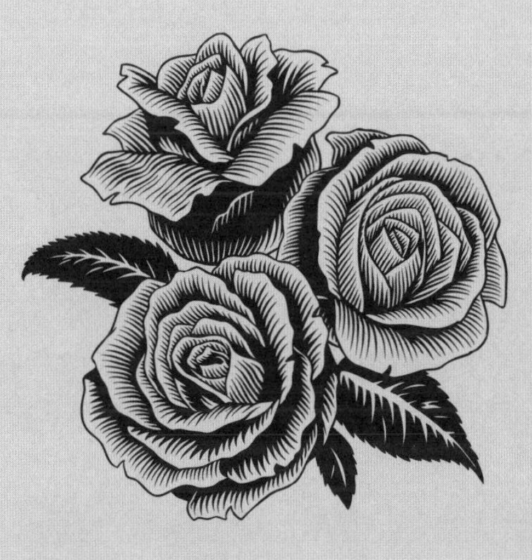

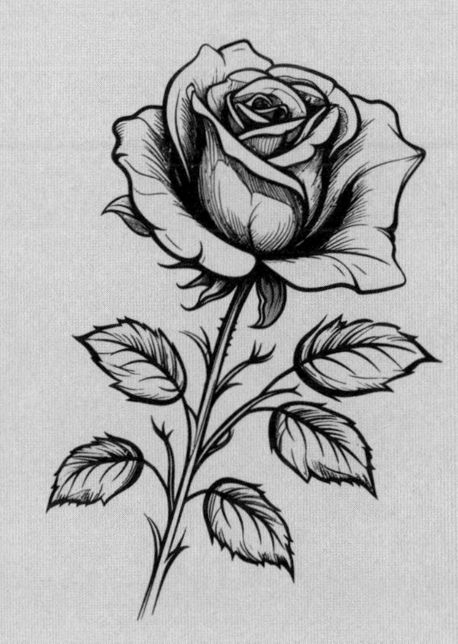

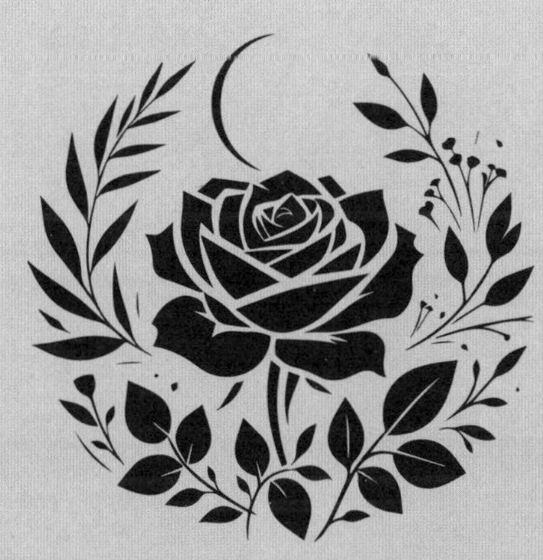

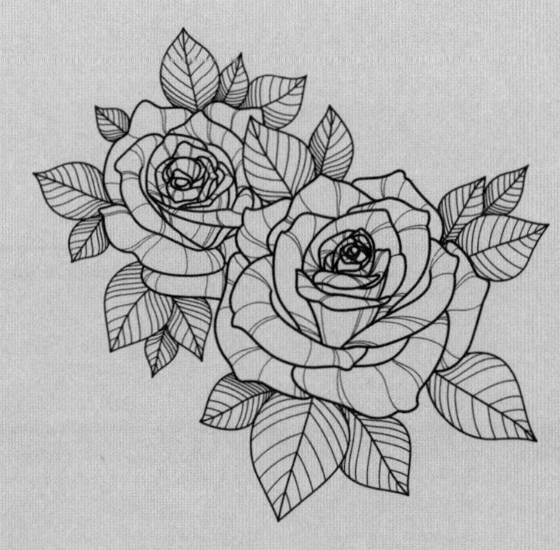

Lily

Purity | Innocence | Peace | Fertility | Abundance

Sacred Origins
Greek, Christian,
Catholic

Used Since
1580 BCE

Tattoo Styles
Fine-line
Black-and-grey realism

Opposite: When paired with the Virgin Mary (top right) the lily's link to purity and fertility is communicated. Multiple flowers within the same piece (top left and bottom right) portray the concept of abundance associated with lilies.

A symbol of purity and innocence, the delicate lily has graced our homes for thousands of years.

Crown of love and beauty

The Greeks prized this bloom above all others, believing it was born from the milk of the mother goddess Hera. Etchings of the lily have been discovered in the remains of a villa in Crete which date back to 1580 BCE. That said, Aphrodite, the goddess of love, was not a fan. She was thought to be responsible for the iconic pistil that protrudes from the centre of the head after she cursed the flower, believing it would take away some of its power. Unfortunately for her the lily's reputation grew, and it became a centrepiece at Greek weddings, often woven into the bride's hair or paired with a sheaf of wheat and made into a crown for her to wear, as a symbol of abundance.

A Christian emblem

With a prominent mention in the Bible at the Sermon of the Mount, the lily became popular in Hebrew scripture and the Catholics soon adopted the white lily as an emblem of the Virgin Mary. Renaissance artists were quick to catch on, creating ornate works of art to illustrate the lily's sacred significance.

How to wear it

The lily is a versatile tattoo design; popular colours are white or pink and the flower can stand alone or be incorporated into a bigger project. On its own, the lily is often seen in a delicate fine-line style suitable for many areas of the arm. The symbol's connection to purity means that it is often paired with images of the Virgin Mary, frequently rendered in a tonal black and grey style.

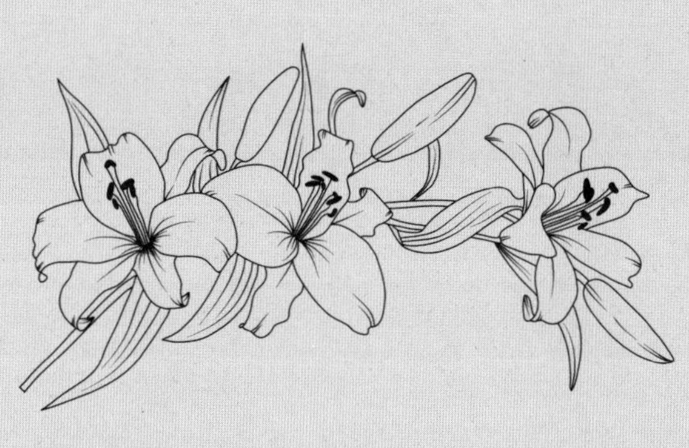

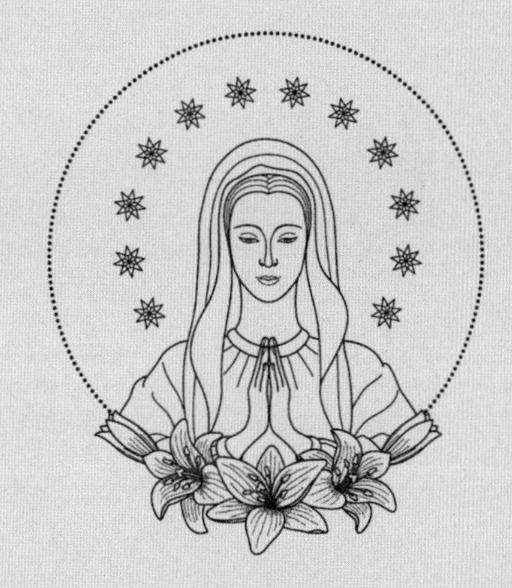

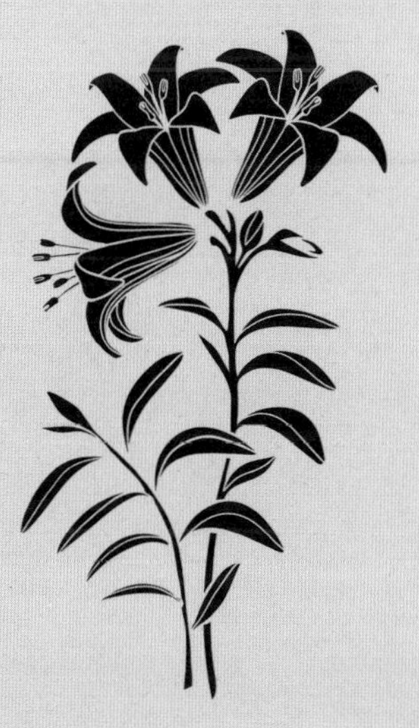

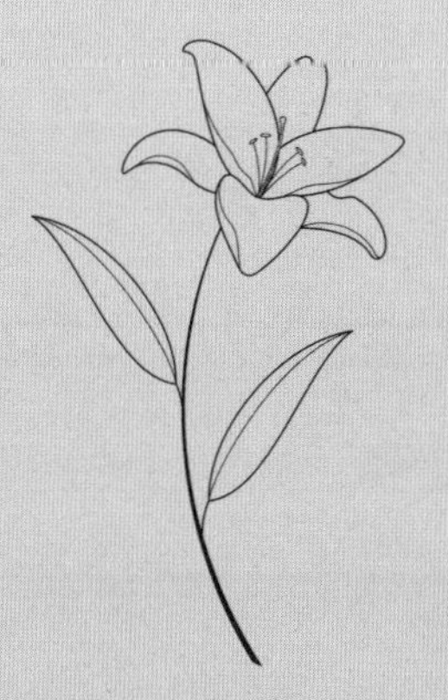

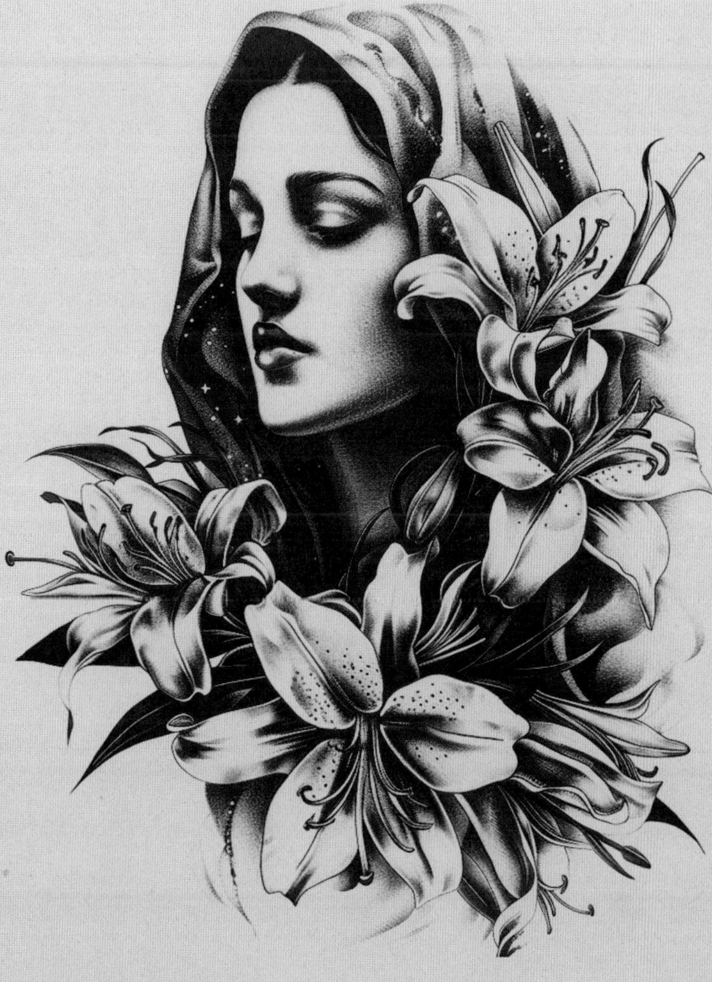

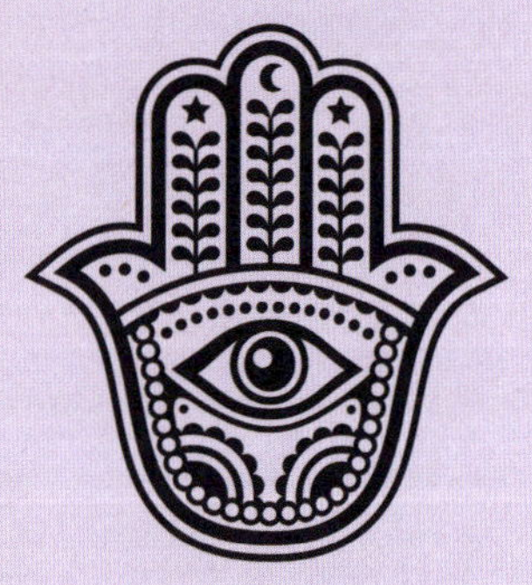

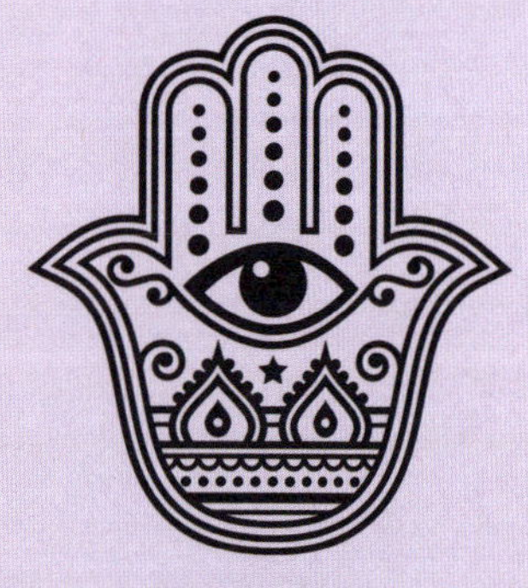

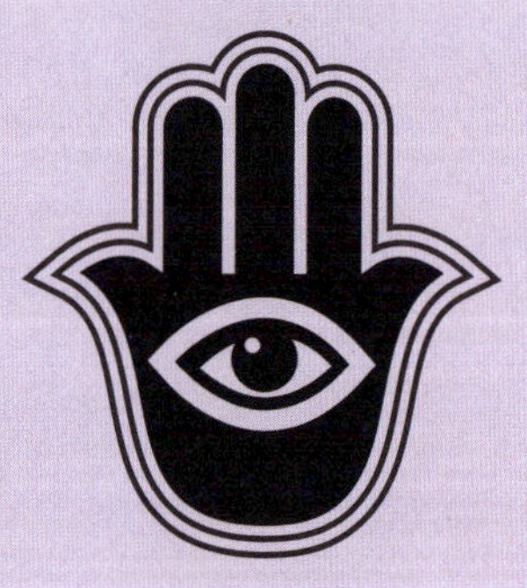

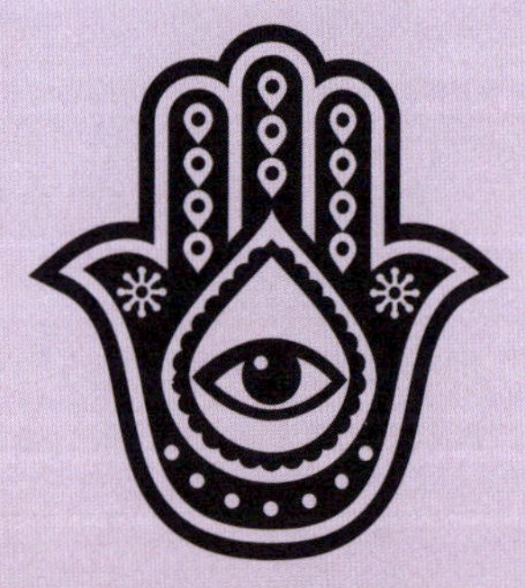

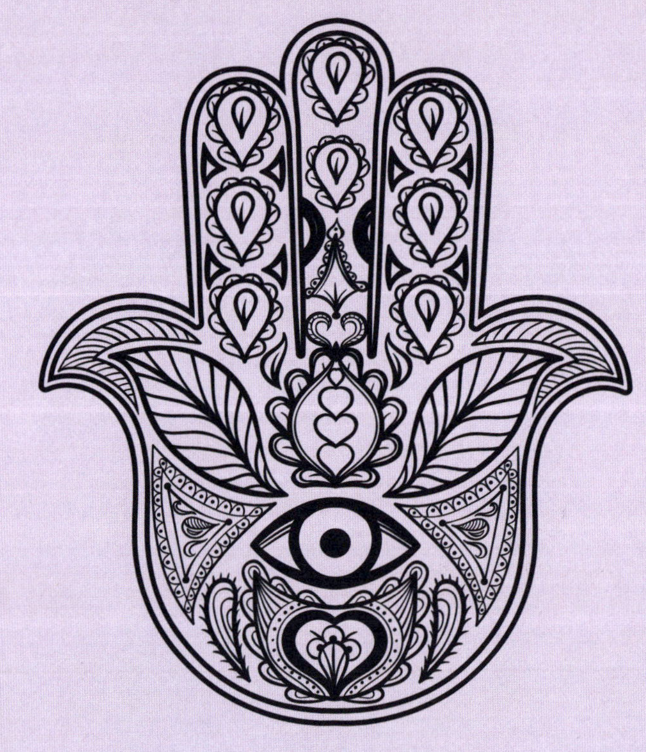

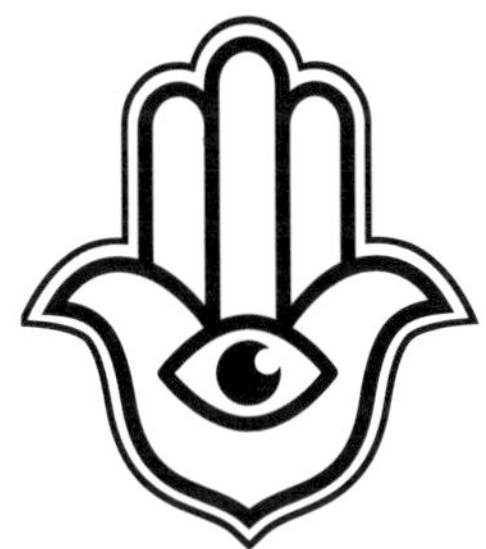

Hamsa

Protection | Luck | Abundance | Strength | Fertility

Sacred Origins
Phoenician, African, Muslim, Jewish

Used Since
2000 BCE

Tattoo Styles
Ornamental
Fine-line
Western traditional

Opposite: When detail is plentiful (top right) the idea of abundance is brought to the fore. Simpler versions of the hamsa (left column) draw focus to the eye, which emphasizes the symbol's protective qualities.

Appearing symmetrical by design, the hamsa, as it is called in Hebrew is a perfectly formed five-fingered hand with a long history.

Deities, prophets and protection

Also known as the hand of Fatima, or the Khamsa in Arabic, this sacred symbol dates back to the 2nd millennium BCE when it first emerged in the city of Carthage on the north coast of Africa, present-day Tunisia.

Originally thought to have been the symbol associated with the Phoenician mother goddess Tanit, the hand was seen as a talisman, providing protection, abundance and a conduit between heaven and earth. Its unique shape captured the imagination of ancient civilizations and, thanks to an increase in trade and travel, its popularity grew. It soon became a religious icon in Judaism, where it was called the hand of Miriam. Medieval Muslims also adopted it, believing the five fingers to represent the Ahl al-Bayt, the Prophet Muhammad's family. This version was named after the Prophet's beloved daughter Fatima.

The hamsa and the evil eye

As the symbol's status grew, new versions emerged with variations to the design, thought to build upon the hamsa's protective energy. The evil eye, which refers to an ancient curse born from envy and delivered by a menacing stare, is a stand-alone symbol of an encircled eye which is often found nestled within the palm of the hamsa hand. This symbol, which emerged thousands of years ago in Asia and Latin America, is thought to reflect negative energy back to the one who has delivered it.

How to wear it

The hamsa is often depicted with the thumb and little finger curling away from the palm to create symmetry and balance, a pose which is also associated with blessings. The hand can be worn facing up or down. If it's protection you seek, then the hamsa should face upwards. When pointing down, it's associated with abundance and it can also bless the wearer with fertility. If the fingers are close together, it is said to increase the flow of prosperity; if spaced apart, it's thought to boost protection. Although colour can be used, most renditions are kept to black.

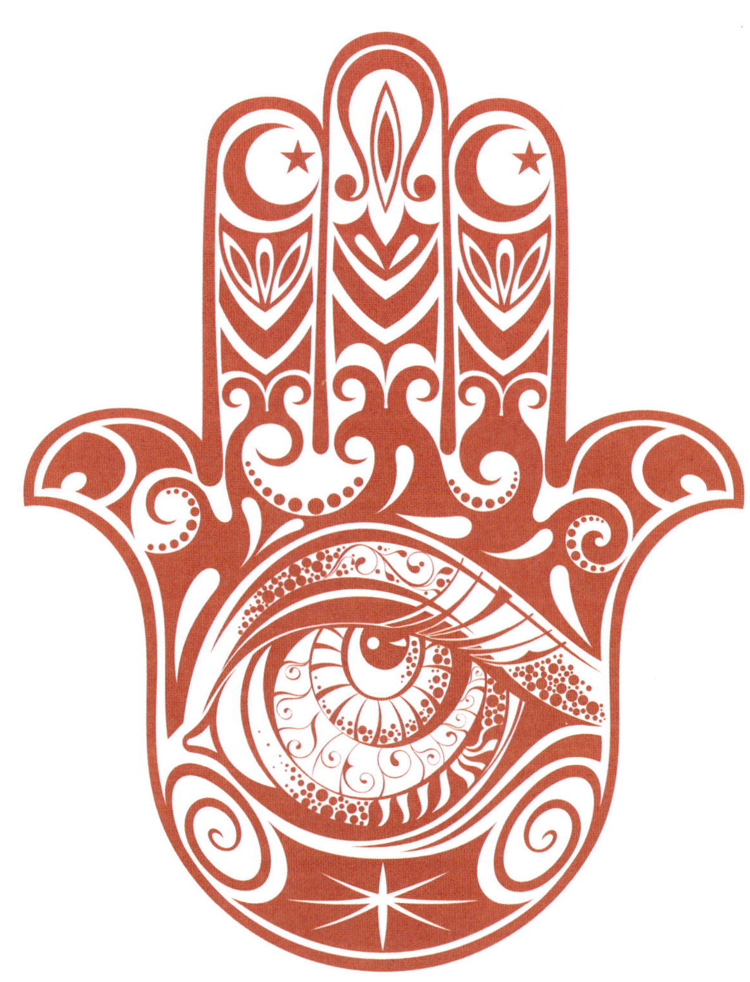

Opposite: The hamsa works at both small scale (bottom) and large scale. This large-scale design (top) incorprates a Merkaba star, which symbolizes spiritual development.

Right: The emphasis of the eye on this hamsa strengthens the idea of protection and of reflecting negative energy.

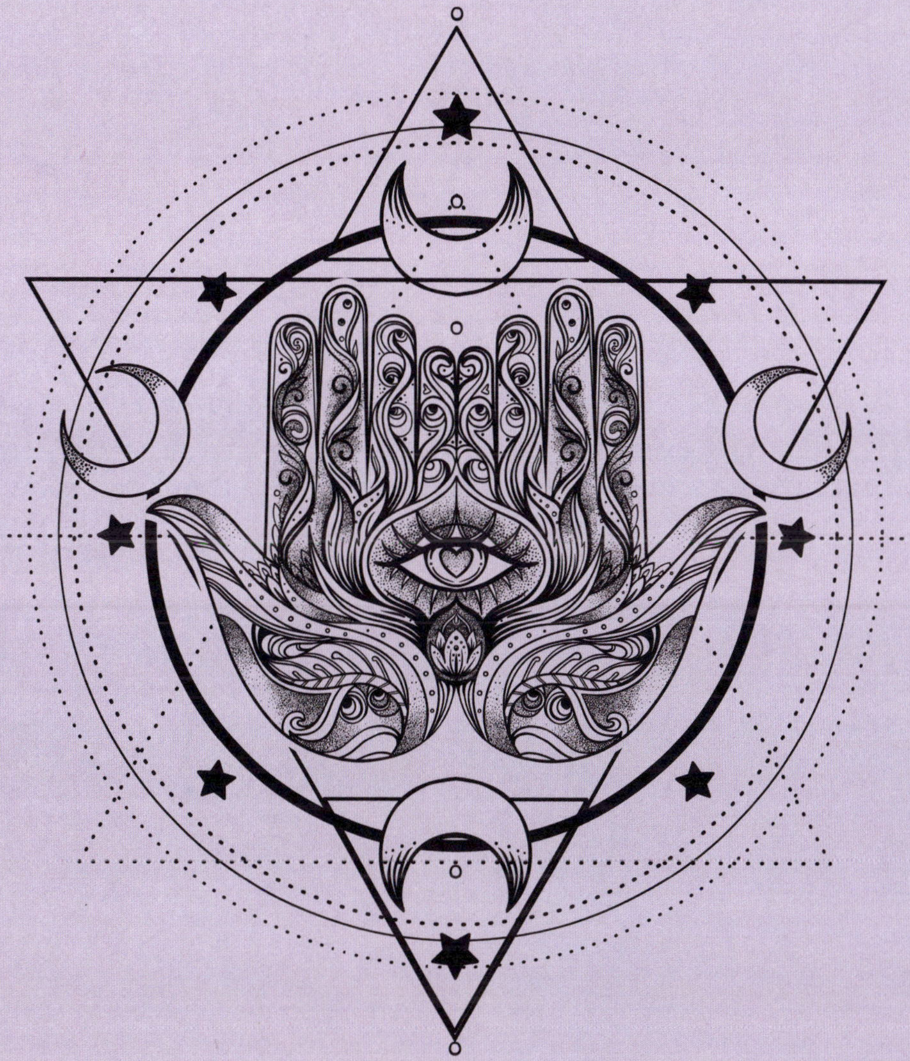

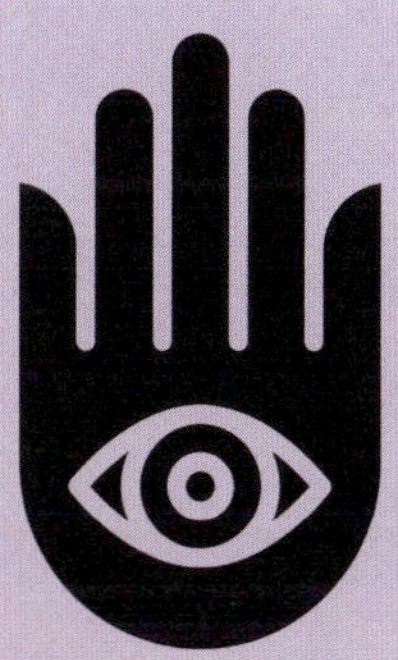

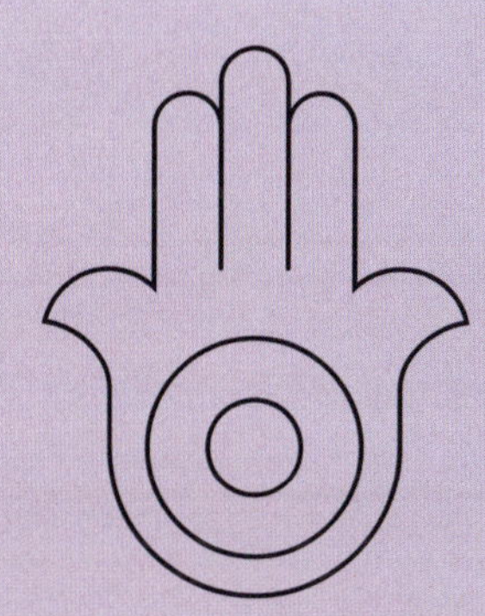

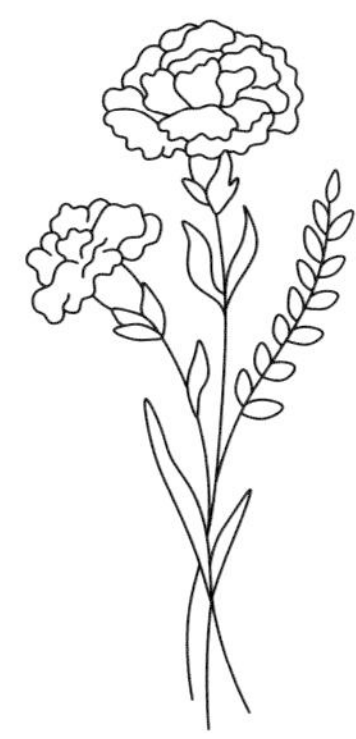

Carnation

Love | Beauty | Purity | Remembrance | Death

Sacred Origins
Greek, Roman, Mexican

Used Since
1st millennium BCE

Tattoo Styles
Fine-line
Western traditional
Watercolour

Synonymous with enduring love, the intricate petals of the carnation make a beautiful tattoo design.

A divine flower

The carnation, revered around the world, has been cultivated for thousands of years. To the ancient Greeks and Romans, it was the epitome of love and beauty and regularly used in festivals to the gods and ceremonies like weddings and funerals.

The flower's Latin name goes some way to explaining its significance. The genus dianthus is derived from the word *dios* meaning divine, and *anthos* meaning flower, while the *caro* part of caryophillus translates as 'flesh' and refers to the pale pink flowers, which were a common hue at the time.

Day of the Dead

This 'divine flower' became prominent in the Middle Ages, when it was adopted by the Christian faith. According to legend, when the Virgin Mary wept for her son, the tears that fell transformed into this bloom, linking the carnation with the purity of a mother's love. To the Mexicans, it is the flower of remembrance and is commonly used to adorn burial mounds and decorate graves and skulls during the Day of the Dead festivities.

How to wear it

This versatile symbol can be filled with a variety of colours, paired with skulls to link to a deceased loved one, or showcased by itself on the forearm, shoulder or leg. It works well in a bold, Western traditional style or in fine-line if the wearer wants a delicate look. Also perfect as a colourful element in a larger design.

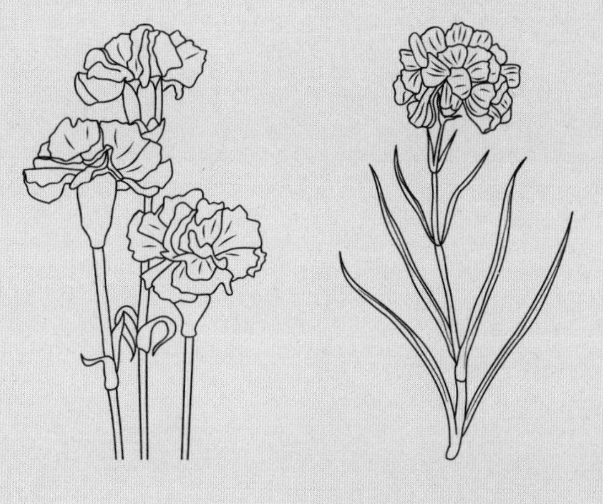 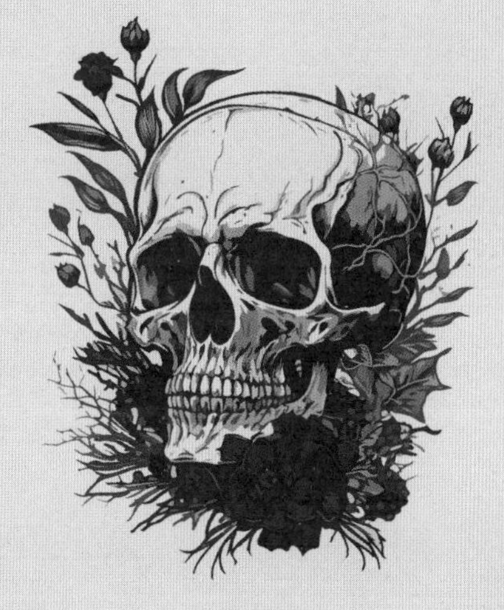

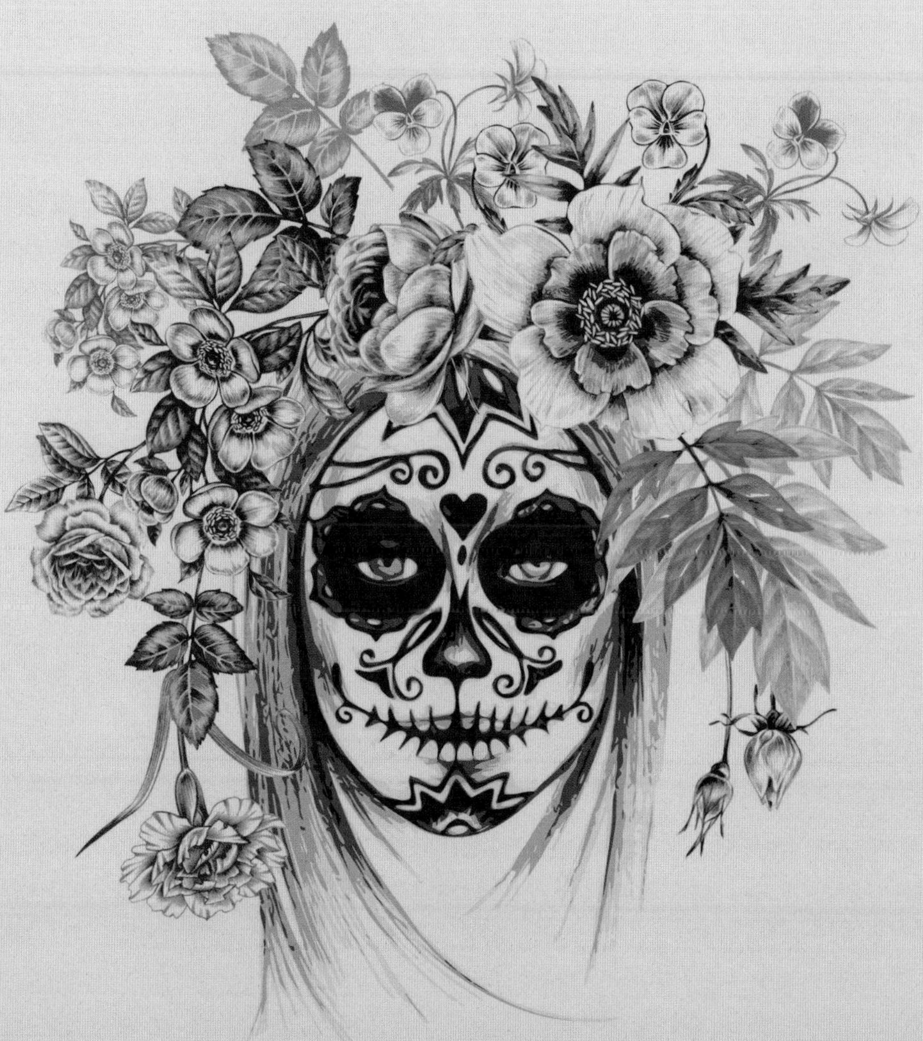

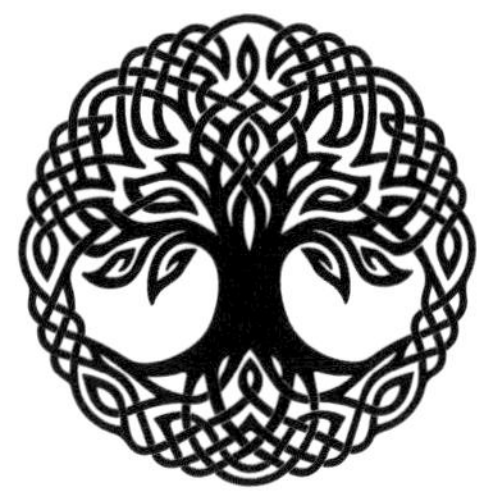

Tree of Life

Life force | Creativity | Energy | Nature | Manifestation

Sacred Origins
Mesopotamian,
Egyptian, Norse, Celtic,
Christian, Jewish

Used Since
7000 BCE

Tattoo Styles
Celtic
Ornamental
Fine-line

Opposite: When combined with Celtic patterning (bottom left), the tree of life can show a link between the earth and the heavens. Rendering the branches and roots in a whimsical style (top left and bottom right) speaks of the creativity associated with the symbol.

The tree of life is a concept that connects humankind to the primal force of nature and the cycles of life and death, uniting heaven and earth and providing balance.

Sentinel of knowledge

A potent archetype which appears in many mythologies throughout the world, the tree of life is universal. Ancient civilizations favoured this symbol and took it to heart. For them the natural world was everything, giving them a sense of belonging and understanding. Trees in particular were silent sentinels, timeless and full of knowledge. Typically depicted at the centre of the earth or holding it up, the tree of life is closely associated with the world tree which features in Norse mythology, and the tree of knowledge, prominent in Christianity, Judaism and Islam. In some cultures, this sacred tree was also the bearer of magical fruit which could grant immortality.

Bridge to other worlds

Crude depictions of the tree of life have been found at excavations in Türkiye, which date back to 7000 BCE, probably the earliest record of the symbol's usage. Indeed, the sacred tree was a popular motif in Mesopotamia and soon spread to Egypt and other civilizations. To the Norse peoples, the tree of life was Yggdrasil, also known as the world tree, a mighty Ash whose never-ending branches connected all the nine realms together. This was the tree that the god Odin hung from for nine days and nights, to receive the gift of wisdom. During this time the tree sustained him, imbuing him with life and energy. To the Celts, this sacred tree provided a bridge to the heavens while also being deeply rooted in the earth, and a link to the dead.

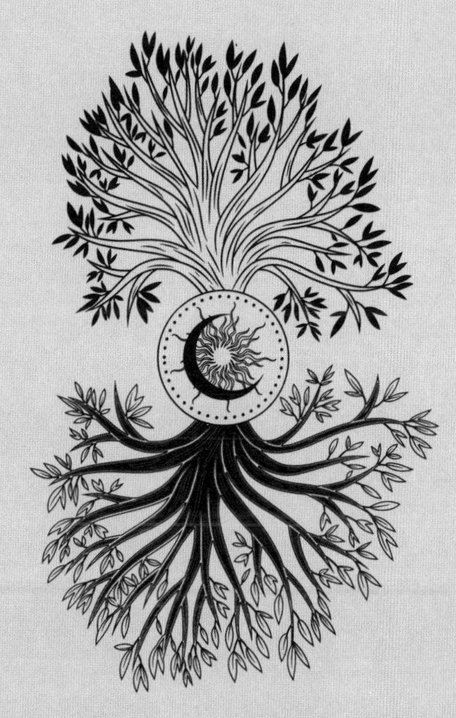

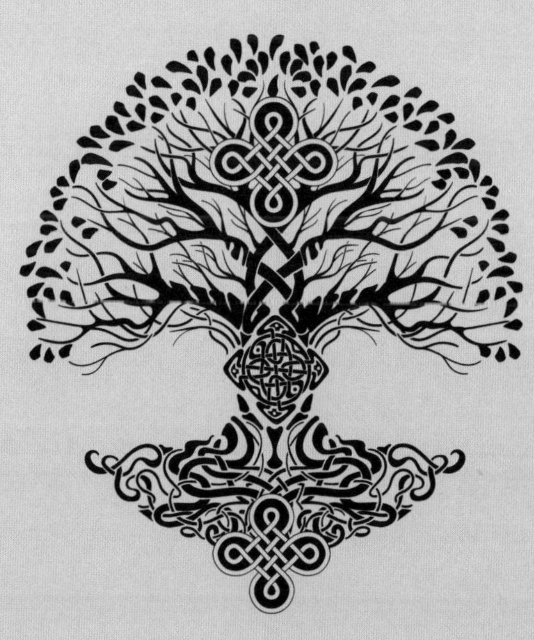

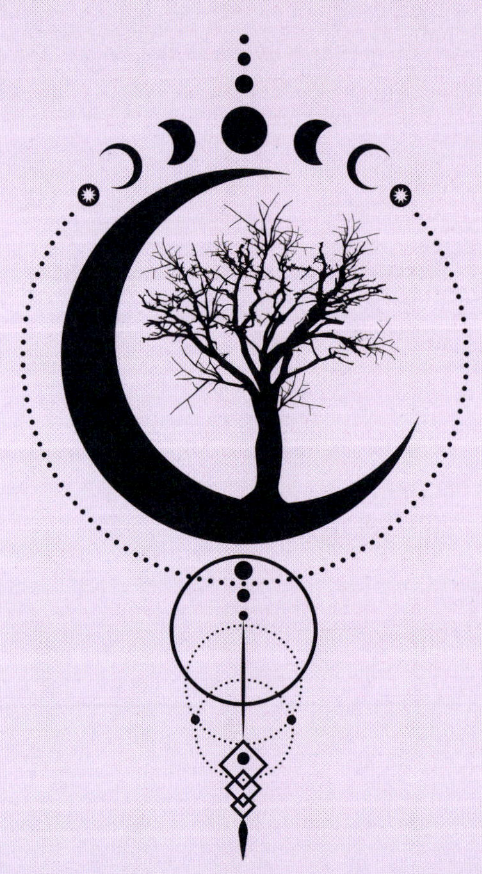

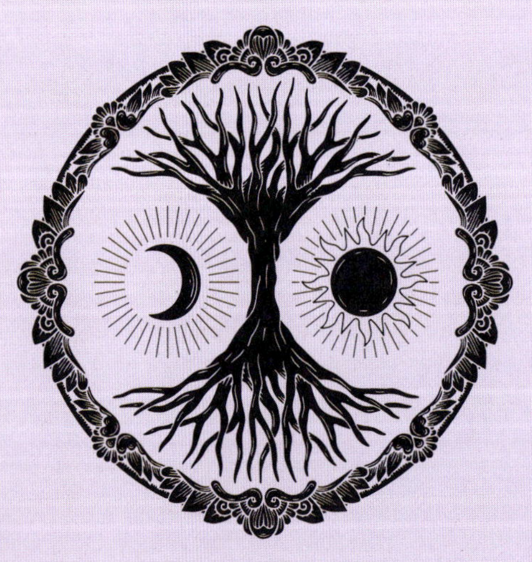

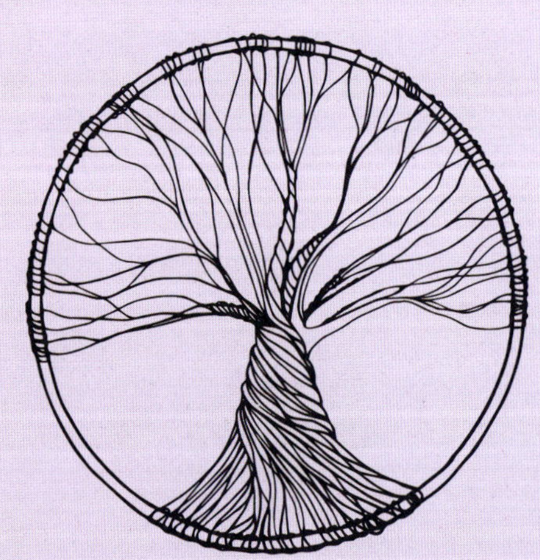

A sacred diagram

Christian and Jewish traditions also held the tree of life in high regard. In the Bible it appears in the Garden of Eden, alongside the tree of knowledge. Here it is protected by an angel so that neither Adam nor Eve can eat from it and gain immortality. In the Kabbalah, the tree of life is a sacred diagram which links the 22 letters of the Hebrew alphabet with the 22 paths and astrological houses. It provides a map which shows how the flow of creativity works, taking this through to manifestation.

How to wear it

The tree of life often appears in a circle with roots sprawling out and linking up to the branches and the heavens above, communicating the link between heaven and earth. Certain styles can be added to illustrate which origin or time period you are taking the inspiration from. The Celtic tree of life, for example, is a popular choice and allows the use of knotwork details in the roots or branches, while a modern approach might adopt a more realistic tree, decorated with foliage, fruit and flowers.

All images: Encapsulating the tree within a circle, or the inclusion of circular imagery, illustrates the circles of life and death associated with the tree of life as well as linking it to the phases of the moon and the balance between day and night.

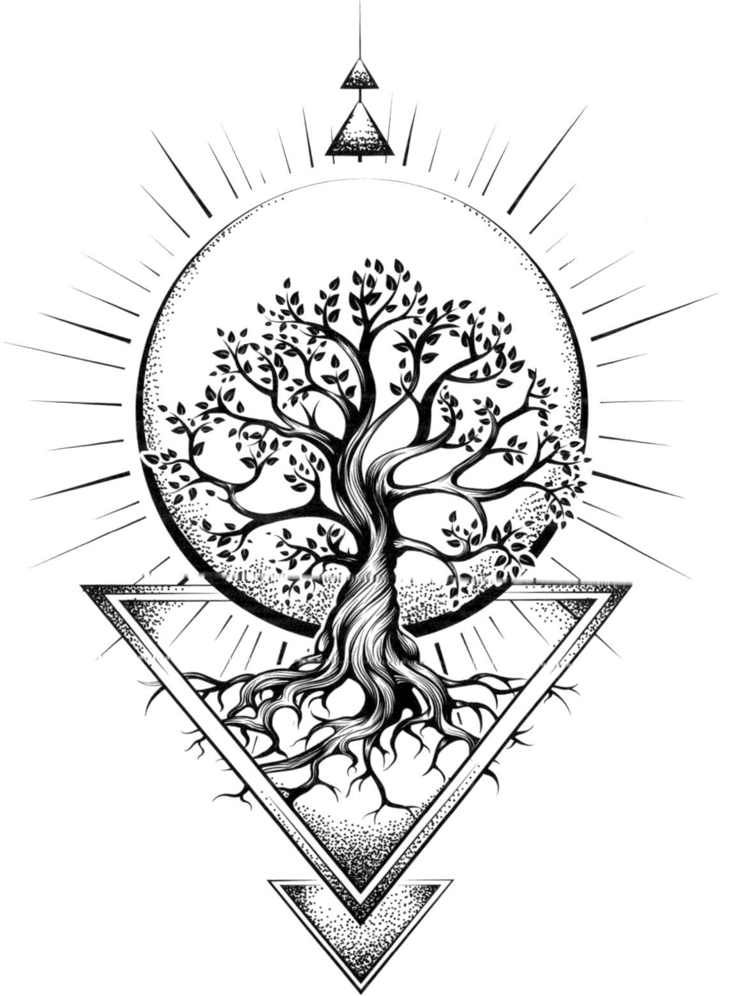

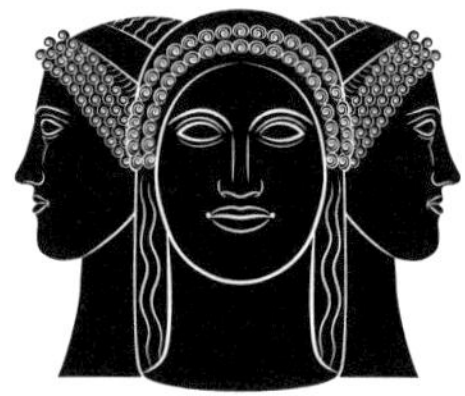

Triple Goddess

Feminine power | Creativity | Magic | Fertility

Sacred Origins
Greek, Celtic

Used Since
19th century

Tattoo Styles
Fine-line
Blackwork

Opposite: The moon phases encircling the goddesses (top) symbolize the stages of womanhood. Celtic patterns (bottom left) entwined with the triple goddess emphasize the symbol's Celtic links.

Today the triple goddess symbol, with its floral-like symmetry, is synonymous with the divine feminine and is held in high regard by many pagan groups.

Triad of deities

In some mythologies, the triple goddess is three separate entities who come together to combine their powers, while for others she is one deity with three specific roles. For example, the Celtic goddess Brigid was a healer, a poetess and a smith. The ancient Greeks believed she was a deity who could shift between shape and form, sometimes appearing as a young maiden, sometimes as a bountiful mother, but most often as an old crone. The Greek goddess Hecate is a prime example of this and is often cited as the first triple goddess. The one thing that all these deities have in common is their triple nature, and this is mirrored in the symbol of the same name which is based upon the three phases of the moon. It's thought that these perfectly emulate the stages of womanhood, going from waxing crescent to a full moon and then waning crescent.

A patriarchal view

The idea of the triple goddess may stem from a number of ancient civilizations, but the symbol itself is more modern, taking prominence in the 19th century thanks to the folklorist and writer Robert Graves. His book *The White Goddess* went into great detail about the different phases of womanhood from a patriarchal standpoint. He amalgamated many European mythical characters into one and described each aspect, from the youthful beauty of the maiden to the plump nurturing characteristics of the mother, and finally the old crone, a wizened creature and an imminent reminder of death. Luckily his views, which seemed to focus on the idea that women were of little value when they reached old age, didn't stand the test of time.

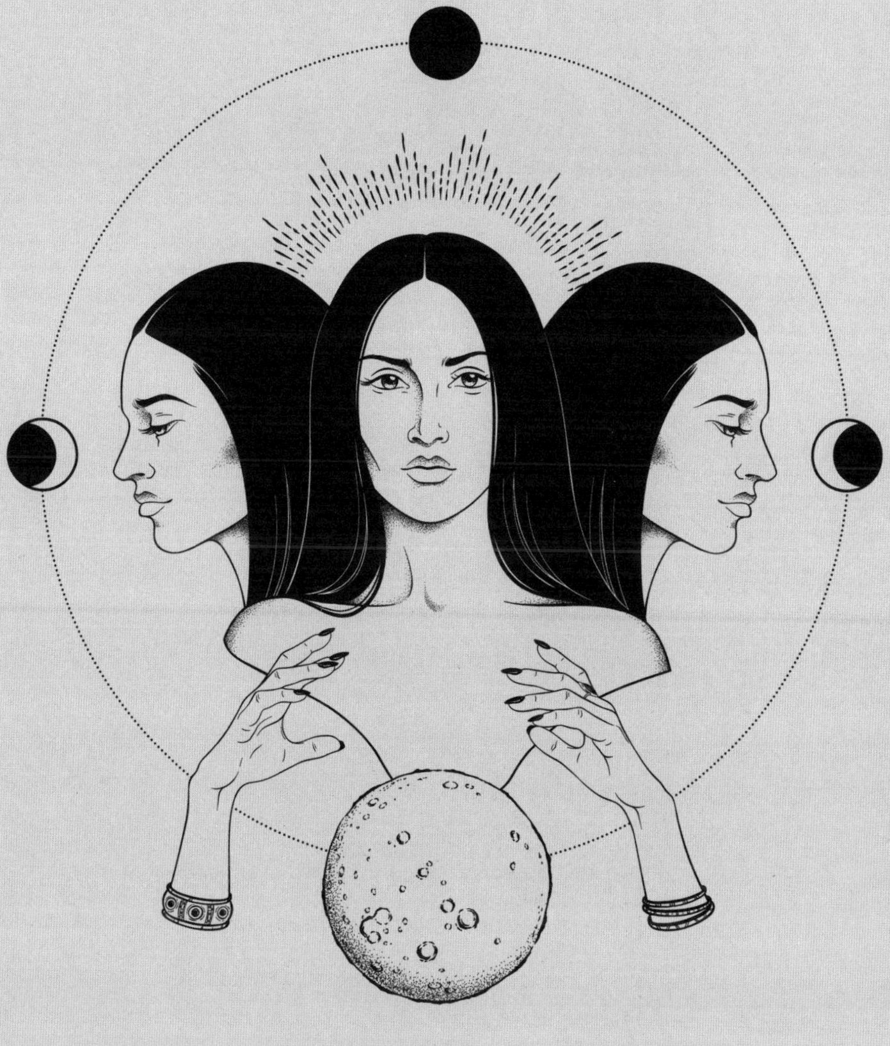

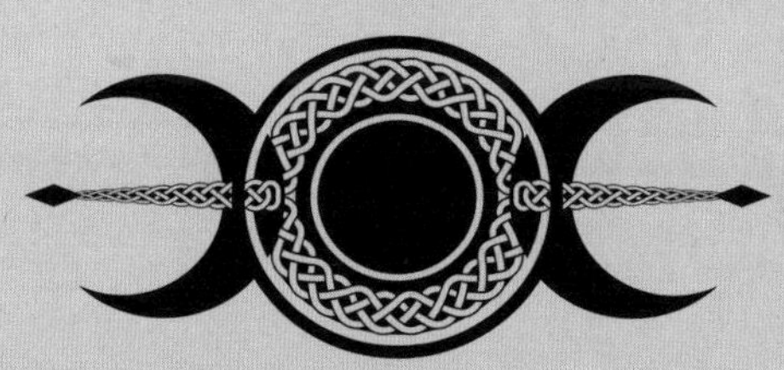

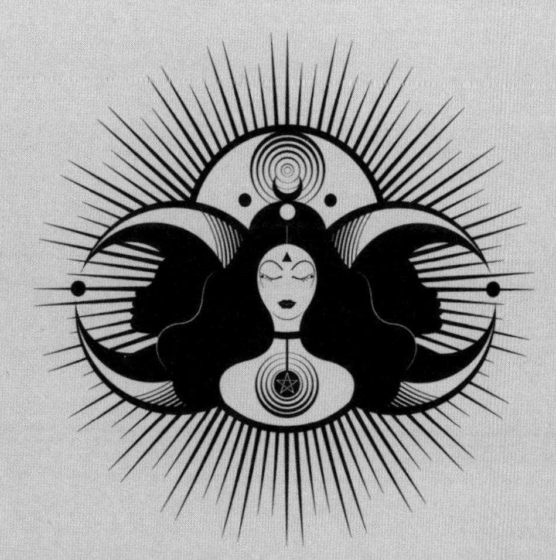

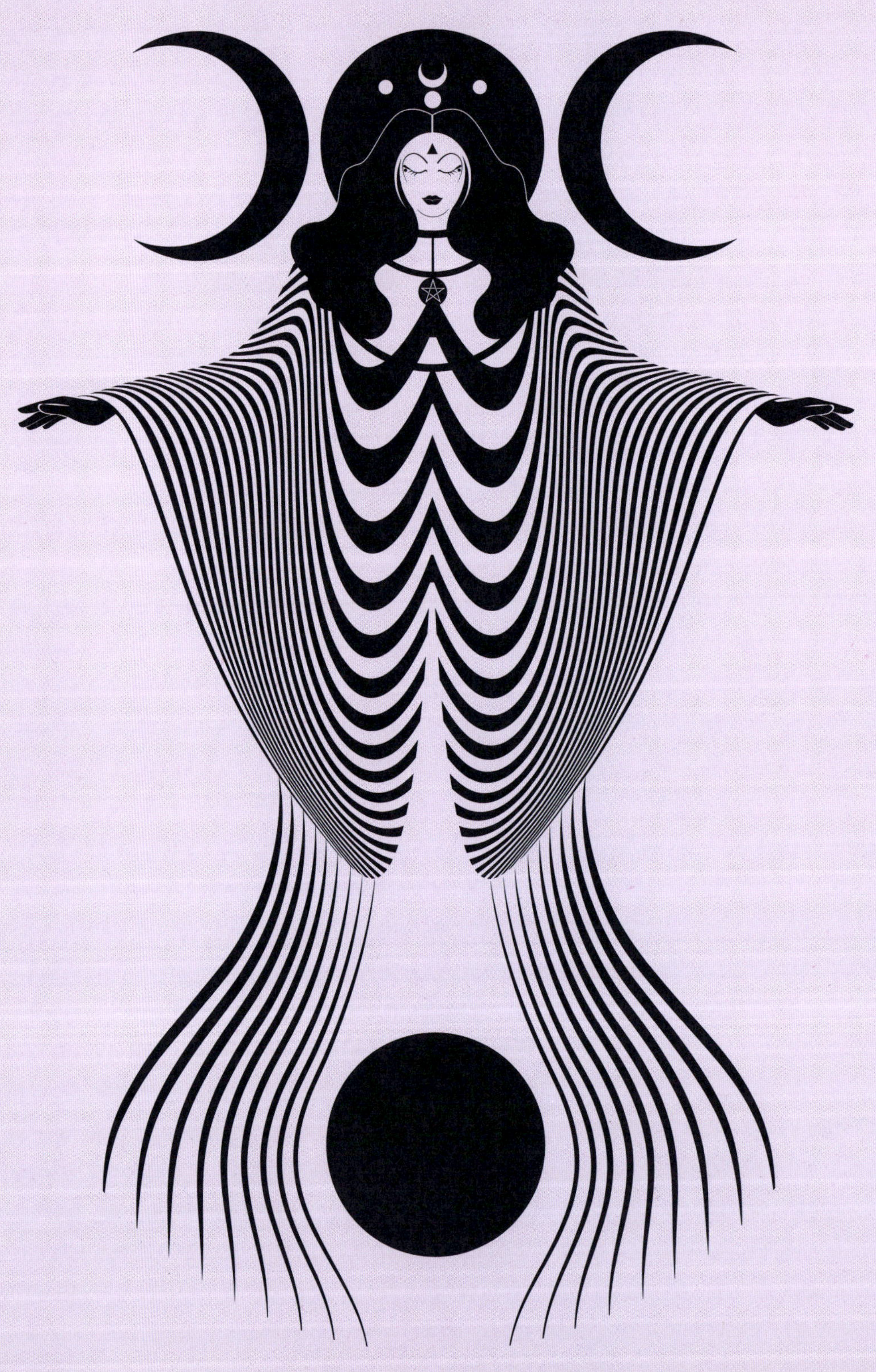

A pagan emblem

The triple goddess is a powerful influence, encompassing all aspects of womanhood
and embracing the positive energy that comes with each. The maiden is full of
youthful exuberance and curiosity; the mother is abundant with creativity and a
nurturing force; the crone is possibly the most powerful of the three, being wise,
graceful and full of good humour.

How to wear it

If rendered simply, this design is perfect for the wrist. More elaborate versions work
well between the shoulder blades, on the chest just under the collar bones or in wider
areas of the arms or legs. It is often adorned with flora and fauna to emphasize new
growth and creative energy. Pentagrams are often incorporated into the central full
moon. The symbol works well in black and grey, especially when small; however, if
heavy floral work is incorporated, this lends itself to a colourful palette.

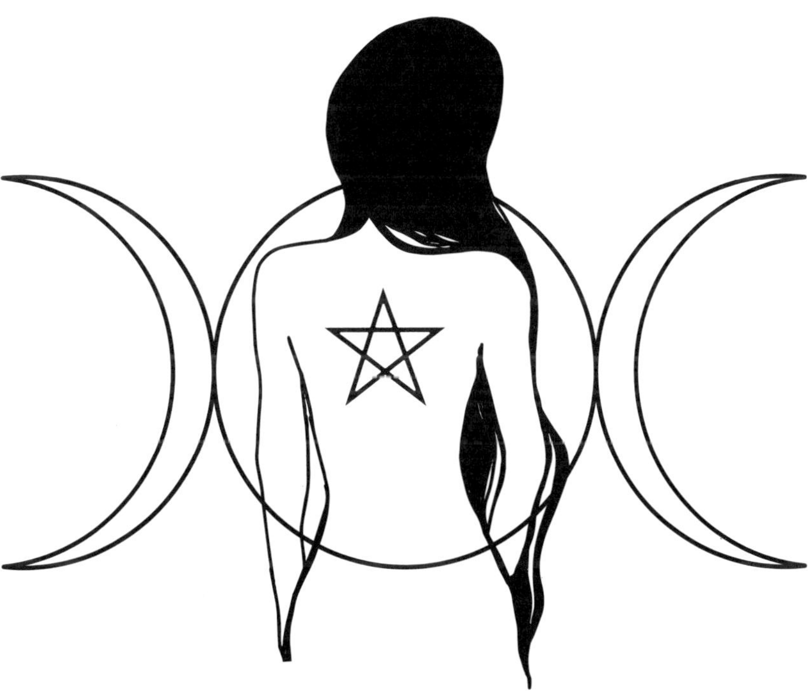

Both images: **At a larger scale
female figures can be included, to
enforce the idea of fertility and
feminine power.**

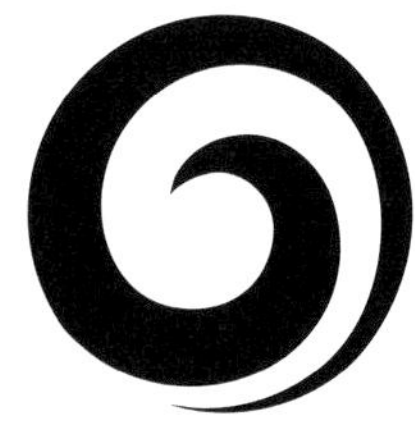

Koru

Life force | Creativity | Energy | Nature | Manifestation

Sacred Origins
Māori

Used Since
Dawn of time

Tattoo Styles
Polynesian

Opposite: The koru shown within a circle (top left) portrays the idea of a relationship. A single unfurling frond (middle right and bottom left) speaks more of the ideas of life and new beginnings.

The meaning of the koru, the Māori word for loop or coil, is related to the ongoing nature of life, rebirth and new beginnings.

The silver frond

Also known as the pītau, the koru is based upon the shape of an unfurling silver frond, a tree fern that is native to Aotearoa (New Zealand). Called silver because the lighter underside of each frond reflects the moonlight at night making it easier to navigate the bush, this beautiful plant was revered and turned into a sacred symbol.

A journey of self-discovery

The name relates to the swirl in this design, which unfurls from a tightly coiled spiral at the centre and gives the impression of movement. The central point represents the start where all life begins and suggests the need to go back to the beginning in a quest for personal growth and self-development. The koru is often seen as a symbol of rejuvenation and represents the perfection and purity that comes with a sense of wholeness. It is commonly worn as a necklace or used in Māori art, from wood and bone carving to weaving and tattooing.

How to wear it

The koru is a simple yet beautiful design that is often seen tattooed at palm size or smaller. The symbol is often tattooed in a Polynesian style, which features bold, pattern-based shapes and areas of solid pure-black ink. Double korus can be tattooed together within a circle to represent a relationship. While the koru itself can be worn as a tattoo by non-Māori, there are some patterns using koru that should not be used. The koru symbol should be treated with respect; research the suitability of the design before you commit.

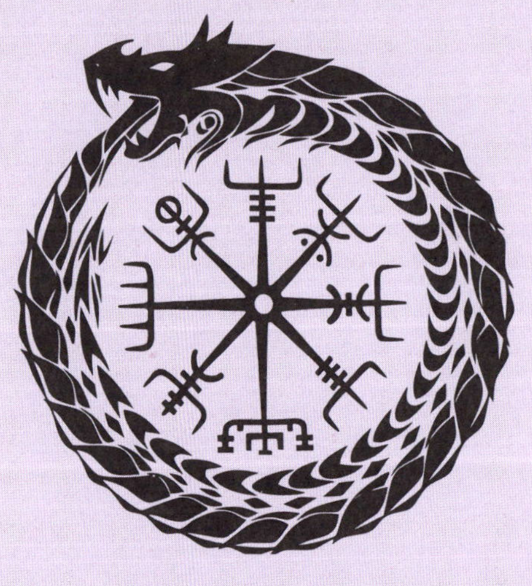

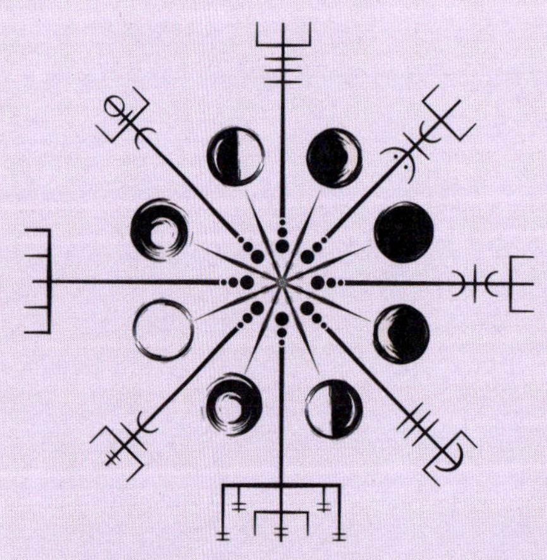

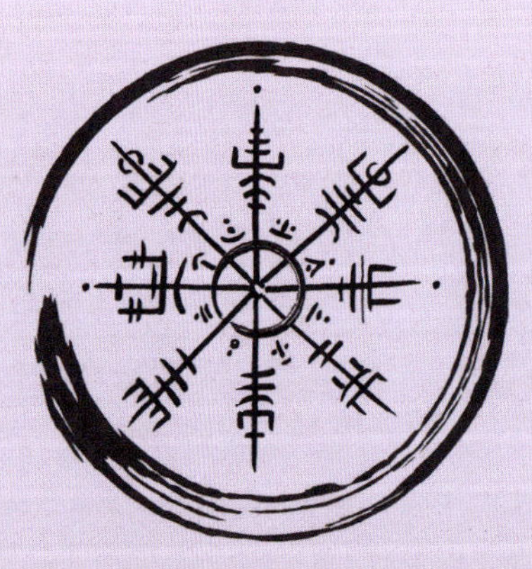

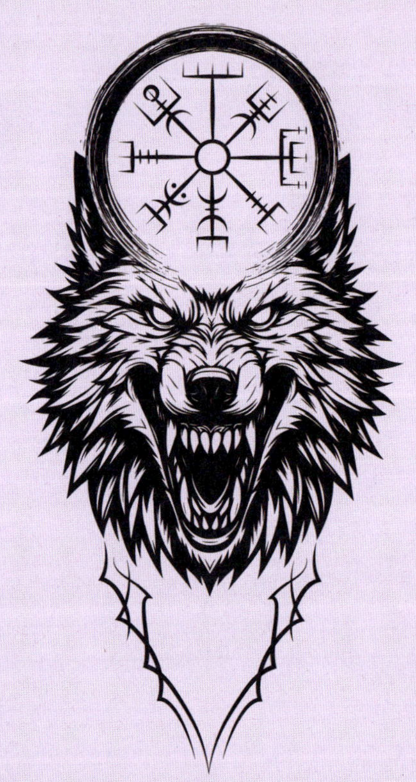

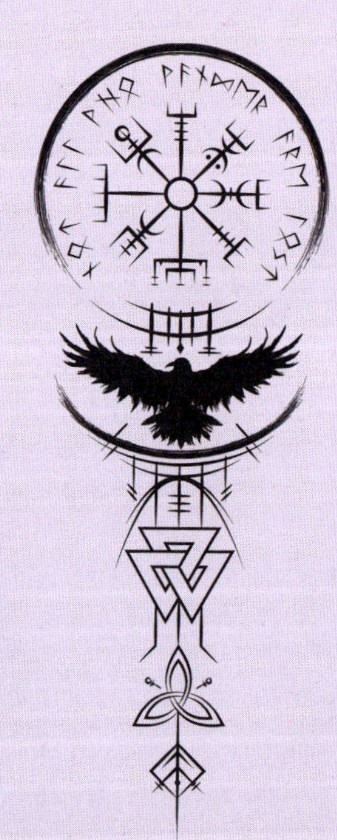

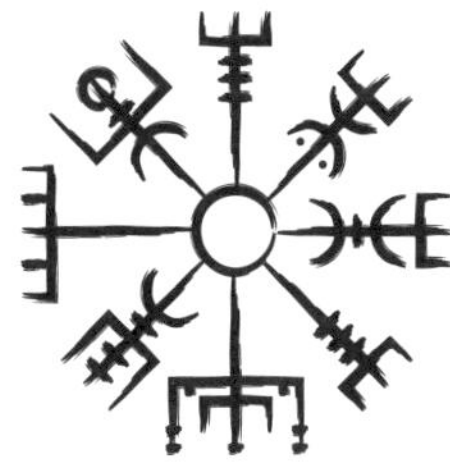

Vegvísir

Guidance | Navigation | Balance | Protection | Strength

Sacred Origins
Icelandic

Used Since
19th century

Tattoo Styles
Black-and-grey realism
Blackwork

Opposite: When vegvísir is accompanied by a wolf or dragon (top right and left), the concept of protection and strength is in abundance.

A popular tattoo choice, the symbol of vegvísir was used as a tool to help people find their way home, physically and metaphorically.

Icelandic origins

Also called the Viking compass, the runic compass and the Odin compass, this intricate symbol was previously believed to have Nordic origins, a theory which has been disproved over time. In truth, the vegvísir finds its roots in three Icelandic grimoires from the 19th century, the most important of these being the *Huld Manuscript* which was written by Geir Vigfússon. Here, the symbol appears with a brief description in Latin which, when translated, says: 'Carry this sign with you and you will not get lost in storms or die of cold bad weather, and will easily find your way from the unknown.'

Occult stars and sigils

It's thought that the symbol was borrowed from the Continent, where similar motifs featuring star-shaped patterns were often used in occult rituals. The confusion comes in the use of staves and lines, which look remarkably like Viking runes, a type of Nordic alphabet which was used as a form of communication. In reality, the lines that appear on this symbol have little to do with runes and were not placed there to create words, rather they are of decorative use to make the symbol look more appealing. Even so, the vegvísir is thought to be packed with magical potential, and was used in spells and rituals during the 1800s.

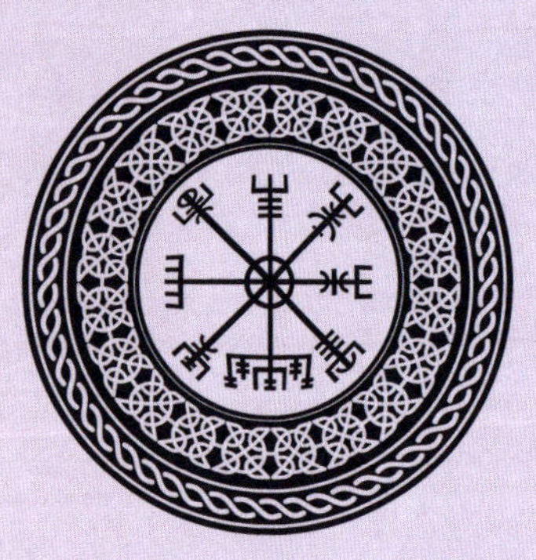 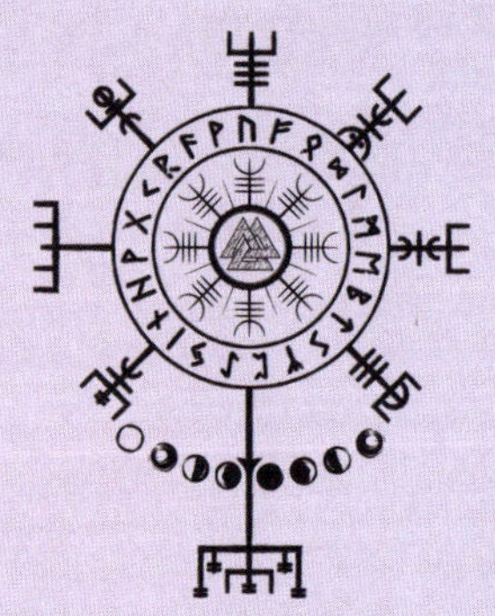 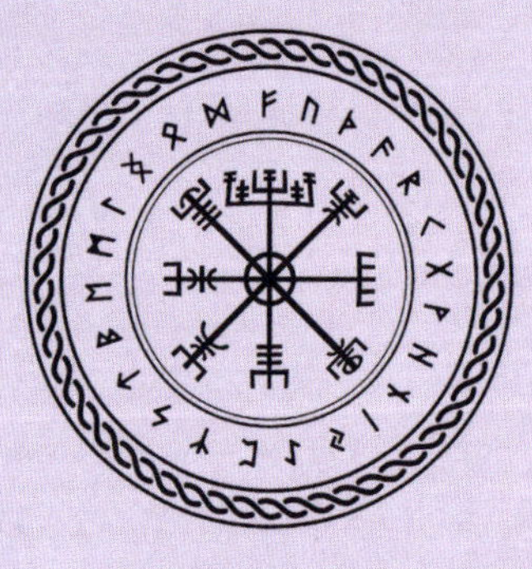

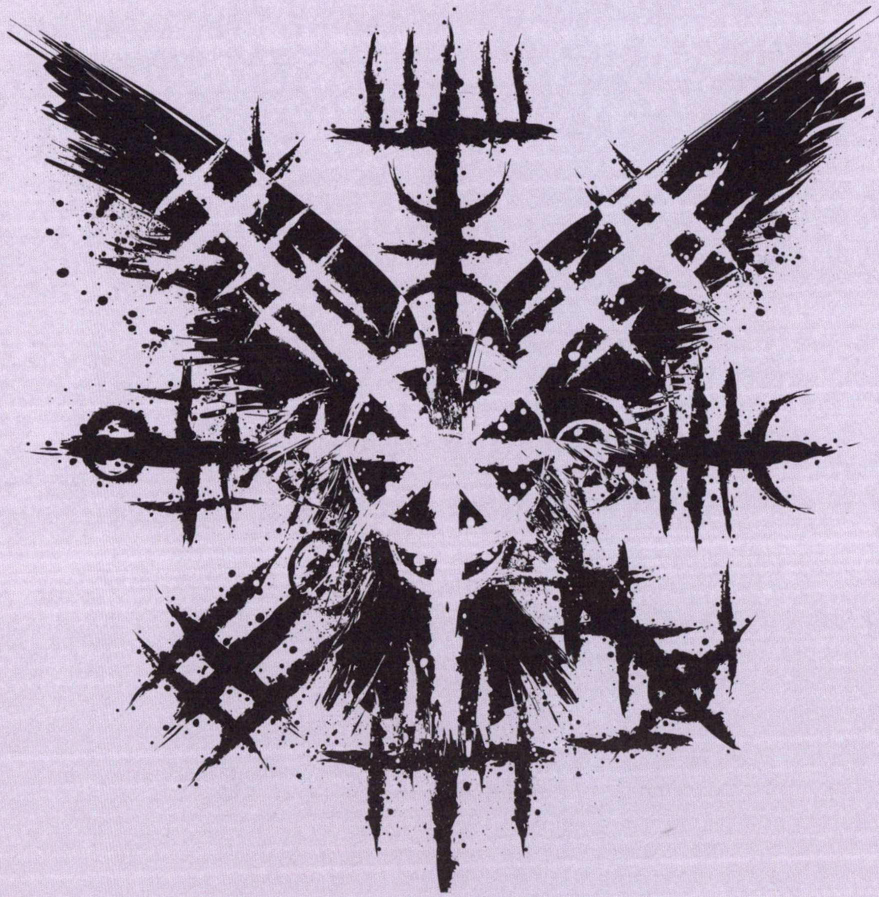

A compass for the mind

While the roots of this symbol may be sketchy, and have no apparent link to
Norse cultures, the meaning remains the same. Its name, an Icelandic word which
translates as 'way finder', hints at the true power of this sigil, a type of compass for
the mind and soul, showing the holder how to navigate the twists and turns of fate
and prevent them from losing their direction in life. The symbol itself is comprised
of eight points, each with their own distinctive design, and it is encircled with what
look like runes. Over time it has evolved and there are many different variations,
some of which include actual runes to enhance the meaning.

How to wear it

This symbol lends itself to a line-based approach,
so that it can be tattooed simply and remain clear
over time. The vegvísir is often seen as part of a
larger, Nordic-inspired design but perhaps serves
its purpose best when placed clearly by itself on the
inner forearm or the wrist. Here it can be easily seen
by the wearer, serving as a reminder to stay balanced
and not stray too far from the path.

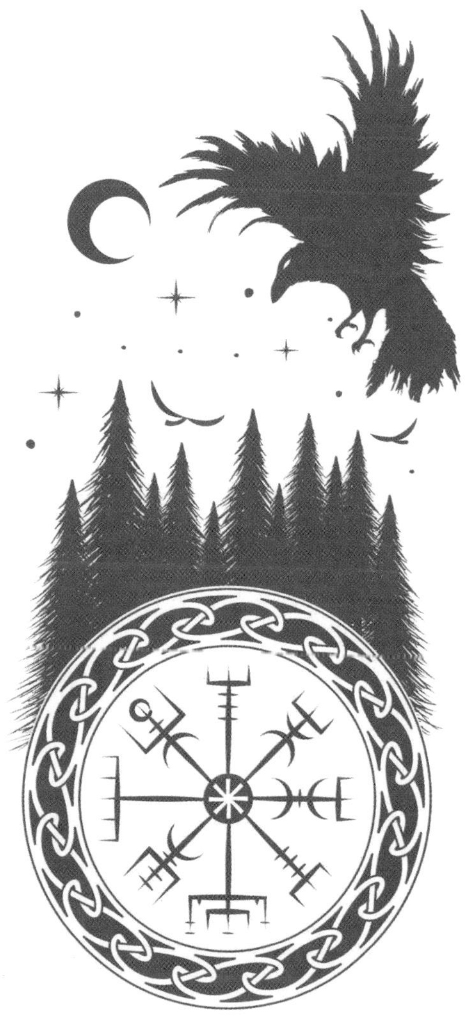

Opposite: **On its own
(top) the vegvísir is a clear
statement of balance and
navigation.**

Right: **The symbol
combined with the moon,
a forest and birds, links
to nature and the wearer's
ability to navigate their
native landscape.**

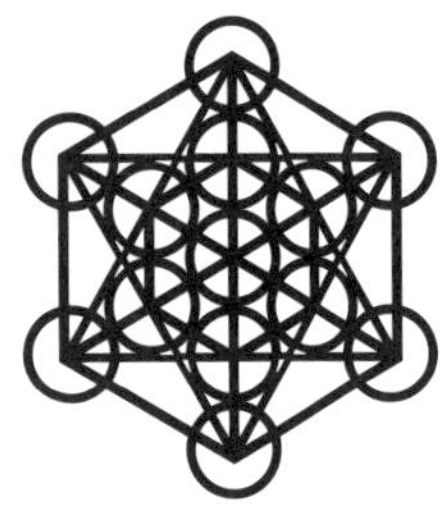

Metatron's Cube

Divinity | Unity | Harmony | Creativity | Positive energy

Sacred Origins
Mystical Judaism
(Kabbalah)

Used Since
13th century

Tattoo Styles
Fine-line
Blackwork

Opposite: The inclusion of planets or movement of the moon with Metatron's cube (top row) helps portray the symbol as a map of the universe. Combining the symbol with open hands (bottom) signifies a connection to life and humanity.

A key symbol in sacred geometry, this captivating design, also known as the flower of life, is considered by some to be the blueprint of all creation.

Map of the Universe

Viewed as a map of the Universe, Metatron's cube has a hypnotic quality and is often used in meditation to connect with the flow of energy and creativity. Comprised of 13 connected circles, the design has a circle at the centre surrounded by six other circles. A hexagon-like outline is formed from the last six circles which surround the inner shape. Lines link each of the circles to each other to illustrate how all things are connected within the Universe. The lines are said to represent the flow of energy between heaven and earth and space and time, while also being masculine in form. The circles within the cube are thought to be feminine. The general flow of the design represents harmony and balance, while the entire cube is a reflection of unity.

A building block

The symbol includes all the known shapes upon earth, including DNA strands and the patterns found in snowflakes. It is also thought to contain the five Platonic solids, regular polygons which the ancient Greek philosopher Plato linked to the four elements of nature – earth, air, fire and water – making them the building blocks of the universe, which is the final element.

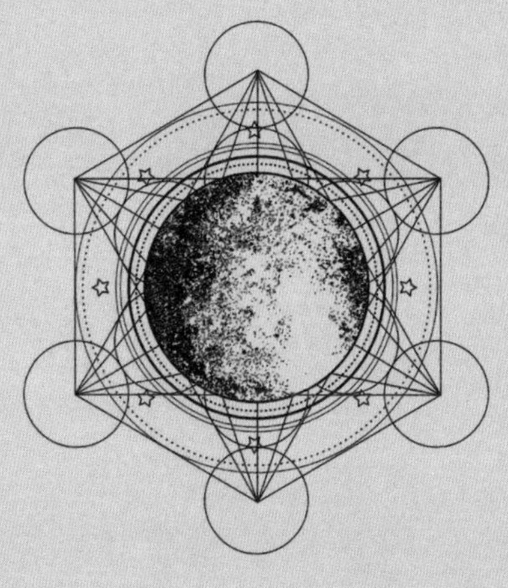

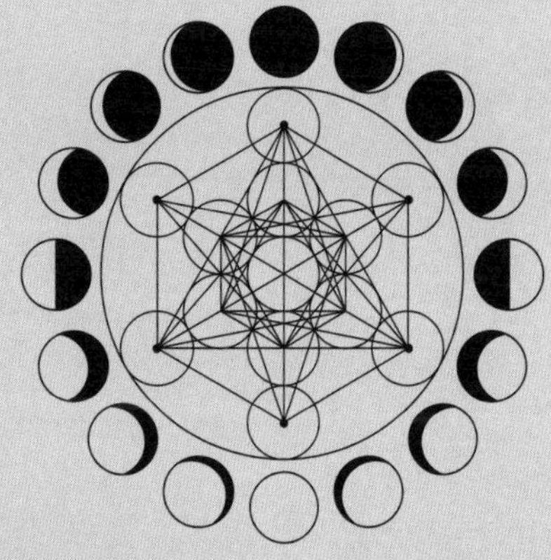

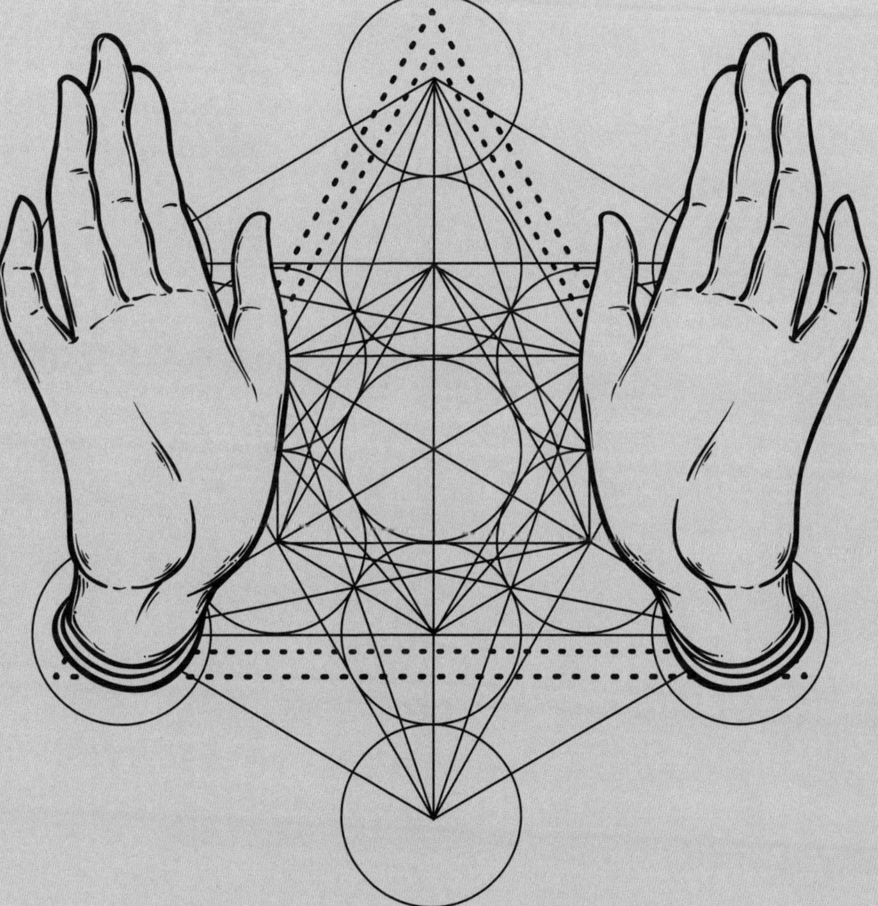

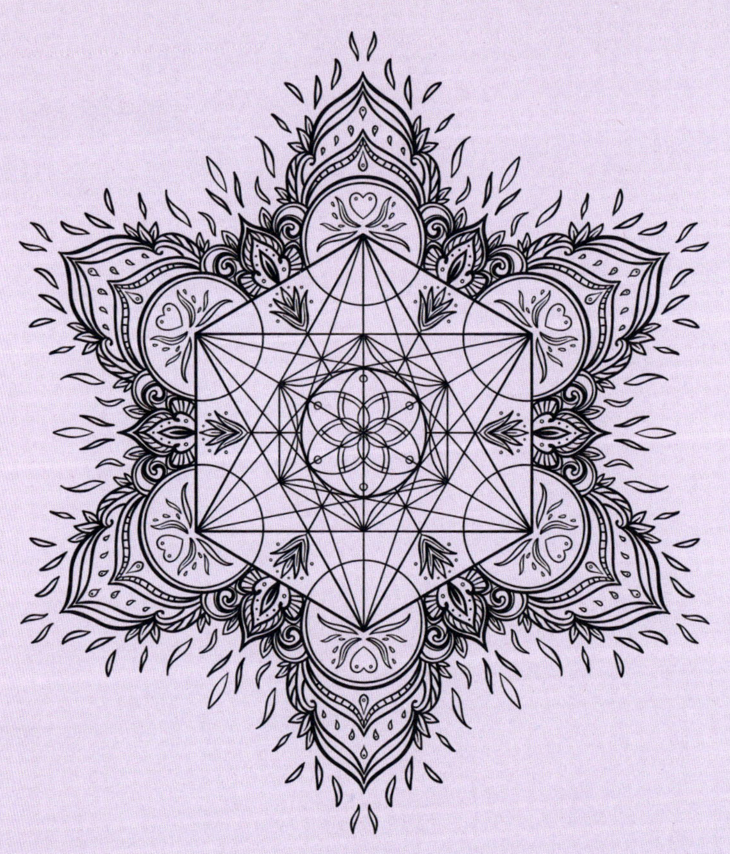

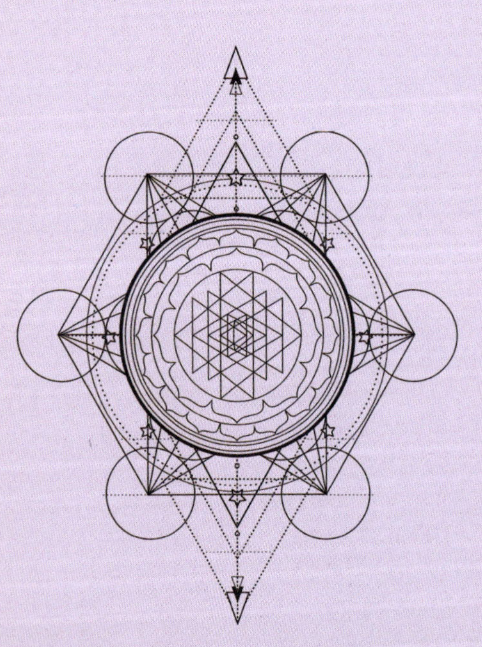

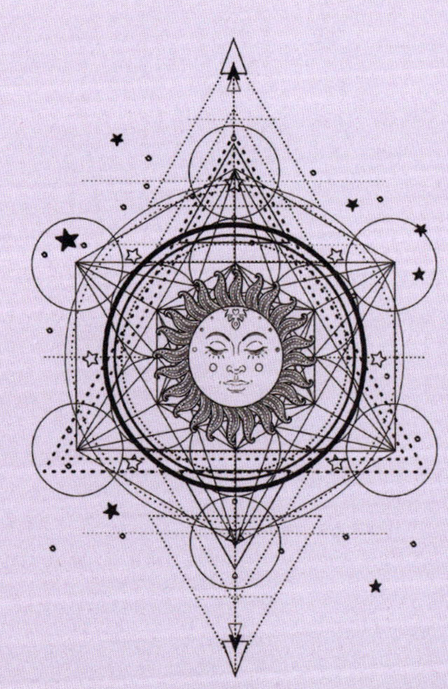

An angel's gift

Various religions and spiritual groups believe that the cube was gifted to humankind
by the Archangel Metatron, who was the first mortal to live on earth. He later
ascended to heaven and became one of the highest-ranking angels at God's side. In
this form Metatron is responsible for keeping a record of the good deeds of humans
and is linked to the tree of life.

The person associated with deciphering this symbol was the Italian 'Fibonacci',
otherwise known as Leonardo Pisano, one of the most talented mathematicians of
the Middle Ages. Since then, the symbol has grown in prominence, and is now used
around the world as a tool to generate positive energy and connect with the divine.

How to wear it

Due to the complexity of linework, this symbol works best on large, flat areas of
the body – the chest or the back, or perhaps parts of the arm or leg if it's a simple
design style. If the cube is appearing at a large scale on its own, or as part of a larger
design, dot-work shading can help bring depth and dynamism to the image without
it becoming illegible.

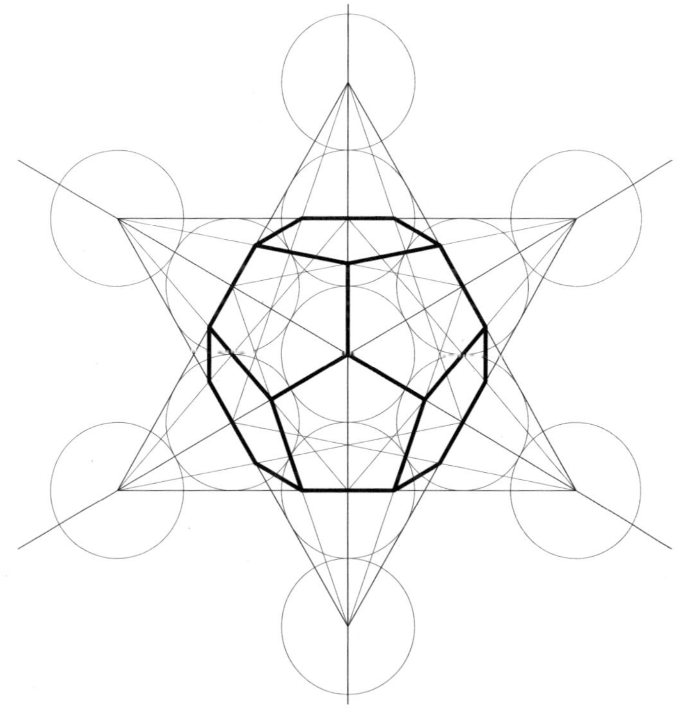

All images: **Metatron's cube is
hugely complex, however further
patterning can be added within
the design if it's shown at large
scale – this approach strengthens
the association with creativity.**

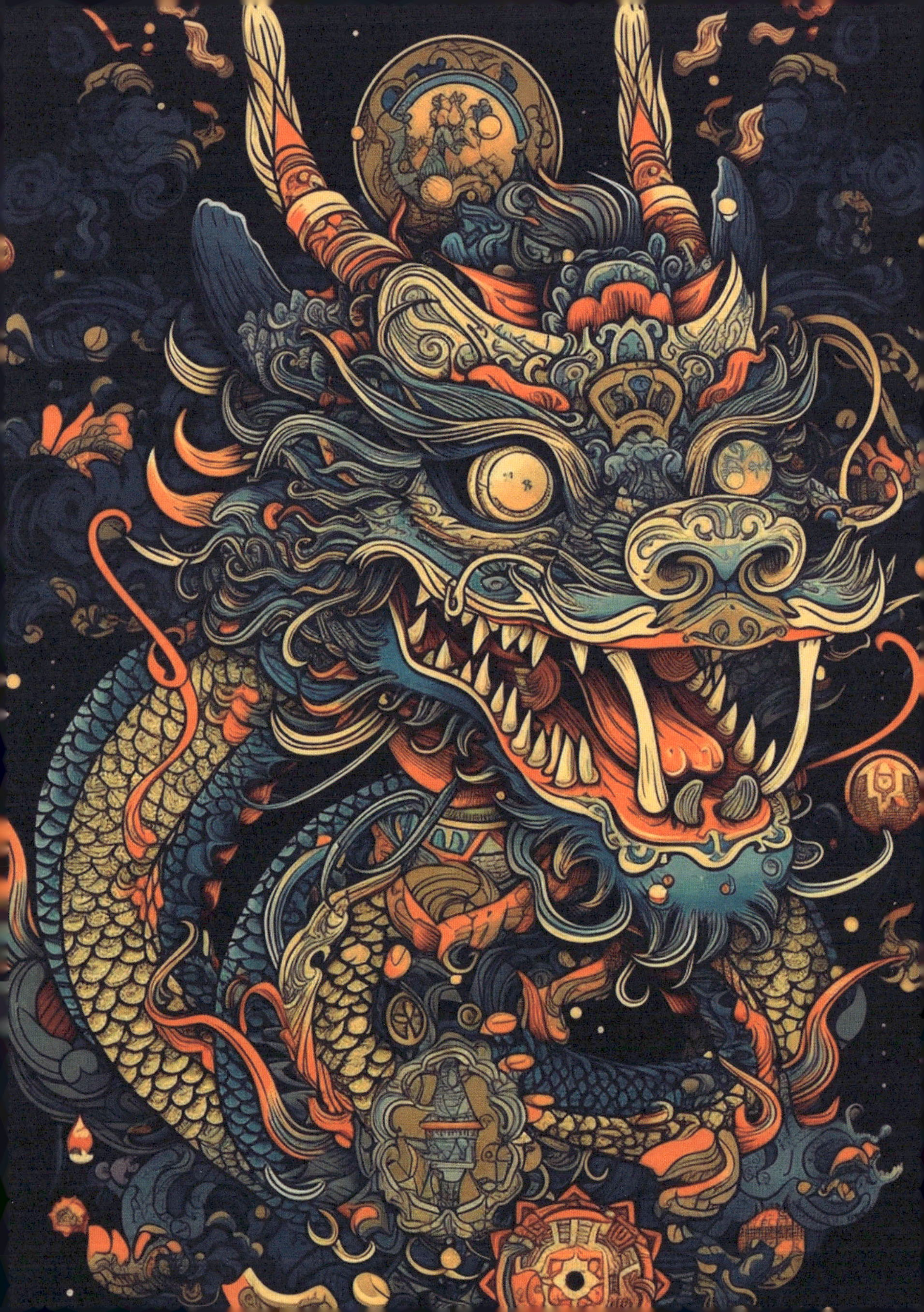

5

Birds and Beasts

Since the beginning of time, we have shared our world with other creatures. We have lived alongside them, finding favour and comfort with some, while fighting others for survival and sustenance. We have tried to dominate them and sometimes failed, but despite the complexity of our relationship with the animal kingdom, there has always been a fascination for the way they live and the strengths, talents and skills that they display.

Many ancient civilizations revered the creatures they encountered, putting them on a pedestal and linking them to their favourite deities. They told stories of their adventures and attributed magical powers to them. Sometimes they invented new, mythic beasts of epic proportions, like winged dragons and birds born from fire, who were often created by taking elements from existing creatures, and they gave them spiritual significance. Within these pages you will find some iconic animals and birds that have become symbols imbued with sacred power. All are unique emblems that make for striking tattoos in a range of styles.

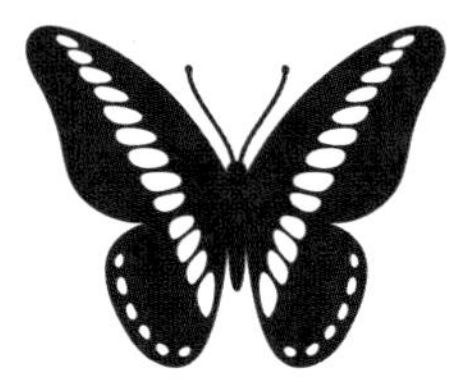

Butterfly

Transformation | Joy | Love | Freedom | Spirit

Sacred Origins
Egyptian, Greek, Celtic,
Christian, Chinese

Used Since
c. 1350 BCE

Tattoo Styles
Western traditional
Fine-line
Black-and-grey realism

Oppposite: From realistic (top left and centre) to abstract (top right), the butterfly consistently proves to be an adaptable symbol. In all styles, it's strongly associated with positivity and transformation.

These delicately beautiful creatures with gossamer-thin wings seem to radiate joy, but the real truth of their magic is in their miraculous transformation.

A painting in an ancient tomb

The ethereal charms of the butterfly have fascinated humankind for millions of years, with the earliest depictions dating back to around 1350 BCE when they were portrayed on an Egyptian tomb. Ancient peoples were transfixed by butterflies and their life cycle of going from caterpillar to cocoon and then emerging fully winged and altogether different, and they came up with a multitude of theories to explain the sacred nature of this insect. To them, the butterfly was a positive symbol associated with freedom, transformation and love.

The soul's journey

The Greek philosopher Aristotle attributed the word 'psyche' to the butterfly, believing that each cocoon was like a tomb, and the winged wonder that broke free was the spirit leaving the body and moving on to the next life. Indeed, the Greeks associated this creature with Pysche, the goddess of the soul. Christians too embraced the idea of resurrection, linking the rebirth of the caterpillar to Christ rising from the dead. In ancient China, the butterfly was seen as a representation of the inner spiritual nature of a person, first mentioned in the story 'Zhuang Zhou Dreams of Being a Butterfly' written around 300 BCE. This early tale went on to inspire many artists and writers.

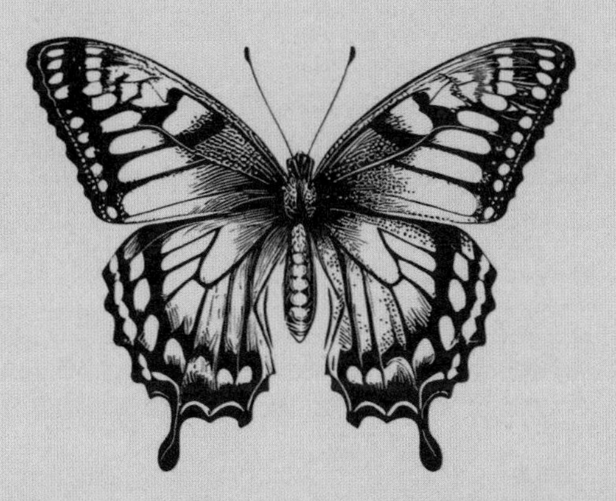

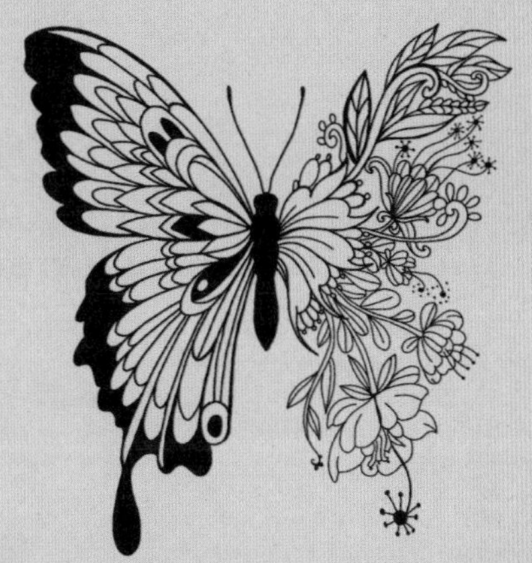

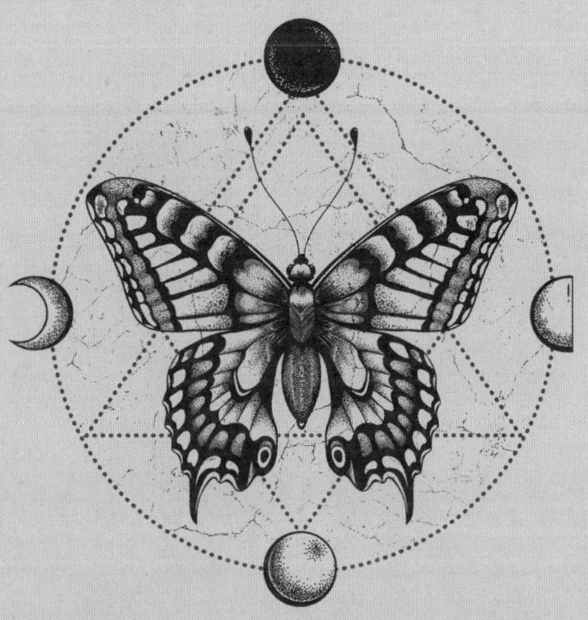

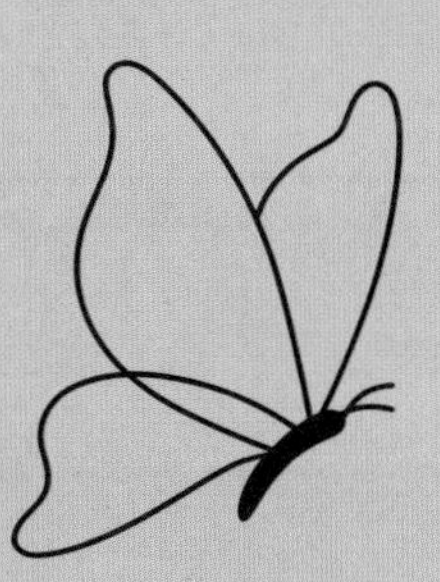

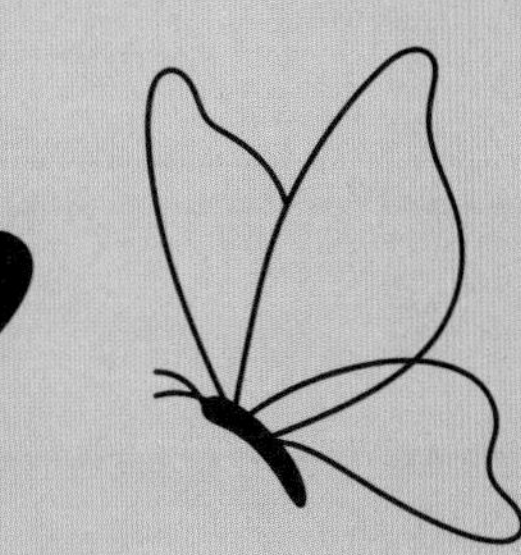

How to wear it

The butterfly can be tattooed in many styles, from Western traditional to modern
geometric – and all that lies in between. It is often positioned on the wrist so
that the wearer is easily reminded of its meaning. However, the versatile nature of
butterfly designs means they will work in many places.

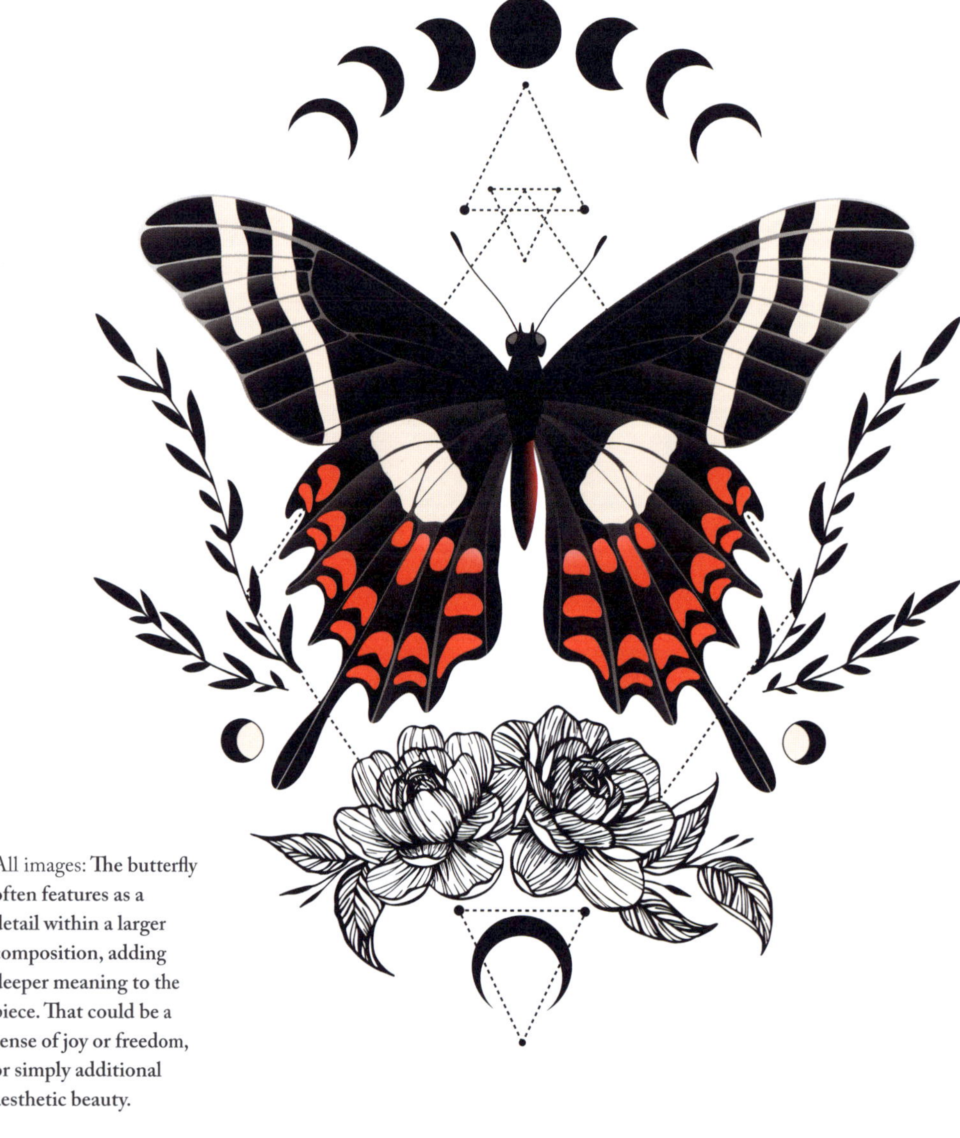

All images: The butterfly
often features as a
detail within a larger
composition, adding
deeper meaning to the
piece. That could be a
sense of joy or freedom,
or simply additional
aesthetic beauty.

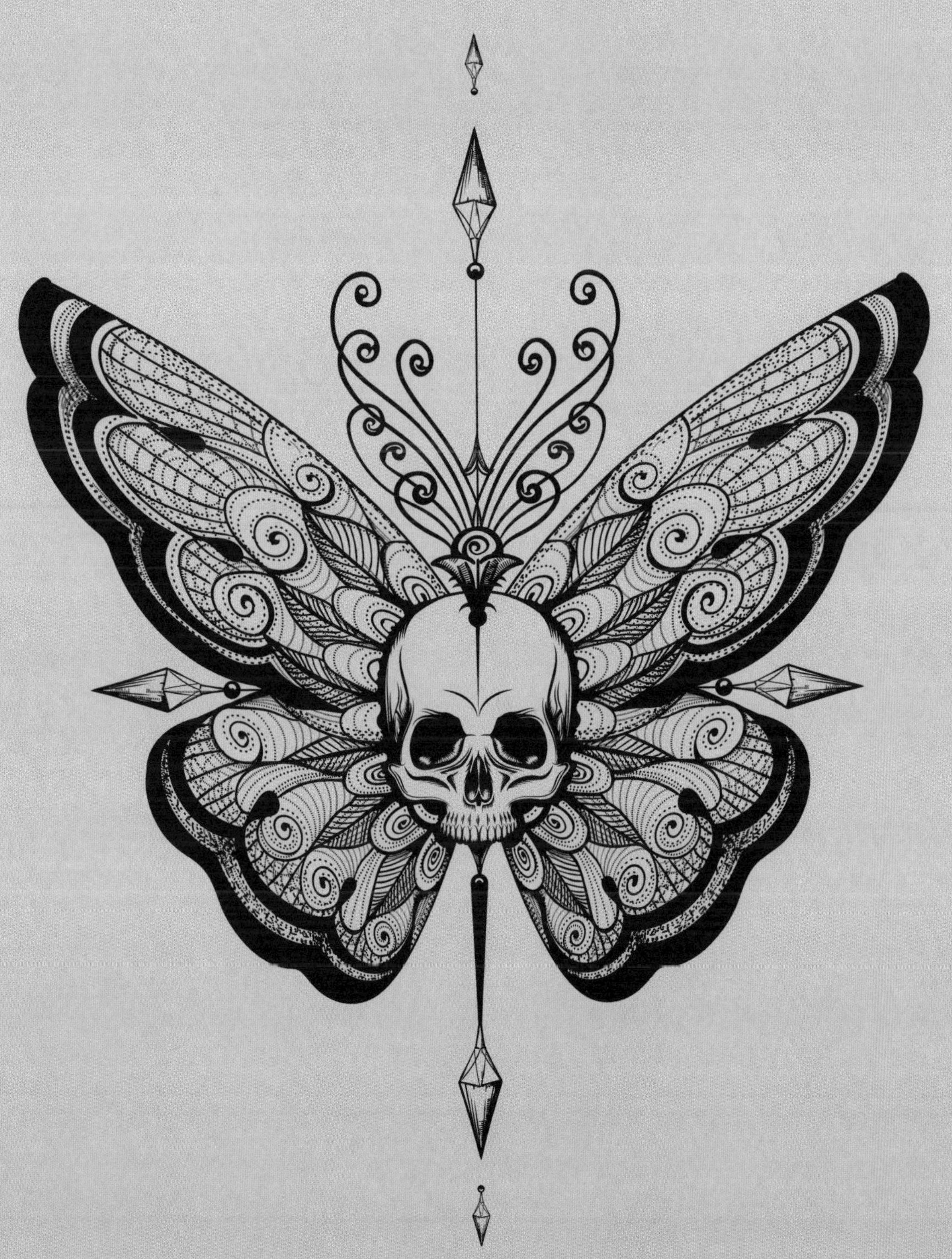

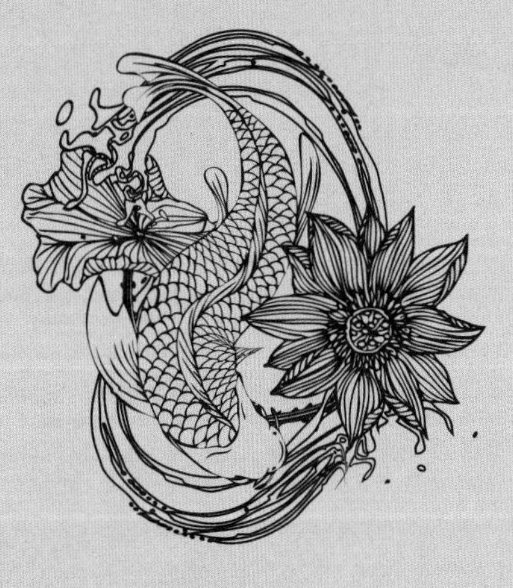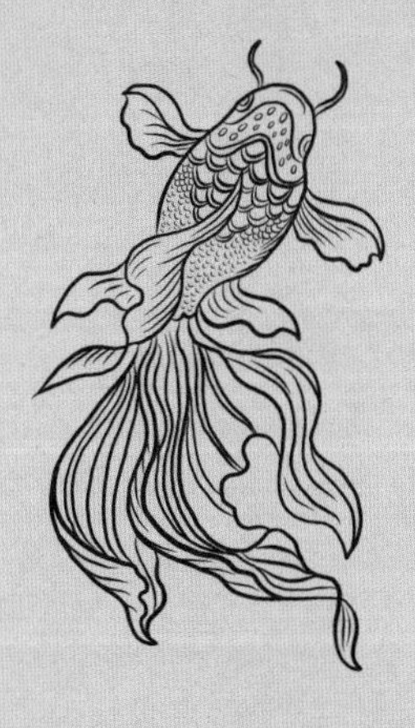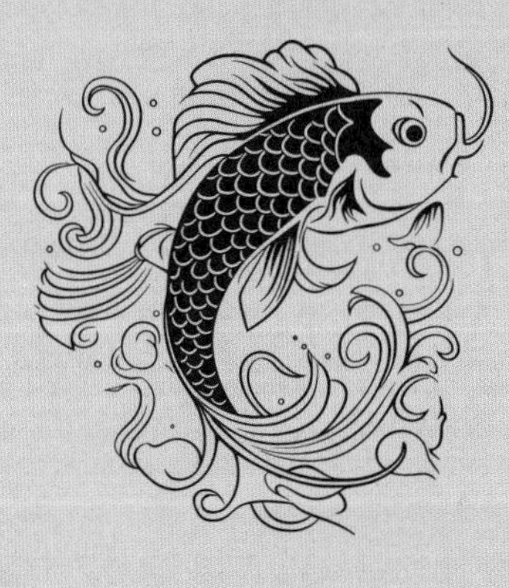

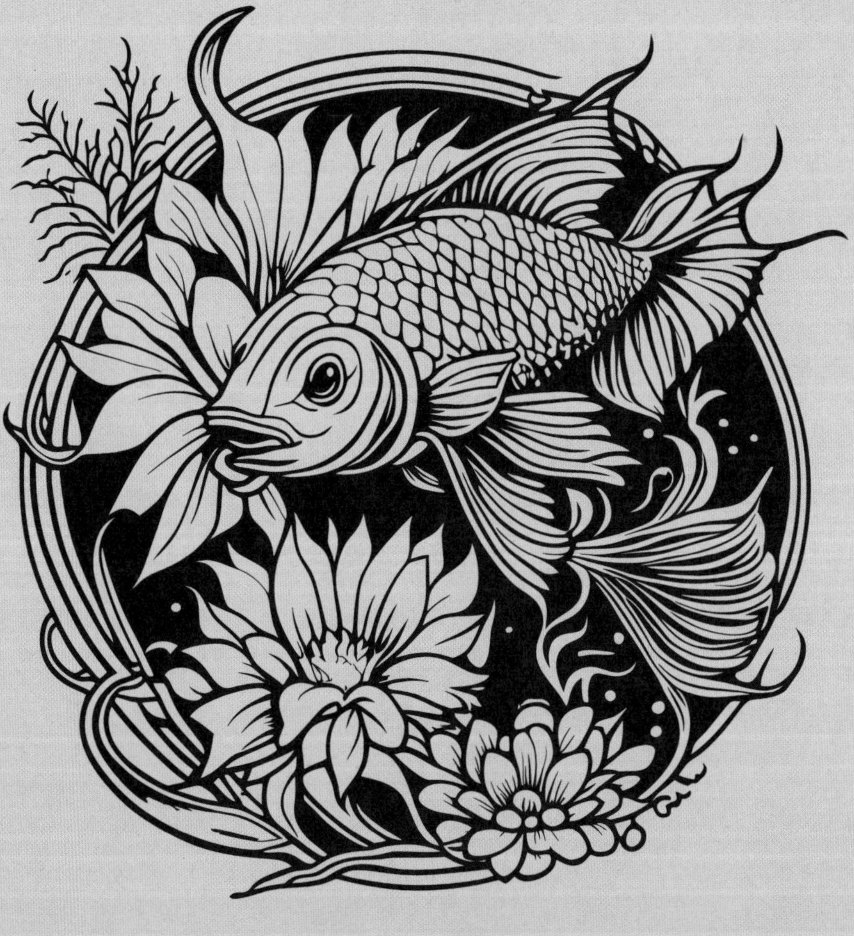

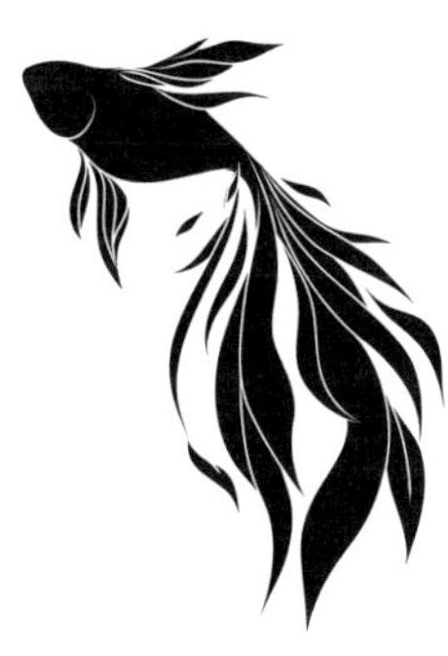

Fish

Faith | Spirituality | Wisdom | Good fortune | Fulfilment

Sacred Origins
Christian, Greek,
Roman, Celtic, Chinese,
Buddhist

Used Since
1st century

Tattoo Styles
Japanese
Fine-line
Western traditional

Opposite: The chosen species of fish defines the meaning of a fish tattoo. A goldfish (top left) communicates a sense of fortune. A carp (bottom) is associated with bounty and abundance.

The fish is an important and sacred symbol for many cultures, although it is most commonly associated with Christianity.

An acrostic with meaning

In the early days of Christianity, the fish was used as a symbol which revealed a person's faith to the initiated, but helped to keep it hidden from prying eyes. It appeared in Christian artwork during the 2nd century, based upon the Greek word for fish, Ichthys. An acrostic was then created, *Iesous Christos theou huios soter*, which translates as the phrase 'Jesus Christ, God's Son, Saviour.'

Sign of faith

This emblem was used to mark underground meeting places and conceal their whereabouts from Roman soldiers. In this form it was often combined with other symbols like bread and wine. The symbol was also carved upon the tombs of the dead to showcase their faith and help them move on to the afterlife, marked on the doors of believers, or worn as jewellery which could be covered if a threat was perceived. It was said that if a stranger should meet another upon the path, they would carve the first arc of the fish into the dirt, and if the stranger responded by drawing the second, then they were in safe company.

The Salmon of Knowledge

Although the fish symbol is largely associated with Christianity, it was used years before by the Romans and Greeks to represent feminine power and often linked to the light of the moon, as the original emblem was formed from two interlocking crescent moons. To the Celts, the sacred fish was the salmon.

Revered by the Druids, this slippery character came to their attention as it leaped up waterfalls in a bid to spawn. The fact that it could dwell in both fresh and saltwater gave it even more significance, and its mastery of air meant it was a creature that could command three realms. Soon the legend evolved of the Salmon of Knowledge, a fish that lived in the Well of Wisdom and had swallowed nuts from the magical hazel tree, absorbing all the wisdom in the universe.

In Chinese culture, the sacred fish was the generous carp, a beautiful, bountiful being, associated with strength and abundance. Tibetan Buddhists prized the golden carp for its ability to traverse the length of two sacred rivers which were imbued by the light of the sun and moon. They believed it was the ultimate symbol of contentment.

How to wear it

Depending on the choice of fish, they can be tattooed in a number of styles. This could be abstract, inspired by Japanese art, Celtic or Western traditional, and they are often positioned on the arm as part of an elaborate sleeve – especially if a Japanese style is chosen. It is safe to assume that the koi fish is the most tattooed of all fish and often features at large scale and in full colour on the body. Some of the most powerful back designs feature koi; this symbol is a staple part of the tattoo vernacular.

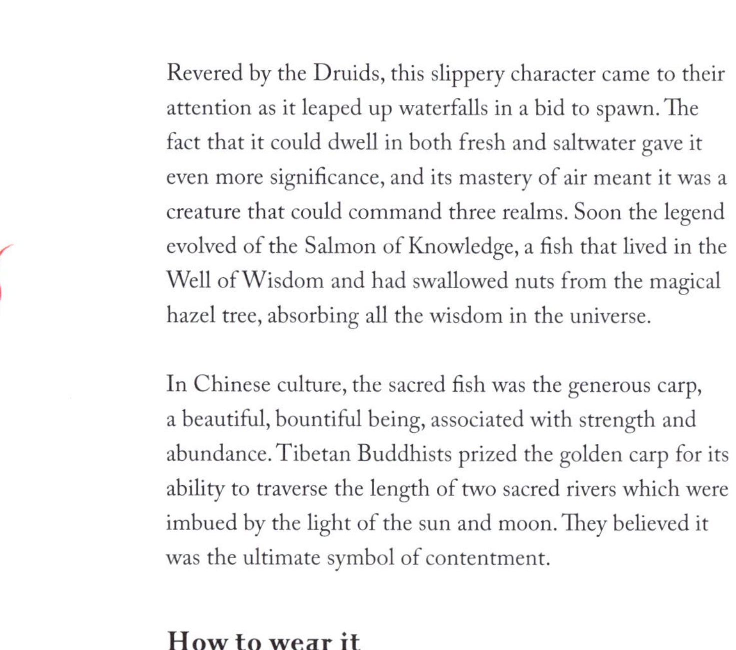

Left and opposite: **A koi fish – a popular choice in Japanese tattooing – shown swimming against the current can indicate perseverance over adversity or overcoming a struggle of fortune.**

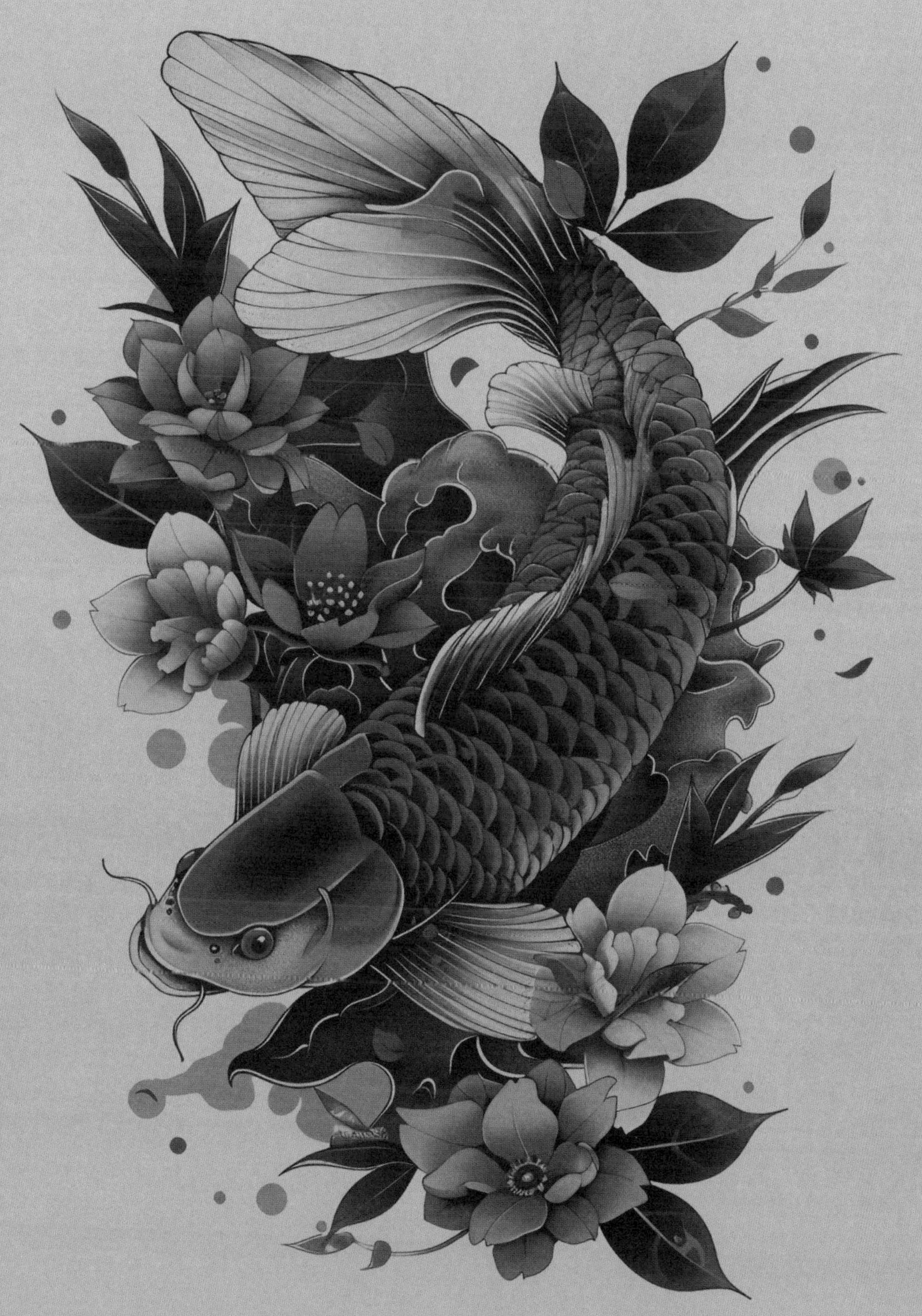

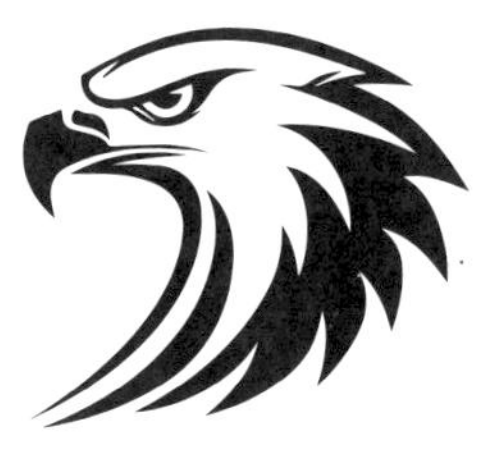

Eagle

Courage | Strength | Imperial power | Freedom | Victory

Sacred Origins
Roman, Greek, Celtic

Used Since
27 BCE (beginning of the Roman Empire)

Tattoo Styles
Western traditional
Fine-line
Black-and-grey realism

Opposite: The eagle – strongly linked to a sense of freedom – works well when tattooed in its realistic form (top). A stylized, Celtic representation (bottom right) links to Celtic culture and its reverence of the eagle. Featuring just the head (bottom left) hints at the concept of courage and victory associated with the symbol.

The ultimate king of the skies, the eagle is a prominent symbol of courage, strength and majesty throughout the world.

Messenger of the gods

The eagle was venerated by ancient cultures, who must have been awestruck at the sheer size and ability of this bird on the wing. To the Greeks, it was associated with Zeus, the king of the gods, and thought to be a personal messenger for the deity. Often pictured at the side of his throne, according to legend it was the trusty eagle who stole the young Prince Ganymede away to Mount Olympus to become the pantheon's cup bearer.

A national emblem and standard

The Celts believed the eagle was one of the oldest and most sacred creatures on earth and a messenger between realms, one of many civilizations who revered the bird's ability to soar through the heavens. Native American tribes prized eagle feathers, as did Highland clan chiefs in Scotland, who wore them as a mark of bravery. To the Romans, the eagle was synonymous with imperial power, used as a standard for the Roman Legion. Held aloft a pole and made of silver or bronze, the eagle was usually depicted with its wings outstretched in a pose to show off its magnificence, while the double-headed eagle was adopted as the symbol of the Byzantine Empire and is still used today on the Albanian flag.

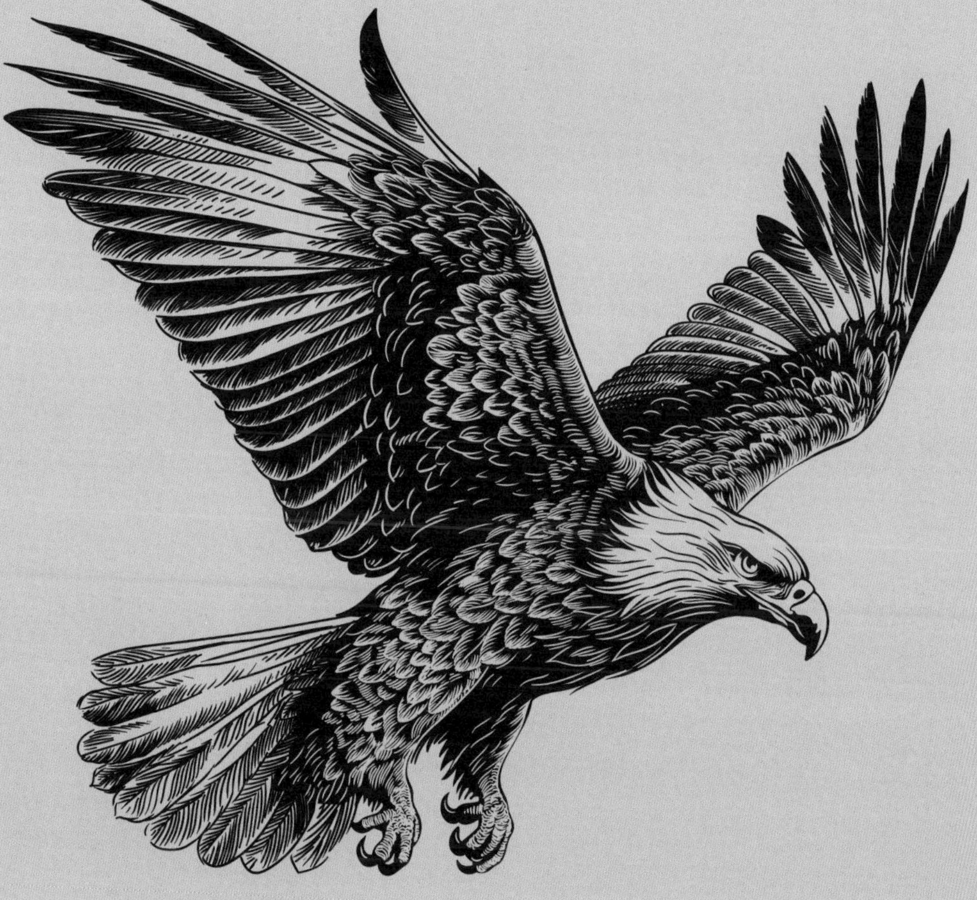

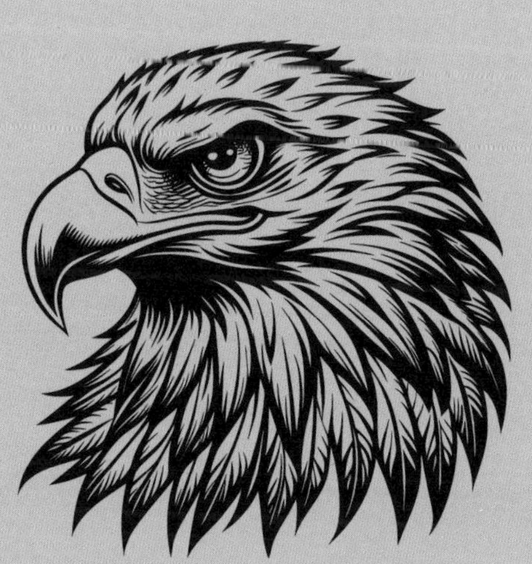

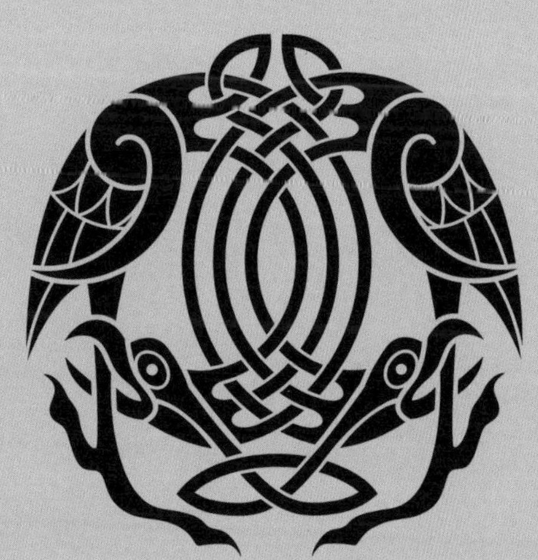

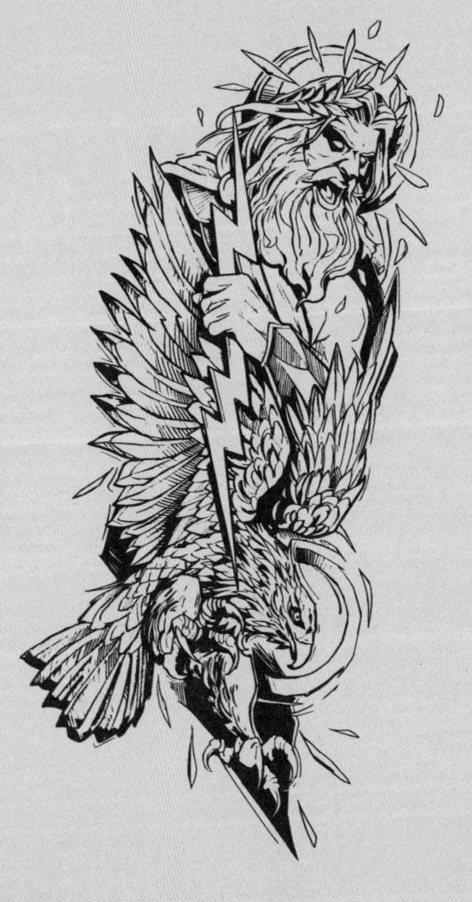

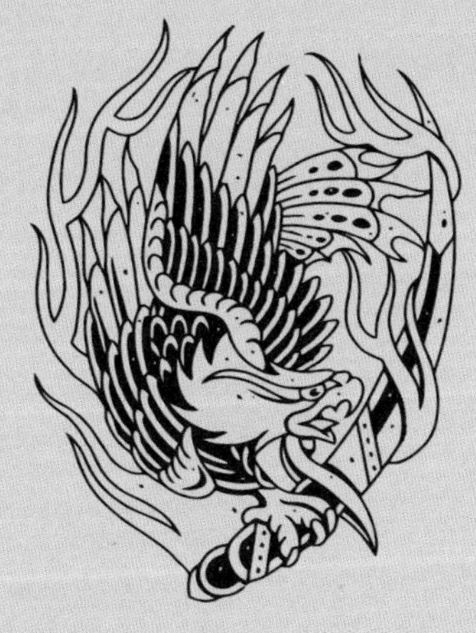

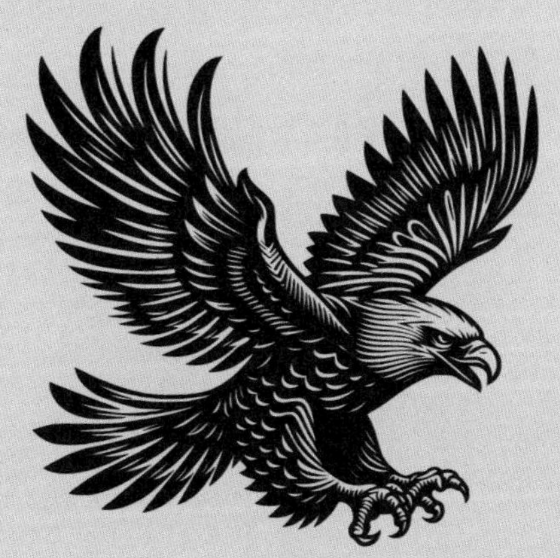

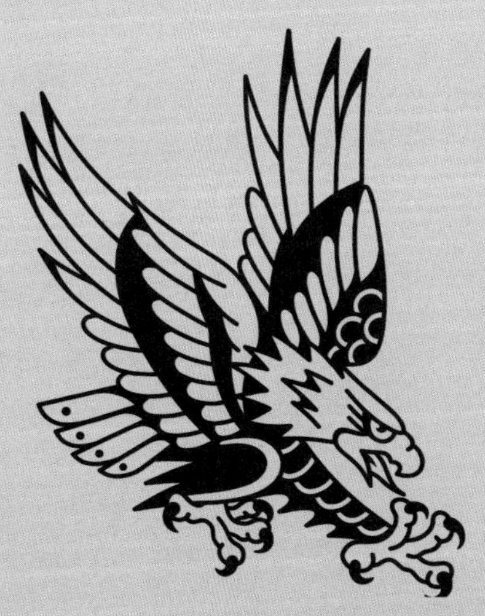

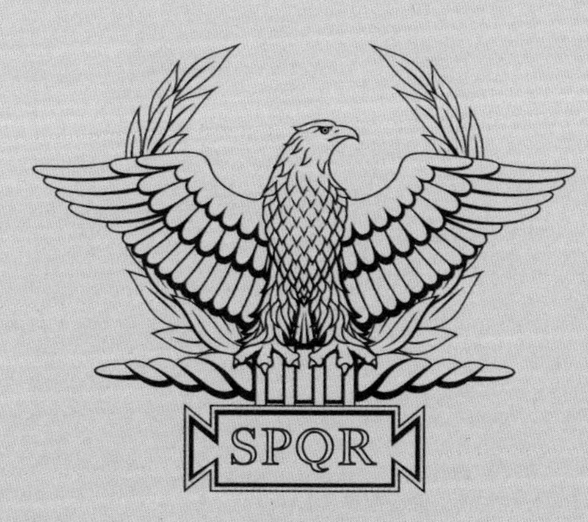
SPQR

How to wear it

The eagle is most often seen tattooed on the arms, chest or back. If the bird is in flight, this suggests attainment of goals and freedom, while an eagle with its claws spread ready to pounce is a sign of dominance and power. There is no style more used when it comes to tattooed eagles than the Western traditional style. Bold lines, heavy black and a strong but limited colour palette is the perfect combination for such an iconic bird.

Opposite: An eagle pictured with Zeus (top left) signifies the strong connection between the king of the gods and the equally strong and majestic bird. The most prolific style choice for the eagle is Western traditional style (bottom left and top right), it doesn't get more iconic.

Right: An eagle in flight and clasping a sword is a clear symbol of strength and freedom.

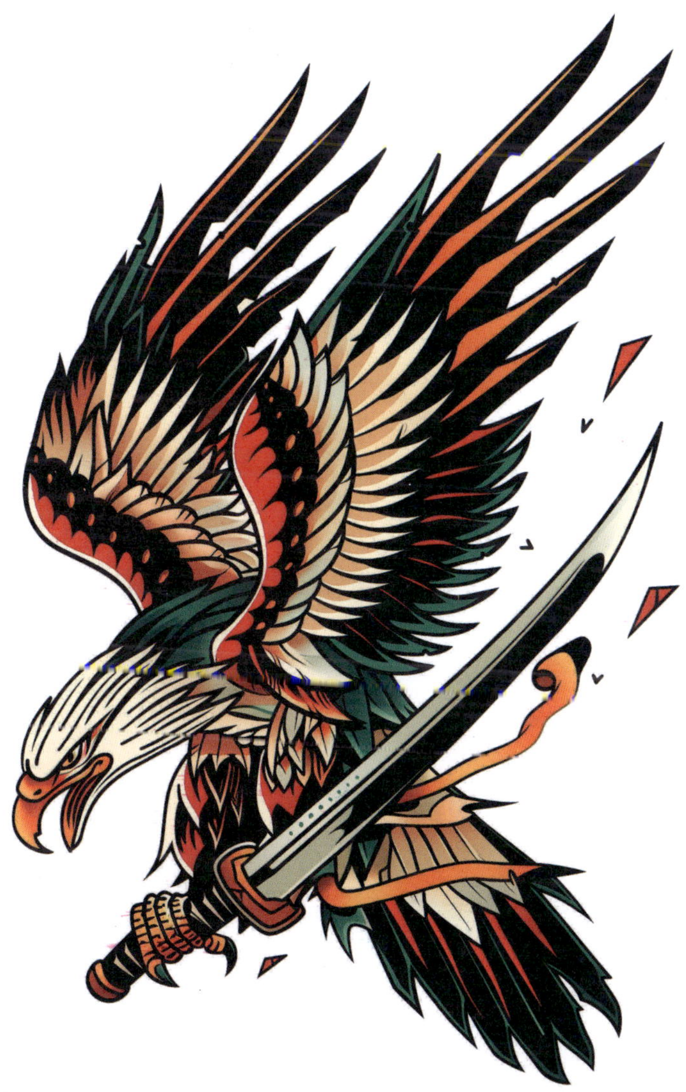

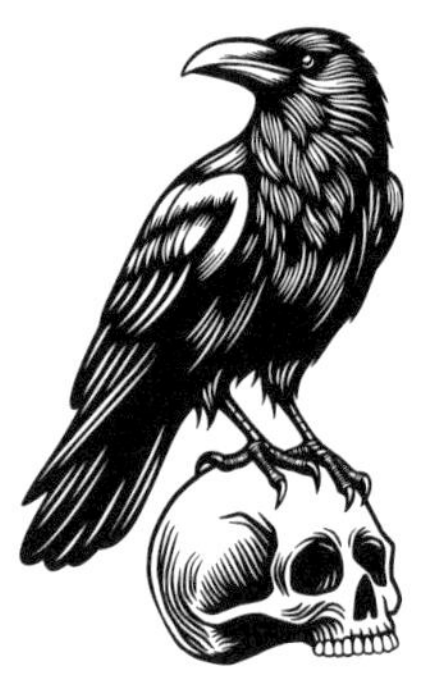

Raven

Mystery | Magic | Superstition | Wisdom | Transformation

Sacred Origins
Greek, Celtic, Norse,
Native American

Used Since
Bronze Age

Tattoo Styles
Western tradtional
Fine-line
Black-and-grey realism

Opposite: Often featuring in a Norse-themed sleeve (bottom right) the raven also works well as a focal symbol or as a background element. A perched pose helps communicate the concept of wisdom.

Crows and ravens, with their glossy black plumage and shrill caws, have frequently been associated with mystery and magic, featuring in the mythologies of many civilizations.

A scorching curse

Mythologies often muddle crows and ravens together as they are similar in appearance and from the same family, but in truth the raven is a much bigger bird. This avian featured in Greek mythology as the cohort of the sun god Apollo, but in this instance, he had white feathers. Being a loyal servant to the god, the crow – or sometimes a raven depending on the version – kept a watchful eye on his lover, the Princess Coronis. When he reported that she had found a mortal man to marry, Apollo was so angry that he set a curse upon the bird which scorched its feathers black and changed its voice to a raucous screech.

Deathly omens and keepers of secrets

To the Celts, both crows and ravens were associated with the triple goddess Morrigan. A powerful deity synonymous with war and death, she would take the form of this bird as she gathered the souls of deceased warriors. The Norse peoples revered the crow as a symbol of their most important god, Odin, although some suggest it was the raven he favoured. It was thought that he had two birds, one upon each shoulder, which were his faithful companions. Each day he would send them out on a mission to visit all the realms and gather knowledge, and each night they would return with stories to fuel his wisdom. This myth went some way to ensure that both the crow and the raven were held in high regard and considered birds of mystery, the keepers of secrets. Some Native American tribes also believed them to be sacred, messengers from

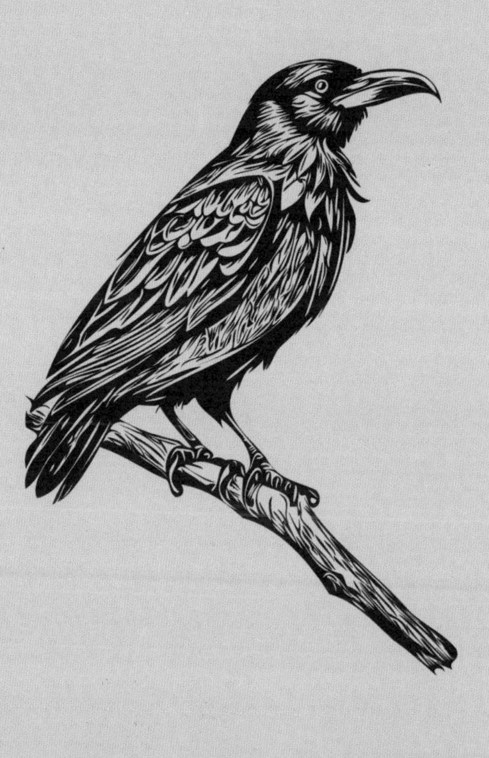

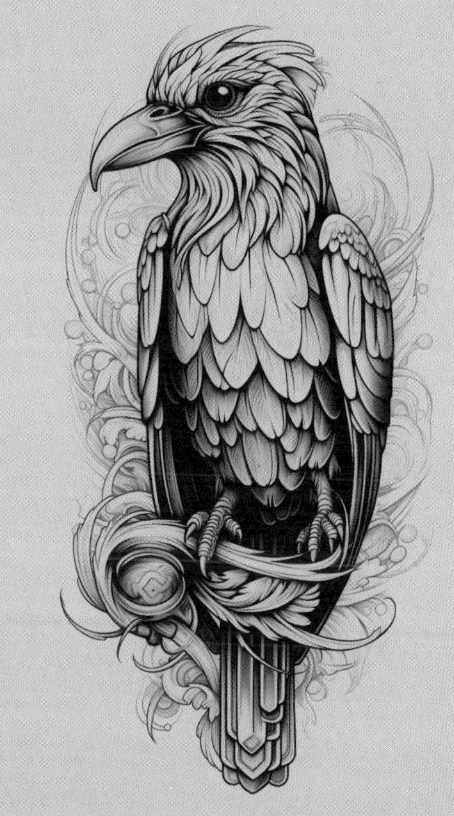

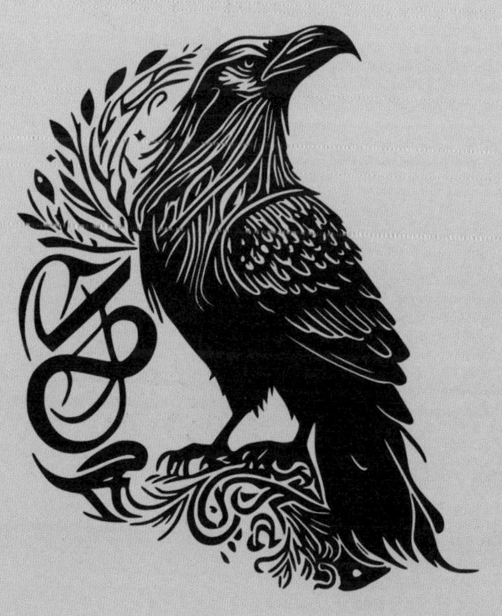

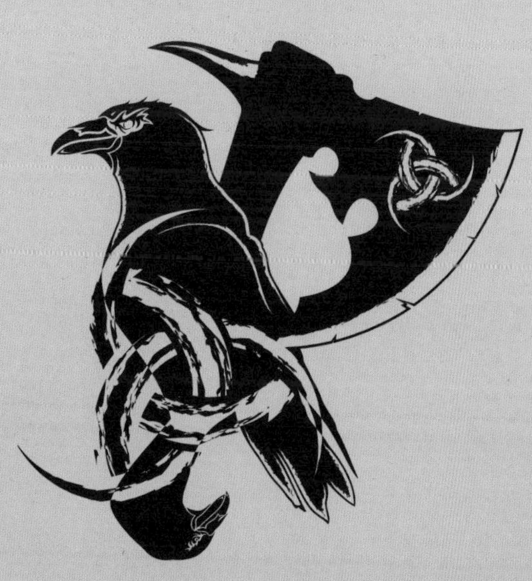

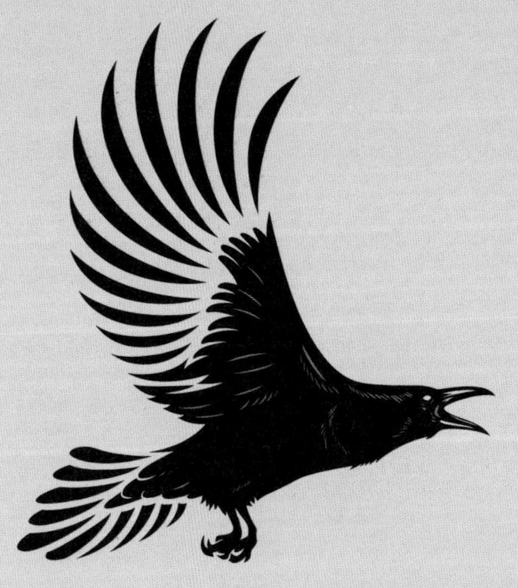

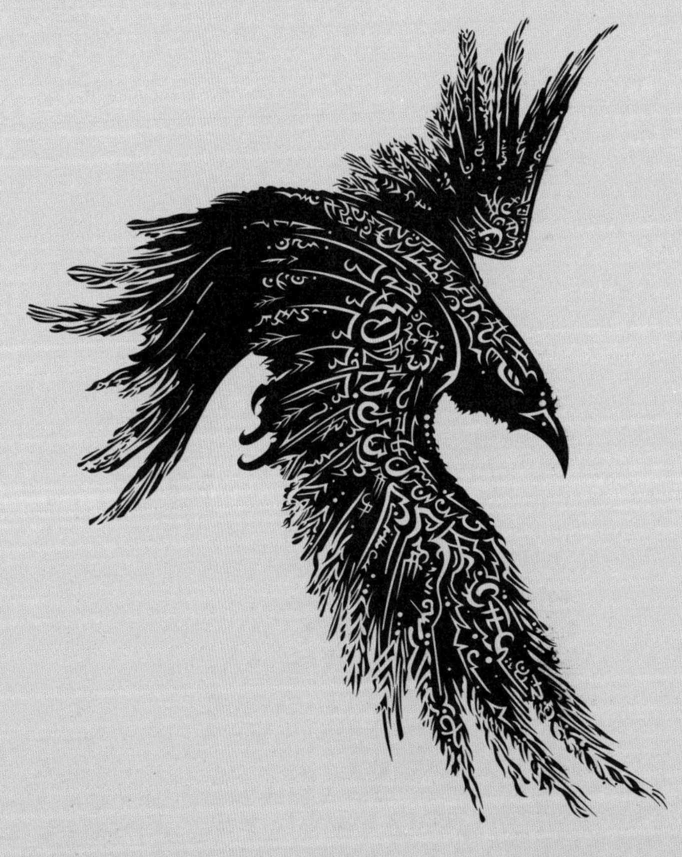
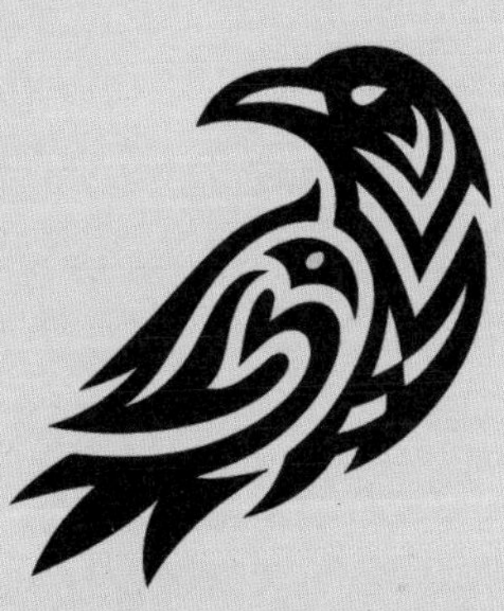
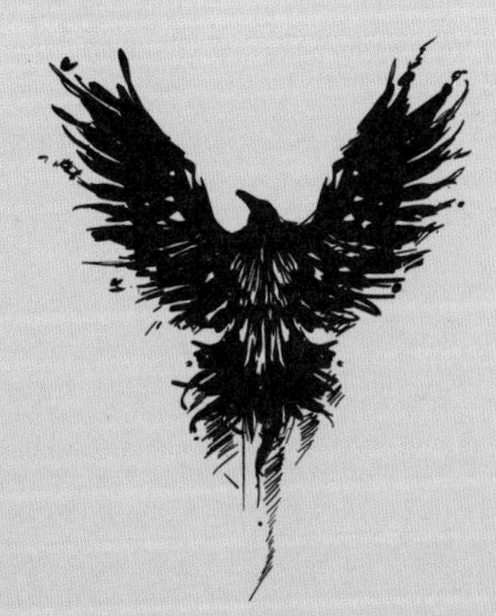

the spirit world, tricksters clothed in feathers and
sometimes an omen of death. Ravens in particular
were seen as wily and often credited with the creation
of the earth.

During the Middle Ages crows were associated with
witches and seen as harbingers of doom, but the root
of this superstition was probably because of the colour
of their feathers and the fact that they raided grain
stores, so were considered a pest by farmers.

How to wear it

Birds work wonderfully as tattoo subject matter, the
dynamic in-flight poses that can be achieved and the
repetition within the feather structures that create
a pattern-like feel lend themselves well to the art
form, and crows/ravens are no exception. Their dark
silhouette means they translate well at small scale;
if a higher level of detail is added they also scale
up successfully. Their dark colouring lends itself to
tattooing them in black and grey, although
sometimes blue tones or a strong eye colour
can work well.

Opposite: **A raven in flight
adds some dynamism to a
design (top left, bottom left,
bottom right). The addition of
a skull communicates a sense
of memorial. The crow or raven
also links to the Celtic goddess
Morrigan (right middle).**

Right: **Ravens and crows
have strong assocations with
intelligence and wiliness.**

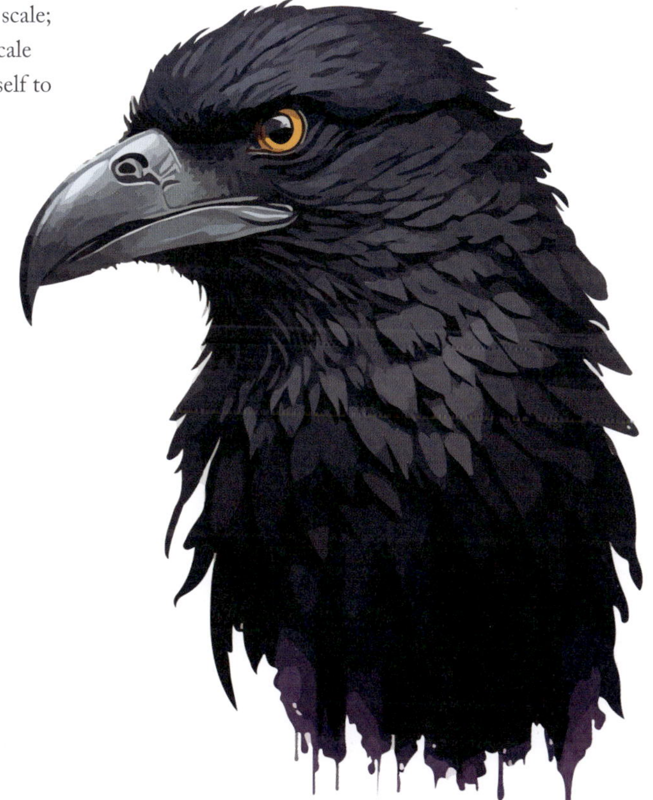

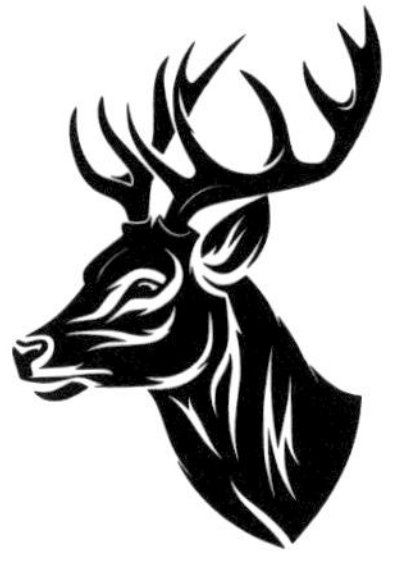

Stag

Strength | Grace | Magic | Nature | Abundance

Sacred Origins
Greek, Roman, Celtic

Used Since
Late Stone Age

Tattoo Styles
Western tradtional
Fine-line
Black-and-grey realism

Opposite: The stag possesses a strong silhouette (right column), its large antlers (top left) are the defining characteristic, communicating strength and animal grace. A simple blackwork representation (bottom right) signifies fertility, prosperity and abundance.

The stag, with its magnificent antlers, holds itself with poise – a symbol of grace, strength and the power of nature.

An emblem of the horned god

It's no surprise that this mighty beast was sacred to the Greek goddess of the hunt, Artemis, and her Roman counterpart Diana. Cave paintings dating back 40,000 years demonstrate the significance of the stag to early civilizations. The Celts prized its antlers, which were often used to create tools and weapons. They believed it was an emblem of prosperity, thanks to its association with the hunt and the meat that it provided to sustain them. Their god of fertility and wild animals, Cernunnos, was linked to the creature, and early depictions of him show antlers protruding from his brow. He wasn't the only one to assume the stag's characteristics; it was commonplace in folklore for characters to shapeshift into this form to flee persecution.

Saint Eustace in the woods

The white stag in particular was synonymous with purity and magic. The Celts believed it to be a symbol of the presence of the Otherworld, while to the Christians it was related to Jesus Christ, thanks to the legend of St Eustace. Once a Roman soldier, Eustace was hunting in the woods when he happened upon a white stag with a cross between its antlers. The sight of this eventually led to his conversion.

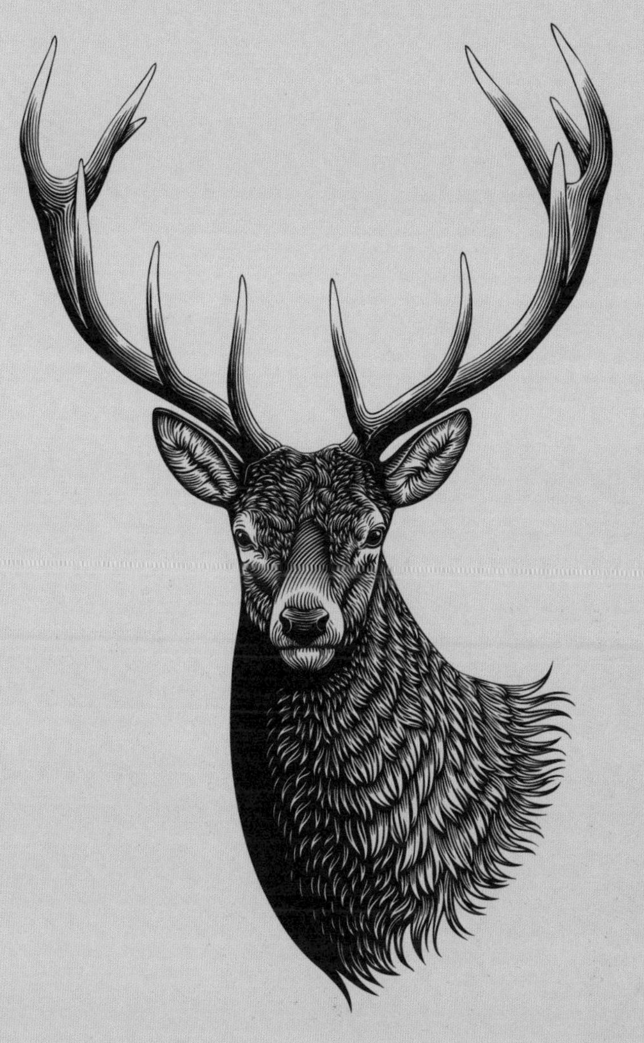

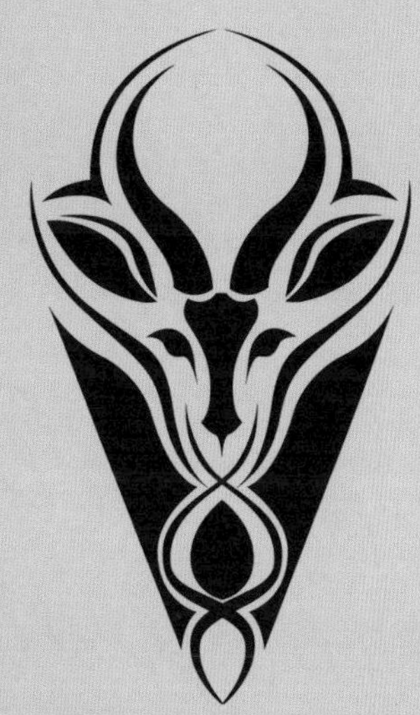

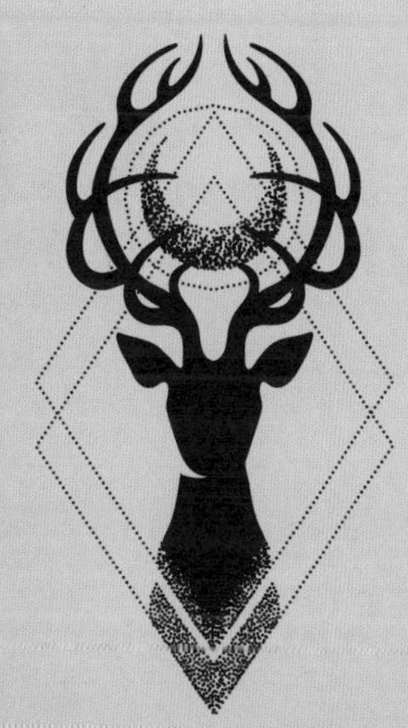

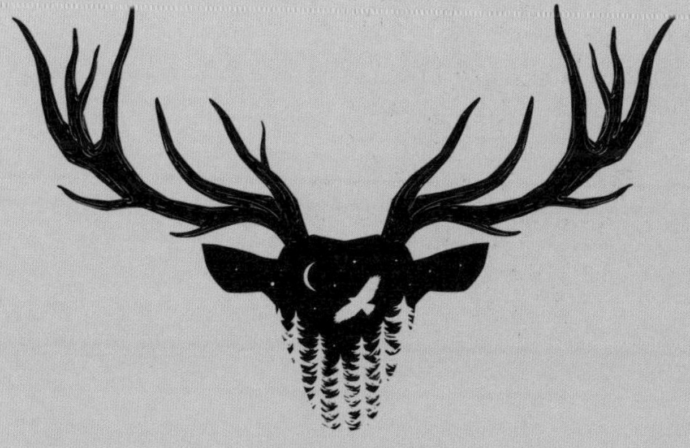

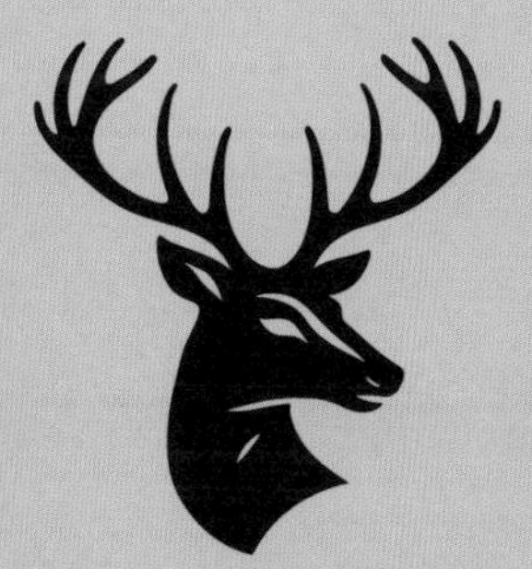

How to wear it

The stag is relatively versatile when it comes to styling. It works well in a bold traditional style but perhaps even better when tattooed in black and grey or a very fine-line style. The stag is often accompanied by other aspects of nature, like trees, and flowers, but its grace and strength is highlighted if it's placed boldly by itself at a reasonable scale.

Opposite: The stylized fine-line portrayal of the stag (top right) adjacent to the more realisic rendering (top left) showcases the versatility of this symbol.

Right: Combining natural flora and fauna with the stag communicates the connection to the power of nature that this symbol holds.

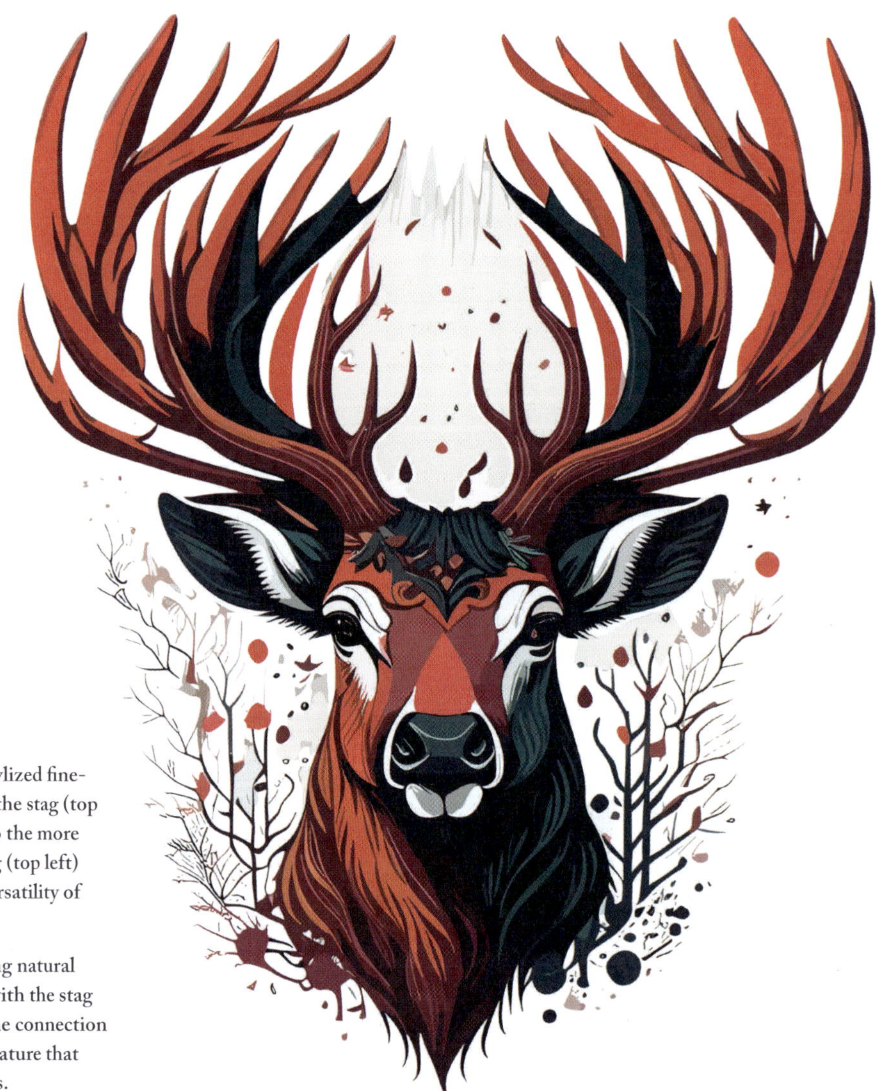

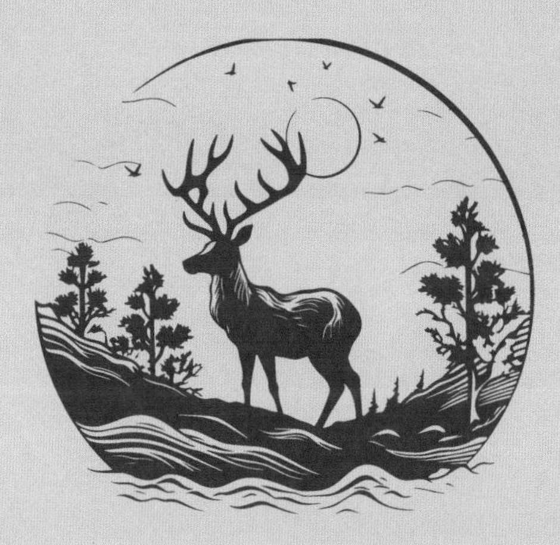

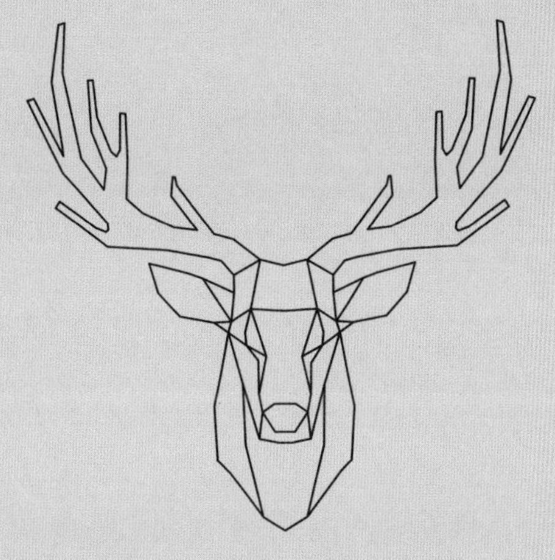

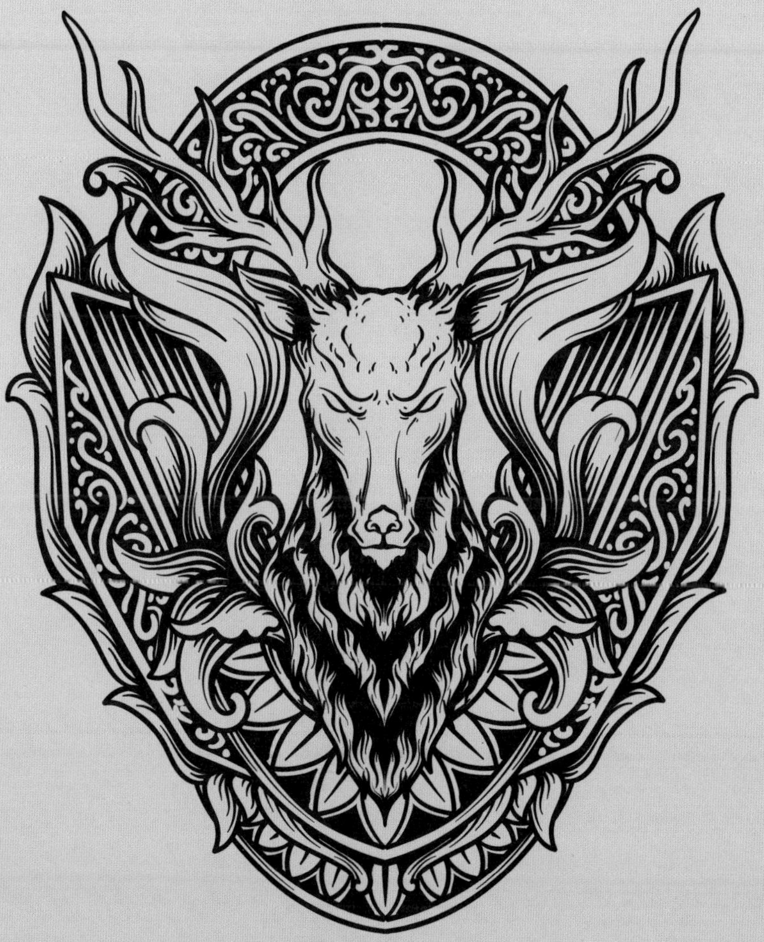

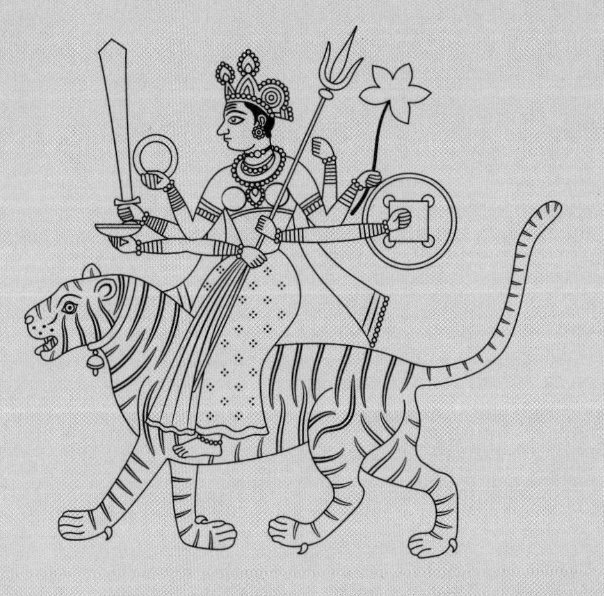

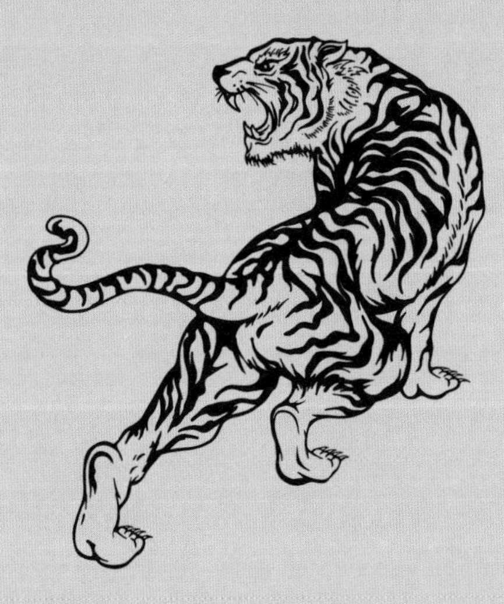

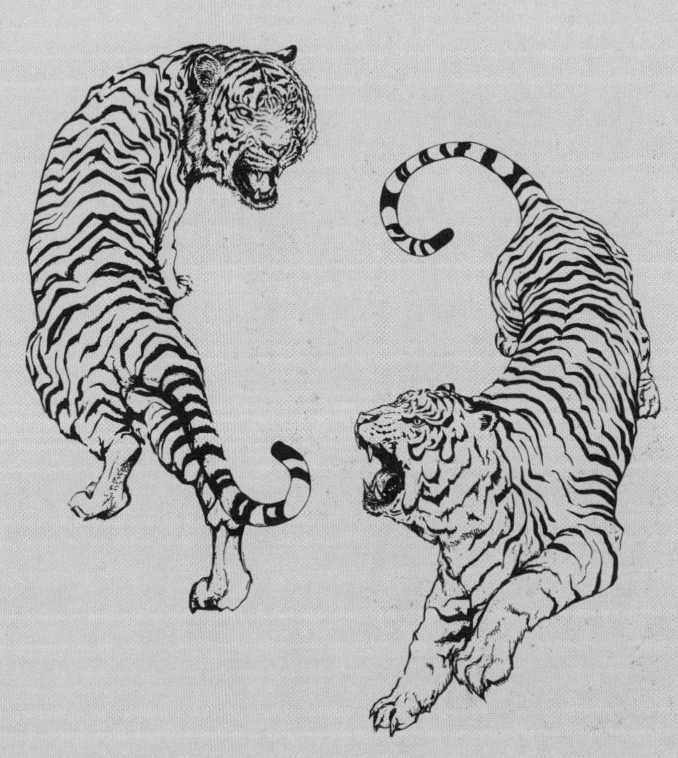

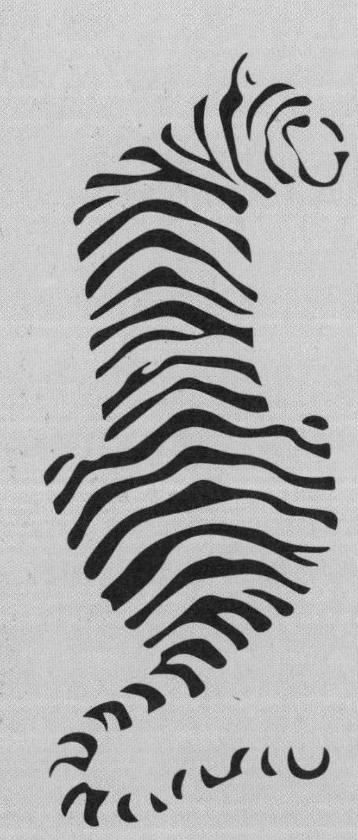

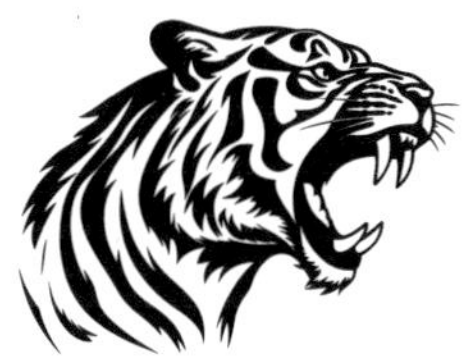

Tiger

Power | Energy | Courage | Abundance | Good fortune

Sacred Origins
Chinese, Taoist, Indian

Used Since
Stone Age

Tattoo Styles
Japanese
Fine-line
Western traditional

Opposite: It's diffiicult to portray a greater sense of power in a tattoo than with a tiger in a Japanese style (top right). More playful images are achievable utilising the tiger's famous stripes (bottom right). The Hindu goddess Durga (top left) is pictured riding a tiger and is a symbol of justice.

The mighty tiger is a powerful symbol around the world, but it is especially revered by the Chinese, who believe the beast to be the perfect embodiment of Yang energy.

Talismans and tokens

Known as the King of the Beasts or the King of the Mountain and associated with masculinity and the radiance of the sun, tiger populations were once dense in southern China and people lived alongside these majestic creatures. Having witnessed first-hand the energy and ferocity of the animal they were instantly enamoured, believing that an image or idol fashioned in the shape of the creature could ward off fire, thieves and evil spirits from the home. As early as the Neolithic Age, tiger-shaped tokens were used as talismans, kept about the person or in their abode, often crafted from bronze or jade. The image of a tiger was also frequently used to decorate porcelain.

The white tiger

Often paired with dragons in artistic renditions, tigers were one of the four sacred beasts, known as the guardians or gods of the cosmos. Each one of these creatures represented a quadrant of the sky and was associated with key components. In this form, the white tiger, known as Baihu, is linked to the season of autumn and the element of metal, with themes of power, fortune and abundance. Here, it plays a key role in maintaining balance within the Universe.

Lords of the forest

The Chinese weren't the only ones to see the spiritual potential of this creature. Indigenous communities in India also celebrated the power of these big cats. Living in tribal groups in the forest, they built 'tiger temples' which were filled with idols of Waghoba, a primeval tiger god, renowned for protection. Some of those early tribes believed that tigers were the owners of the forest, and that worshipping them would keep them happy and secure a hefty amount of rainfall for the crops. The Hindu warrior goddess Durga, the protective mother of the Universe and a representation of the divine feminine, was also associated with the tiger and often pictured riding on one. In this form the tiger was a symbol of unlimited power, and the ability to uphold justice.

How to wear it

The position and style of a tiger design says a lot about the symbol's meaning. A roaring tiger denotes courage and strength, while a prowling tiger suggests patience and striving to reach a goal. Full-body depictions are often chosen in the Japanese style and used in many back-piece designs. It's popular to tattoo a tiger climbing up rock formations with a bold sun providing a colourful backdrop.

Opposite: **Depicted with a growling expression, the simple, bold style of this tiger effectively communicates courage, strength and power.**

Right: **A tiger battling a snake can be used as an analogy for the struggle between brute strength and power (the tiger) and cunning (snake).**

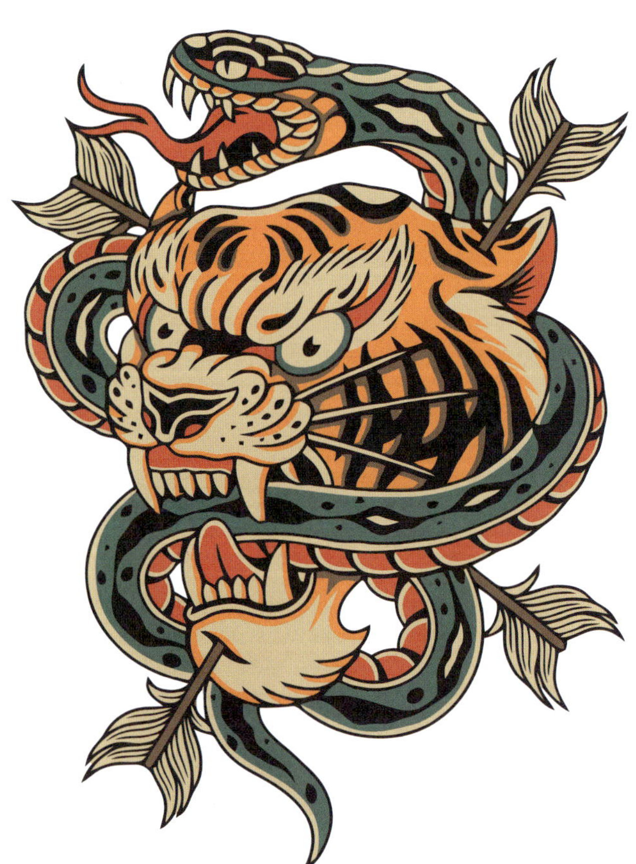

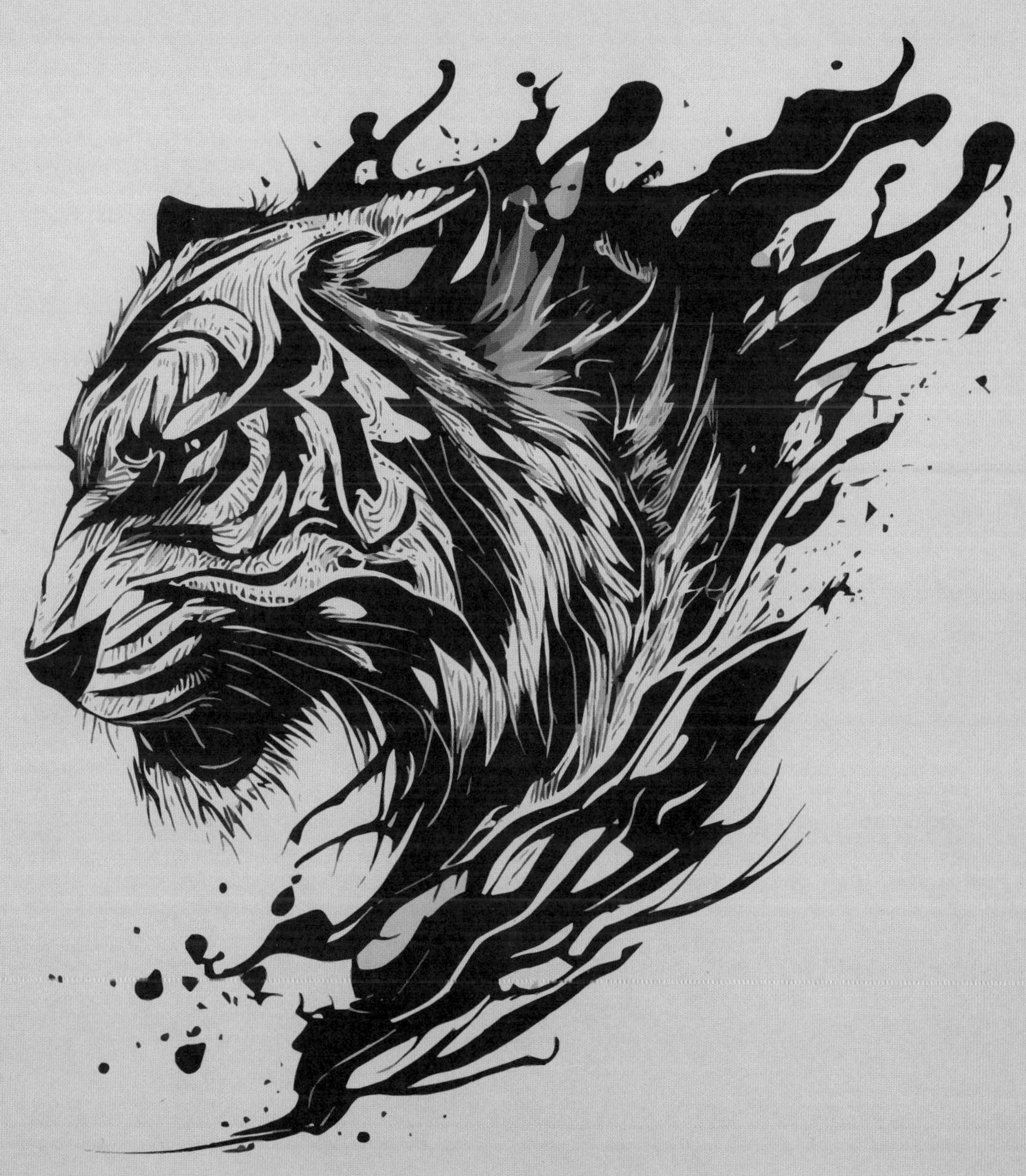

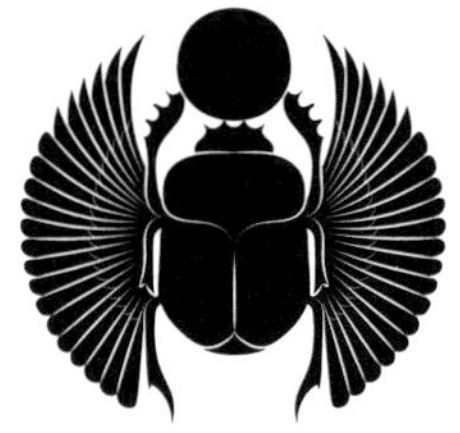

Scarab Beetle

Rebirth | Resurrection | Creativity | Positive energy

Sacred Origins
Egyptian

Used Since
Mid 3rd millennium BCE

Tattoo Styles
Black-and-grey realism
Fine-line
Blackwork

Opposite: A large scarab combined with the moon phases and the sun and moon (top right) emphasizes the connection to the cyles of life. A simple blackwork scarab (bottom row) speaks of positivity and creativity. Combined with the Eye of Horus and an ankh (middle left), the symbol signifies the Egyptian association to the afterlife.

Synonymous with rebirth and the cycles of life, the scarab beetle was revered by the ancient Egyptians and believed to have links with the gods.

Balls of dung and the light of the sun

The Egyptians likened the scarab beetle to the dung beetle, a creature known for rolling balls of dung along the ground to lay its eggs inside. They believed this practice mirrored the movements of the sun upon the horizon. Because of this, they associated the scarab with their god Khepri, who governed the rising sun. Khepri was often depicted with the head of a scarab, but he wasn't the only deity linked to the beetle. Atum and Re, two separate entities that came together to form the singular Atum-Re, were thought to represent the primordial creative force, the sun's vitality, and were also associated with this symbol.

Amulets for the dead

Scarabs first appeared as stone seals and amulets during the 6th dynasty of the Old Kingdom, with one of the most famous depictions belonging to the female pharaoh Hatshepsut. This ornate beetle was fashioned from gold and adorned with precious gems. Most commonly scarabs were used as amulets for the dead and placed upon coffins to secure safe passage to the afterlife. Sometimes they were placed over the heart during the process of mummification.

How to wear it

Scarab designs work nicely in a fine-line style with dot-work shading; however, a bolder look can work well too and colour can be introduced. They are often enhanced with a solar orb or the Eye of Horus. This symbol works at palm size or smaller and can be placed on many areas of the body.

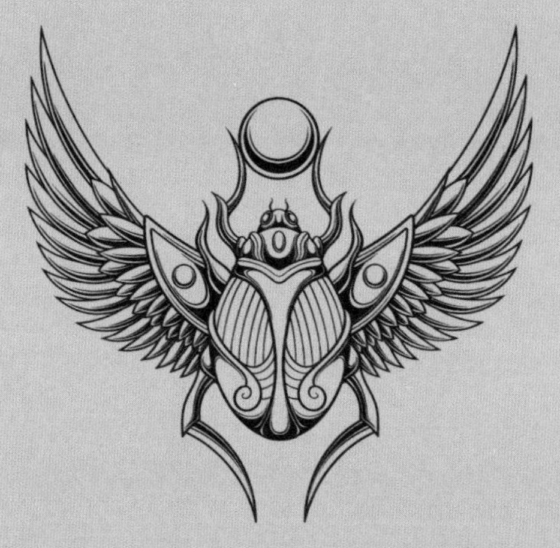

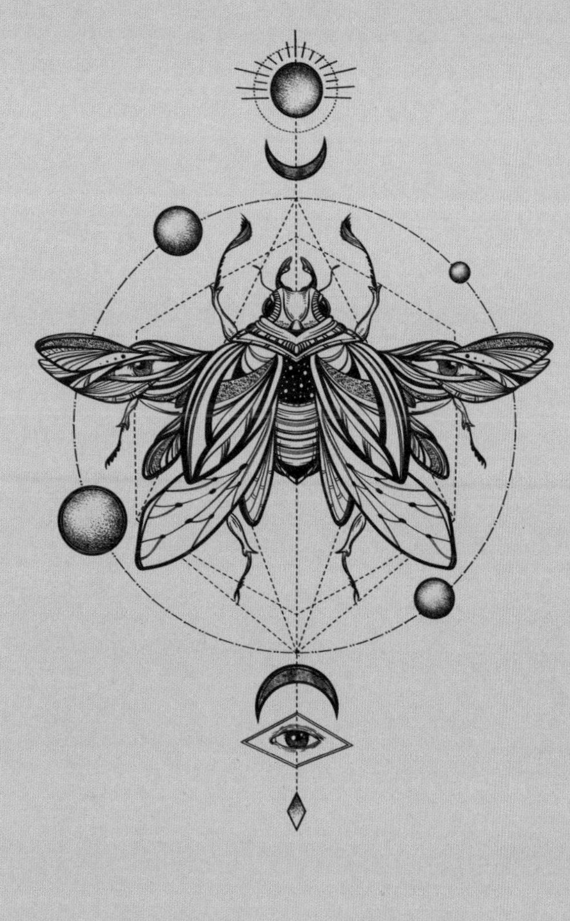

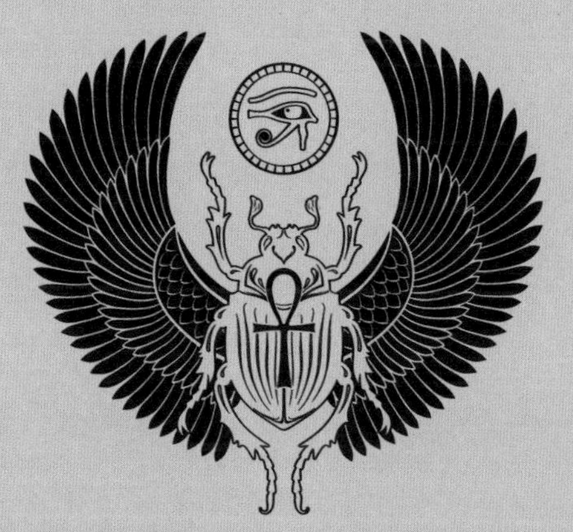

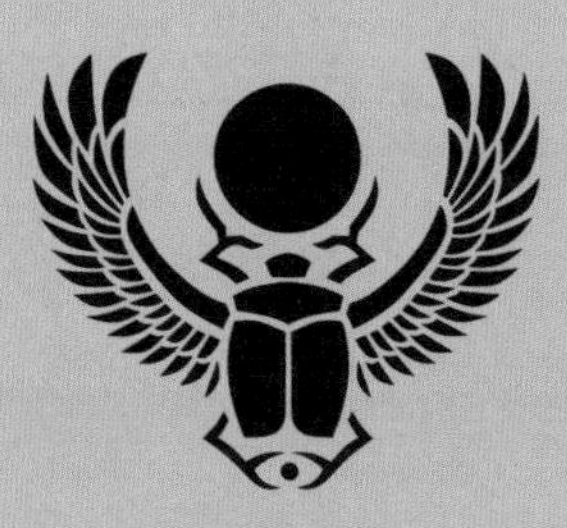

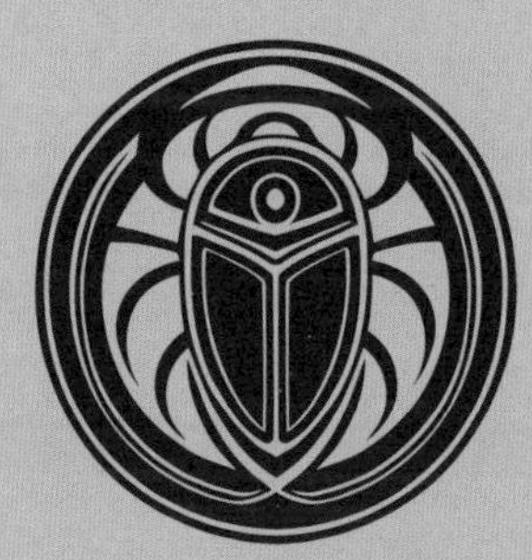

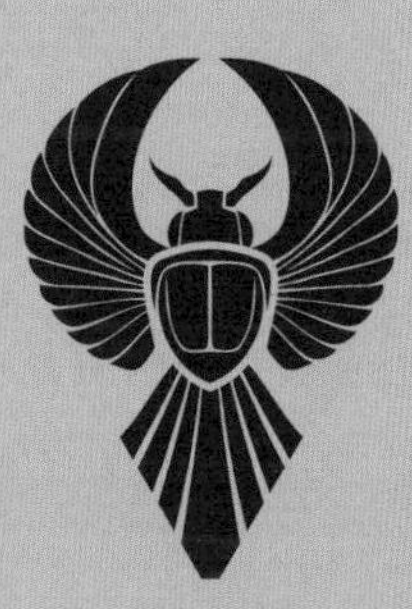

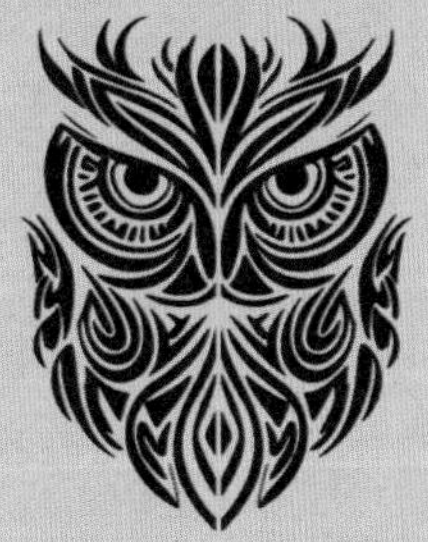

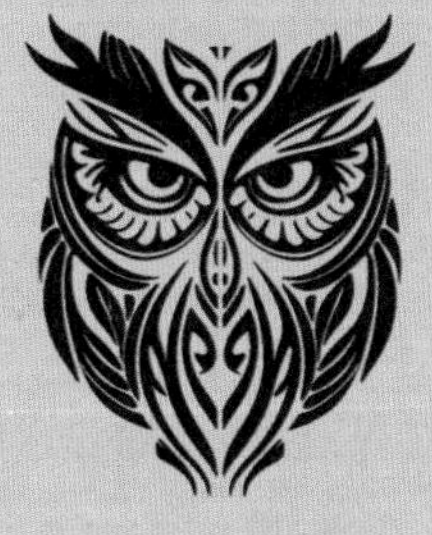

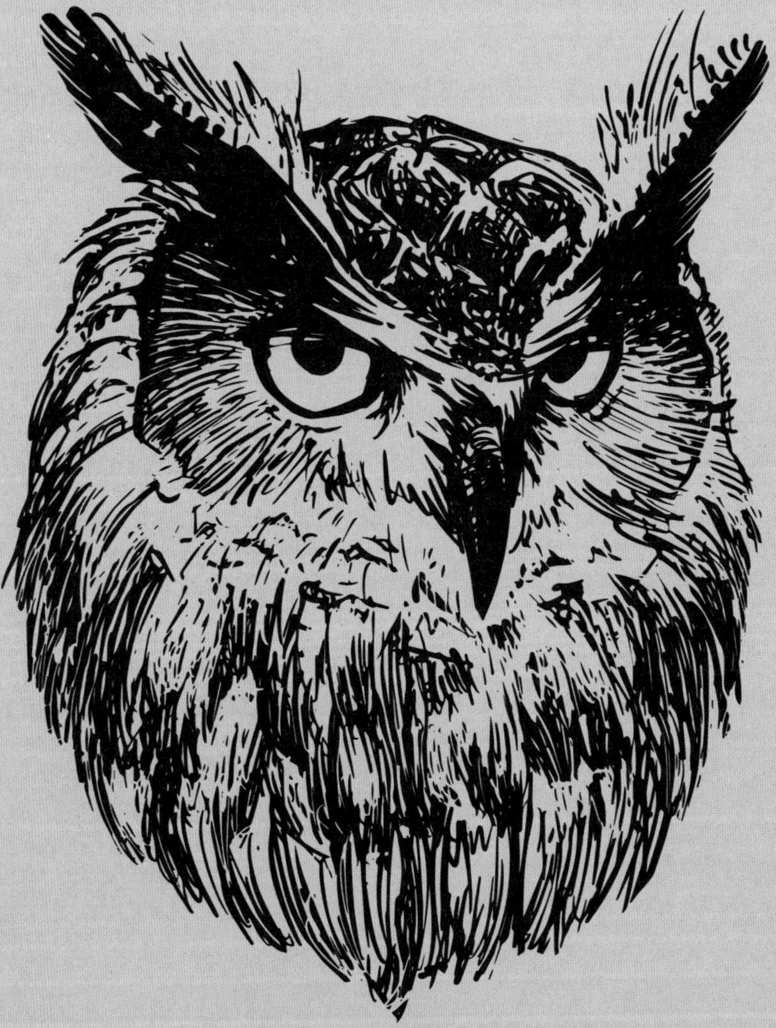

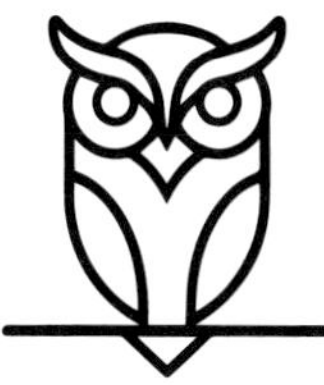

Owl

Wisdom | Intuition | Magic | Protection | Psychic power

Sacred Origins
Greek, Roman

Used Since
*c.*480–420 BCE (the owl
of Athena/Minerva)

Tattoo Styles
Western traditional
Black-and-grey realism

**With large, bright eyes and silent nocturnal flight,
the enigmatic and ethereal owl is a creature that
divides opinions.**

Athena's favourite

The owl was both revered and feared by ancient civilizations, who acknowledged
its many talents and gifts by making it a key feature in mythology. To the
Greeks, the owl was synonymous with wisdom and the ability to see beyond
the veil. Chosen by the goddess Athena as her companion after she rejected the
crafty crow, she favoured the little owl for its quiet strength and discernment,
making it an emblem of hidden knowledge and power. To cement the idea
that it was sacred, the bird was protected within the Acropolis at the time.
Often seen adorning shields and weaponry as an emblem of victory, it was
considered a positive omen if one flew overhead during the march to battle.
The symbol of the little owl was a common sight in Athens and even appeared
on coinage to reinforce its significance. The bird was also depicted in sculptures
and artwork sitting upon the shoulder of the goddess Athena or her Roman
counterpart Minerva.

Witches in disguise

The Romans viewed owls with some trepidation. Being a creature of the night,
it was thought the bird could offer protection and repel the forces of evil, and
dead owls were often nailed to doors to keep harmful influences at bay. The
Romans believed that witches had the ability to shapeshift into owls and would
then feast upon the blood of the innocent, a superstition that spread throughout
Europe. In the Middle Ages the owl was generally feared. Its haunting screech
was an omen of death at worst – or a sign of a storm to come.

The eyes have it

Owls' eggs were considered the cure for most ailments, including drunkenness, and were often consumed to improve eyesight. Indeed, the eyes of the owl were its most striking feature, and probably the reason it gained such a mystical reputation. To many ancient civilizations it was a messenger, able to traverse the realms and carry the spirits of the dead to their final resting place. Today, the owl is recognized as a symbol of intelligence, insight and intuition.

How to wear it

Owls in flight, with a symmetrical spread-winged stance, are often chosen for large areas like the back or chest, while a smaller owl, perched on a branch, could be tattooed on the wrist or most areas of the arm. In a Western traditional style, the owl is often accompanied with other images like flowers, plants or a banner – it's also popular to combine the owl with a skull on the chest to add mystery to the design.

Opposite: **Focus on the eyes of the owl (top right) sheds light on wisdom, the attribute most commonly associated with the owl. The incorporation of Athena (top) links to Greek myths and hints at quiet strength and discernment.**

Right: **An owl combined with a skull can be a way to remember a lost loved one.**

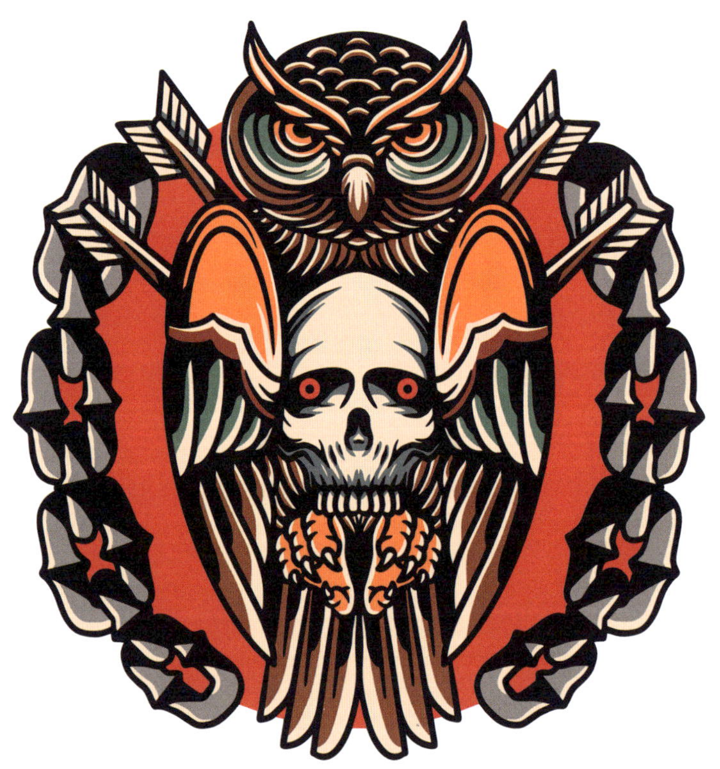

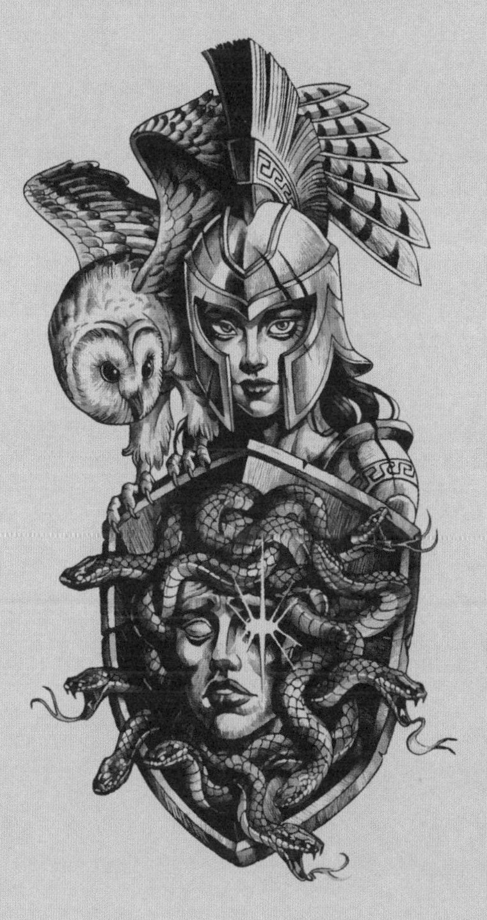

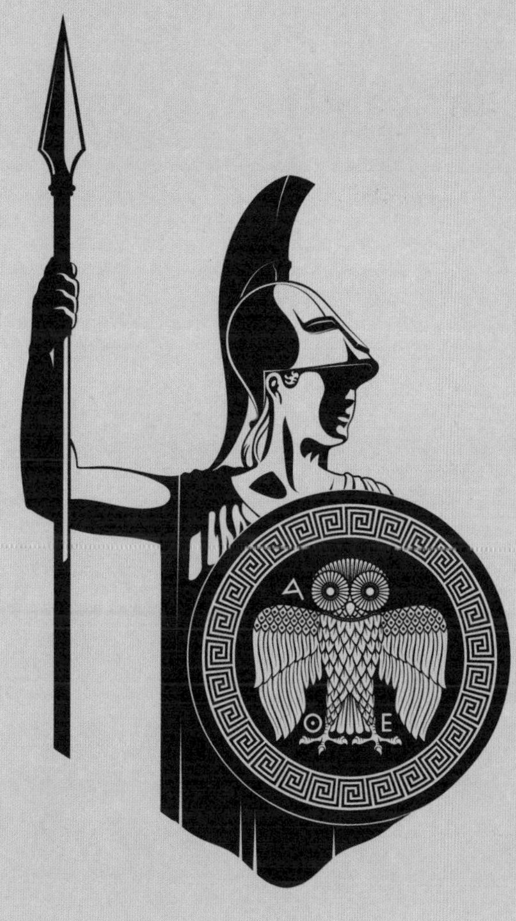

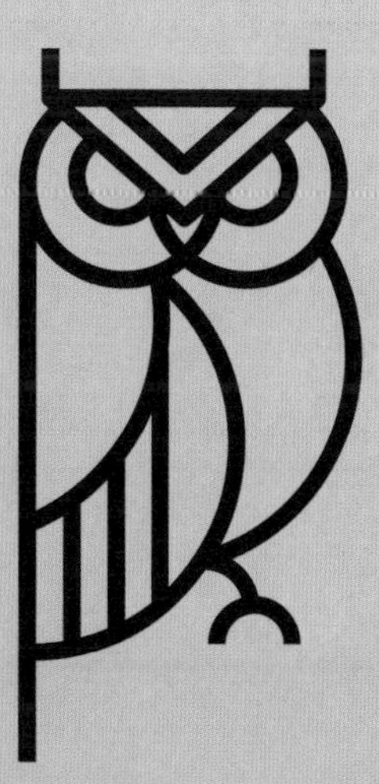

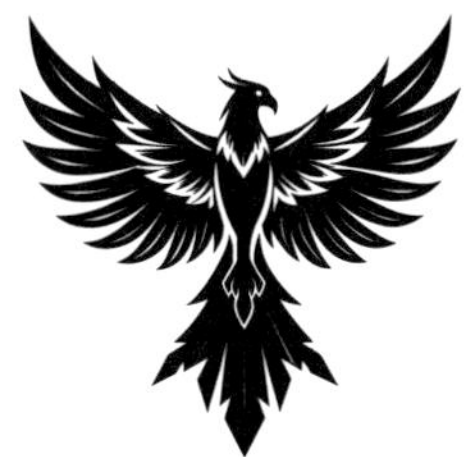

Phoenix

Rebirth | Transformation | Immortality | Resilience | Rejuvenation

Sacred Origins
Egyptian, Roman, Greek

Used Since
5th century BCE

Tattoo Styles
Japanese
Fine-line

The iconic image of a phoenix rising from the ashes is a symbol of rebirth and reinvention.

From the flames
The idea of the dramatic rebirth of the phoenix stems from ancient Egypt, where the bird was associated with the worship of the sun. Born from the smouldering fire of its predecessor, the phoenix, with its gold and scarlet feathers and huge size, was a mythical creature imbued with the magic of life.

City of the Sun
According to legend, this glorious firebird had a lifespan that stretched to well over 500 years. When the time came for it to leave the earth, the phoenix would build a pyre made from aromatic sticks and boughs, then set it alight and let the flames consume it whole. As the embers flickered and waned, a new phoenix would emerge. It would then anoint the ashes of the previous bird in an egg of myrrh, and carry them to Heliopolis, known as the City of the Sun. Here it would lay them upon the altar, in the temple of the sun god Re. To the Egyptians, the phoenix was a symbol of immortality and the cycles of life. It was also adopted by the Roman Empire as an emblem used on coinage to represent the eternal city of Rome.

How to wear it
The symbol of the phoenix lends itself to a colourful palette, and the feathers offer a lot of opportunity to create an elaborate composition; it's a popular choice for going large scale. The phoenix is often seen as a full-back design with feathers flowing just beyond the back and trailing down both arms or the legs.

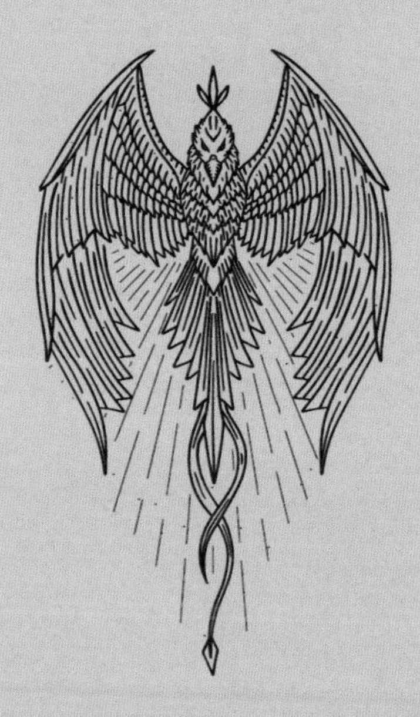

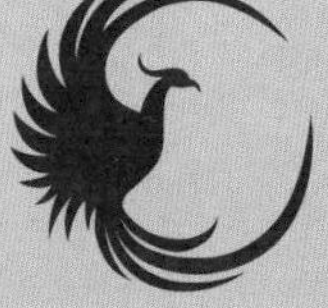

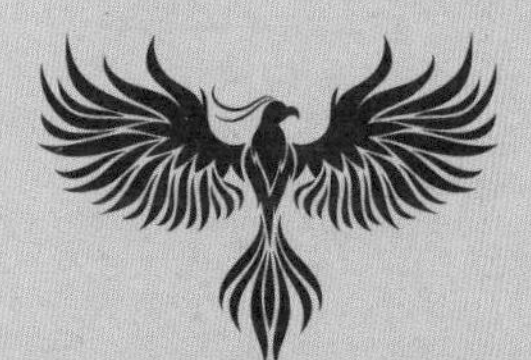

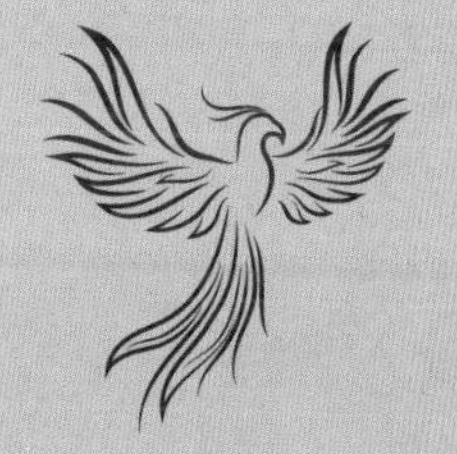

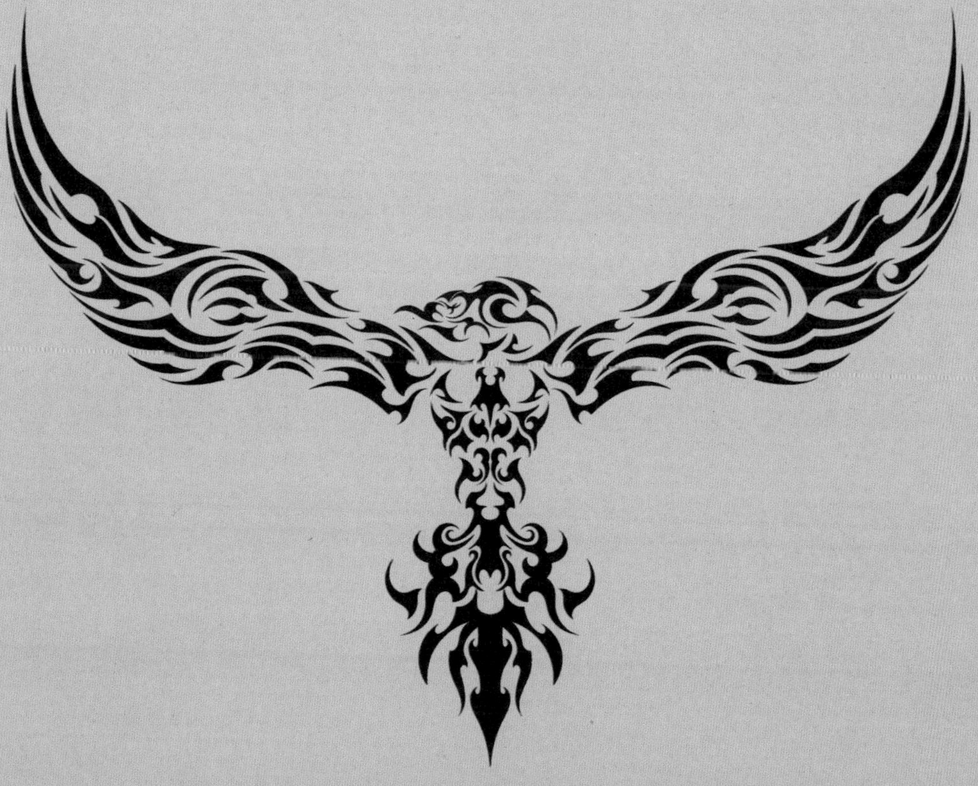

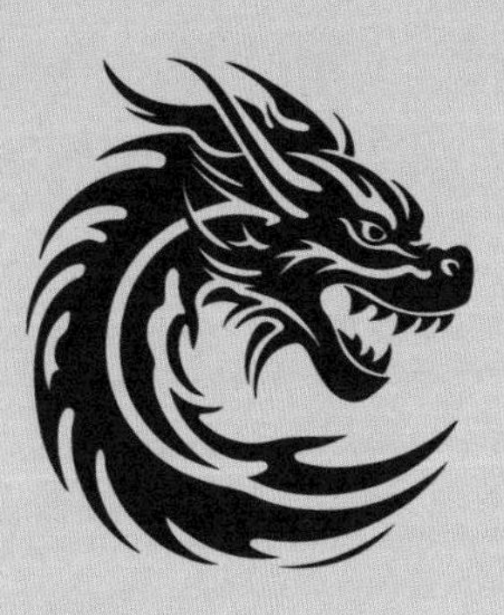
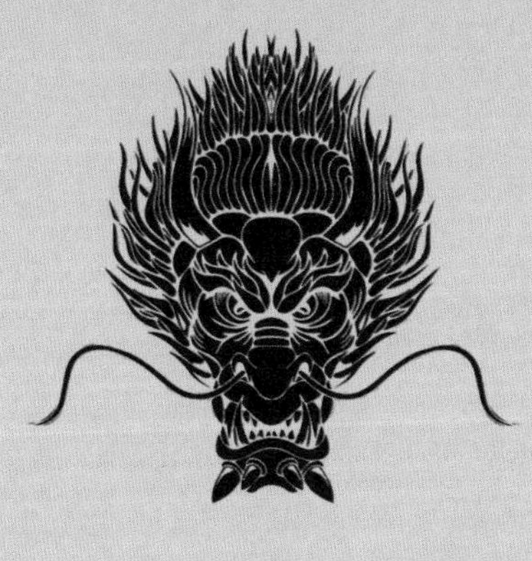
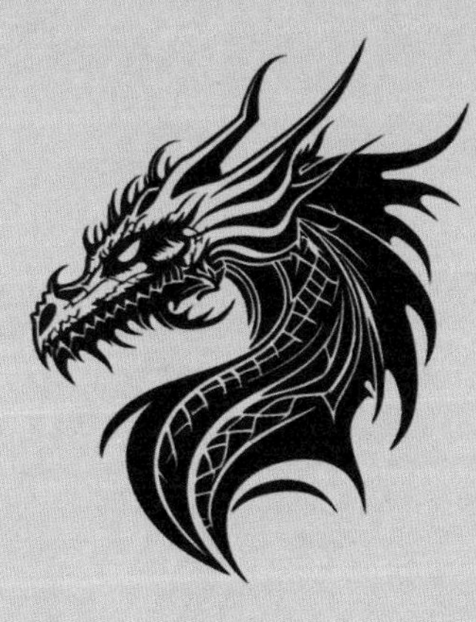
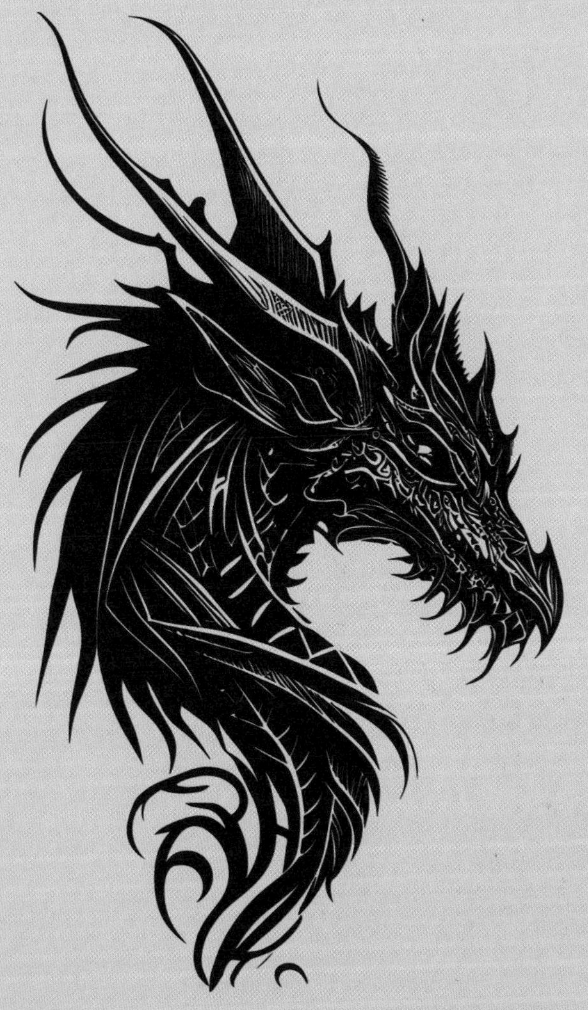
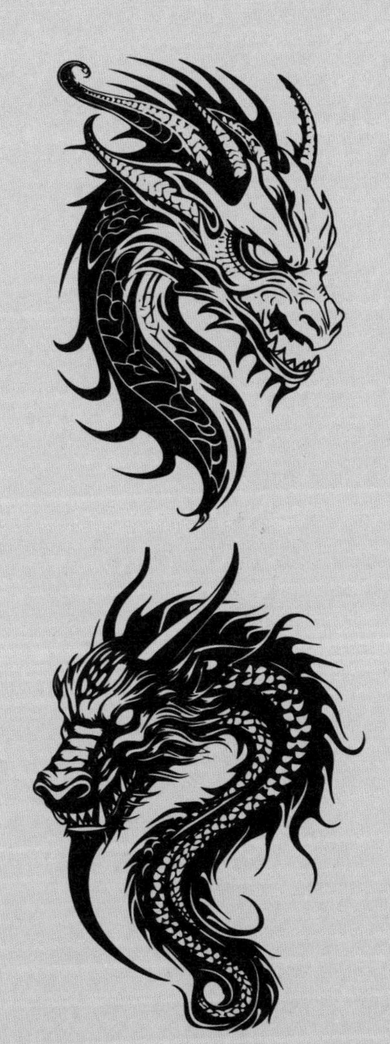

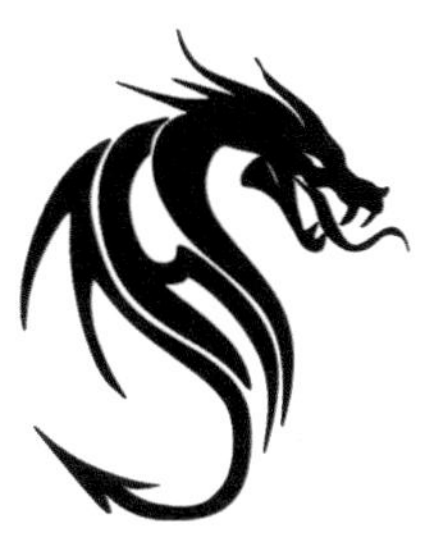

Dragon

Power | Good fortune | Protection | Strength

Sacred Origins
Chinese, Japanese,
Celtic, Christian

Used Since
Stone Age

Tattoo Styles
Japanese
Western traditional
Fine-line
Black-and-grey realism

Opposite: Whether using just the head or the full body, the concept of power and strength intrinsic to a dragon always comes across, making it a hugely popular symbol in tattooing.

The dragon is a mythical creature that divides opinion: a benevolent presence or a vicious fire-breathing beast?

A symbol of nobility

In the East, the dragon is seen as an auspicious omen and a symbol of hope and kindness. Synonymous with imperial rule and nobility, it was thought that the earliest emperors were closely related to this beast, with some even manifesting in this form. According to one legend, when the Yellow Emperor, Huangdi, came to the end of his reign, he was immortalized as a dragon and ascended to the heavens. This winged creature was considered a symbol of wealth and good fortune, and could be found in artwork and adorning palace walls. Emperors would sit on 'dragon thrones' and wear 'dragon robes' to demonstrate their status and power. The claws of the beast depicted upon garments could distinguish the position of the wearer. Emperors were the only ones allowed to wear the five-clawed dragon, while the four-clawed version was reserved for princes, and other high-ranking officials. Peasants were only permitted to clothe themselves in three-clawed dragons, this being the lowliest form of the creature.

The Chinese zodiac

According to one famous tale, the Jade emperor of legend set a quest for all the creatures to decide the order of the Chinese zodiac. Whoever should reach his gates first would be the leader of the pack. Most assumed this would be the dragon, but the rat, ox, tiger and rabbit arrived first. When asked why he was late, the dragon explained that he had heard of a village suffering from a drought so he had stopped to make rain for them.

Terrifying fiend and cave-dwelling hoarder

In the West, the dragon is seen as a fire-breathing demonic monster, a creature
that brings havoc and destruction. To the Norse peoples he was Nidhogg, the
'curse striker', an enormous snake-like being that gnawed at the roots of the world
tree which held the nine realms aloft. He was so powerful that even the gods could
not defeat him. In Arthurian legend dragons were led by avarice and greed, and
often protected huge hoards of treasure. They were always a menace to be defeated,
an opinion which the Christians reinforced, referring to Satan as a dragon and
alluding to the evil nature of serpent-like creatures. The Celts saw a different side
– they believed that dragons were cave-dwelling beings, linked to the earth. They
celebrated their powerful nature and harnessed it during battle. Today the dragon
is the battle standard of the Welsh and an emblem of strength, courage and power.

How to wear it

Dragon designs are considered one of the most powerful tattoos you can get, and
are a firm favourite among many tattoo artists. They are a statement piece and often
get prime real estate on the body, whether it's a full back, full front or a sleeve. The
choice of dragon dictates the style. Japanese or Chinese dragons are often bold and
colourful, while winged dragons, also known as wyverns, are usually given
 a more realistic design style.

Opposite: **Western-style dragon renderings often show the beast with huge wings, and may incorporate Celtic patterning (middle left). The more decorative dragons of the East are often wingless with flowing manes and intricate scale designs (top and bottom left).**

Right: **In the East, dragons are a symbol of good fortune and power.**

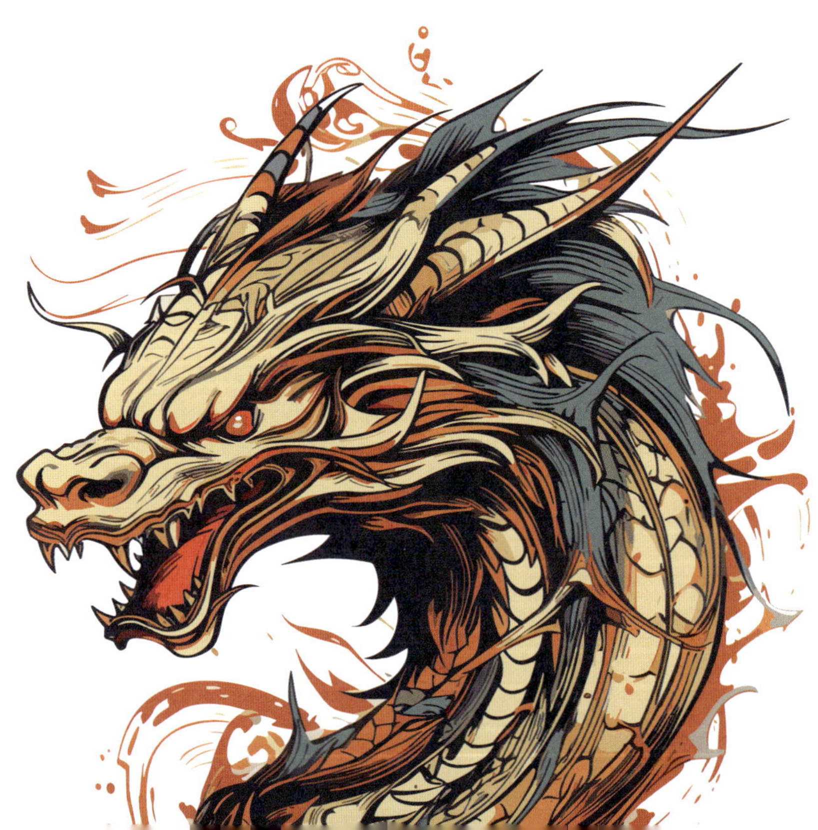

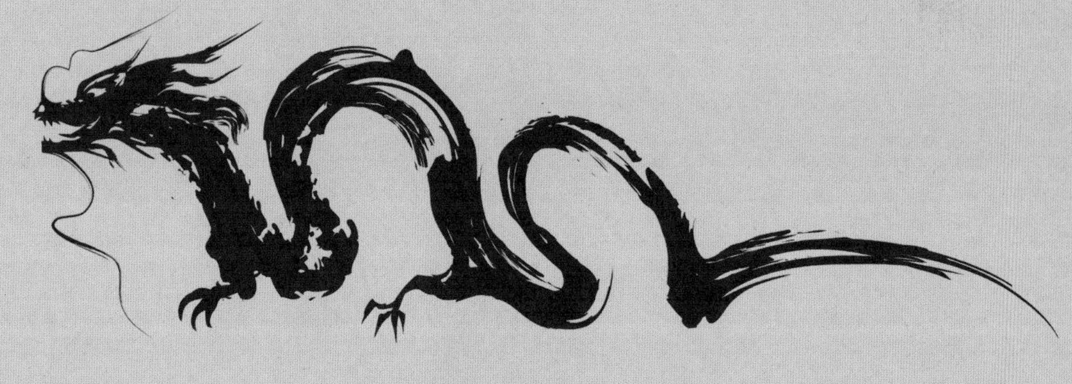

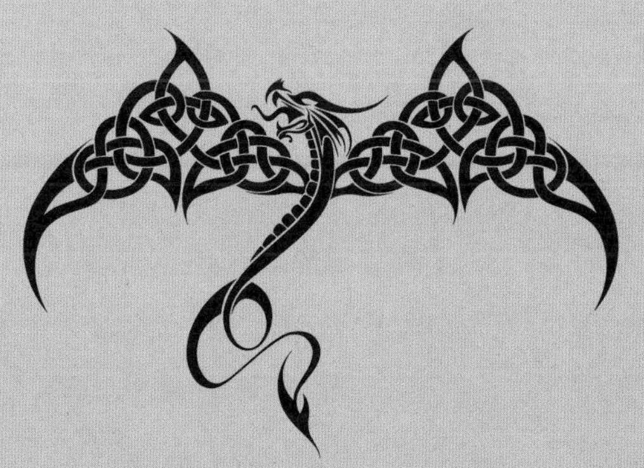

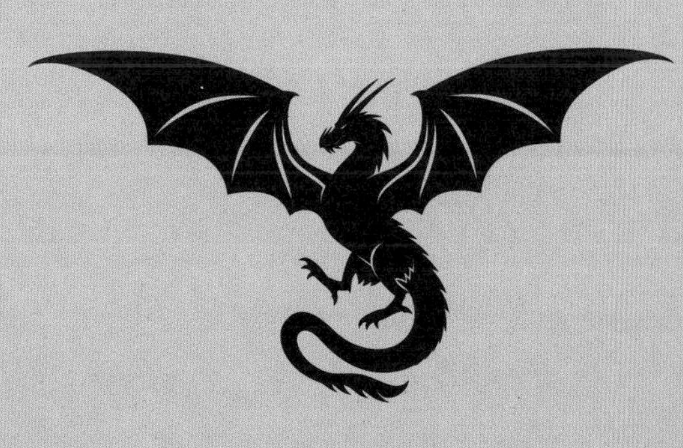

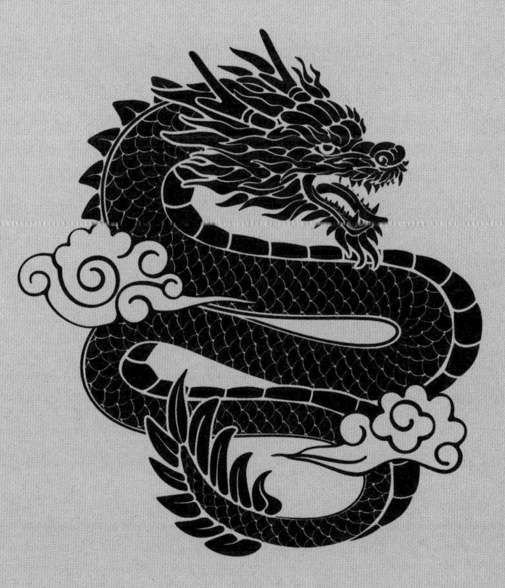

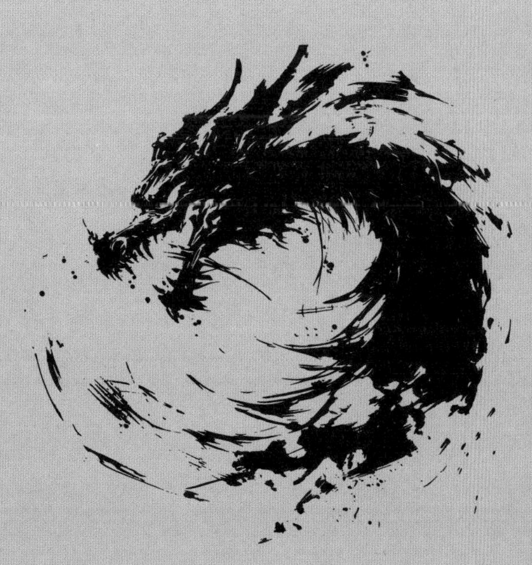

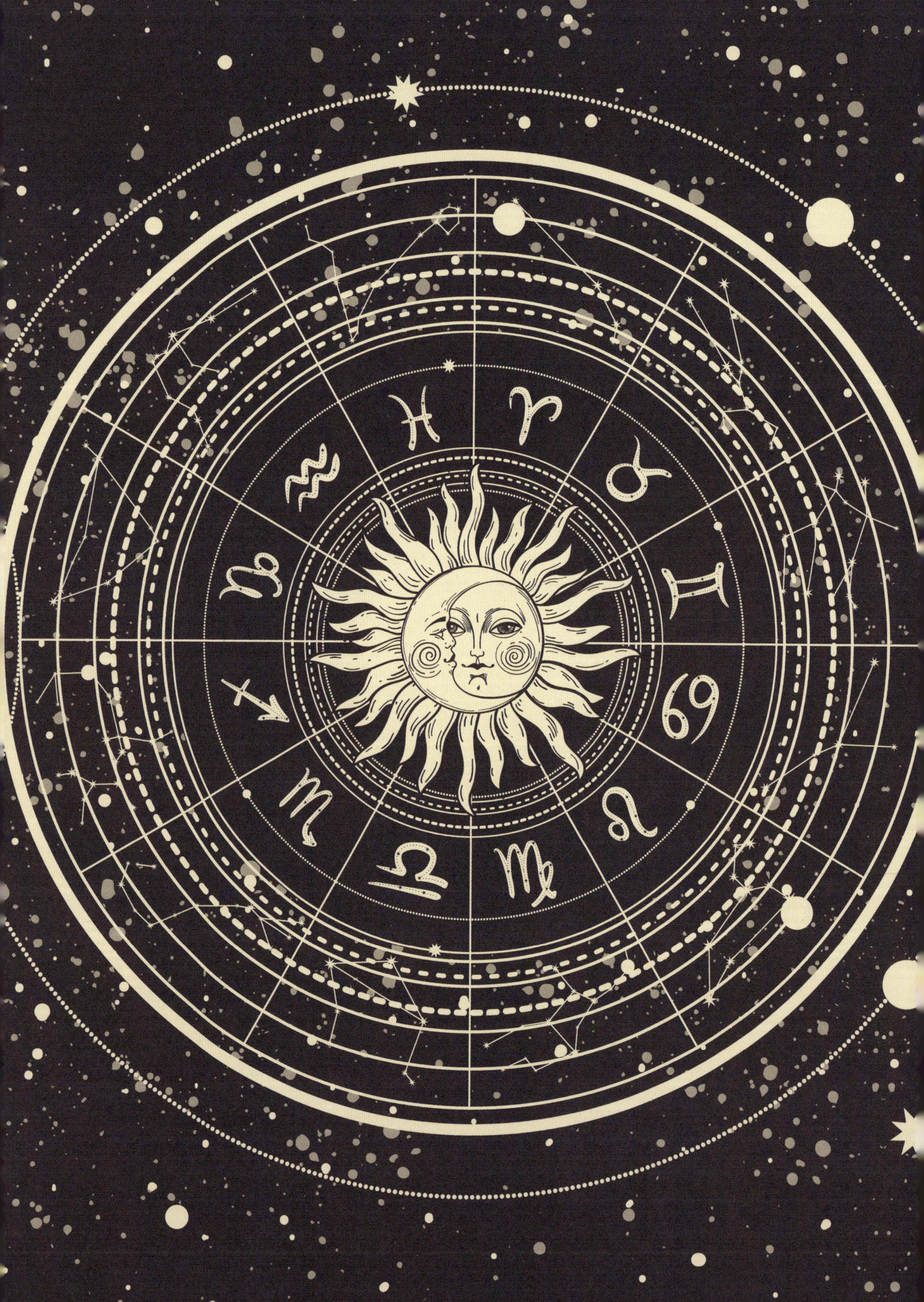

6

Stars, Myths and the Zodiac

The night sky has been a source of fascination for millennia. When early humans made their homes upon the rocky landscape and looked up at the stars, they must have marvelled at the plethora of patterns and shapes, the vivid brightness of the moon in its full glory and how the heavens seemed to come alive in darkness. They began to note each twinkling formation, giving them names and narratives that matched with their beliefs. They charted the positions too. The Babylonians were the first to split the sky into 12 sections, each associated with a constellation, and the Greeks quickly followed suit in the 2nd century BCE, taking their discoveries and assigning specific names, symbols and stories to enhance their meaning.

From this moment on, the star signs and their symbols have captivated human hearts and minds, taking on a sacred resonance which is enhanced by the myths and beliefs of ancient civilizations. The glyphs and figures associated with each constellation are imbued with meaning, making them a popular tattoo choice for those who want to add a cosmic feel to their design. Whether you're looking to wear a starry emblem that's personal to you or seeking astrological inspiration, the 12 symbols that follow have history, myth and magic to offer.

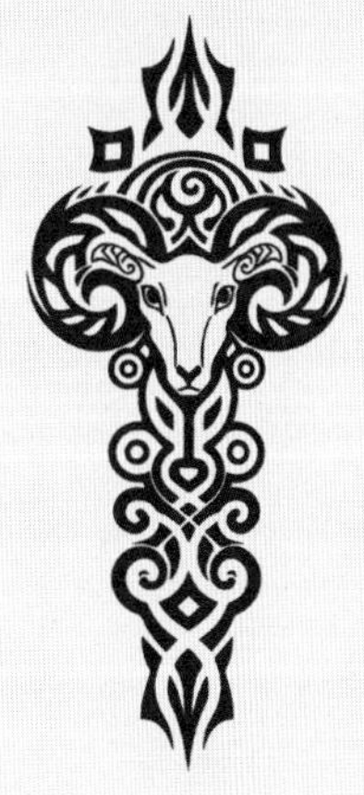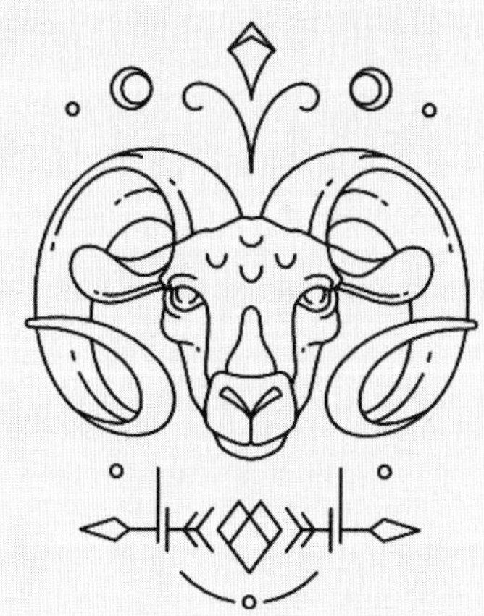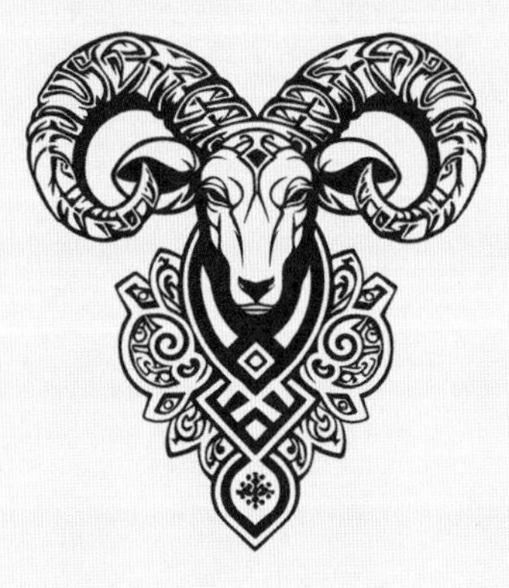

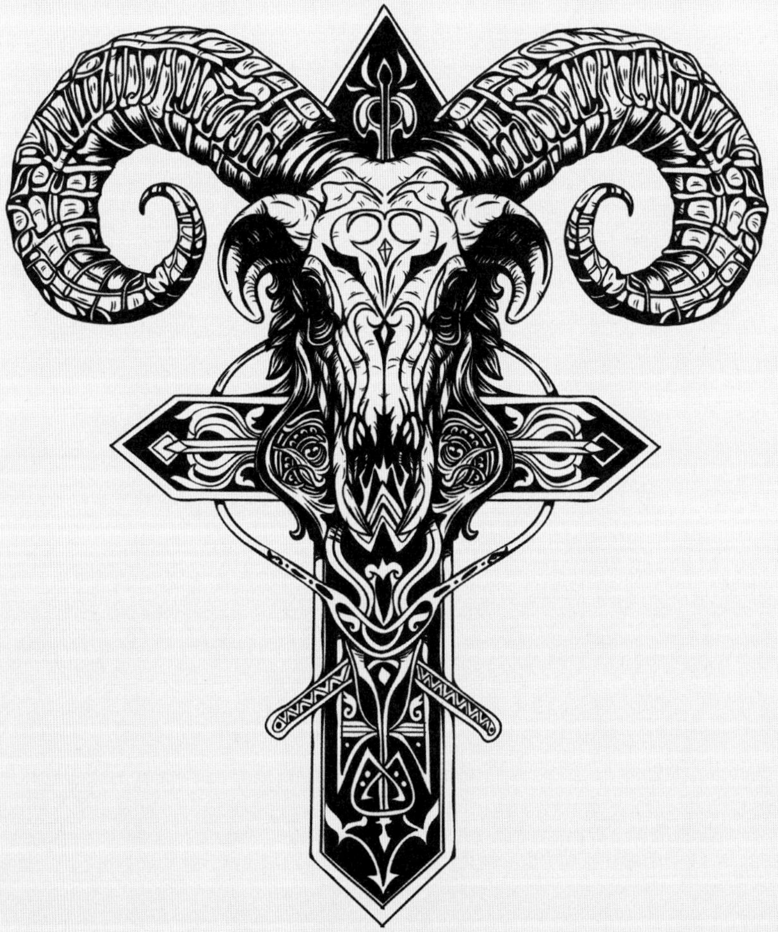

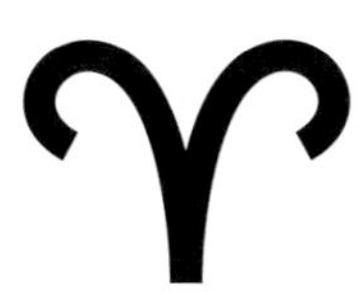

Aries (21 March to 19 April)

Courage | Leadership | Passion | Action | Assertiveness

Sacred Origins
Egyptian, Greek,
Roman

Used Since
3rd millennium BCE

Tattoo Styles
Japanese
Fine-line

Opposite: The ornate pattern surrounds on these Aries symbols (top) accentuate the leadership and power of the ram. The cross within this Aries head (bottom) denotes faith, and is a nod to the proactive energy associated with this zodiac sign.

Aries is the first of the 12 astrological signs to charge through the heavens, so it's no surprise the ram is associated with leadership.

Amun's amulets
A bold fire sign, the Aries symbol and the beast related to it make a popular tattoo choice and not just for those born under the sign. The ram's head was a popular icon in ancient Egypt, where it was associated with a range of deities, including the god of the sky, Amun, who was often pictured with rams' horns. Lapis pendants of rams' heads have been discovered dating back to the 3rd millennium BCE and were worn as protective amulets. The constellation and the associated Greek myth are both synonymous with courage and action, and the ruling planet Mars reinforces the assertive power and passion of this sign.

The Golden Fleece
According to Greek legend, the ram came to the rescue of the children of the King of Athamus, whose lives were threatened by their evil stepmother. Fleeing the kingdom with them upon his back, he soared through the heavens. The ram was revered for its brave action, and as a mark of respect it was sacrificed to Zeus. Its fleece became the Golden Fleece of legend, while its body was transformed into a cluster of stars that formed the constellation Aries.

How to wear it
As with all astrological symbols, Aries can be tattooed as the constellation using simple dots and lines, but more often, a depiction of the ram itself is chosen. This stylish curly horned motif is just too appealing to leave out. Aries works well in a bold outlined style, or a fine-line approach with placement ranging from large-scale back pieces to smaller iterations on the wrist or inner forearm.

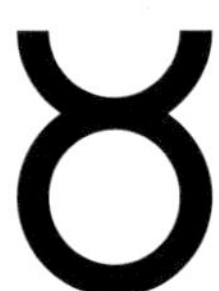

Taurus (20 April to 20 May)

Strength | Determination | Resilience | Honour | Fertility

Sacred Origins
Babylonian, Sumerian,
Egyptian, Greek

Used Since
2nd century BCE

Tattoo Styles
Western traditional
Blackwork
Fine-line

Opposite: The bull with upturned crescent moons (top right) signifies mystical energy and a link to the star sign. The charging bull (middle left) suggests force of will and fortitude. A woman sporting bull's horns and pictured with the Taurus constellation (bottom right) wears a wilful expression, which highlights the tenacious energy of this symbol.

Those born under the astrological sign of Taurus may be considered bullish, but in truth the sign and any related mythology is a testament to the sheer will and determination of this sturdy creature.

An early symbol

From the Early Dynastic Period to the Chaldean Period, the bull was venerated and associated with a range of Mesopotamian deities. The Mesopotamian shepherd and cattle god Dumuzi carried the epithet 'Wild Bull', while the Babylonian moon god Sin, who embodied the form of the crescent moon, was linked to the bull.

Bull of Heaven

The beast's horns were seen as a representation of the orb in this phase. The storm god Ishkur, also known as Adad, was gifted the moniker 'Bull of Heaven'. It was thought that the sounds of tremulous thunder rolling in were not dissimilar to a bull's deep bellowing, and so the two were inextricably linked. To the ancient Egyptians, this horned beauty was associated with the god of fertility, Apis; bull's head amulets were fashioned out of precious stones and carried to imbue a person with strength and virility.

The healing bull

In the Japanese region of Aizu, the red bull known as Akabeko is worshipped. According to local legend, this sacred creature was thought to have saved the entire region from a smallpox epidemic around a thousand years ago and is celebrated to this day with commemorative statues and papier-mâché tokens which are decorated with spots, to illustrate recovery from disease.

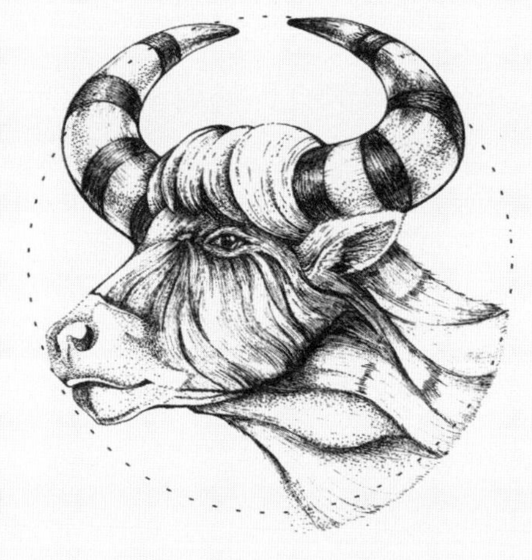

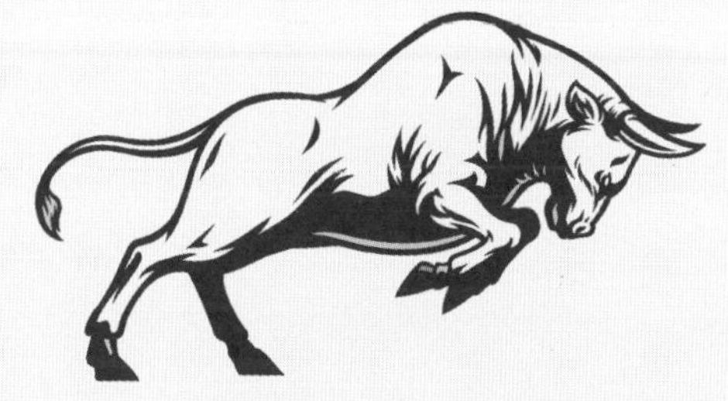

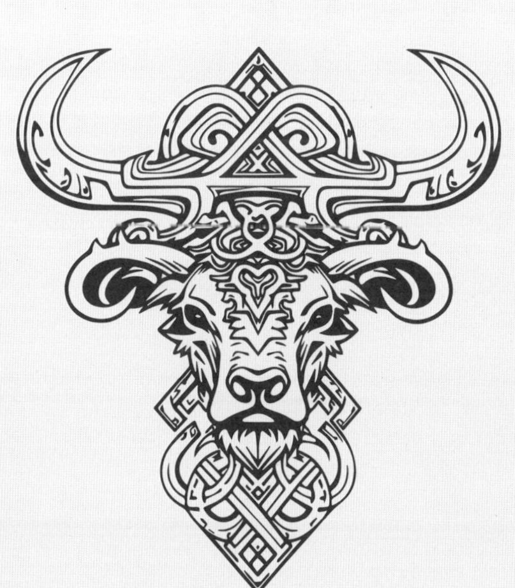

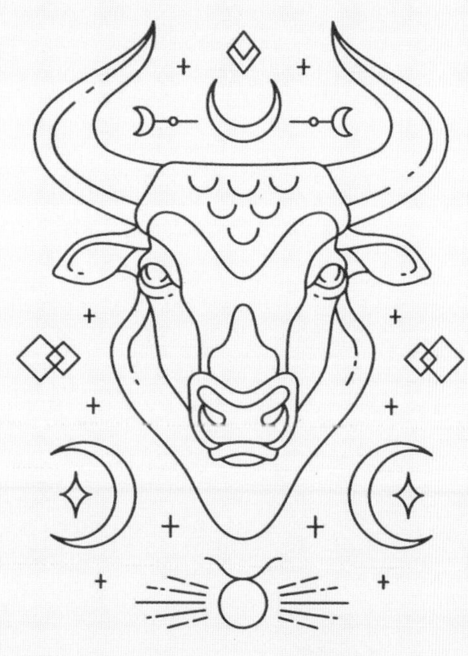

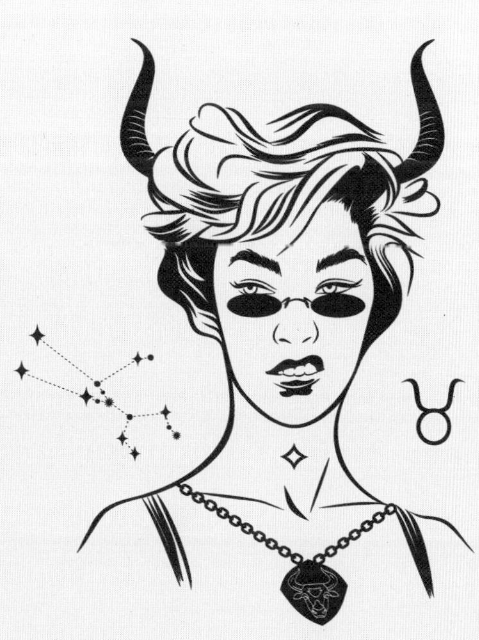

The white bull of Crete

To the ancient Greeks, Taurus the bull and the corresponding constellation was associated with the father god Zeus. When the god fell in love with the mortal Princess Europa, he transformed into a majestic white bull and whisked her away to the island of Crete to seduce her. Here he revealed his true nature, and the princess reciprocated his advances. From that moment on, Taurus the bull was recognized as a divine creature, honoured for its strength and resilience and cast into the heavens as the mighty constellation of the same name.

How to wear it

Bull tattoos lend themselves to bold black outlines and heavy black shading, which helps to communicate the power of this mighty creature. Full-body depictions are popular, with the chest and back being prime locations on the body. More stylized or abstract renditions, often just showing the bull's head, can be used in smaller areas. Designs that incorporate other symbols, such as flora and fauna, highlight the earthy nature of this sign.

Opposite: This Taurus symbol promotes a peaceful zen energy as it sits within a mandala-style frame.

Below: This bull, with steam-filled nostrils, denotes power and determination.

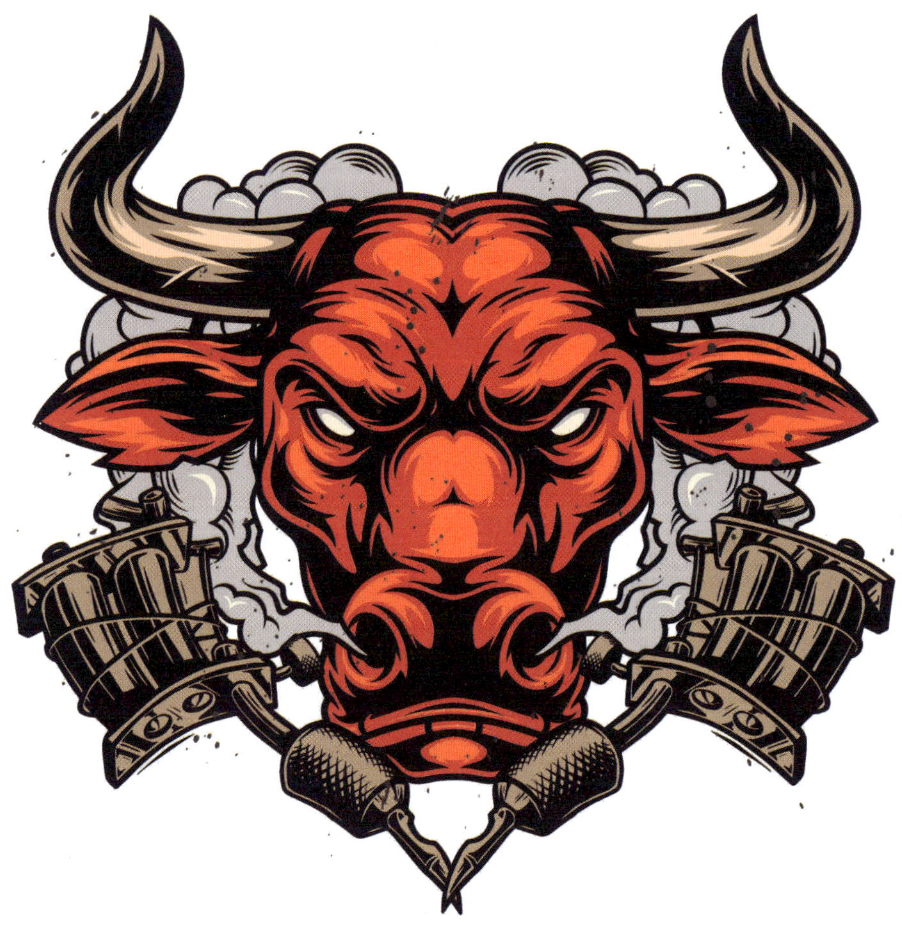

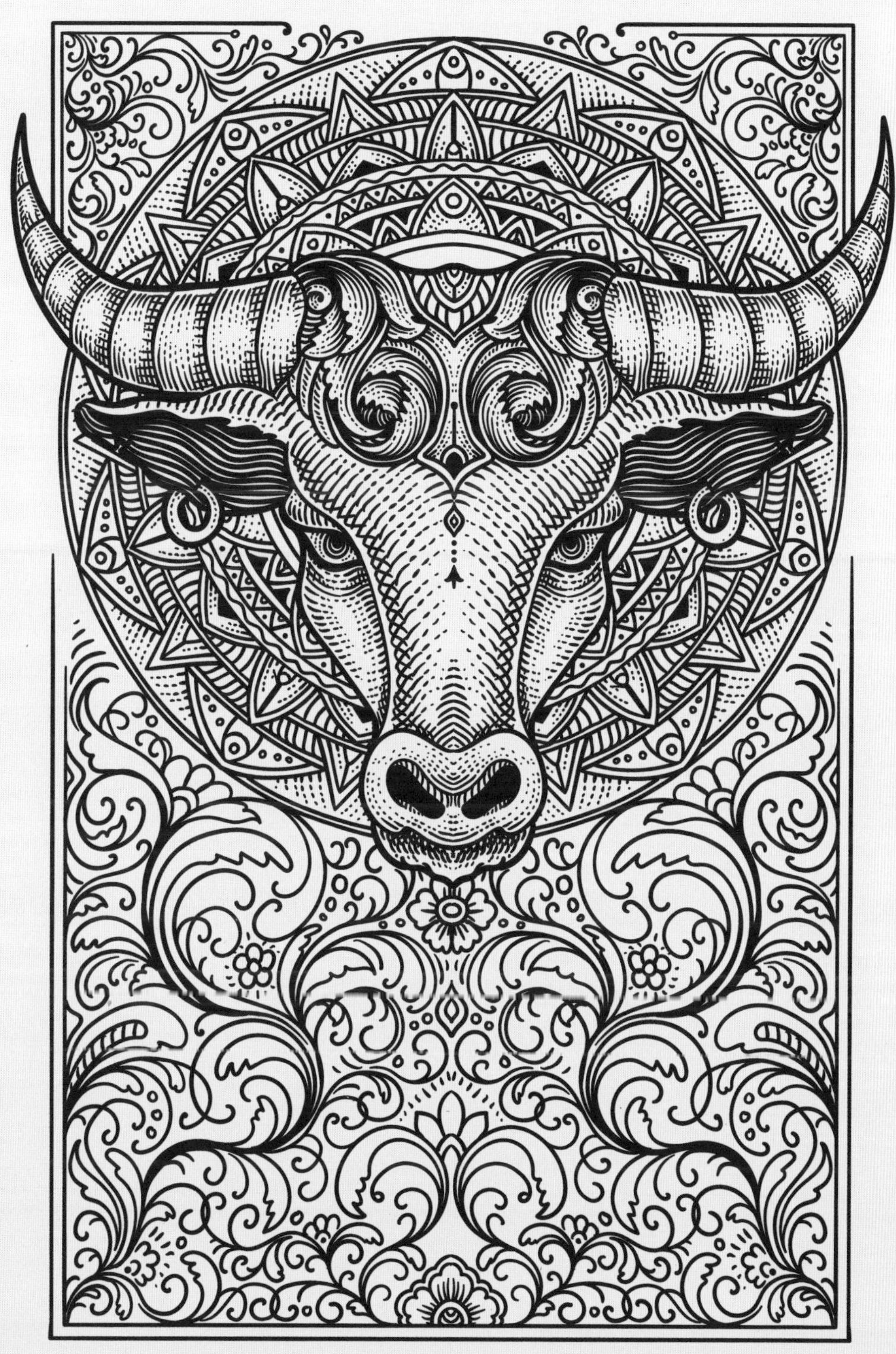

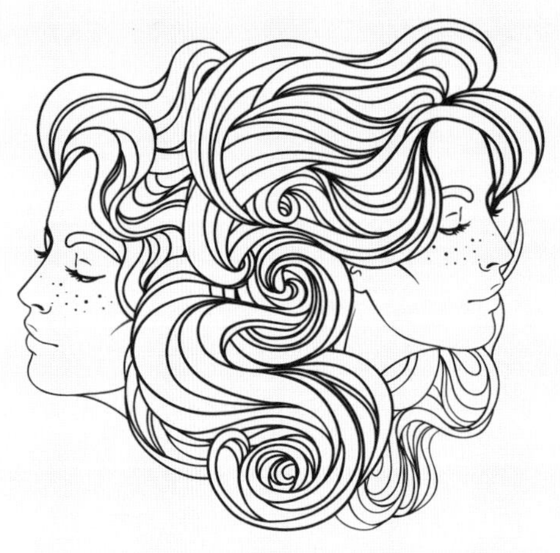

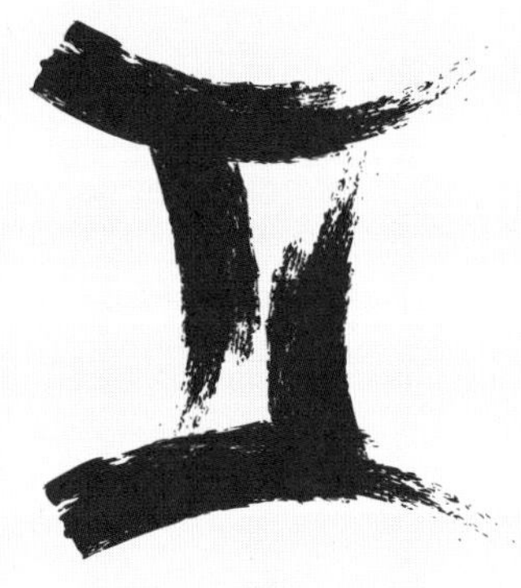

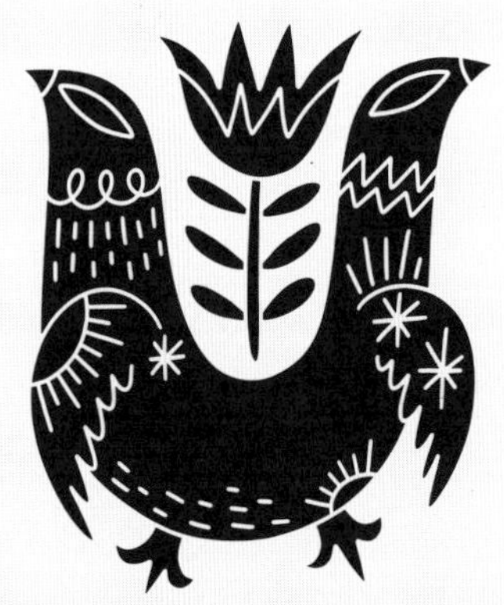

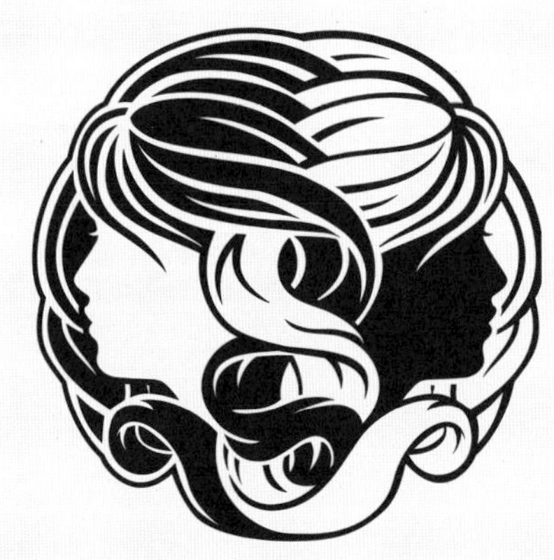

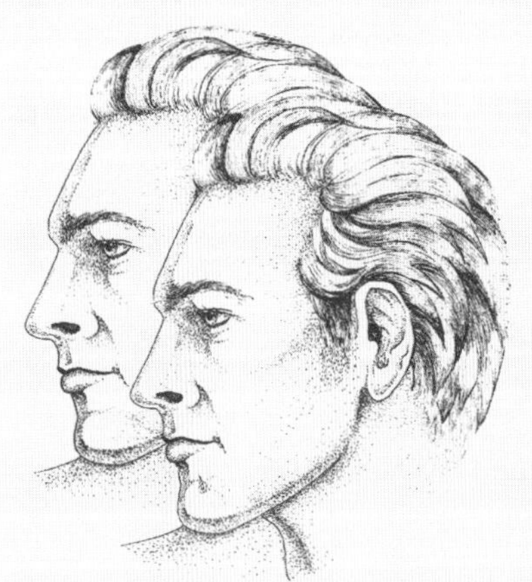

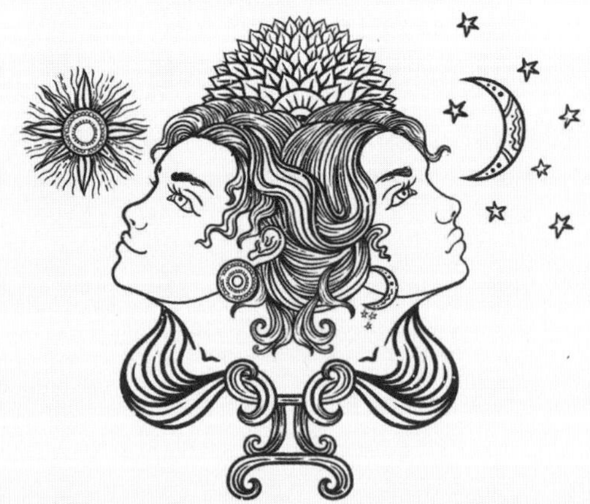

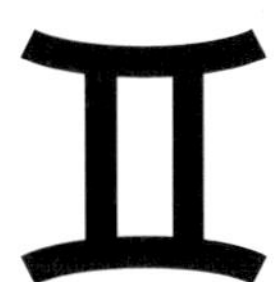

Gemini (21 May to 21 June)

Duality | Unity | Balance | Harmony | Contrast

Sacred Origins
Egyptian, African,
Greek, Roman

Used Since
2nd century BCE

Tattoo Styles
Fine-line
Blackwork

Opposite: A simple Gemini glyph in a brushwork style (top right) gives this symbol a Southeast Asian feeling. The interconnected birds along with the flower (middle left) suggest a link to nature and accentuate the element of air, which is connected with this zodiac sign. Gemini symbols using two heads (bottom and middle right) reinforce the dual nature of the sign.

In mythologies around the world, the notion of twins is sacred and thought to reflect the dual nature in all of us.

Children of the sky

Two halves make a whole, while being opposites. When they are reunited, it brings balance and harmony to the world. To the ancient Egyptians, the sign of Gemini was represented either by a pair of goats or a man and woman holding hands; this pairing was known as Mithuna in Sanskrit. In southeast Africa, the Baronga tribe believed that twins were blessed and had the ability to control the weather – they called them children of the sky.

The Dioscuri

The Greeks had their own myth which centred around twin brothers Castor and Polydeuces, known as the Dioscuri. Although they emerged from the womb together, Polydeuces was the son of Zeus, while Castor was mortal. In the story, Castor loses his life when the twins enter into combat with another pair of brothers. Polydeuces is so taken with grief that he asks Zeus to gift his twin immortality. The god takes both brothers and casts them into the heavens as the twinkling constellation Gemini.

How to wear it

The Gemini glyph, which consists of two gently curving horizontal lines connected by two straight vertical ones, is often tattooed to represent the nature of duality. Being small in size, it is perfect for wrists or ankles. More artistic interpretations might include two connected faces which mirror one another. This approach works well tattooed in a very delicate fine-line style with stippled shading often used to give dimension to the faces.

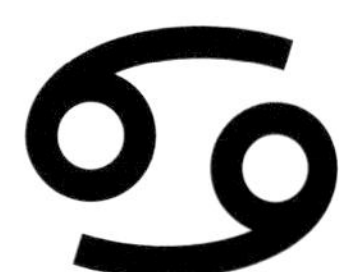

Cancer (22 June to 22 July)

Protection | Sensitivity | Inner strength | Womanhood

Sacred Origins
Chinese, Greek

Used Since
2nd century BCE

Tattoo Styles
Blackwork
Fine-line
Western traditional

Opposite: The encircled crab (bottom right) suggests a link to the eternal nature of life, while the crab with the moon (middle left) is associated with mystical energy. The crab holding a mandala style jewel (middle right) connects this symbol to inner wisdom and enlightenment.

A creature of land and sea, the crab hides its softer side within but can also provide a nasty nip. It is contradictory, like the constellation which is the dimmest in the sky but contains one of the brightest star clusters.

The element of water

Throughout the world the crab is seen as a symbol synonymous with protection, thanks to its hard shell. Couple this with its shoreline habitat, and it's no surprise that it is linked with the element of water.

Cancer and Hydra

To the Chinese, the crab was also associated with the moon, and Yin energy. Sent by the gods to kill the hero Hou Yi, it was eventually defeated by his wife, the goddess of the moon. This is not dissimilar to the Greek myth which explains the existence of the Cancer constellation. In this story, the crab comes to the aid of the Hydra, a venomous nine-headed water serpent who is fighting the hero Heracles. Pinching at his heels, the tiny creature does its best to assist but is crushed beneath his sandalled foot. The goddess Hera takes pity on it and transforms the broken body into a constellation of stars in the night sky.

How to wear it

Crab tattoos are versatile and can be tattooed in a variety of styles, from bold to fine, stylized to realistic, geometric or even purely pattern based. Some artists choose to use the shell-shaped body as a framework to work within, perhaps adding a scene or the symbol's constellation inside it. The inclusion of water is popular but the symbol works just as well on its own. Black ink alone can be used but some of the most striking designs use bright and bold colour.

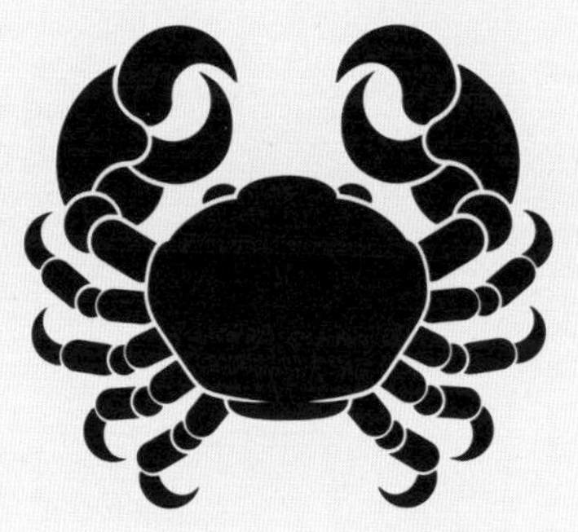

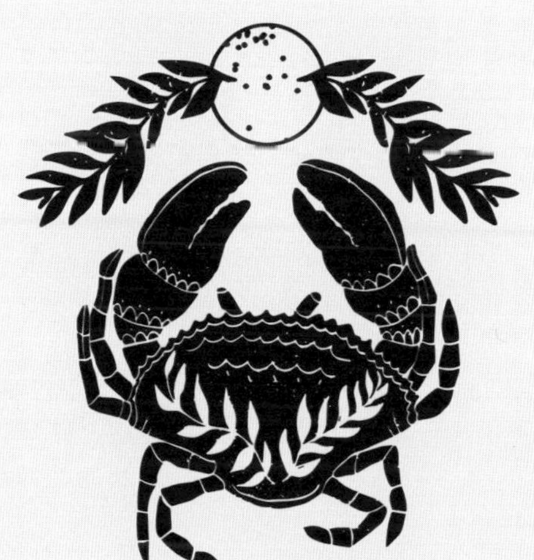

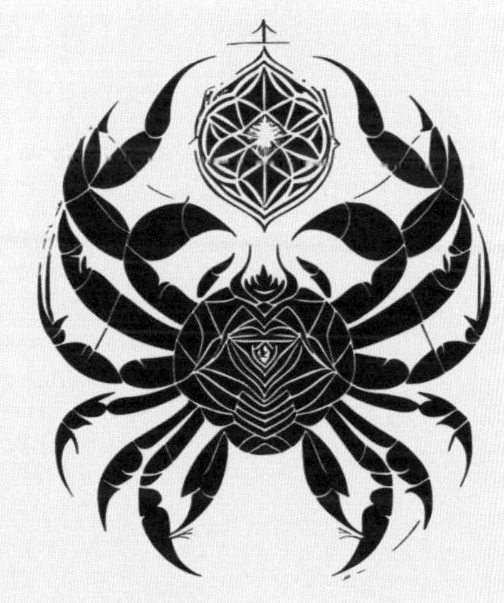

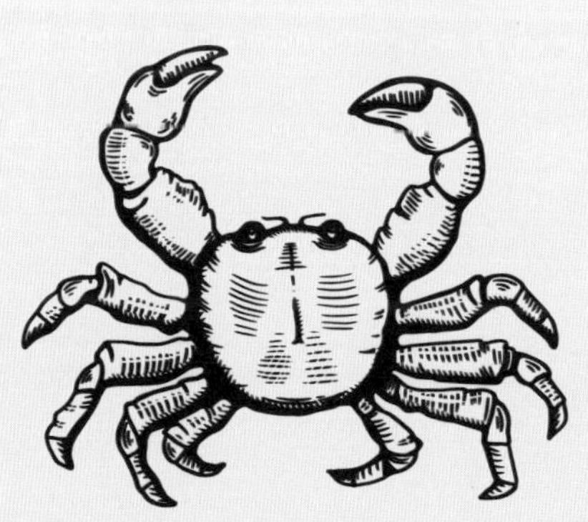

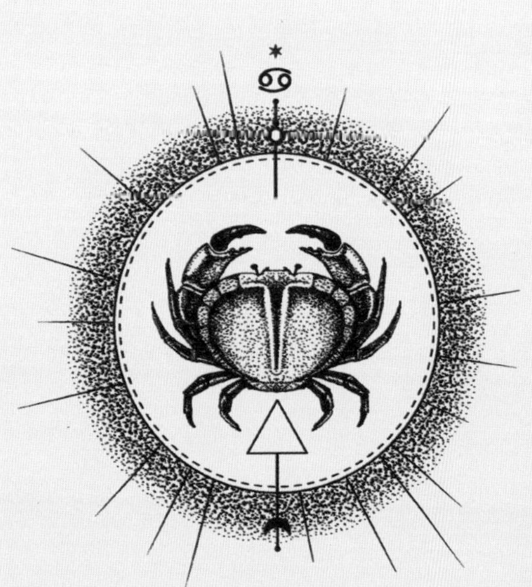

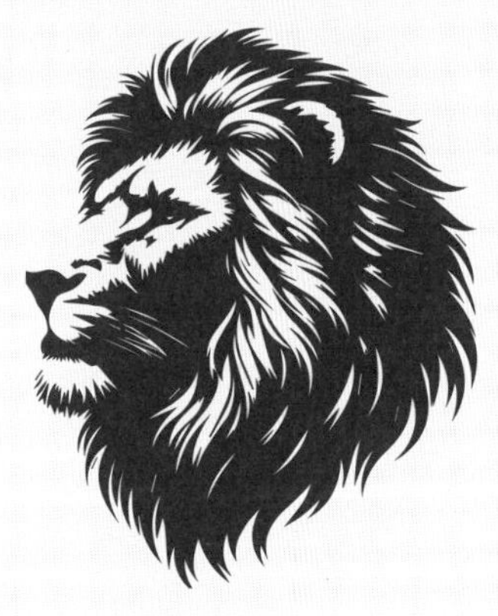
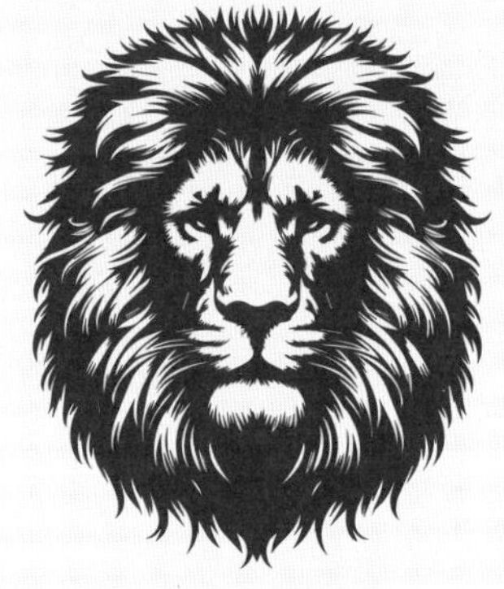
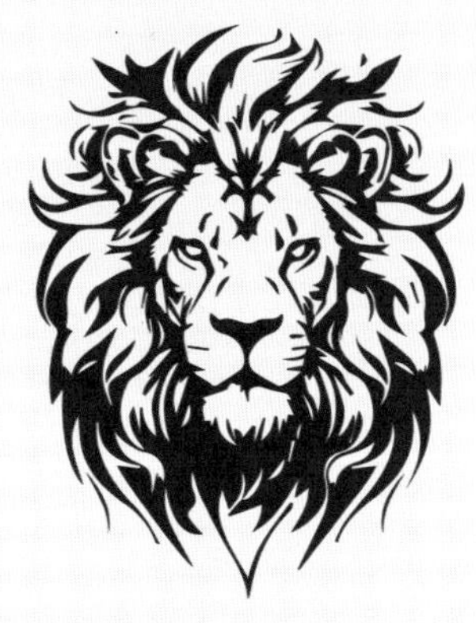
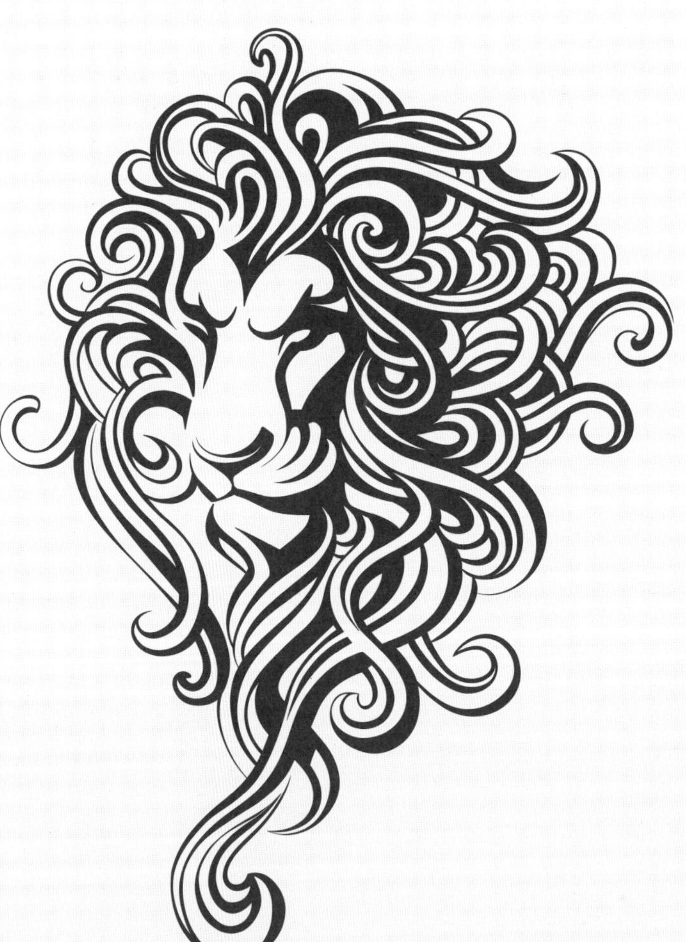
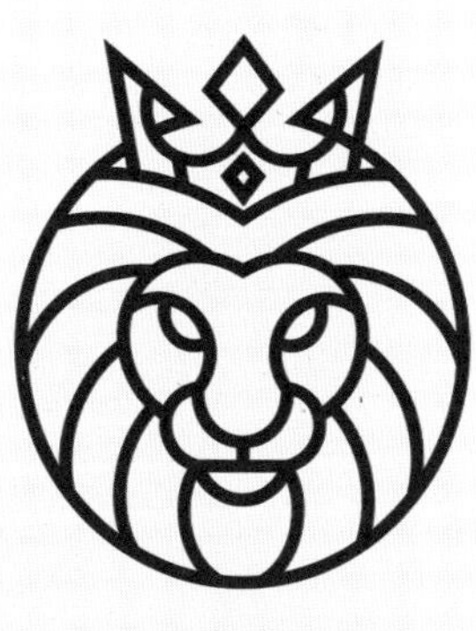
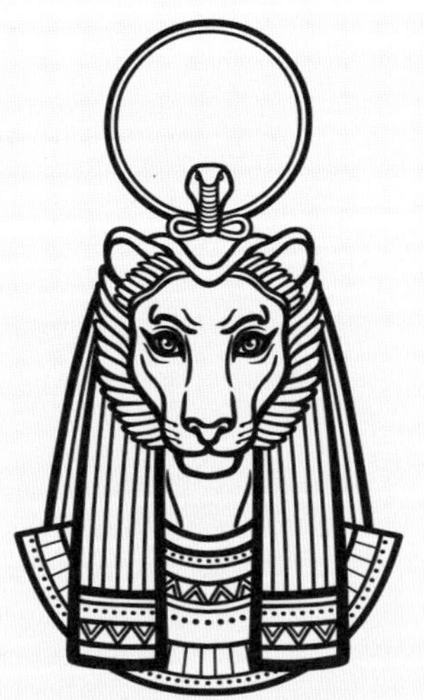

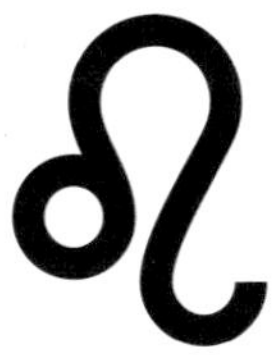

Leo (23 July to 22 Aug)

Courage | Confidence | Strength | Power | Wisdom

Sacred Origins
Chinese, Japanese,
Egyptian, Babylonian,
Greek, Roman

Used Since
2nd century BCE

Tattoo Styles
Black-and-grey realism
Blackwork
Fine-line
Western traditional

Opposite: Leo heads (top) accentuate the lion's mane and reinforce the power and strength of this symbol. A crowned Leo (middle right) is synonymous with authority and gives a regal feel to the symbol. An Egyptian-style Leo (bottom right) has features reminiscent of the lion-headed goddess Sekhmet, who was associated with strength and protection.

The mighty lion holds court around the world as the king of the beasts and a symbol of strength and bravery.

An ancient icon

This cultural icon can be found peering from heraldry, adorning statues and featuring on buildings of eminence, being a motif that has been around for thousands of years. Wall paintings and figurines crafted from clay and ivory are just some of the lion artefacts that have been uncovered in archaeological excavations, with one of the most famous discoveries unearthed in Germany's Swabian Jura Mountains, in the Vogelherd Cave. This lion sculpture fashioned from a mammoth's ivory tusk dates back at least 40,000 years.

Lion dancing

In Egypt the lion was associated with the goddess Sekhmet; a fierce warrior goddess, she was embraced for her protective influence and often depicted with the head of this big cat. In the East, these creatures were revered for their power and wisdom. The Han Dynasty demonstrated their strength and authority with a colourful 'lion dance', which was thought to promote good fortune, while in Japan statues of lions known as koma-inu guarded the temples and shrines.

The Nemean lion

To the ancient Greeks, the colossal Nemean lion was a terrifying creature with supernatural strength who pillaged the land at will. Some say he was born from the goddess Hera, a magical creation that she had made to bring about the end of Zeus, while others suggest he was the offspring of the monster god Typhon. Whatever his origins, his rampage needed to end and so the gods sent Heracles to defeat him, as one of his twelve labours. The hero killed the lion with his bare hands – Hera, beside herself with grief, cast his broken form into the heavens as a vibrant constellation. The Romans swiftly caught on to the narrative and gave the pattern of stars the name 'Leo'. Like the lion of legend, those born under this sign are thought to be confident, courageous and never short of admirers.

How to wear it

Leo, the lion, is a powerful symbol that often takes centre stage in sleeves or full-back or chest tattoos. Realistic interpretations are popular, with additions like a crown and roses to highlight the 'King of the Beasts' moniker, or a sun to link to the zodiac sign. Also popular in Japanese-style tattooing, koma-inu are often tattooed in pairs as part of a large-scale design or a full-body suit. These depictions can be very colourful, while the more realistic approach tends to suit a monochrome palette.

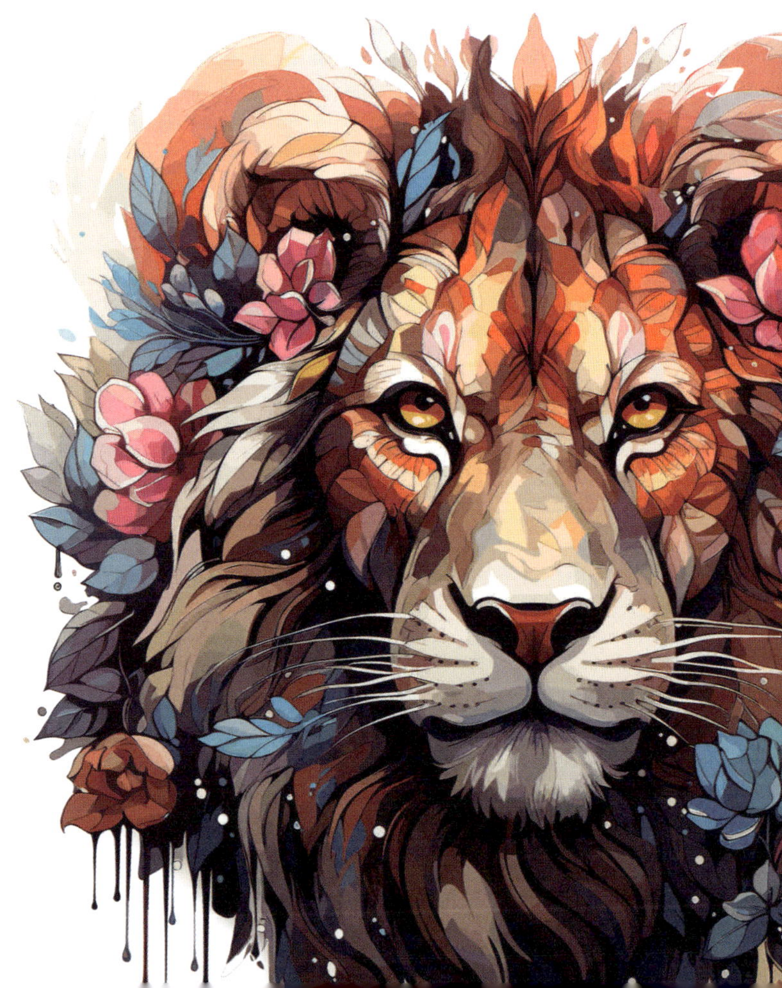

Opposite: A floral interpretation of the Leo symbol (bottom right) denotes natural beauty, while a realistic rendering (bottom left) portrays the animal's natural grace, power and potential.

Right: This colourful Leo head adorned with flowers accentuates the generous nature of this star sign and constrasts the strength of the lion with the fragility of flowers.

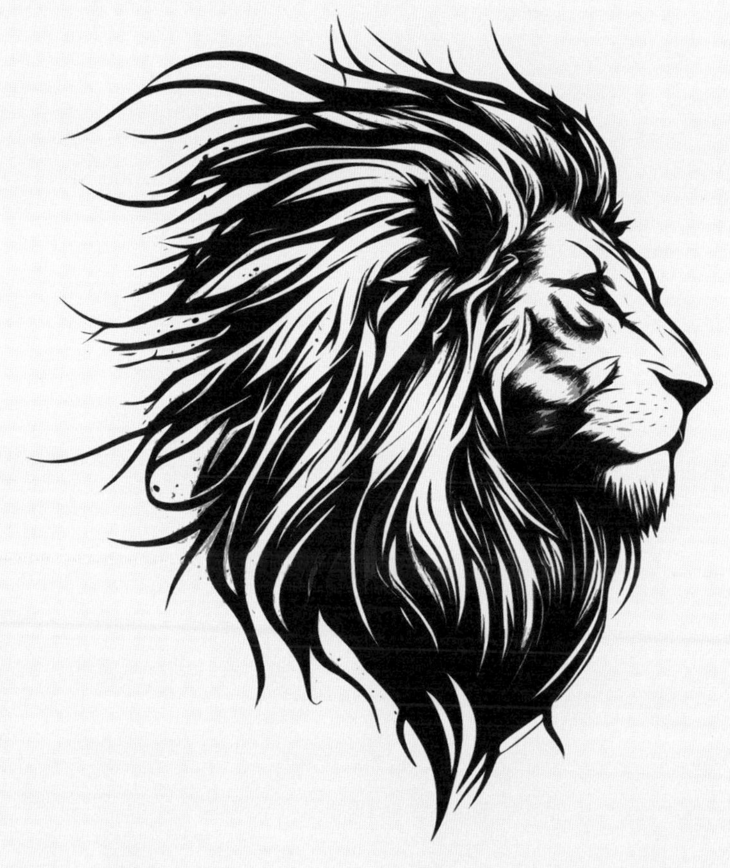

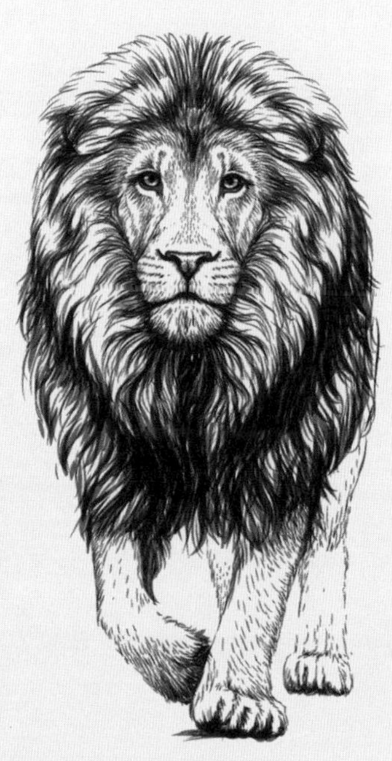

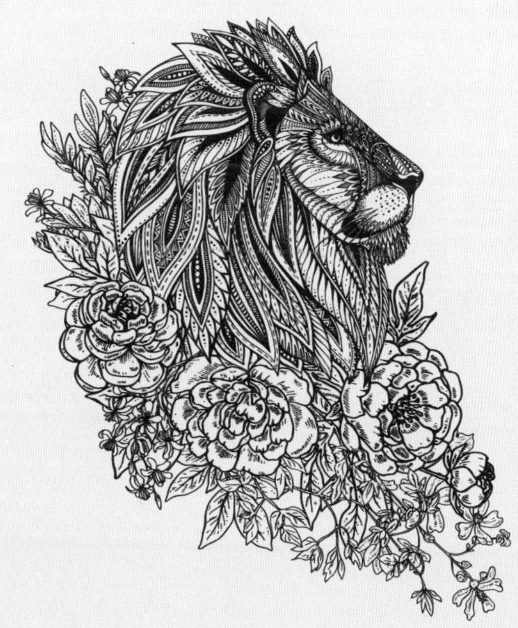

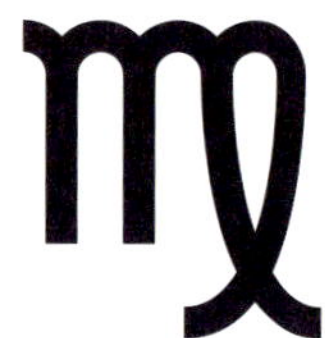

Virgo (23 Aug to 22 Sept)

Fertility | Growth | Abundance | Femininity | Creativity

Sacred Origins
Babylonian, Greek,
Roman

Used Since
2nd century BCE

Tattoo Styles
Fine-line
Blackwork

Opposite: These Virgo heads (left column) accentuate the feminine nature of the sign; the incorporation of wheat sheaves draws a link to the earth and agriculture. Virgo shown within diamonds and circles (top right) highlights the power of beauty and the eternal cycles of nature. The fertility goddess (bottom right) stands with her arms outstretched in a welcoming pose.

Virgo marks an important phase in agriculture, making the astrological sign and the associated constellation synonymous with growth and abundance.

Goddess of fertility

The sixth sign of the zodiac, which as a constellation resembles a box tilted on its side, is a representation of a fertility goddess carrying a sheaf of wheat. To the Babylonians, she was Ishtar, the feisty goddess of war synonymous with love and fertility, while to the ancient Greeks, she was associated with the goddess of the harvest, Demeter, and her beautiful daughter Persephone.

A seasonal virgin

According to legend, Persephone was kidnapped by the god of the Underworld, Hades, who held her captive in his realm. Demeter was so distraught she abandoned her role as an earth goddess to search for her lost daughter. Zeus intervened and demanded that Hades return the maiden, but as Persephone had already eaten from an Underworld fruit, the pomegranate, she was destined to return for six months of the year to represent the six seeds she had consumed. Virgo's disappearance from the sky during the winter and early spring coincides with Persephone's visits to the Underworld.

How to wear it

In tattoo form, a feminine style is often chosen to represent Virgo. Tattoos frequently show a maiden's face, adorned with flowers to represent the sign's link to fertility and the harvest. Commonly tattooed in a delicate, elegant style, using a dot-work approach for shading, Virgo tattoos can work in many areas, but if a full figure is shown, a sleeve or at least a half-sleeve design, or a large, flat area like the back is best.

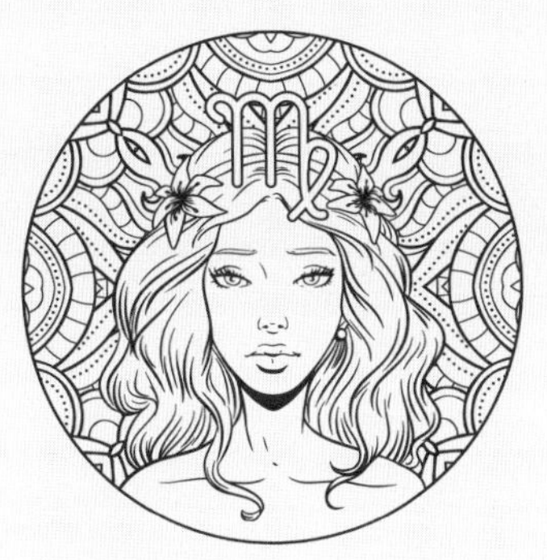

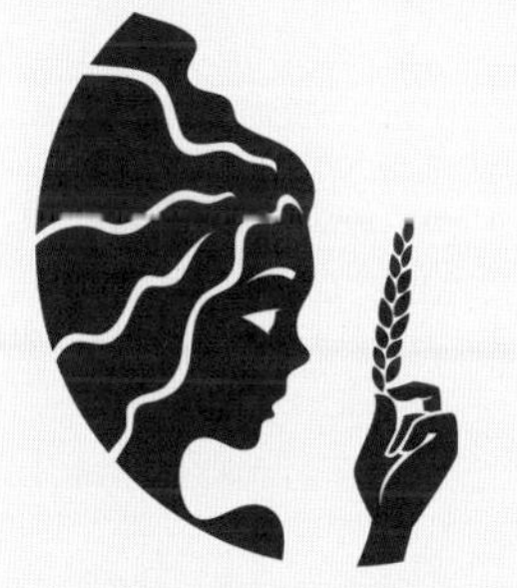

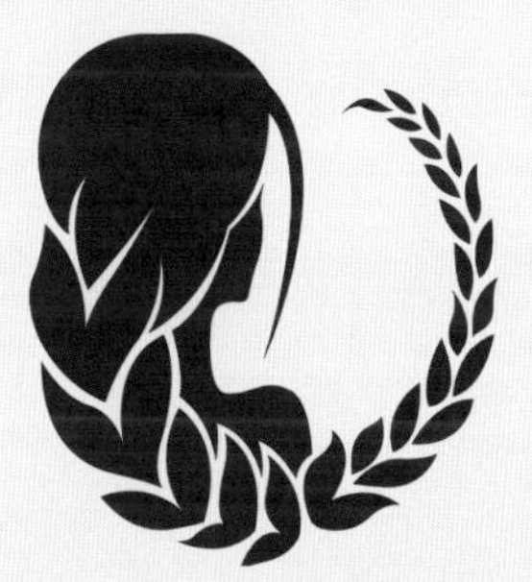

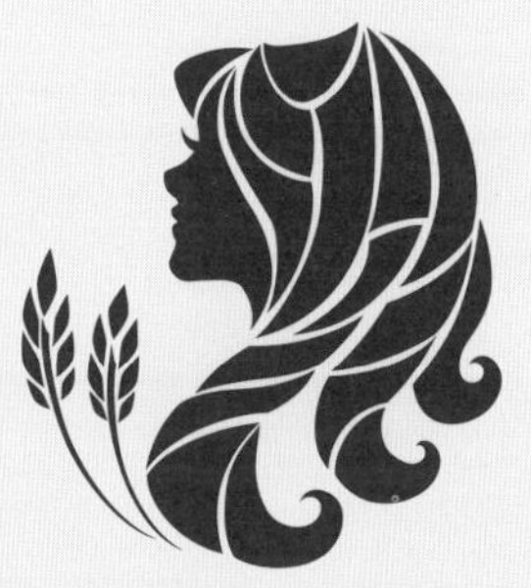

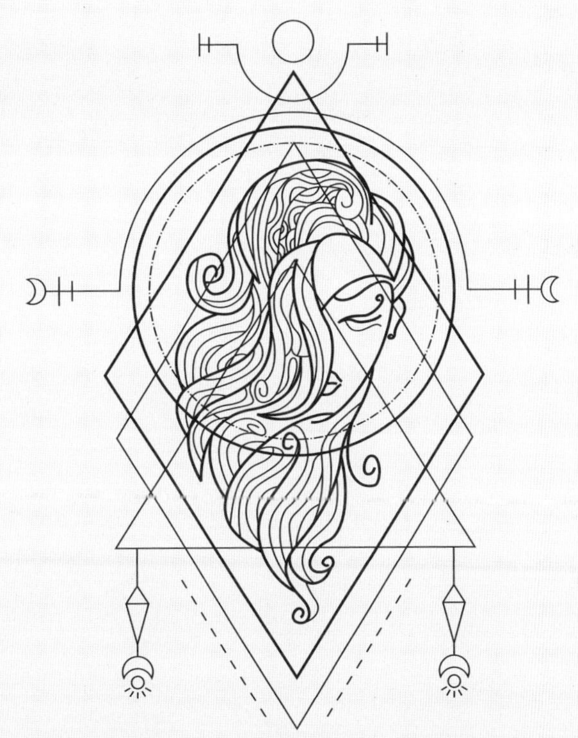

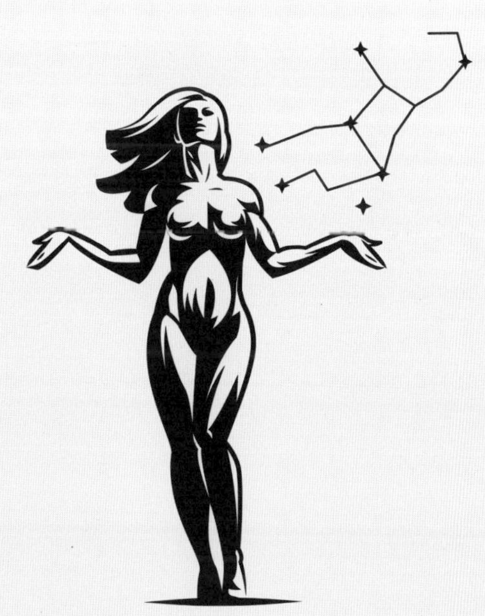

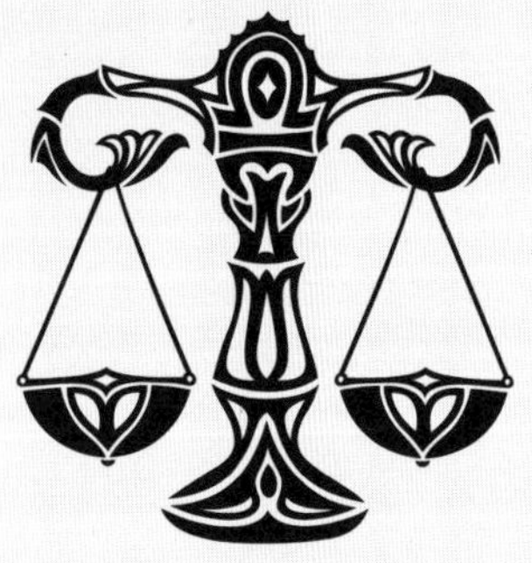 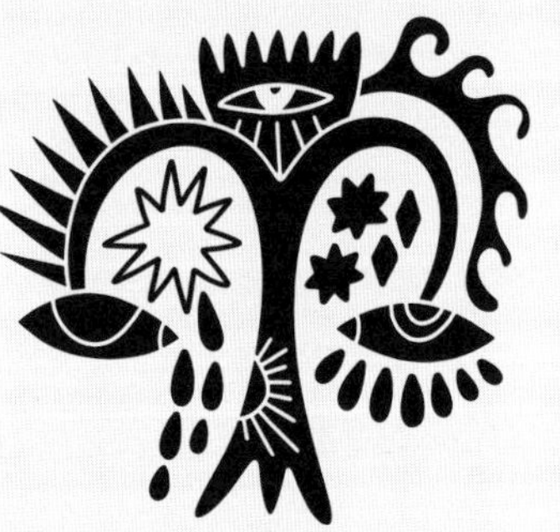 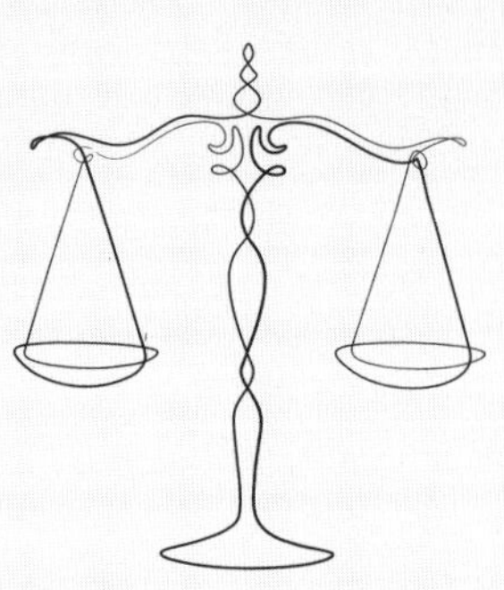

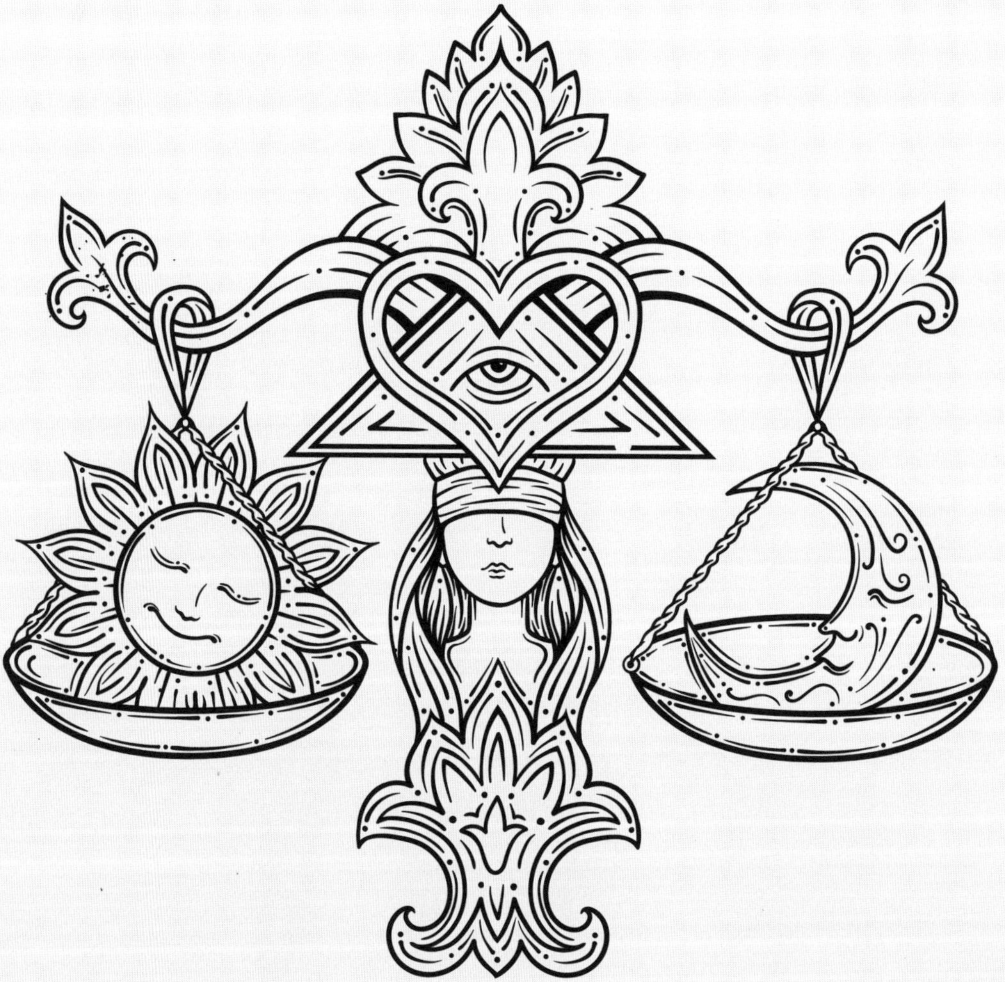

Libra (23 Sept to 23 Oct)

Balance | Justice | Law | Order | Judgement

Sacred Origins
Babylonian, Greek, Roman

Used Since
2nd century BCE

Tattoo Styles
Fine-line
Blackwork

The sign of the scales is recognized as a symbol of equilibrium, justice and order around the world.

Balance between the seasons

To the ancient Babylonians, the constellation of Libra was a turning point in the farming calendar. It marked the transition from the warm summer months to a colder, darker period, and drew a line of balance between the seasons.

A deity of justice

In Roman mythology, the scales of Libra were associated with the goddess Justitia (also known as Lustitia). She governed the realms of justice and order, and was depicted blindfolded, carrying a sword and the scales. The Emperor Tiberius was so enthused by her power that he commissioned a temple in her honour to be built in Rome, while the Emperor Vespasian had coins minted that were adorned with her image.

To the ancient Greeks, Libra was a symbol of the goddess Themis. A primordial being associated with divine law, she would weigh the fates of mortals in her scales in order to dispense judgement fairly.

How to wear it

The scales associated with this symbol offer a fantastic device within which to illustrate. Items can be placed in each side of the scales to support the concept of balance and communicate a bespoke meaning for the wearer. Symbols like a skull, the sun or the moon enhance the idea of divine law. Libra can be tattooed in many ways, however a fine-line style works very well if showing the scales.

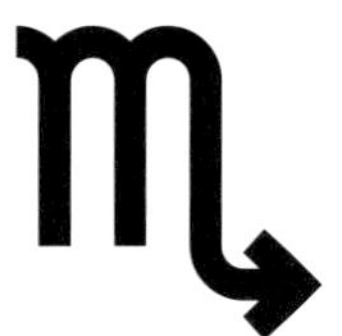

Scorpio (24 Oct to 21 Nov)

Resilience | Strength | Mystery | Power | Transformation

Sacred Origins
Babylonian, Sumerian, Egyptian, Greek

Used Since
2nd century BCE

Tattoo Styles
Western traditional
Fine-line
Blackwork

Opposite: The isolation of the tail (middle left) puts the focus on its sting, suggesting caution. A realistic interpretation of the scorpion (bottom), accentuates the creature's power and might.

The mysterious scorpion is the symbol of this zodiac sign, a creature which divides opinions.

Denizen of the dark

Synonymous with resilience, the scorpion was recognized by early civilizations as a powerful totem, associated with protection and transformation. Its venomous sting meant it was feared, but its ability to shed its exoskeleton was akin to a type of rebirth and seen as magical. This arachnid craved the security of shadowy spaces, making it a denizen of the dark and a creature of the Underworld. The Babylonians were quick to catch on to this idea, introducing the concept of scorpion men in the ancient text *The Epic of Gilgamesh*. These hybrid beasts who guarded the gates of the sun god Shamash had the head and upper torso of a man while the rest of their body resembled a scorpion.

A potent talisman

To the ancient Egyptians, the scorpion was a sacred symbol of protection and a cohort of the goddess of the dead, Selket, who was often depicted as a scorpion from the shoulders up, or with the deadly creature sitting aloft her head. Keeper of the canopic jar, used during the process of mummification to contain the internal organs of the deceased, her image was usually carved into tombs or painted on the walls. The scorpion, being her close associate, was venerated and used in talismans and amulets to keep evil forces at bay.

Orion's downfall

The ancient Greeks were responsible for taking the beast and placing it in the skies. According to myth, Orion the hunter became a little too big for his sandals after spending many months plundering the earth and competing with

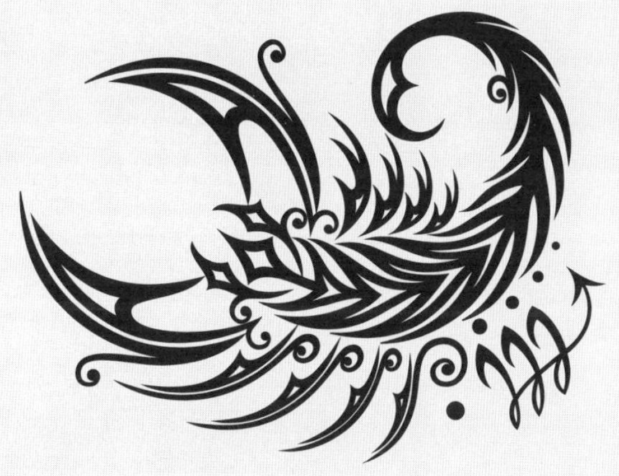
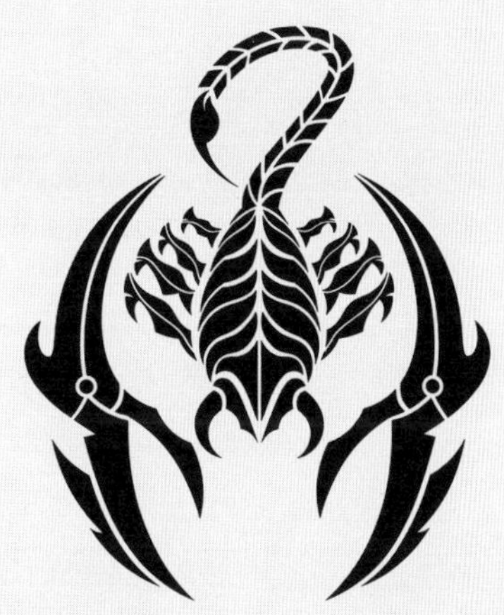

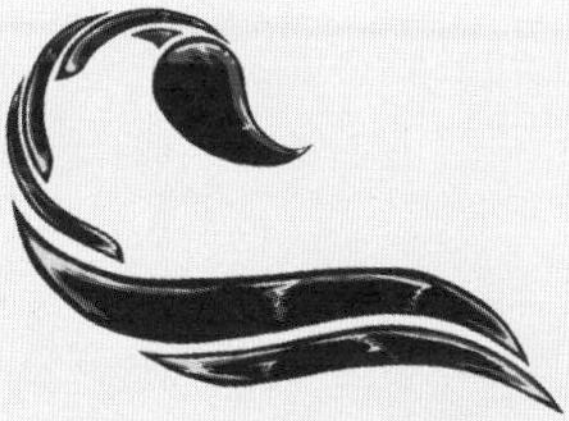

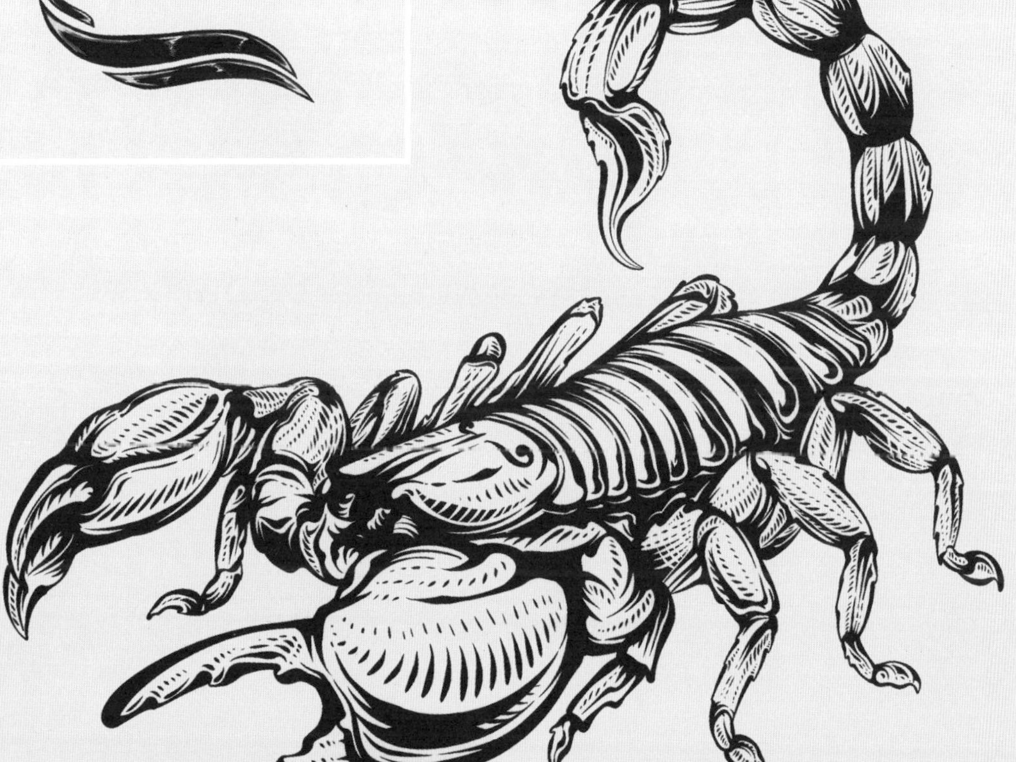

the goddess Artemis for kills. His insatiable appetite for blood became an obsession, and so the primordial earth goddess Gaia stepped in. She created the scorpion to put an end to the hunter, which it did swiftly with a lash of its tail. Orion and the scorpion were honoured in the stars as two separate constellations. Legend has it that they never appear at the same time, thanks to their careful placement. It was thought that Zeus arranged it this way, so that the two enemies would never need to fight again.

How to wear it

Designs can be abstract or realistic when tattooing the scorpion. The symbol is a staple in the Western traditional style, with many collectors making sure it features as part of their assortment of tattoos. It works well in bold black, or with a minimal palette, perhaps just one colour to accompany black. The stinging tail is usually a prominent feature of all styles. Some people prefer to use the zodiac glyph as a small and simple tattoo that can be placed discreetly on the wrist, ankle or finger.

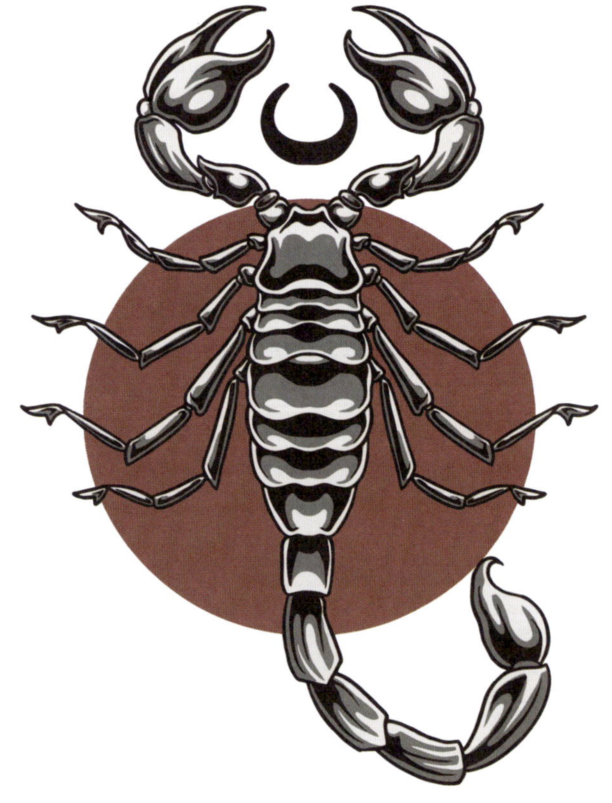

Opposite: This scorpion sits within a large crescent moon, drawing a link to the psychic and secretive nature of this zodiac sign.

Right: The crescent moon sitting between the scorpion's claws denotes mystical power and provides a link to the subconscious.

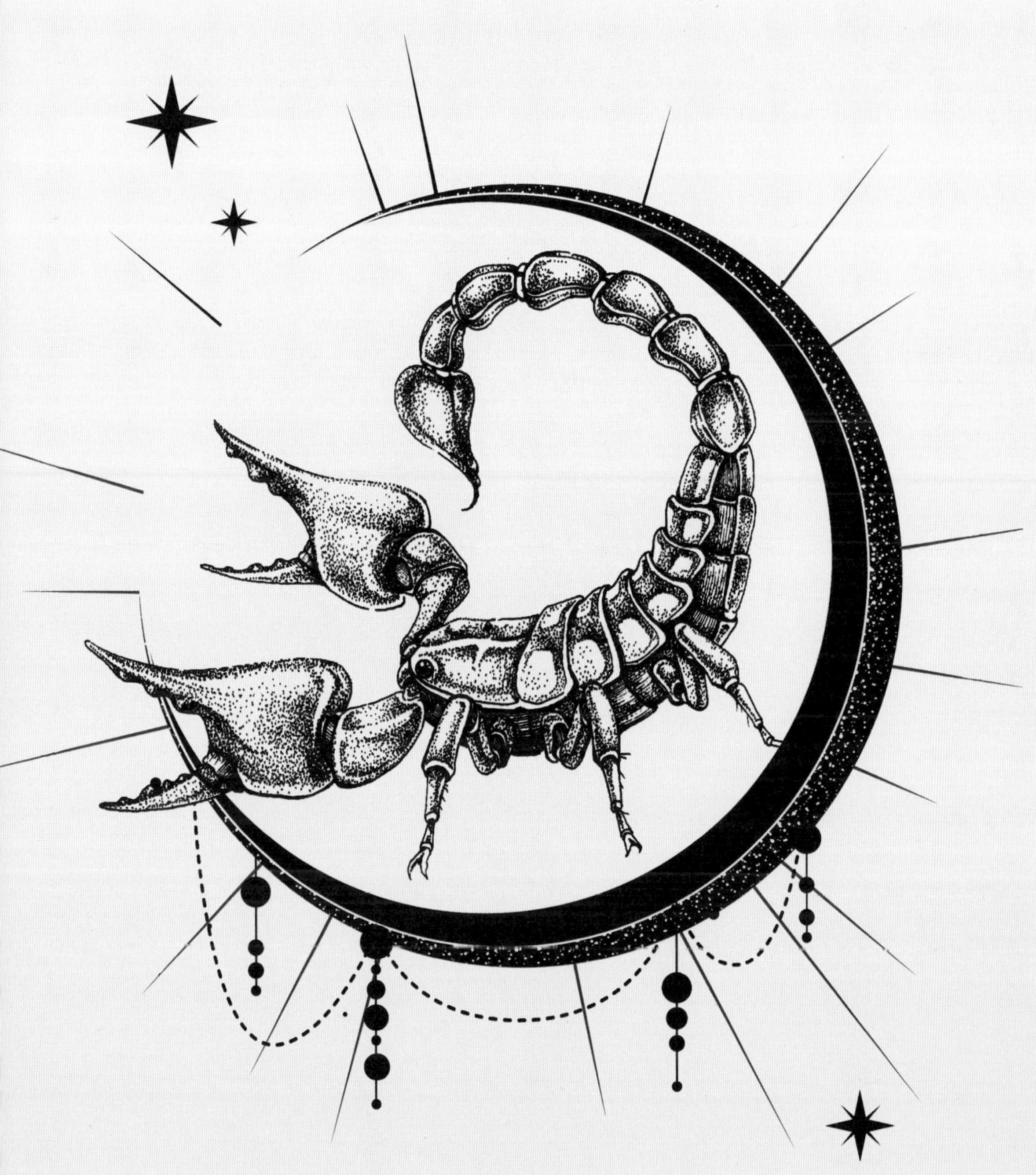

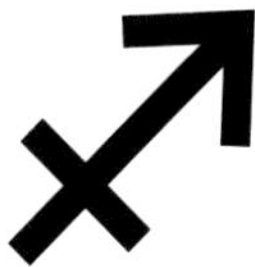

Sagittarius (22 Nov to 21 Dec)

Focus | Determination | Bravery | Freedom | Adventure

Sacred Origins
Babylonian, Egyptian,
Greek

Used Since
2nd century BCE

Tattoo Styles
Fine-line
Blackwork
Western traditional

Opposite: The archer in this image is a woman (top left), giving the symbol feminine strength and energy. The arrow within the compass (top right) gives the sign direction, and points to focus and guidance. The arrow ready to be fired by a centaur (bottom right and left) is a nod to the proactive adventurous energy associated with the sign.

The mythical archer was an important constellation to early civilizations and a symbol of energy and focus.

Centaur and god

Depicted as a centaur with his arrow primed and ready, he was Nergal, the Babylonian god of war, who governed the Underworld. In this guise the archer was a powerful influence ready to step into the midst of conflict upon earth. The ancient Egyptians believed Sagittarius to be a wild centaur-like beast with the head of a lion. Cave murals dating back over 2,000 years were discovered in the Temple of Esna, on the west bank of the Nile, depicting images of the archer.

Teacher and guide

The Greeks likened Sagittarius to the centaur Chiron, a wise, learned teacher and advisor to many fabled heroes including Achilles and Asclepius, but there is some dispute as to the true roots of the symbol. What can be agreed upon is the nature of the archer being adventurous, brave and determined in his aim.

How to wear it

The archer, being a creature of myth, allows for artistic renditions which can be elaborate and warrant a prominent position on the body. In this style, black and grey or fine-line style with stippled shading works well, as does a bold traditional style. If the wearer wanted a simpler approach, they could opt for just the bow and arrow or the zodiac glyph to capture the spirit of the sign.

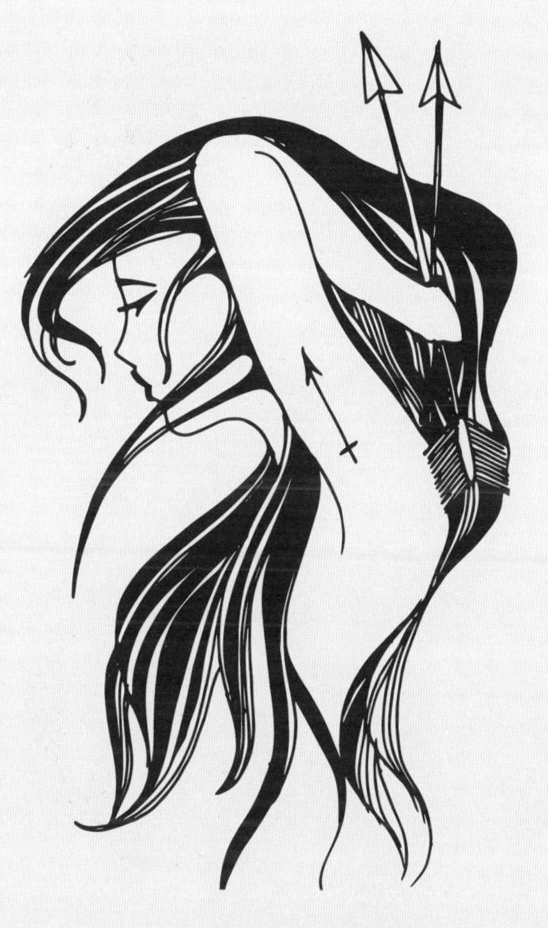

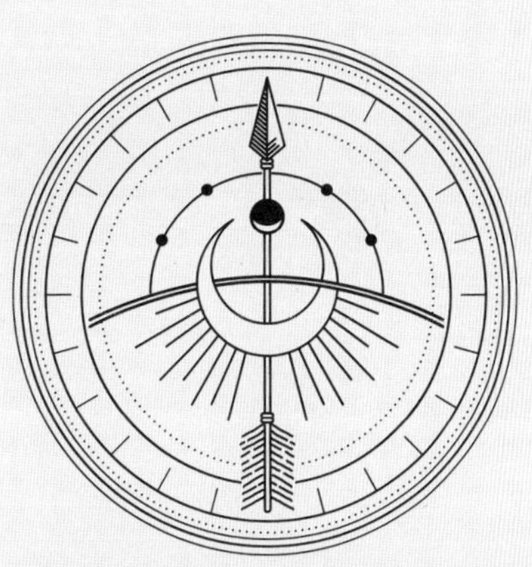

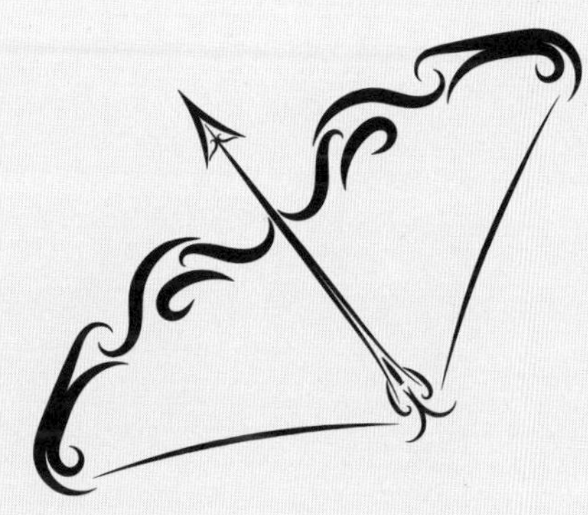

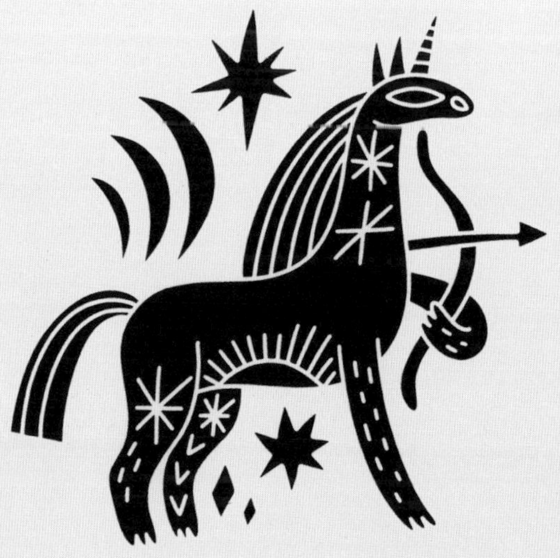

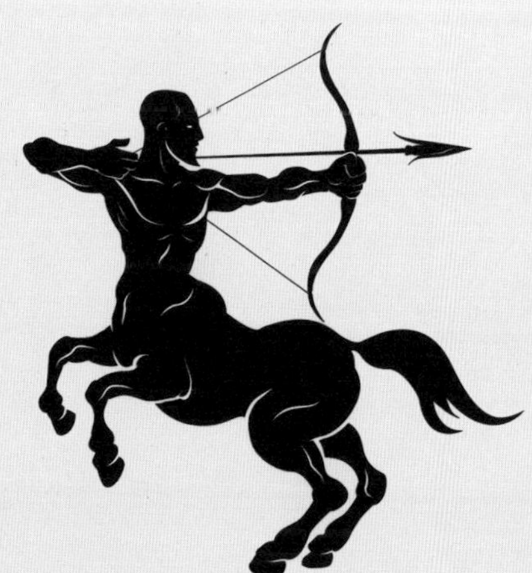

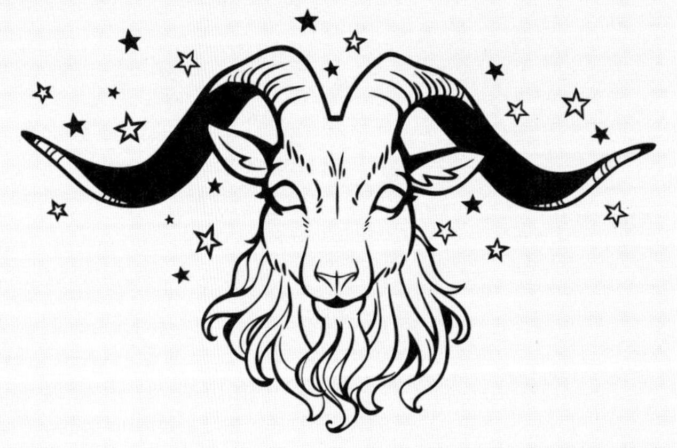

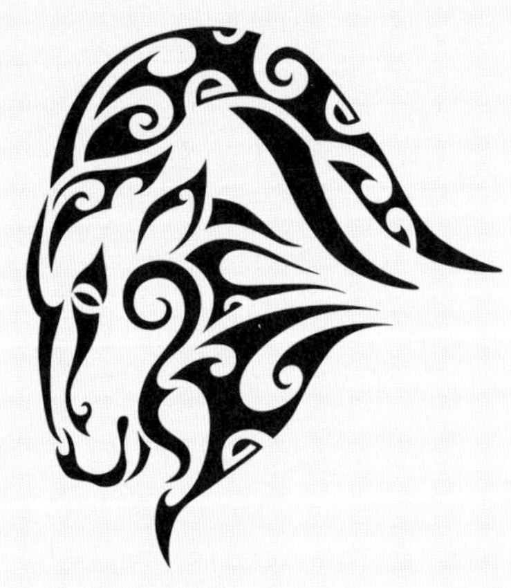

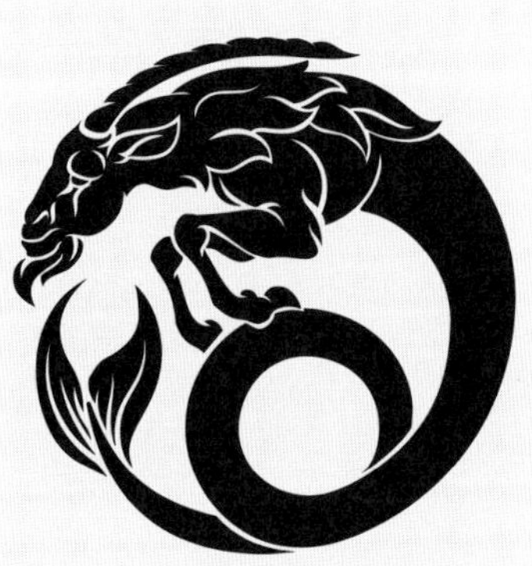

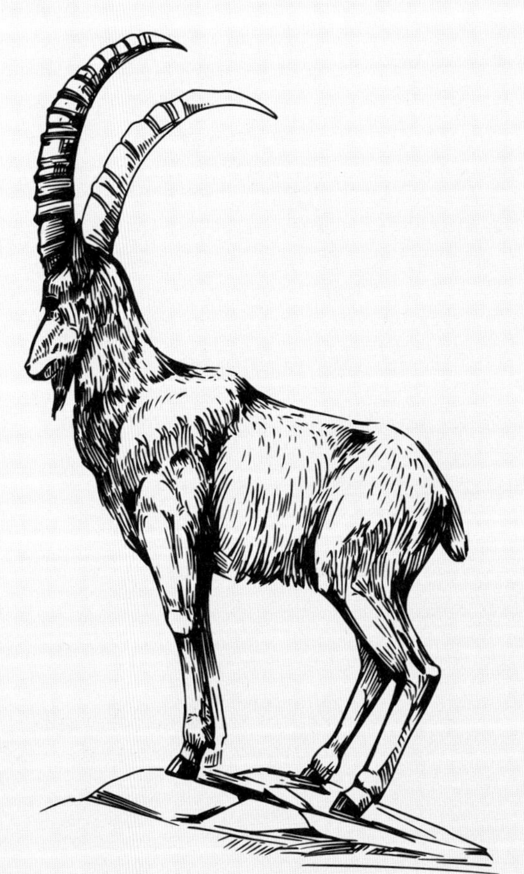

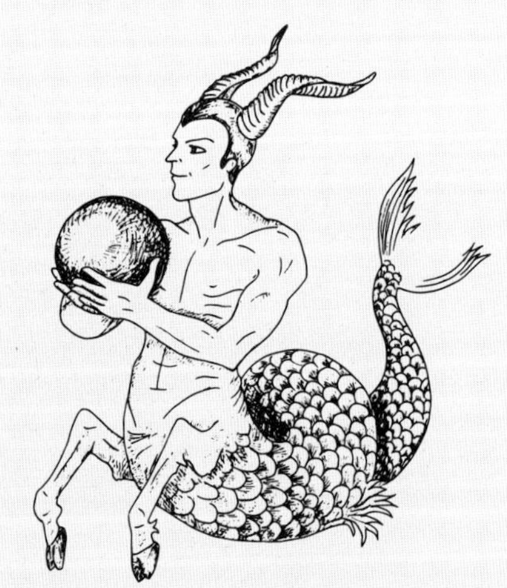

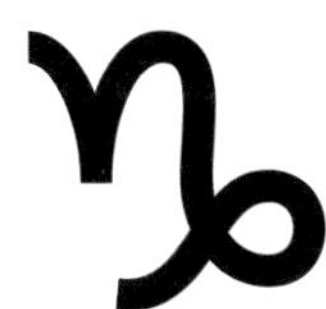

Capricorn (22 Dec to 19 Jan)

Discipline | Strength | Duty | Wisdom | Transformation

Sacred Origins
Babylonian, Greek

Used Since
2nd century BCE

Tattoo Styles
Western traditional
Fine-line
Black-and-grey realism
Polynesian

Opposite: A smattering of stars surrounds this goat's head (top left), giving this Capricorn an otherworldly feel. The circular form of this Capricorn symbol (middle right) is a nod to the ongoing cyclical nature of life. Capricorn as a nymph-like creature, holding the world in his hands (bottom right), is synonymous with wisdom.

Capricornus, meaning 'horned goat' in Latin, is the tenth sign of the zodiac and the smallest constellation.

A wise old sea goat

Capricorn may be small, but what it lacks in size it makes up for in mythological roots. First noted in Babylonian star catalogues before 1000 BCE, the sea goat with its fishy tail represents the Babylonian god Ea, also known as Enki, who was associated with wisdom, medicine and the ocean.

Pan's disguise

To the Greeks, the horned one was thought to be a version of the nature god Pan, who was often depicted with the legs of a goat. According to legend, when the monster Typhon charged his way through Mount Olympus, Pan quickly leaped into the sea to escape his clutches, transforming into a type of sea goat. That said, there are other claims to the starry crown of Capricorn. Some scholars believe that the goat is a representation of Amalthea, the goat-nymph that suckled the father of the Greek gods, Zeus, when he was an infant. Either way, the constellation and the associated zodiac sign are synonymous with discipline, strength and a sense of duty.

How to wear it

The sea goat is such a unique image that it suits being shown in full, in all its glory. The symbol is often decorated with flowers and plants, as well as water-like forms. For a truly cosmic feel, stars and the governing planet Saturn can also be included. Traditional, fine, realistic, and even Polynesian styles all complement this striking symbol.

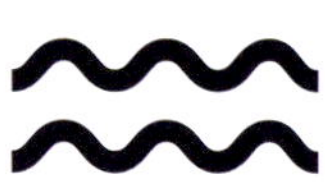

Aquarius (20 Jan to 18 Feb)

Individualism | Eccentricity | Eternal optimism | Youthfulness

Sacred Origins
Arabic, Babylonian,
Egyptian, Greek

Used Since
2nd century BCE

Tattoo Styles
Fine-line
Black-and-grey realism

Aquarius, the water bearer, is said to be the most compassionate sign of the zodiac.

The cup bearer

The eleventh sign of the zodiac and one of the oldest constellations, Aquarius is a large group of stars known as the cup bearer or the water bearer, thought to represent a man pouring liquid from an amphora into the mouth of Pisces, the southern fish. Ancient civilizations would have noted that this constellation rose to prominence during the rainy season in the Middle East, and so a link with water was established.

The Egyptians believed the figure in the sky was their god of the Nile, Hapi, who was responsible for the annual flooding of the river, while the Babylonians believed it to be Gula, the Great One, also known as the irrigator. Early depictions portray him carrying an overflowing urn which quenched the earth with rain.

The god and the Trojan prince

To the Greeks, this sparkling image was the handsome Trojan prince, Ganymede, who captured the heart of Zeus. The besotted deity did all he could to catch the youth's eye, including transforming into a mighty eagle. In the end he whisked him away to Mount Olympus, promising life eternal and everlasting youth if the prince would become his cup bearer. A pact was made and Ganymede took his place at Zeus's side for many years, until one day the god finally wavered in his affections, and the prince was surplus to requirements. Even so, Zeus honoured his word, giving Ganymede immortality by transforming him into the epic constellation Aquarius and placing him in the heavens for all to see.

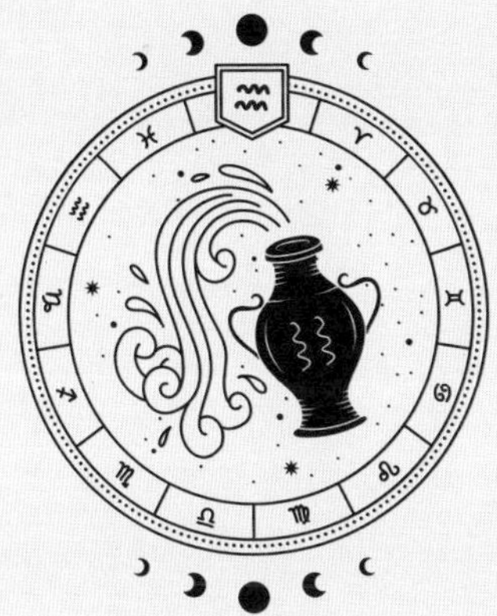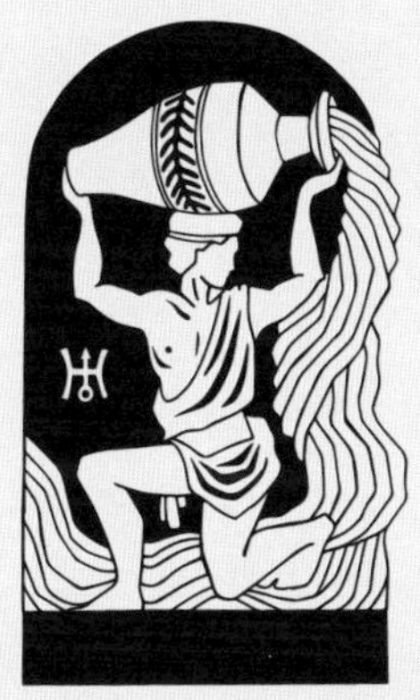

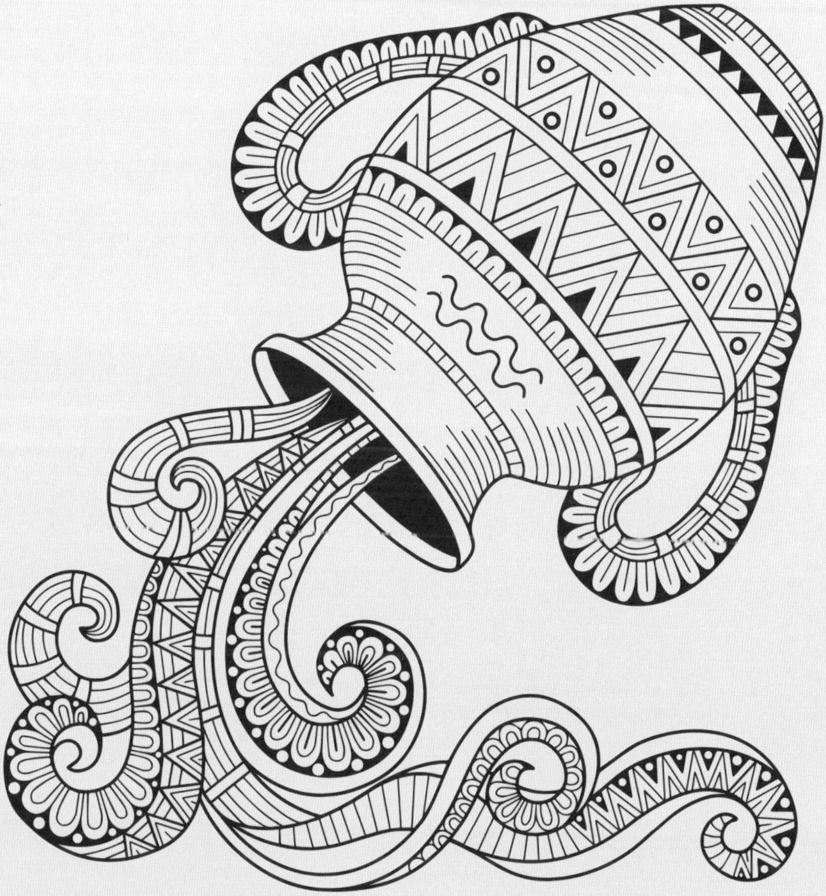

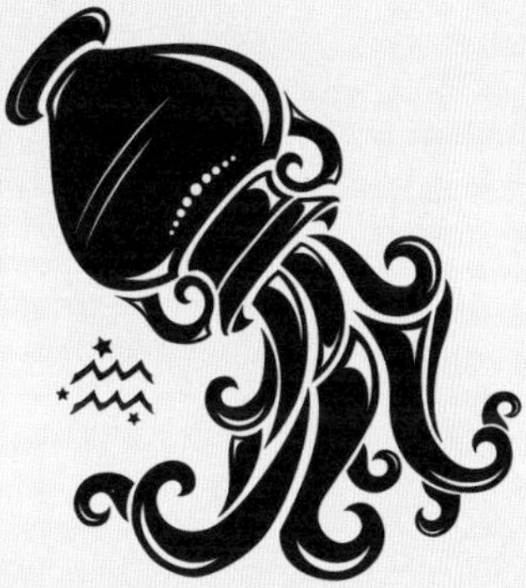

The element of air

Aquarius is often mistaken as a water sign, being the cup bearer, but in truth it is
a fixed air sign that finds its place in the darkest section of the sky known as the
'celestial sea'. Add to that the symbols glyph, which is taken from the Egyptian
hieroglyph for 'water' and confusion abounds, which seems somehow fitting for a
revolutionary sign synonymous with eccentricity and individualism.

How to wear it

Aquarius tattoo symbols often incorporate water into the design. An overflowing
jug is a popular choice, often being poured by a male – or sometimes female – figure.
This approach works well on either the arm, leg or back. An esoteric approach may
include astronomical aspects, including planets and stars. The stacked waves of the
sign's glyph are often tattooed discreetly on the wrist, inner forearm or ankle.

Opposite: **Depictions of Ganymede, Zeus's cup bearer (top and bottom left), link the symbol to Greek myth.**

Right: This abstract depiction of water overflowing from a jug uses dot-work shading in one half and fine-line polygonal shapes in the other – an interesting twist on the symbol for Aquarius.

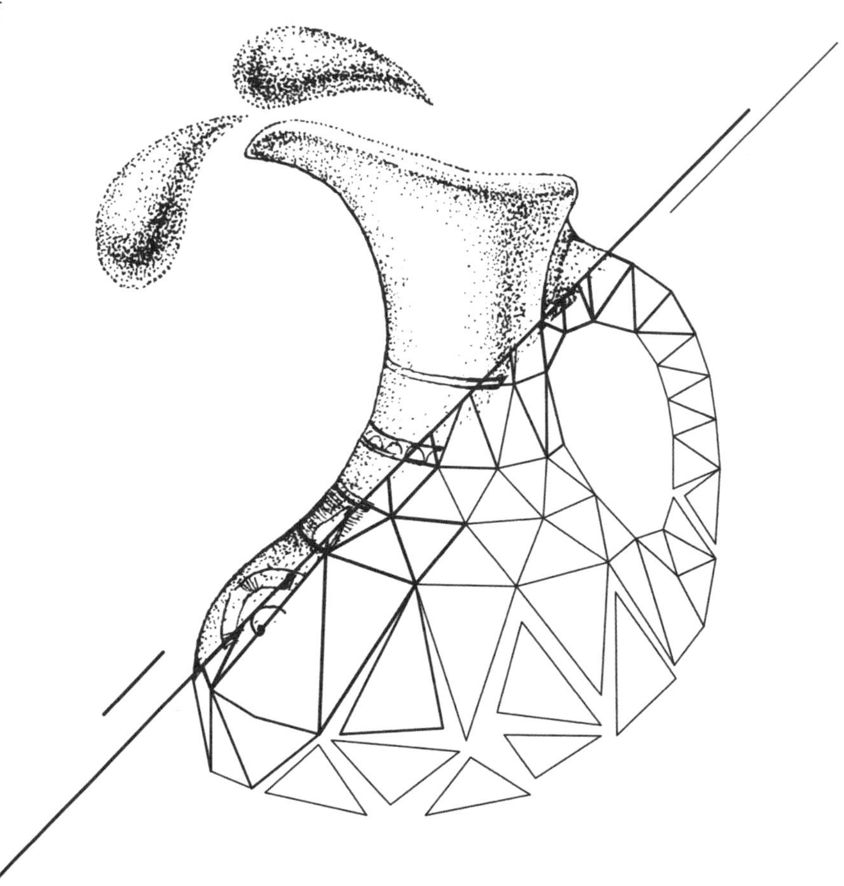

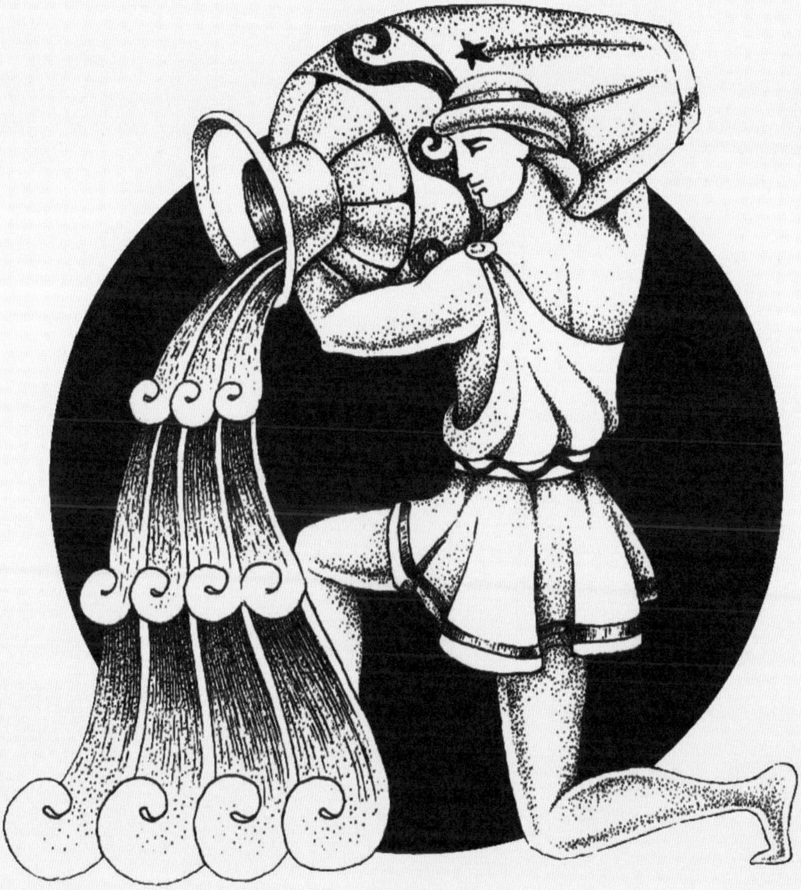

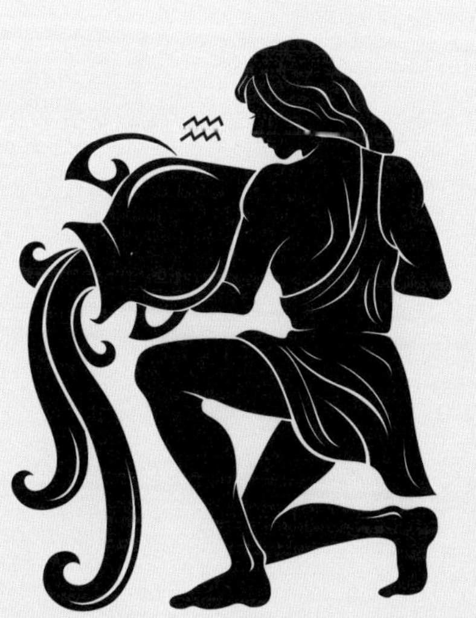

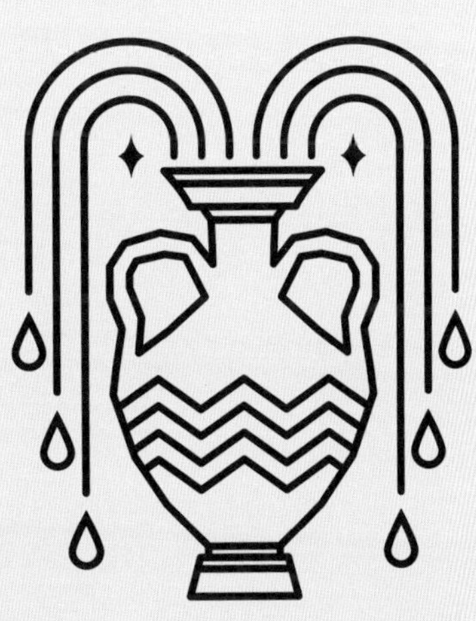

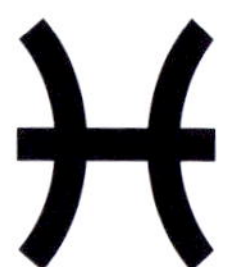

Pisces (19 Feb to 20 March)

Intuition | Imagination | Empathy | Kindness | Creativity

Sacred Origins
Indian, Babylonian, Greek

Used Since
2nd century BCE

Tattoo Styles
Fine-line
Blackwork
Japanese

Opposite: The Pisces motif, the fish, can be depicted in different styles depending on the wearer's preference. An ornate style (top left) emphasizes creativity and imagination. A Yin Yang symbol at the heart of a design (bottom) is at odds with the ethereal nature of this zodiac sign and provides a sense of balance and stability.

The two fish in this symbol are tied together in a timeless dance amid the waves, and represent the ability to delve deep within the subconscious mind.

Cast in stone
The earliest depiction of the Pisces symbol was uncovered in Ratnagiri in the state of Maharashtra, in Western India, in the form of a petroglyph which shows two fish swimming in opposite directions connected by a cord. This 12,000-year-old representation is a perfect match for the Pisces motif and suggests that there was knowledge of astrological signs and constellations in the Ice Age. This sign, like all the others, was recognized by the Babylonians and noted in the 2nd century BCE by the Greek astronomer Ptolemy.

Aphrodite's escape
The myth that was created as a narrative to complement the constellation involves the goddess of love and beauty Aphrodite and her son Eros, saved from the monster Typhon by two enormous fish sent by Zeus. The goddess and her son tied the tails of the fish together so that they would not lose sight of each other, and then swam to safety on their backs. The fish were honoured with the gift of immortality and placed in the heavens as the constellation Pisces.

How to wear it
A circular composition is often seen in Pisces tattoos, created by two fish circling each other. High detail or simplified elegance can both work well, but consideration should be given to the tattoo's final size if an elaborate approach is chosen. Some people choose the simple insignia of the sign, framing it with waves to link to the element of water.

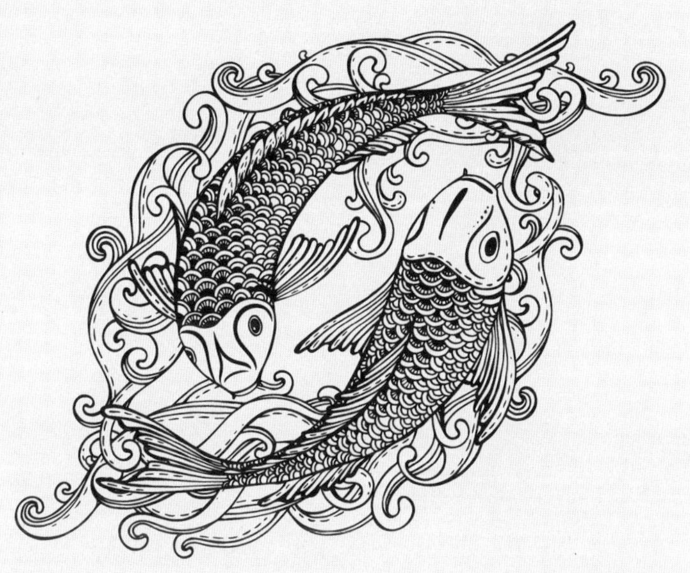
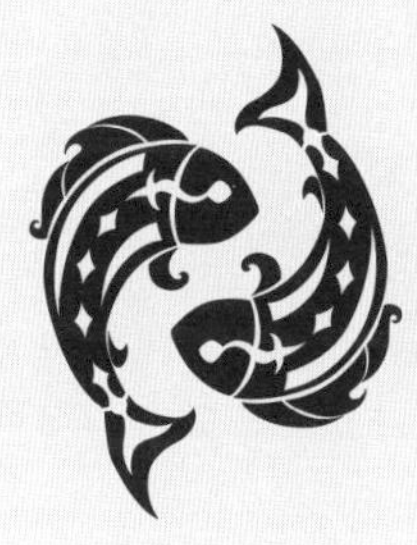
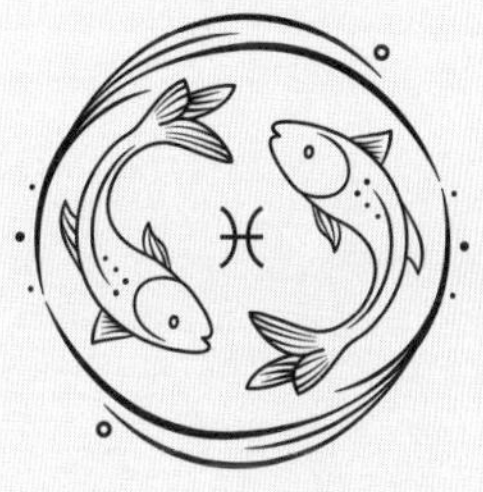

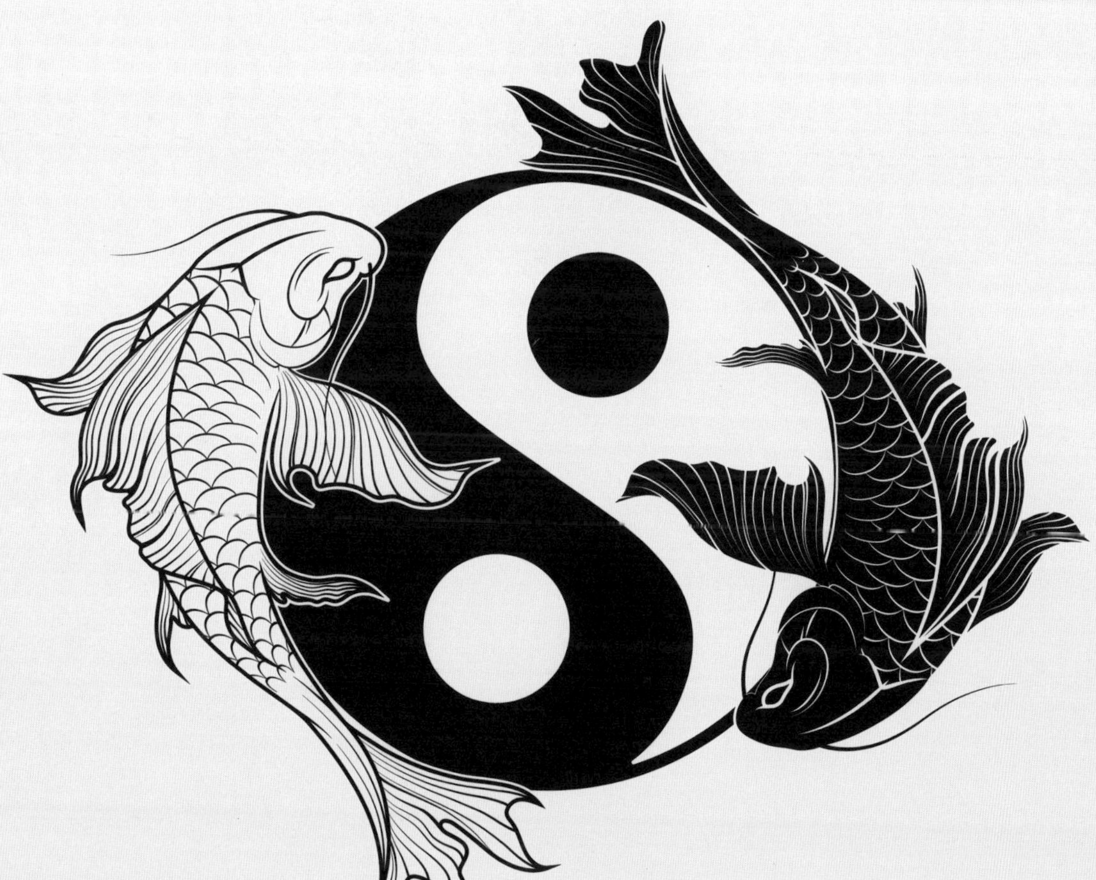

Index